The Types of Economic
Policies under Capitalism

Historical Materialism Book Series

The Historical Materialism Book Series is a major publishing initiative of the radical left. The capitalist crisis of the twenty-first century has been met by a resurgence of interest in critical Marxist theory. At the same time, the publishing institutions committed to Marxism have contracted markedly since the high point of the 1970s. The Historical Materialism Book Series is dedicated to addressing this situation by making available important works of Marxist theory. The aim of the series is to publish important theoretical contributions as the basis for vigorous intellectual debate and exchange on the left.

The peer-reviewed series publishes original monographs, translated texts, and reprints of classics across the bounds of academic disciplinary agendas and across the divisions of the left. The series is particularly concerned to encourage the internationalization of Marxist debate and aims to translate significant studies from beyond the English-speaking world.

For a full list of titles in the Historical Materialism Book Series
available in paperback from Haymarket Books, visit:
https://www.haymarketbooks.org/series_collections/1-historical-materialism

The Types of Economic Policies under Capitalism

Kôzô Uno

Translated by
Thomas T. Sekine

Edited by
John R. Bell

Haymarket Books
Chicago, IL

First published in 2016 by Brill Academic Publishers, The Netherlands
© 2016 Koninklijke Brill NV, Leiden, The Netherlands

Published in paperback in 2018 by
Haymarket Books
P.O. Box 180165
Chicago, IL 60618
773-583-7884
www.haymarketbooks.org

ISBN: 978-1-60846-802-7

Trade distribution:
In the US, Consortium Book Sales, www.cbsd.com
In Canada, Publishers Group Canada, www.pgcbooks.ca
In the UK, Turnaround Publisher Services, www.turnaround-uk.com
All other countries, Ingram Publisher Services International, ips_intlsales@
ingramcontent.com

Cover design by Jamie Kerry of Belle Étoile Studios and Ragina Johnson.

This book was published with the generous support of Lannan Foundation
and the Wallace Action Fund.

Printed in Canada by union labor.

10 9 8 7 6 5 4 3 2 1

Library of Congress Cataloging-in-Publication data is available.

Contents

APPENDICES
Two Essays by Thomas T. Sekine

List of Tables

Foreword to the Revised Edition of 1971

The origin of this book goes back to my lecture notes at Tôhoku Imperial University, Faculty of Letters and Law, where I taught a course on Economic Policy, between 1925 and 1935. At first, the notes were not organised in the present form. The latter, however, evolved as I continued to teach the same course repetitively over the ten-year period, during which I constantly added revisions and new materials. Thus, in the spring of 1936, I could publish the first half of the book, up to and including Part II on the Stage of Liberalism, as *Volume I* of *Keizai-Seisakuron* [here translated as *The Types of Economic Policies under Capitalism*]. It was then expected that the second half, consisting of Part III on the Stage of Imperialism, would follow in due course as *Volume II* of the same book. Yet, towards the end of 1937, the so-called Popular-Front Incident [*Jinmin-Sensen Jiken*] occurred, followed by the wholesale arrest of those who were then referred to as *Rônôha* professors including me, in February 1938. Such circumstances made it impossible for me to carry on working on the second half of the book. When in 1940, after the second trial, I was finally acquitted as not having been guilty of subversion, the Imperial University voted for my reinstatement, which, however, was opposed by the Ministry of Education. This provided me with a suitable pretext to resign from the university, and to move to a private institute for economic research. I welcomed that option, having been convinced, even as I was interrogated by the public prosecutor, that I no longer lived in a climate of intellectual freedom adequate for the pursuit of scientific truth.

With the end of the Pacific War, a more favourable climate returned to Japan, and I was pleased to obtain a position at the University of Tokyo, in the newly opened Institute of Social Science. By that time, however, my interest had shifted to the empirical/historical analysis of Japanese capitalism and I undertook, as my first task, an in-depth study of the land-tax system [*Chiso-Kaisei*], which the Meiji Government introduced in 1873. Thus, a gap opened between my concentration on this new theme and the resumption of my interrupted work on the economic policies of imperialism. In the meantime, the revival of interest in Marx's *Capital* among Japanese scholars led to active debates on theoretical issues of Marxian economics, and, in that context, my new book, entitled *Value Theory* (1946), attracted a number of criticisms. In the course of responding to these criticisms, I felt that my path was diverging even further from a concentrated study on imperialism, leaving a gap that I did not have the opportunity to fill until after a new edition of *Keizai-Seisakuron*, *Volume I*, appeared in 1948. Several years afterwards, however, the University of Tokyo undertook to pub-

lish a series of textbooks in economics, and I was assigned as my contribution
a one-volume treatise on economic policy. I gladly accepted that challenge, and
completed this book in its present form in 1954, the first half of which consisted
of a condensed version of the previously published *Keizai-Seisakuron, Volume I*,
while the newly written second part dealt with economic policies in the stage of
imperialism. The latter half, however, had to be much shorter, and far less substantial, than what I had contemplated earlier when I discontinued teaching
my course on Economic Policy at Tôhoku 18 years before. Given the prevailing circumstances, the best I could do then was to add a few bits of relevant
new information on this subject to that which my old manuscript already contained. Thus, I am keenly conscious of the fact that this book fails to be fully
up to date as a treatise on the history of economic policies under capitalism. I
regret also that, even in the present revision, I have not been able to overcome
its shortcomings.

In partial apologia, however, I would like to say that my approach to the subject of economic policy has always been quite different from its conventional
treatment. During the ten prewar years when I devoted myself to the teaching of Economic Policy at Tôhoku, I was, at the same time, wholly engrossed
in efforts to learn from Marx's *Capital*, a book which deeply fascinated me, the
basic idea of what economics was all about as social science; for I was totally
disappointed with what I had myself been taught as 'economic theory' at uni-
versities (in Japan as in Germany), which were then predominantly under the
influence of the now defunct German historical school. I was convinced that I
could not possibly offer a satisfactory course in any branch of economics, short
of being myself convincingly enlightened on that matter. Thus, my teaching of
Economic Policy then had to be carried out concurrently with my own in-depth
study of Marx's *Capital*. It so happened that, during the first half of that period,
Capital became, for the first time, the object of intense controversy between
the economists of the Marxist, and the non-Marxist, persuasion in this country;
and, in the second half, the Marxists were themselves divided into two oppos-
ing camps on the basis of another controversy, which pertained to the nature
of Japanese capitalism. Although I did not directly participate in either of these
strident debates myself, I could certainly learn a great deal from both of them.
The fact that the socialist movement in Japan was then gaining momentum,
and tending towards the formation of political parties, rendered these debates
all the more urgent and consuming.

Unlike the many Marxist participants in the controversy, however, I was
primarily interested in discovering the meaning of economic policies under
capitalism in the light of the economic theory that Marx taught in *Capital*. In
other words, rather than trying to make direct use of Marx's economic theory

as an instrument of political practice (including the formulation and implementation of economic policies), I was concerned with identifying the place
that economic policy should occupy in the study of economics as a whole. To
my mind, addressing that problem would entail a parallel attempt to account
for the contrasting methodologies employed by the two best-known classics in
Marxian economics: Marx's *Capital* and Lenin's *Imperialism*. Struggling with
Capital while concurrently giving a course on Economic Policy imposed on
me a task which was invariably bypassed by other Marxist economists, who
primarily aimed at interpreting the economics of *Capital* for the novice in
a textbook fashion. In my isolated reflection, however, I was led to the conclusion that *Capital* essentially advanced what I call *Genriron*, or a logically
closed (and hence pure and general) theory of capitalism, and, in that light,
I arrived at a dawning awareness of how I might solve many difficult problems
which had previously perplexed me. I was further led to the conclusion that
the problems of imperialism that Lenin explored with prodigious insight were
essentially stage-theoretic ones, and that we could address in a similar fashion the problems of mercantilism and liberalism, which appeared earlier in
the development of capitalism. The stage-theoretic determinations in each of
these cases were there to mediate between *Genriron* (i.e. the economic theory of capitalism) and the empirical/historical analysis of the actual course
of capitalist development (i.e. the economic history thereof). In other words,
an empirical/historical analysis of the capitalist economy in real time would
enable us to comprehend the true nature of its current evolution, and would
then provide us with a scientific referent in the light of which we might choose
the tactics and strategies for our impending political practice, if and only if
these were informed by *Genriron* through the mediation of the stages-theory.
It was in this way, moreover, that I understood the relationship between economics and the materialist conception of history – a way that was contrary to
that which was usually believed correct. Since a fully transparent explication
of the 'economic' base of a society, which the materialist conception claims
to consist of the totality of its production-relations, could be accomplished
only in the light of *Genriron*, the pure theory of capitalism, it was economics that would validate the materialist conception of history (at least insofar
as it pertained to capitalism), and not the other way round. Thus, instead of
accepting the materialist conception of history simply as a matter of faith, and
then considering economics as an application of its principles specifically to
capitalism, I concluded that economics, which in its *Genriron* unambiguously
exposes the totality of the capitalist production-relations, validates that conception in its 'epitome' insofar as it pertains to capitalism as a historical society.

Though quite insufficient as regards the documentation of historical details, the present book intends to convey to the reader my main thesis that theory and history cannot be directly joined, in economics, but rather can only be joined through the mediation of stage-theoretic determinations such as will be described in what follows. That thesis has survived unaltered since the first time that this book was published years ago. In the present revision, I limited myself to removing some obvious errors in reasoning, documentation, phrasing and typography. In accomplishing that work, I have been most generously assisted by Messrs. Shirô Tohara (University of Tokyo), Tsuneo Mori (Meiji University), Hiroshi Watanabe (Tôhoku Universtiy) and Katsuyuki Amano (Hosei University), to all of whom I wish to express my sincere gratitude. The other novelty of this revised edition is that it contains an Appendix, in which I briefly state my thoughts on the nature of capitalist development *after* the First World War, a theme which I left unexplored in the previous edition of this book. For, only more recently have I fully convinced myself that the stage of imperialism cannot be extended beyond the war of 1914–18, without undermining its consistency.

6 December 1970

Introduction

1   The Commodity-Economy and Economic Policies

Some authors propose to define economic policies as those instruments of the state which inspire the economic life of society with a definite orientation, and which, on that basis, aim at achieving a particular set of desired goals.[1] A broad description of this kind, however, hardly clarifies the significance of economic policies in the capitalist society in which one lives. By being far too general to hold any substantive content, it ignores the fact that economic policies under capitalism always pursue specific ends with specific means. Not only does a general statement of that kind fail to critically expose the objective ground for the policies that are actually implemented, but it also creates the false impression that one might be able to learn from science the method of prescribing an ideal policy. Indeed, current economic policies are frequently criticised as being 'unscientific' on the basis of such a premise. Yet, the objective factor that calls such economic policies into being is never seriously questioned, so that they are, in most cases, merely endured without their significance ever being understood. Economic policies are, however, never, in fact, practised in an empty space, i.e. in the absence of the objective conditions that call them into being. Even if individual policies pursue some arbitrary aims, others will correct them, in such ways that the whole gamut of economic policies, in any period of capitalist history, always points to a definite goal, and this quite independently of the subjective aspirations of policymakers or of the abstract discourses of prolix scholars.*

*A nation such as Japan which joined the league of already established capitalist nations in the late nineteenth century had to import economic policies and institutions from advanced Western countries together with the capitalist mode of production, so that the primary duty of the academic economists was, for some time, regarded as the conducting of studies of economic policies practised elsewhere in the world so that they might be adapted to the Japanese context. Similar conditions prevailed in Germany vis-à-vis Great Britain earlier in the nineteenth century. In both cases, the excessive preoccupation with policy issues on the part of academics tended to obstruct the development of theoretical economics for an extended period of time. More recently, the popularity of so-called 'modern economics' [a preferred Japanese

---

1   Sauda Kiichirô 1922, p. 125.

appellation of 'bourgeois economics' – T.S.] revives the false idea that pure economic theory may be immediately applied to formulate policy prescriptions. Such a vulgar view seems to have influenced even Marxists in more than a few instances. This shows the urgency of clarifying the relationship between theory and policy in the Marxian context, the relation which has so far been left ambiguous.

Our present economic life adopts the *form* of the commodity-economy, or, more precisely, that of the capitalist commodity-economy. A national economy with a given population, more or less related to other national economies by means of external trade, is not a mere collection of nondescript individuals. Some are capitalists and others are workers. There are also landlords and peasants as well as members of intermediate classes or incidental social groups. Their economic life differs, depending on the position that they occupy in society. Surely one cannot 'inspire the economic life of society with a definite orientation' without due consideration of these differences. For the same economic policy is bound to exert dissimilar influences on those occupying differing economic positions.

Further, the nation's annual product, which sustains its economic life, presupposes definite social relations of production, as determined by the capitalist mode of production and the specifically commodity-economic mechanism of distribution that it entails. No economic policy operates except in conjunction with the capitalist laws that govern the production and distribution of goods, i.e. except in ways that either enhance or mitigate the working of such laws. In other words, no effective policy can directly strike at production and/or distribution as such, circumventing or blocking the laws of capitalism. This is not to deny that the complex economic life operated by the capitalist commodity-economy requires some purely technical and generally applicable conventions or rules, such as the standard of weights and measures, for instance. The adoption of such conventions no doubt becomes more and more important with the development of capitalism, as an effective functioning of the commodity-economy itself calls for them.

Yet technical rules or conventions designed to meet the requirements of an ordered social life are different from economic policies, and do not even form the subject matter of economic studies in general. If such conventions were examined in the same way as, say, customs policies, neither the one nor the other would be properly understood. It is true that whenever the imposition of a tariff is proposed, it is invariably rationalised on the grounds of a common benefit, be it the development of the national economy or the stabilisation of the market. If, for that reason, such an economic policy is treated as being the same type of choice as the adoption of the standard of weights and measures, the historically specific nature of the tariff will certainly escape notice. Perhaps the distinction between the adoption of purely technical rules and economic policies is quite apparent in this particular instance; but there are other more intricate cases as well. For example, monetary and financial institutions combine the merely technical with specifically economic aspects that are by no means easy to disentangle.

The quantity of money necessary for the circulation of commodities can never, in practice, be technically determined, nor can the supply of currency be regulated accordingly. Since it is commodities themselves that generate money, and let it circulate as currency, the quantity of the latter must be regulated by the commodity-economy itself. Yet, the fact that the authorities determine the standard of price, by specifying the gold content of a unit of the currency, leads to the popular confusion that the authorities can also determine and enforce an optimum supply of money. If, as at present, much of the circulating medium takes the form of inconvertible paper currency issued by the central bank, the confusion will be even more firmly entrenched. Thus, it is thought that the supply of the currency ought to be so regulated as to minimise the fluctuation of its value, and so the monetary policy that purports to aim at such a public benefit tends to be widely acclaimed.* However, the very fluctuation of the price level, which calls for the stabilisation of what is referred to as the currency value, betrays the technical impossibility of finely adjusting the supply of money. Indeed the stabilisation of prices, if successful, would establish a rule or convention which would be desirable to all. However, there is an economic aspect to the matter as well. An anti-inflationary policy, for example, is never introduced because the stability of prices is generally desired so as to achieve a public benefit. Even if the policy, by chance, turned out to be effective in achieving price stability, the latter is merely its by-product and not its original aim. A policy to combat inflation is introduced when the development of capitalism itself is threatened by inflation, particularly by fiscal inflation of the kind experienced in Japan immediately after the Second World War. A runaway inflation caused by fiscal irresponsibility impeded the formation of idle funds convertible into capital, and eventually frustrated the accumulation of capital (and of fixed capital in particular). The overriding purpose of the anti-inflationary policy then adopted was clearly the rehabilitation of capitalism, which required restraint in public finance. The latter, in turn, entailed the stabilisation of the currency value. To interpret the policy as a mere pursuit of stable currency that would benefit everyone is to ignore the specifically economic reason for which the inflation, so far left unopposed, was now suddenly viewed as a threat to the system. If the policymakers are motivated by such an interpretation, they only naïvely serve the sectional interest of the capitalist class, being unaware of the significance of the changing economic climate.

* Policies that aim at controlling inflation or deflation are often called monetary (or currency) policies and appear to concern themselves only with the supply of the currency. To be effective, however, they must regulate the demand and supply of idle funds by influencing the activities of credit institutions. Only because credits assume the form of currency which circulates in the market does one get the impression that the supply of currency is being regulated. As we experienced in this country after the war, it is quite possible that the abundance of currency and the shortage of loanable funds (convertible into capital) can simultaneously occur, so that the two functions of money must always be clearly distinguished. For, if they are confused, financial policies aimed at controlling credit institutions will be subordinated to the monetary policy, which has for its primary concern the regulation of the total supply of currency.

The preservation of the social relations consistent with capitalism demands certain technical rules that are universally applicable; but such rules can effectively be enforced only when they agree with the laws of capitalism. An economic policy that assists the operation of these laws often proclaims as its goal the attainment of a certain technical norm, which merely follows as a by-product of the policy motivated, in fact, by other considerations. This relation, however, is by no means simple. Indeed, an individual economic policy, taken in isolation from others, does not normally enable us to determine its true social significance. Precisely for this reason, a wholesale denunciation of all the currently enforced economic policies as class-antagonistic, in such a way that they invariably benefit capitalists at the expense of workers and peasants, does not shed light on anything either. Such an ideological determinism ignores the specific character of individual policies, condemning them all regardless of their particular circumstances. It is futile to directly apply abstract theoretical principles to interpret concrete economic policies, and to overlook the objective ground that calls for them in each specific case. By failing to expose the concrete circumstances that motivate particular policies, such a blind dogmatism also fails to specify what social practice may be most usefully set against them. Scientific economics cannot be used either to defend or to denounce individual economic policies. For economic policies that supplement the laws of the commodity-economy cannot be comprehended, until the specific commodity-economic forms* under which the policies operate are exposed together with that which lies behind these forms.

*Since the scale of social production and circulation has remarkably expanded with the recent development of the capitalist commodity-economy, statistical data are now widely available in many aspects of economic life. Behind the numbers, however, lies the specifically commodity-economic *form* of operation of economic life. Without the knowledge of this *form*, these statistical data cannot hope to contribute towards a scientific analysis however refined may be the mathematical method that is adopted in processing them. On the contrary, an uncritical focus on statistics diverts one's attention from the real forces at work.

These forms must surely be objectively determined in the light of the historical development of capitalism. For only under capitalism does the commodity-economy tend to govern a whole society, subjecting its development to forms that are peculiarly commodity-economic. In capitalist society, not only the means of production but also the articles of consumption are produced as commodities. This does not simply mean that the products are traded or exchanged as commodities. It also means that the very process of the production of wealth, which hinges upon the commodification of labour-power, is subject to the commodity-economy's automatic regulation, in such a way that the direct producers can no longer produce their own means of livelihood. The commodity-form dictates not only the relation between the capitalist and his/her workers, but also the allocation of capital and labour in the production of use-values that are socially necessary. It is this fact that inspires capitalist society with its typically forceful motive for the advancement of productive powers. The productive powers of labour are, however, not developed directly for the purpose of securing the affluence or comfort of the population, but rather for the purpose of reducing the value of labour-power as a commodity. For that enables an increase in the production of surplus value, the ultimate source of profit accruing to capital. The advancement of productive powers is, for that reason, realised in capitalist society with a speed and scope unheard of in previous societies.

In its original sense, the word *commodity-economy* simply connotes that products are exchanged as commodities. As such, however, the commodity-economy has always operated on the periphery of a society, the economic life of which is fundamentally governed by other principles. This is because the commodity is a *form* that arises between separate economic communities to regulate their external relations, even though its subsequent development may impinge on the internal working of those trading communities. Capitalist society administers the whole of its economic life by a *form* that originates outside it, i.e. by applying the method of external regulation to its internal relations. It carries out the labour-and-production process existing commonly in all societies and vital to human existence, the process in which humans work on nature with a view to acquiring therefrom both the means of livelihood and of production, in a manner that is economically more rational than in any past society. This economic rationality is realised by the conversion of labour-power into a commodity.

Unlike other commodities, however, labour-power is not a product. It is, therefore, a very special kind of commodity, if it is a commodity at all. Thus, even if it is said that labour-power is converted into a commodity in capitalist society, capital cannot for that reason produce it at will. Nor can it be sold by the workers in the same way as any other ordinary product. The conversion of labour-power into a commodity in capitalist society is secured via the recurrent process, in which the workers purchase their means of livelihood (as products of capital and hence of labour) as commodities, with the money wages that they receive from the capitalist. In return for these wages, the workers have sold their labour-power to the capitalist, labour-power which they can reproduce only in their individual consumption process. The workers thus end by buying back from the capitalist the means of livelihood, which they themselves have produced. This, without any doubt, is quite different from the condition of simple commodity production, in which individual producers trade among themselves the products of their own labour, be they means of production or articles of consumption. The workers are compelled to sell their labour-power in order to purchase their means of livelihood as commodities. This compulsion presupposes the fact that they are denuded of property, and do not possess the means of production with which to produce their own livelihood. Only when this commodity-economic relation thus descends to the core of society, i.e. to the very process of reproduction of its direct producers, is the capitalist mode of production well established. That, in turn, tends to universalise the form of the commodity in the whole of society.

In societies not founded on the commodity-form, the means of production were, in principle, left in the hands of the direct producers (though in the special case of slavery, both the means of production and the slaves themselves belonged to the masters). Medieval society, out of which capitalism emerged, abided by this principle, the peasants being directly tied to land, which constituted their principal means of production. It was precisely for this reason that feudal society required the exercise of extra-economic compulsion to cement a master-servant relation. Capitalist society could formally dispense with this master-servant relation because of the conversion of labour-power into a commodity. Yet even capitalist society maintained, in substance, the subordination of the direct producers to their employer, by virtue of their separation from the means of production.

The process of excluding the direct producers from their means of production, however, could not be accomplished in one stroke. A definite historical epoch, characterised by a particular style of economic policies, had to elapse before capitalism irrevocably superseded the preceding regime, demonstrating the marked superiority of the peculiarly capitalist-social method over the traditional, isolated methods of production in the enhancement of the productive powers. Indeed, the capitalist method of production, which had emerged in Western Europe, particularly in England, in the sixteenth and seventeenth centuries, could firmly establish itself only in the course of the Industrial Revolution, which occurred towards the end of the eighteenth century. It was modern mechanised industry, the offspring of the Industrial Revolution, that finally secured for capital the conversion of labour-power into a commodity – labour-power which capital could not directly produce but which, to some extent, could be made to reproduce itself as a commodity on an expanding scale. This enabled capitalism to govern a whole historical society. Yet, even in that case, the capitalist organisation of society was never complete and thorough, with traditional social relations remaining here and there, and to a greater or lesser extent. This meant, however, that capitalism occupied a position which allowed it to eliminate the remainder in due course.

It is, however, a matter of no negligible importance that capitalism thus acquired the tendency to reproduce by itself the social regime congenial to its own operation. It is this fact that not only provides economic theory with its objective foundation, but also enables it to scientifically understand the relation between capitalism and its economic policies. Briefly, it means that the need for economic policies tends to disappear with the perfection of the capitalist commodity-economy. However, even this tendency, though remarkable at a certain stage of capitalist development, is never meant to be consummated. For, as already stated, labour-power does not become a commodity, nor do even ordinary products become commodities, because of some necessity inherent in the development of human life in society. The commodity-form arises rather in the interstices between independent communities, and, in due course, permeates their economic lives from the outside, as they are integrated into a larger society. From the point of view of social life, therefore, the commodity-form is essentially an alien and transitory form. This fact explains, on the one hand, why even such a thing as labour-power which is not a product, and which cannot be produced as a commodity, can still assume the *extraneous form* of the commodity under capitalism, and, on the other, why concrete historical conditions may not enable the development of capitalism to completely 'commodify' all aspects of society.

Indeed, past the middle of the nineteenth century, the prior tendency for capitalist social relations to universalise themselves was frustrated, instead giving rise to the formation of organised monopoly. The swift development of so-called monopoly capital depended on, firstly, the drastic intensification of labour made possible by an increasing population of wage-workers; secondly, the extended absorption of the products of the surviving handicraft sector into the capitalist market; and thirdly, and in particular, the expropriation of smaller capitalist enterprises by larger ones. In view of the enormous profit thus obtained, monopoly capital was no longer obliged to contribute to the further disintegration of traditional social relations. This may be interpreted as a reversal of the earlier tendency of capitalist development. The fact that the capitalist mode of production historically marks the three stages of its birth, (self-sustained) growth and decline stems from its 'absurd' (or unreasonable) foundation, that is to say, from the conversion of labour-power into a commodity. It is because of the peculiarity of this fact that capitalist society always requires economic policies as indispensable, supplementary support for its capacity to self-organise.

Thus, a scientific analysis of economic policies demands, first of all, a general determination of the changing historical context, which the development of the capitalist commodity-economy must necessarily undergo. It is a common fallacy to expect science to help prescribe some useful economic policies in an empty space. Science cannot arbitrarily take individual policies out of their historical context and evaluate them. The study of economic policies as a branch of economics has its own peculiar task and method, which will be described in the following section.

2   The Task and Method of the Study of Economic Policies

It is popularly believed that the study of economic policies consists of a scientific search for policy prescriptions that might be applied to solve various economic problems of the day. This, as already stated, is a fallacy stemming from the misconception of the nature of the (capitalist) commodity-economy, and of the scope of economics that scientifically exposes it. Such a misconception betrays the lack of appreciation of the peculiar status of the social sciences which, unlike the natural sciences, do not permit a technical application of their knowledge.

Yet this point has frequently been overlooked not only by the uninitiated but also by fully trained economists themselves. Thus, in Japan for instance, it has long become customary for the economists to subdivide the domain of

economic policy into such specialised branches as commercial, industrial, agricultural, colonial and other policies, following the traditional German style;
that is to say, without avoiding this popular fallacy. Specialised policy studies
in the tradition of the late German historical school have surely not been altogether futile. Indeed, this school, which had devoted particular attention to the
study of 'social policies' [*sozialpolitik*] since the 1870s, produced a monumental
accumulation of scholarly works. Yet, for precisely that reason, it contributed all
the more to investing the popular fallacy with a misleading, pseudo-scientific
appearance.

It is not without reason that the study of economics developed a strong
policy orientation in Germany. When capitalism emerged there during the
1830s and 1840s, that nation had not yet achieved political unification. The
need to accelerate its capitalist development under the overriding influence
of Great Britain impelled German economics to concentrate, on the one hand,
on historical investigations, and, on the other, on policy formulations. Britain
had already ascended to the liberal stage of capitalism, when Germany had
only entered the nascent phase of its development. Having successfully undergone the Industrial Revolution at the turn of the century, Britain was by then
already divesting itself of the mercantilist policies of the earlier epoch. In contrast, a still largely agricultural Germany found itself under pressure to rapidly
industrialise its economy, by expeditiously 'importing' the modern mechanised industry that had already come of age in Britain. Given such international relations, German reaction to Britain's classical political economy, which
expressly rejected mercantilist economic policies, was predictably negative, as
was demonstrated by Friedrich List's major work of 1841, *The National System
of Political Economy*.

Yet even classical political economy, against which List spoke, was not aware
of the reason why its theoretical system had to presuppose a society in which
capitalist production-relations were fully developed. In the light of the factual
development of capitalism in Britain in the early nineteenth century, which
was increasingly outgrowing the mercantilist policies of the earlier period, classical political economy simply took the perfection of capitalist society as its
ideological goal, and constructed its theoretical system accordingly. Indeed,
such a theoretical system turned out to be a fitting tool for the critique of mercantilism. The image of capitalism as it should be was perhaps less emphasised
in Ricardo than in Adam Smith. Yet even Ricardo never conceived of capitalism
as a historically transient society; he too viewed it as a realisation of a natural
order, so that even its failings were to be countenanced and borne as part of
human destiny. Friedrich List, who at the dawn of German capitalism reacted
strongly against the liberal thought of Adam Smith and inaugurated the histor-

ical school in economics, understood, however, very little of the real nature of the limitations of classical political economy. Operating at the purely practical level, List had no conception of capitalist society as a specific historical form. He thus resorted to a general theory of economic development, propounding a questionable stage-theoretic necessity for an agricultural nation, for example, to transform itself into an industrial one at a certain point in history.* Such a pseudo-scientific theory was to dominate German economics for a long time afterwards.

* According to List, the development of society undergoes the stages of (i) the primitive state; (ii) pastoral life; (iii) agriculture; (iv) agriculture coupled with manufacture, and, finally, (v) agriculture, in company with manufacture and commerce. He took the last stage, in which the three forms of economic activity develop harmoniously, to be the final and ideal state, believing that only in that stage could free international trade be realised. He clearly failed to understand why the capitalist commodity-economy mediated the transition of an agricultural nation to an agricultural-manufacturing nation. This historical fact was not understood by the classical school either, though the latter was not, for that reason, deterred from developing (if not completing) a body of economic theory. In the case of List, his failure to comprehend the historical necessity of capitalism prevented him from developing *any* economic theory at all, which rendered his stages-theory wholly arbitrary.

In using the concept of history to critically overcome the political economy of the classical school, Marx, who took an interest in political economy in Germany a little later than List, went far beyond him and his followers, and established, in the end, the system of economic theory in *Capital*. By locating not only capitalist society but also classical political economy, which proposed to study it, in its historical context, Marx indicated the method whereby systematic economic theory could be brought to completion. This method (unlike the classical one) did not claim the perfectibility of capitalism as such. It instead stipulated merely that a complete statement of economic theory required the presupposition of a perfectly developed capitalist society, while admitting the fact that real capitalism remained always a particular (and hence transient) historical society. The reader may refer to chapters 10 and 37 of *Capital*, Vol. III, for Marx's conception of a purely capitalist society.

Supplementary remarks: It is, however, never absolutely clear to me what Marx meant by 'the economic law of motion of modern society', the exposition of which he considered to be the ultimate aim of *Capital*, especially when the method of this exposition is said to be 'dialectical'. By 'economic law' Marx seems to imply not only the law of motion of a purely capitalist society but also that which regulates the process of the 'transformation of the economic conditions of production which can be determined with the precision of natural science',[2] i.e. the process of transition of one society to another. I am, however, unconvinced that economic theory can account for the latter process. Elsewhere, I have explained at length why I believe this to be impossible, commenting exhaustively on the text of 'Historical Tendency of Capital Accumulation'.[3]

The problem boils down to this: in what way can the economic law that is supposed to govern and regulate capitalist society *transform* itself into a new law that does nothing of the kind? Is there any logical explanation to this transformation? It seems to me that Marx merely infers the transition of capitalism to a new society from his materialistic conception of history, that is to say, by ascribing to his economic theory of capital accumulation a 'historical tendency' parallel to the 'primitive accumulation' which created conditions that were conducive to the subsequent evolution of capitalism. However, it seems apparent that, in so doing, he has failed to apply the principle of historical materialism unambiguously, as indeed he fails to explain how his so-called 'contradiction between productive forces and production-relations' relates to his other concept of 'the mode of production'. It is this kind of ambiguous 'historical' approach that, in my view, deters Marx from developing a satisfactory theory of periodic crises in *Capital*.

Although virtually all Marxists, economists and philosophers alike seem to interpret this ambiguous method of Marx (as illustrated by the section on 'Historical Tendency') to be his dialectical method, I believe, on the contrary, that it vitiates the true dialectical logic inherent in the economic theory of a purely capitalist society, and seriously detracts from the scientific character of *Capital*. I certainly do not wish to claim infallibility for my own contention. If it is erroneous, however, I would like to have it logically refuted rather than merely being denounced as un-Marxist and dismissed.

Concerning the significance of the dialectical method, I wish to emphasise the fact that Marx did not propose that his materialistic conception of history constituted scientific knowledge in and of itself; rather, he sought to partially validate it through economics. This seems to impose a certain restriction on the scope of application of this conception of history. For, as Marx himself established, economics focuses on the study of the capitalist commodity-economy as a historical society. Of course, the materialistic conception of history cannot be simply reduced to a commodity-economic conception of history. Yet it seems to me that the concrete operation of the dialectical logic must be found in the working of the theoretical system of a purely capitalist society. I wish to return to this important problem (pertaining to the relationship between the economic theory of capitalism and historical materialism) later. For the moment, as we begin the

---

2   Marx 1970, p. 21.

3   Marx 1987, *Capital*, Vol. I, Part VIII, Chapter 32.

study of economic policies, however, I wish to especially warn against the facile blend (sometimes believed to be the 'dialectic') of the logical and the historical so common in Marxist literature.

The policy-oriented political economy of List, which responded to the practical need of German industry as capitalism emerged in that country in the 1830s and 40s, thus made little contribution to scientific knowledge. Nor did its counsel prove effective even in Germany, which remained predominantly agricultural up to the 1860s, and which, consequently, leant towards the liberal doctrine of the Manchester style. That was not all. Since the unification of the empire in the early 1870s, the development of capitalism in Germany had entered a new phase, and visibly accelerated its pace. Under the circumstances, the historical school too had to grow out of its old *stufentheorie*, and to address itself to economic policies of the new kind, generically known as the *sozialpolitik*. The Association for studies in such policies [*Verein für Sozialpolitik*], which was inaugurated in 1873, dominated German economic studies in the era of finance-capital, vesting its economic policies with a suitable academic aura. At this point, the old teaching of List that depicted capitalism as a harmonious combination of agriculture and manufacture hardly impressed anyone. Even in Germany, the capitalist economy was manifesting its perverse effects, the containment of which called for practical solutions. The tide of socialism that demanded a once-and-for-all eradication of capitalist contradictions could be counteracted only by the admission of the need for the state to undertake eclectic 'social policies', which included economic policies.

The school of *sozialpolitik* adhered to the historical method. As illustrated by Schmoller's study of mercantilism,* however, this method consisted of deducing appropriate economic policies for the present from the study of past policies, the application of which were presumed to have been either correct or incorrect. It was believed that a scientific pursuit, through an ongoing process of trial and error, would eventually converge to a more or less correct solution. This approach, unlike the one of List, did not directly confront Britain's classical political economy. It instead willingly forsook any scientific analysis of capitalist society as such, and buried economic theory in a welter of historical contingencies. Economics, thus preoccupied full-time with the formulation of policy measures for practical solutions of current social problems, did not seek to comprehend that these were merely manifestations of the fundamental (logical) contradictions inherent in capitalism. It totally ignored its own nature as a social science, and applied itself to a limitless approximation to truth in history, in much the same way as natural science is presumed to approach truth pertaining to nature. Yet, in reality, capitalism no longer appeared as permanent as the natural order, its historical transience becoming increasingly obvious. It was not understood, however, that even the general and permanent aspects of social life in history could be accounted for only in the light of the peculiar form of the historically specific process known as capitalism. It is, of course, true that even capitalist society, in its peculiar functioning, abides by the general norms of economic life common to all societies. However, the problems of capitalism, insofar as they reflect its peculiar development, cannot be comprehended from the point of view of these general norms; nor can the norms be grasped in their true generality, unmediated by the commodity-economic forms of capitalism. Historical investigations that ignore the particular significance of capitalist society in the history of humankind, and thus overlook the commodity-economic forms which govern that society, can never be defended scientifically. That oversight is precisely that which characterises the study of economic policies in the tradition of the German historical school. That school, consequently, has never risen above the conventional wisdom of the practical person.**

* After defining mercantilism as a set of policies for the formation of the modern nation-state, Schmoller writes as follows: 'Whether such policies were implemented in each individual case correctly or incorrectly depended on the knowledge and discretion of the leaders of the state. Whether the policies were as a whole vindicated or not depended on whether or not they accompanied a general upward trend of national economic life'.[4] According to him, mercantilism was to be criticised for its excesses due to 'the misguided application of the powers of the state' and 'the technical imperfection of means'.[5] As I will show later, however, the historical meaning of mercantilist policies consisted precisely of the tendency of their being applied in excess.

** Confronted with Max Weber's criticism, which I shall mention presently, the followers of Schmoller tended to escape to such vague terms as 'the will to live'[6] and to 'the synthesis of the collective and individual benefits in the light of economic effectiveness',[7] where their master used to refer more concretely to 'the peoples and their age',[8] in the hope of describing the aim of economic policies in what would appear as more abstract-general terms. In this country, Professor Kumagai echoed the same tendency by aspiring for 'a system of economic policies conducive to public welfare'.[9]

---

4   Schmoller 1884, p. 59.
5   Schmoller 1900, II, p. 694.
6   Voigt 1928.
7   Wilbrandt 1924.
8   Schmoller 1911.
9   Hisao Kumagai 1964, *Keizai-Seisakuron no Tenkai*, p. 15.

The practical orientation of the historical school, however, has been criticised by the supporters of the thesis, according to which the definition of the end (purpose) of economic policies should fall outside the scope of economics considered as empirical science. Max Weber, in his article 'Objectivity in Social Science and Social Policy', expands on this thesis, which implies a novel epistemology in economic studies.[10] According to Weber, the scientific study of economic policies must be limited to the search for the means that are appropriate for the achievement of a proposed end, and the estimation of the chances and costs of attaining the end by certain available criteria. Thus, even though such a study might indirectly question the setting of the end itself, the adoption or rejection of the end must be left to the individual value judgement of the policymaker (the acting and willing person). If this value judgement is ever subjected to a scientific scrutiny, it is merely to make the policymaker more aware of the consequences of his/her choice, as the espousal of certain values involves the rejection of certain others; but the act of choice is a matter of his/her personal responsibility and not of the scientist's. The scientist himself/herself can, of course, propose a policy on practical grounds; but then he/she does so as an individual and not as a scientist, because, in proposing a policy, his/her personal value judgement cannot be avoided; a value judgement does not belong to his/her scientific activity proper. Even though, by experience, the scientist can more easily discover appropriate means for the implementation of the policy, and see its objective consequences more clearly, he/she is not, for that reason, free from cultural values and ethical imperatives in his/her choice of the end of the policy. Thus argues Weber.

The fundamental defect of this thesis lies in its failure to recognise the fact that the end of economic policies is, in essence, predetermined by the given historical conditions and the social relations of the age, and cannot be dictated by the subjective choice and value judgement of the policymaker. Of course, as I have already remarked, an individual policy may be adopted and pursued to serve the subjectively chosen end of a particular person, which may be contrary to the general trend of the society. Such a policy, however, is bound to be corrected by others in such a way that the total process of historical development ends always by reflecting a definite set of social relations. Thus, even if all individual policies are each introduced by the policymakers' subjective decision, that does not contradict the fact that *together* they form an objective process in history, and pursue an objectively determined end, and that the policymakers are merely made to play their historically assigned role unawares. This point

---

10   Weber 1949, pp. 50–112.

may be challenged by the claim that the adoption of a proper policy goal is, in fact, decisive to the subsequent development of the state. For example, Germany's protective commercial policy in the first half of the nineteenth century may be credited for its later, successful industrialisation, while the failure of Portugal and Spain to establish the capitalist method of production, despite their early exposure to international trade, may be attributed to the absence of judicious policy guidance by the state. In that regard, however, the case of England, the country in which the development of capitalism proved to be most successful, was not in any way different. It is important to understand that even England's mercantilist policies did not constitute an exception. For they were not guided either by any clear conception of the underlying economic trend, which remained hidden underneath the conflicts of interest that prevailed among various social groups. It only so happened that the process through which that conflict was actually resolved, often in an unexpected manner, determined the direction towards which the mercantilist policies, on the whole, groped haphazardly. All this is not to deny the fact that individual policies were always adopted, case by case, in the light of the best available knowledge of the day.

From this, however, it does not follow that the correct direction in which economic policies may be pursued can be scientifically predicted. The development of capitalism itself is not a general and permanent process, the scientific analysis of which teaches us how to formulate proper economic policies for its most effective operation. On the contrary, policies are always formulated and vigorously promoted by sectional interests, which fail to see the teleological development of capitalism. Therefore, the policies that are actually adopted do not, in general, realise the end originally intended by the real economic process itself. On the contrary, they often yield unexpected results. It is, thus, impossible to say, for example, that German economic policies in the nineteenth century were correctly formulated or that they realised their ends as originally intended.

To say, as I have said, that arbitrary policies would be corrected by other policies implies that the actual trend of capitalist development cannot be affected by any arbitrary choice of economic policies. Yet that must not be interpreted to be an assertion of a simple determinism; for the actual process exhibits, in each period, a high degree of complexity, which cannot be lightly set aside just because it is not easily captured by general characterisations. It is for this reason that the intensive study of economic policies undertaken by List and Schmoller, on the one hand, and by Max Weber, on the other, must be given due credit. These authors are criticised only because they embarked upon the study of policies without situating this task within economic studies in general, that is to say, without a prior knowledge of the relationship between theory, policy and history in economics. It is a matter of fundamental importance to have a clear idea as to how the scientific study of economics is to be brought to bear on practical issues. Though I have already referred to this matter in passing, I believe it necessary to discuss it in more systematic terms in the following section.

3   The Study of Economic Policies and Economics

In a society founded on capitalist production, its economic activity is always mediated by the commodity-form, and is never carried out directly, i.e. unmediated by that form. Thus, in principle, individuals relate themselves socially only through the sale and the purchase of commodities. The relation between the capitalists and the workers, which fundamentally characterises this society, rests on the conversion of labour-power into a commodity, and this in turn makes the production-process in this society radically commodity-economic. It goes without saying that the capitalists are related to one another by commodity exchanges, but their relationship with the landlords too is mediated by the market. Therefore, the three major classes of the capitalists, the workers, and the landlords form among themselves the governing social relations in commodity-economic terms; and into these basic social relations are integrated other members of capitalist society too, be they those traditional merchants and small producers, such as craftsmen and peasants, who continue to survive, or the professionals and parasites of various kinds who proliferate as capitalist society becomes increasingly more complex. This would mean that the behaviour of individuals, though always motivated by their subjective considerations, is, in fact, directly or indirectly regulated by the laws of the commodity-economy and proves to be effective only insofar as it conforms to these laws. The latter, in turn, emerge as a large number of independent individuals repeatedly strive to achieve their own self-seeking and myopic goals by the process of trial and error. For the totality of their acts, plied each independently, ends by forging stable social relations that suit capitalist society.

This peculiar nature of capitalist economic laws all too often fails to be adequately comprehended. Economic theory exposes the general principles of capitalist society only by following the operation of these laws in an imagined, purely capitalist context, that is to say, only from the perspective of the social relations that the three major interacting classes tend increasingly to form. Yet the operation of commodity-economic laws cannot be artificially separated from their many disturbing factors, in the same way as the operation of natural-scientific laws may be isolated under the condition of controlled experiment in the laboratory; for we cannot make capitalism work ideally, except by reinforcing, in our thought, its automatic tendency to restore equilibrium, a tendency which is ensured by the automatic working of the price mechanism, correcting the social imbalances that the anarchic commodity production, undertaken by competing firms, necessarily engenders. In other words, economics does not describe the laws of capitalism as externally imposed, even though the working of the laws appears to the individual producers as constraining their action from the outside. It is precisely for that reason that economics cannot, even after having discovered the laws of capitalism, apply them back to it extraneously for its arbitrary control. The failure to grasp this fundamental relation between the anarchic form of the commodity-economy and the capitalist laws that reflect its essence was bound to lead to this popular fallacy of the role of economic policies. This fallacy, since it is devoid of sense, contains no more theoretical substance than the erratic reference to, say, the so-called 'law' of demand and supply. In the (capitalist) commodity-economy, production is anarchic in form but not so in essence. Economics possesses a systematic theory based on the fact that capitalism as a global (all-embracing) commodity-economy is self-regulatory.* That sort of theory, as it turns out, could not be built on the fragmentary knowledge derived from the study of the imperfectly operating 'commodity-economies', which always existed to a limited extent on the periphery of many pre-capitalist societies.

* It must not be forgotten that even the purely theoretical exposition of the capitalist commodity-economy presupposes the working of the law of value, which corrects the imbalances of commodity production only *ex post facto*. The economic laws are enforced through this corrective process, in which social imbalances tend to be removed, as individual producers pursue their profits. No economic law directly enforces itself, without undergoing this uniquely commodity-economic mechanism of self-regulation. If, for example, technical progress occurs in the course of capital accumulation, not only the inter-industry relations (including those between the sector that produces means of production and the sector that produces articles of consumption, as distinguished in the so-called reproduction-schemes), but also the relations between the classes (first between the capitalists and the wage-workers, then between the capitalists and the landowners as well) will be significantly affected, so that the development of the capitalist economy will be subject to many forms of unevenness; but biases and irregularities will be corrected by the motion of prices through which the law of value enforces itself automatically. In the meantime, no one can appropriate this law and use it as a practical tool for the control of capitalism from without. The popular exponents

of economic policies seem to believe, quite incorrectly, in the technical and judicious 'application' of economic laws, as if the latter were, in essence, the same as laws of the natural sciences.

The fallacy of such beliefs becomes evident if one considers the commodity-form of labour-power, which is a product neither of labour nor of capital. Needless to say, the motion of prices alone cannot regulate the demand and supply of labour-power. A rise or a fall in its price does not enable capital to produce more or less of it. It is thus only in the cyclical process of capital accumulation, periodically disrupted by industrial crises, that the demand for labour-power can be indirectly adjusted to the supply of it. Indeed, the natural growth of labour-power, originating only in the family life of individual workers, cannot necessarily be made to conform to the requirements of capital, except in a roundabout fashion through the working of the law of relative surplus population. In other words, even capital has to resort to an indirect method (such as the law of population) in order to maintain the commodity-form of labour-power and, thus, to ensure the working of the law of value. It is here that the true cause of industrial crises under capitalism must be located.

Of course, an economic crisis can, in practice, occur for reasons other than the difficulty that capital has in ensuring the availability of labour-power as a commodity. For example, inter-industry imbalances or 'disproportions' may actually lead to a crisis, since such contingent factors as the condition of foreign trade can always intervene in practice. Moreover, it is expected that the concrete form of the manifestation of a crisis differs from one stage of capitalist development to another. However, an explanation of economic crises in the light of contingent factors is never theoretically satisfactory, nor scientifically adequate. In this respect, Marx, too, has to be blamed to some extent; for he failed to demonstrate the theoretical necessity of capitalist crises owing to his undue preoccupation with contingent factors. Confronted with the massive 'industrial reserve army', Marx could not clearly see the connection between the law of surplus population and economic crises, and subscribed to the thesis of immiseration, which then appeared more empirically plausible; but that, in my judgement, made it impossible for him to formulate a correct theory of economic crises, even though he made a number of pertinent remarks related thereto, and even though he indicated profound insights into the law of relative surplus population peculiar to capitalism.

If, as Marx thought, the working population were always available in the form of an industrial reserve army, the reason for the cyclical development of modern industry would tend to be attributed to factors that are extraneous to the logic of capitalism, such as the opening up of a new market. Marx's reference in *Capital*, Vol. II, to intersectoral disproportions as a plausible cause of crises, which has found many followers, stems also from his failure to see the full import of the law of population. The intersectoral condition of the reproduction schemes, which capitalist society too (as all other societies) must always satisfy in order to exist as a historical society, cannot be presumed to suffer regular (and periodic) violations, unless the historical presence of capitalism as a commodity-economy itself is to be negated. Marx's formulation of the 'excess of capital' in *Capital*, Vol. III, too, is also less than defensible for the same reason. In my book, *Theory of Economic Crises under Capitalism* (1953), I have developed what I consider to be a theoretically more defensible explanation of economic crises, based on the idea that the fundamental contradictions of the capitalist mode of production must be derived from the conversion of labour-power into a commodity.

As capitalism began in history, however, social relations based on the conversion of labour-power into a commodity had not yet been well established. It was only during its subsequent stage of self-sustained development that capitalism gradually tended to materialise its purer form, which economic theory must always presuppose. Yet even this tendency had not been consummated, before another phase of development set in to frustrate and to reverse it. Such circumstances suggest that the conversion of labour-power into a commodity, which capitalism had to accomplish in its phase of birth and autonomous growth, was by no means the natural outcome of any human society. It was, on the contrary, an exceptional turn of events. The modern wage-worker is, of course, neither a slave nor a serf. Yet his freedom from the traditional master-servant relation does not imply freedom from a class relation. Capitalism only conceals it by means of the conversion of labour-power into a commodity, thus realising the limiting case of class society. This society, known also as 'civil society', openly espouses classless human relations based on freedom and equality, as the commodity-economy transforms even human relations into relations between material objects (like commodities) quite indifferent to social stratification. It is through this 'reification' of human relations that the commodity-economy organises a historical society, a society which achieves the spectacular advancement of its productive powers by means of reified laws, and which also exposes, for the first time, the structure of its material base in economic theory.

In the formative period of capitalism, however, the operation of commodity-economic laws was as yet limited to preparing their own foundation, that is to say, to expediting the society-wide conversion of labour-power into a commodity. Only in the subsequent period of autonomous growth, as already remarked, did the laws become self-dependent and capable of securing their own operative conditions under the capitalist regime, which was now firmly established. These stages of formation and self-expansion of capitalism were most clearly represented by the Great Britain of the seventeenth and eighteenth as well as by the first half of the nineteenth century; but, as other countries, such as Germany, the United States and France, became capitalist in the latter half of the nineteenth century, the hitherto clearly discernible tendency of real capitalist society to approach its pure image appeared to lose its momentum. These newcomers could directly import from Britain the advanced methods of production as already embodied in mechanised, large-scale industry, even in the nascent period of their capitalisms. This meant that the social process that accompanied the commodification of labour-power in those nations unfolded quite differently from what was experienced earlier in Great Britain.

Although capitalism originally grew out of international trade centring around Spain, Portugal and the Netherlands, these countries soon dropped out of the forefront of world economic history, given their inability to lead the development of capitalism. Great Britain alone, having successfully implanted the capitalist method of production, exhibited the most typical form of the two early stages of capitalist development. Yet Britain too had to lose its hegemonic supremacy to Germany and the United States, in the second half of the nineteenth century, as the imperialist stage evolved. The advanced methods of production that these countries cultivated were then made available to Russia and Japan, when the latter subsequently joined the capitalist orbit. Thus, the introduction of capitalism did not occur uniformly in all nations. Instead, the introductory process differed from one case to another, depending on the date on which it began and the various historical circumstances specific to each country. It, therefore, becomes obvious that the evolution of the capitalist method of production in those countries, which played the leading part in the world-historic development of capitalism, is of particular importance to the study of economic policies.

The following picture then emerges. Notwithstanding national differences in historical and economic conditions, the mercantilist policies of England in the seventeenth and eighteenth centuries most typically represented the world-historic stage of formation of capitalism. Other countries followed England as they practised more or less similar policies; but the Industrial Revolution, which intervened towards the end of the eighteenth century, unmistakably established Britain's supremacy as the centre of the capitalist world, a position that was consolidated and maintained throughout the second stage of capitalist development known as the age of liberalism. Yet, as capitalism entered the last stage of its world-historic development, with the coming of age of German industry towards the end of the nineteenth century, the development of all capitalist countries was, directly or indirectly, affected by the economic prowess of Germany; and, thus, other nations tended to adopt economic policies in the German-style. The goals of such policies were never set by the value judgement of individuals, as Max Weber would have liked to believe, nor did such policies achieve their ends because of the appropriateness of their 'scientifically' devised means. Both the ends and the means of the economic policies then pursued were dictated by the interest of the dominant form of capital, known as finance-capital, which was specific to the world-historic stage of imperialism. The economic policies of capitalist society, just as its socio-economic relations, were thus without any doubt historically shaped, even though the forces that shaped them were bound to be buried underneath the anarchic form of the commodity-economy and may not be immediately apparent. This being the case, the policies that did not serve the interest of the dominant form of capital, if they were ever put into practice, did not fail to be subsequently corrected by counteracting policies. It, therefore, seemed to follow that capital conceded sometimes to the political thrust of landed property, sometimes to the wishes of small producers and other interest groups, and sometimes even to the vigorous demands of the working classes. Yet it was, in principle, possible to determine the ends and the means of economic policies, specific to each of the world-historic stages of development of capitalism, when they were practised in the country that most typically represented that stage. A scientific study of economic policies thus finds its ultimate justification in view of the fact that, in such contexts, the objective grounds for such policies could be grasped quite unambiguously.*

* It is obvious that the scientific study of economic policies cannot be viewed as an immediate extension of the economic theory of capitalism. Classical political economy could not formulate abstract economic theory, until capitalism became self-regulating, that is, after it concluded its formative period and entered the liberal stage. Marx recognised this fact, and took the tendency of capitalism to approach its pure image, divesting itself of the remains of earlier societies, to be the essential condition for economic theory to be objectively grounded. In reality, however, real capitalism in history never achieved theoretical purity in its actual operation. That is the case not only in the mercantilist and the imperialist stages, but even in the liberal stage as well, in which the ideal image of laissez-faire and free competition was most closely approximated. Therefore, such theoretical laws as the laws of value and of average profit are not expected to operate in the context of the stages with the same rigour or self-repetitiveness as they must do in the context of a purely capitalist society. Instead, the operation of these laws must become blunted, or less stringent, to the extent that it is impeded by the concrete-specific circumstances typical of each stage. It thus becomes quite possible for the operating mode of imperialism, for example, to become quite different in Britain and Germany, even though, at the end of the nineteenth and the beginning of the twentieth century, the two countries equally embodied the imperialist economic policies in their most typical form – typical in the sense that they served as the referent, in the light of which the historical significance of imperialist policies in other countries must be understood. It can be said, in the same spirit, that Great Britain most typically rep-

resented the stages of mercantilism in the seventeenth and eighteenth centuries, and of liberalism in the mid-nineteenth century, as a consequence of the set of economic policies it adopted in each of those eras. On the other hand, neither mercantilism nor liberalism ever took their typical form in Japan, as its capitalism underwent the periods of birth and self-propelled growth broadly during the world-historic stage of imperialism. The economic policies that Japan and other similar nations adopted in the course of their historical development cannot be studied scientifically without due reference to the stage-theoretic types, as these are defined by the earlier experience of Britain and Germany in the world-historic development of capitalism.

Neither the pure theory of capitalism nor the typified stages of capitalist development can offer scientific guidance for the designing of concrete economic policies. It is perfectly obvious that economic policies under capitalism were, in fact, implemented in all its stages of development with hardly any conscious knowledge of its inner logic. If the idea of 'laissez-faire' espoused by the followers of Adam Smith found wide support at one stage, it was not because the historical meaning of free competition was understood by the public, but merely because it agreed with the interests of the then dominant capitalist class, which took advantage of the precepts of the existing economic theory. Moreover, classical economic theory, the systematic formulation of which was assisted by the development of capitalism itself, had not as yet been objectively grounded. That is to say, it was not understood as revealing the inner laws of capitalism. Thus, laissez-faire policies were advocated and practised by the political parties which represented the capitalist interest, but were also fiercely opposed by the parties representing the interest of other classes. Liberalism, too, forced its way through to victory against the persistent opposition of the old, privileged classes. So far as the economic policies of imperialism were concerned, the same situation repeated itself even more flagrantly; for a theoretical weapon comparable to classical political economy was not available in that era. Had the true economic theory been sought, it would have vindicated Marxism, and would have exposed the historical limitations of the policies that were being actually designed and implemented. In the stage of imperialism, economic theories, which failed to criticise the capitalist regime, degenerated into mere tools of the apologists of one kind or another. Neither the historical school, which propounded *sozialpolitik*, nor the marginal utility school, which lucubrated on social welfare, had the slightest conception of what 'capital' really meant. It was clearly a far cry for them to come to grips with a scientific comprehension of imperialism.

  Marxism is often called scientific socialism, but the true sense of this expression is frequently misunderstood. Although the pure theory of capitalism, which constitutes the scientific core of Marxism, is designed to expose the objective logic of capital, and that is what socialism is meant to overcome, this fact alone does not (and should not) in any sense uniquely determine our socialist practice. The socialist movement must, of course, be guided and directed by a political party which represents it; but the party cannot achieve its aim by simply advocating the necessity of a socialist society as the natural sequel to capitalism. Neither does the working class automatically adopt a socialist ideology and define itself as its revolutionary agent. The workers acquire class consciousness in organised political activities led by a socialist party. In the stage of imperialism, in particular, a socialist party must, in order to be effective, formulate its programme in concrete terms and counteract the policies of other parties. Instead of merely denouncing the policies of the opposition, however, the socialist party should expose their concealed ulterior motives in the light of historically objective conditions. The analysis of such conditions is bound to be much more involved than a mere recapitulation of the general theory of capitalism.

Since capitalism in various countries attains different degrees of development at different times and retains a multiplicity of traditional elements, it is futile for a socialist party to simply lecture on the theoretical class structure of capitalist society in general. Yet, the analysis of current conditions which is required will not be 'scientific' if it is not linked with the general theory of capitalism through the mediation of appropriate stage-theoretic determinations. Even a scientifically precise and sophisticated analysis of the current conjuncture, however, cannot, by itself, determine the strategies and tactics of a socialist party. The latter must strategically adapt to day-to-day changes in social conditions. It must be guided by practical judgement based on information pertaining to the current state of affairs gathered by its own organisations, and also on the party's considered evaluation of its own internal strength and solidarity. Such practical judgements cannot be determined scientifically even by Marxism just because it is called 'scientific socialism'.* The strategy of the party is frequently constrained by the extent to which it can mobilise its resources, and that depends on many contingent factors. Furthermore, the party's action must always consider the interests of various social groups, which are related in various complex ways with the three major classes of capitalist society. Even a fully defensible, scientific analysis of current economic conditions would be able to capture the conduct of such groups only in broad terms.

* Economists of a Marxist persuasion have consistently held the opposite view, believing the positions of the Marxist party to be unquestionably 'scientific', and misconceiving their role to lie in the provision of an uncompromising defence of the party's

platform. Many *Kôzaha* Marxists have been scrupulously faithful to the party's view of Japanese capitalism. Their preconception that Marx and Lenin are infallible and that their writings are above criticism does not, however, demonstrate a true respect for the greatness of Marx or of Lenin. *Capital* and *Imperialism* are, of course, works that must be carefully studied; but economists are surely not obliged to accept such portions of these books that they themselves cannot fully comprehend. Perhaps the positions of the party may not be lightly criticised by someone like myself who, as a theorist, must maintain a certain distance from the political movement for socialism. However, if the party advances a position allegedly based on the writings of Marx and/or Lenin, everyone, including economists outside the movement, should be entitled to question whether or not the relevant parts of these writings are free from errors and ambiguities. To claim the infallibility of the party because it is inspired by 'scientific socialism' is not only futile but also positively harmful to the Marxist movement itself. One must not overestimate the importance of socialist (and, thus, ideological) pronouncements in *Capital* at the expense of that work's more important scientific contributions.

This important point has not been firmly understood within the tradition of Marxist political movements. The position of the German Social Democrats towards the end of the nineteenth century, when they confronted the question of tariffs, illustrates this failure.[11] Marx's own view, it seems to me, is clear enough from the speech that he gave in 1848 on the problems of free trade.[12] Marxism cannot, of course, simply endorse an economic policy that contributes to the development of capitalism; but that does not mean that it should oppose any capitalist policy as automatically incompatible with the interests of the working class. Since the aim of a socialist party is to change society by means of an organised political movement, it should either support or oppose economic policies, depending on their usefulness to its strategic aim.* The party's decision in this regard is strictly pragmatic, even though it should be made, as far as possible, in the light of a scrupulous analysis of current economic, juridical and political conditions, so as to be worthy of the mantle of scientific socialism. This is so because even the finest scientific analysis does not permit one to foretell all the consequences of a particular economic policy, which may turn out to be either conducive or detrimental to the political movement that is presided over by a socialist party. The latter must, therefore, depend on practical judgement, which necessarily involves fallible

---

11   See 'The Tariff Argument of the German Socialist Party' in my book entitled *Introduction to the Agricultural Problems* (Uno 1947).
12   Marx 1976, 'Speech on the Question of Free Trade'.

decisions. Yet that is precisely the specific role assigned to the party. If the present economic policies of the state are judged to be 'imperialist' in the stage-theoretic sense, it is, of course, out of the question for Marxism to simply accept them on the grounds that they are historically inevitable; but to systematic-ally oppose them as 'reactionary' does not make Marxism any more scientific. Instead, it would only reveal an ignorance of the limits within which stage-theoretic determinations are useful. Neither the pure theory nor the stages-theory can, by themselves, unambiguously determine the effects of individual economic policies, contrary to the belief of doctrinaire Marxists. Yet this point touches upon a more fundamental issue relating to the practical significance of economics as a social-scientific discipline. This issue cannot be satisfactorily addressed, without further methodological inquiry into the nature of econom-ics.

* Here again I must stress the fact that Marxism, because it is said to be 'scientific social-ism', cannot dispense with the practical judgement (strategy) of a political party in adopting its stance with regard to economic policy. For neither the pure theory nor the stages-theory – and, indeed, not even the most credible analysis of the current situ-ation – can unambiguously determine what a particular policy actually entails. Instead of admitting this important limitation, Marxism has often covered it up under such slo-gans as the 'dialectical unity of theory and practice'. We must, however, categorically reject the view that the knowledge of society may be utilised for political movements in the same way as the knowledge of nature can be technically applied to enrich our lives. The investigation of this difficult connection between the knowledge of society and social practice should constitute the main theme of Marxist philosophy. Yet, the latter has systematically neglected this kind of investigation without even realising the presence of the issue. On the whole, Marxists have taken this issue too lightly, hiding it under the cover of such a complacent dogma as 'Marxism is a science'.

Economics may be said to have more or less established its method of theor-etical inquiry with Marx's *Capital*, which extended the works of the classical school. I say 'more or less' since the method thus established pertains only to the purely theoretical part of economics. It is true that *Capital* contains detailed historical accounts of capitalism in its birth (specifically as the process of prim-itive accumulation) and in its subsequent phase of autonomous growth. These historical accounts are, however, essentially of a nature that is conducive to pre-paring the ground for, and offering illustrative comments on, the exposition of the pure theory of capitalism, and do not provide us with determinations of what I would call the stages-theory of capitalist development. This is the case, even though I have found Marx's historical accounts to be highly suggestive of, and useful for, a more detailed elaboration of the latter kind of theory. It is my view that the method of study in the specialised branches of applied economics (including economic policies, public finance, financial institutions, etc.) has not, so far, been laid down in clear enough terms. Yet none of these specialised subjects can be adequately grasped in the light of purely theoretical determinations alone, even though the latter must always be held firmly in mind in all economic studies. Nor does it seem to be generally understood that the theory can really become pure and systematic only when it, for its part, renounces direct reference to either concrete-historical or stage-characteristic particulars.*

* Actually *Capital*, as it stands, is not as systematic as I would like it to be, nor can it be said to have achieved the purity or abstractness that a truly systematic theory requires, though my own interpretation on this point may not be shared widely. Nevertheless, it is my firm belief that *Capital*, on the whole, prepares the ground for the pure and general theory of capitalism.

Apart from the general theory of capitalism, economics involves a wide range of specialised fields. It is my view that all these fields must be studied, in the first instance, with reference to the world-historic stage of capitalist development, that is to say, with reference to the country which most typically represented the particular stage of development of capitalism, together with its international relations. It is not the detailed economic history of the referent country that is in question here, but rather the stage-characteristic determinations that the country most unambiguously exhibits. The question, therefore, boils down to how such determinations (of the world-historic stages of capitalist development) are obtained. Clearly, the theory of any particular developmental stage of capitalism will have to consist of a plausible synthesis of many specialised economic studies, and cannot stand apart from them. For instance, a concrete-synthetic theory of the (bourgeois) state will have to be elaborated, with the assistance of political and juridical studies that relate to the specific developmental stage of capitalism in question. In other words, the stage-theoretic determinations are expected to emerge from the common insights made available by all these specialised studies. The study of economic policies must, however, constitute the core of all these studies, inasmuch as, and to the extent that, they directly bear upon the specific developmental stage of the evolution of capitalism. This relation, as I see it, is, to some extent, borne out by the historical connection of economic theory and economic policies. It was, indeed, during the period in which capitalism increasingly purified itself in fact that economic theory emerged from earlier debates on various economic policies, as if to achieve a more synthetic view on them. The same circumstances gave rise to the false conception (which persists even to this day) that economic theory has the power to endorse or to prescribe economic policies. This conception, false as it is, is not entirely baseless, since economic policies are always there to ensure the most effective functioning of the capitalist commodity-economy, as theory would envisage it. The fact that the three stages of capitalist development are to be distinguished by the three types of economic policies, known as mercantilism, liberalism and imperialism, seems to me to lend support to this contention. I might also remark, in passing, that economics can relate with other social-scientific disciplines, such as law and politics, only at the stage-theoretic level, the level at which economics manifests its policy orientation.

It can be said that economic studies, too, ultimately aim at 'praxis' in some sense. Yet, the fact that economics, unlike a natural science, consists of the three parts at distinct levels of abstraction (i.e. the pure theory, stages-theory and empirical/historical analyses of capitalism) militates against any technical application of its knowledge. It is for that reason that economics lays the foundation for all other historical and social sciences, while indicating the correct way in which the latter may relate to political practice. This statement may sound paradoxical in the first instance. It must, nevertheless, be well understood that the study of economic policies under capitalism (as that of the economic theory of capitalism) cannot be made scientifically objective, nor truly useful to political practice, unless it transcends the vulgar pragmatism that seeks to directly connect theory to practice.

The classical school laid the foundation for a system of economic theory by extricating itself from active policy concerns. Marx's economic doctrine followed the same path but went further, until, in the end, it established a logically self-conclusive system of economic theory. This it did in the spirit of a criticism of capitalist society itself. That is not to say that either classical liberalism or Marxist socialism was by itself powerful enough to ensure the scientific objectivity of economics. Yet the realisation that capitalism, the object of inquiry, constituted a once-and-for-all historical process, which undergoes the stages of birth, growth and decline, contains its own negation. In other words, capitalism cannot be scientifically (objectively) grasped, unless its end is foreseen at the outset. The significance of this crucial point will be overlooked, if one merely sees and stresses the ideological motivation of either classical or Marx's economics. By simply labelling economics as socialist or Marxist, one may easily overlook the true value of Marx's approach. Marx made a truly significant step towards the completion of economic theory, based on his exhaustive critique of past economic doctrines, which confirmed his initial insight that capitalism constituted a historically transient society. The economic theory that we arrive at, by scrupulously following Marx's 'critique of political economy', is both convincing and understandable to anyone because of its true scientific objectivity.

Surely, that scientific objectivity lends strong support to the cause of a socialist party, but that does not mean that the party is enabled to make a technical use of Marx's economic theory with a view to prescribing or implementing a particular economic policy. For even though the economic theory of capitalism shows what needs to be changed and by whom in general terms, it neither teaches a practical lesson applicable in a concrete-historical context, nor does it offer a specific judgement with regard to the suitability of individual economic policies. Even when a concrete analysis of current economic conditions can be linked to general theory by the mediation of the stages-theory, this is by no means sufficient for political practice. Even Max Weber's epistemological critique of economic policies did not amount to anything more than a glorification of conventional wisdom, due to his lack of appreciation of the historically objective conditions under which the economic policies of capitalism are constrained, as I have already mentioned.* Marxist economics, too, cannot escape the same criticism, if it purports to apply the pure theory of capitalism directly to the analysis of current economic conditions, without the mediation of stages-theory. Indeed the neglect of the stages-theory of capitalist development not only vitiates the integrity of the pure economic theory of capitalism, but also leaves the task of a Marxist political party completely undefined.

* Max Weber, in the already quoted article, claims that concept-formation in the social sciences is to be assisted by 'ideal types'. Fundamental concepts in economics, however, cannot be constructed from such a subjective point of view. Weber must have completely overlooked the actual process in which economic theory emerged hand in hand with the formation of capitalism in the sixteenth and seventeenth century, the point that Marx especially emphasised. It is beyond any doubt that economics as a social science defined its fundamental concepts objectively in the historical process of development of capitalism itself. The basic concepts of the circulation forms (such as the commodity, money and capital), of wage-labour, and of landed property under capitalism, all of these present themselves unambiguously as capitalism emerges as a historical society, divesting itself of traditional and non commodity-economic relations. They are not 'arrived at by the analytical accentuation of certain elements of reality',[13] nor do they imply 'one-sidedly emphasised viewpoints'[14] as Weber claims.

13   Weber 1949, p. 90.
14   Ibid.

Weber specifically illustrates his ideal types in reference to the ideas of 'the market', 'handicraft' and 'capitalistic culture'. However, the idea of the market, for example, would be empty of substance if one failed to understand the real process whereby the demand and supply of capitalistically-produced commodities realise their market values through the motion of prices, while being constrained by the production-process of capital. Weber simply explains his idea of the market as follows:

> It is thus the 'idea' of a historically given modern society, based on an exchange economy, which is developed for us by quite the same logical principles as are used in constructing the idea of the medieval 'city economy' as a 'generic' concept. When we do that, we construct the concept of 'city economy' not as an average of the economic structures actually existing in all the cities observed, but as an *ideal type*. An ideal type is formed by the one-sided *accentuation* of one or more points of view and by the synthesis of a great many diffuse, discrete, more or less present and occasionally absent *concrete individual* phenomena, which are arranged according to those one-sidedly emphasised viewpoints into a unified analytical construct [*gedankenbild*]. In its conceptual purity, this mental construct cannot be found empirically anywhere in reality. It is a *utopia*. Historical research faces the task of determining in each individual case, the extent to which this ideal construct approximates to, or diverges from, reality, that is to say, to what extent, for example, the economic structure of a certain city is to be classified as a 'city economy'. When carefully applied, those concepts are particularly useful in research and exposition.[15]

There is no mention here of the mechanism that actualises market values, as it is only vaguely and conventionally conceived as a feature of an 'exchange economy'. Although Marx in *Capital* is not fully successful in the exposition of this particular mechanism, there is no doubt, in his case, that he intends to deduce it from the objective working of capitalist society.

I have quoted above a fairly long passage from Weber in order to clearly contrast the difference between his concept-formation and mine, because some authors believe that my idea of a purely capitalist society is quite similar to Weber's idea of the market. The quoted passage makes it immediately apparent that Weber, in explaining 'the market', talks extensively of the medieval 'city-economy'. This reveals his external approach to the concept: an ideal type of the market can be proposed because an ideal type of the city economy is plausible. Yet I must state quite emphatically that the concept of a purely capitalist society cannot possibly be inferred from an 'idea' of

---

15   Weber 1949, p. 90.

the city economy. On the contrary, a scientific analysis of the city economy requires economic concepts that can be established only in the process of the development of capitalism. It is perfectly obvious that a city economy, whether in the ancient or in the medieval age, could not form a historical society. How does Weber propose to synthesise a historical society by combining such partial ideal-types as the city economy? Weber's ideal type of the market merely refers to a set of commodity transactions in a definite place with no explanation of how the market in its full development properly functions, how limited its function was in medieval cities, and so on and so forth.

The idea of a purely capitalist society, which Marx clearly alluded to and which I have proposed to bring out more explicitly, is an objective reality, a reality that increasingly made its appearance in the actual process of capitalist development beginning in the seventeenth and eighteenth century. Great economists then arrived at their theoretical concepts, while being assisted by this self-disclosure of objective reality, not arbitrarily 'by analytical accentuation of certain elements of reality'. Surely a description of reality from a particular point of view does not enable anyone to appropriate general, scientific concepts. Even Marx was less than fully rigorous when he persisted in his socialist point of view. Adam Smith's liberalism contributed to a scientific understanding of reality to the extent that it enabled him to criticise mercantilist dogma, and Marx's socialism played the same role to the extent that it enabled him to criticise capitalism. In other words, an ideology serves science (objective knowledge) only when it criticises the dominant ideology of the age, which passes for the unquestioned *pre*supposition of science, not when its own espousal demands the name of science. This important relation between an ideology and objective social science is totally overlooked by the vulgar claim of a 'value-free' vantage point. He who claims to be value-free is only naïvely unconscious of the extent to which his own social life is dictated by conventional ideology. Scientific objectivity in matters of real social life cannot be reached by a self-complacent individual of this sort.

Max Weber's view was most probably influenced by the neo-Kantian philosophy of his day, which reasserted the critique of the cognitive capacity of the mind undertaken earlier by Kant himself in reference to the natural sciences. Indeed, Weber seemed to have inherited the neo-Kantian practice of wholly ignoring Marx's economic theory, while bitterly attacking the materialist conception of history, which only served as the guiding thread to it. Even in the article in question Weber 'intentionally avoided' discussion of Marx's economic theory 'in order not to complicate the exposition ... and in order not to forestall discussions on the Marxian literature' which were to appear in the same *Journal* under his own editorship.[16] However, I know for a fact

---

16   Weber 1949, p. 103.

that Weber 'intentionally avoided' confrontation with Marx's economic theory even where excuses of this type would not apply.

Whereas the conceptual framework of economic theory is fundamentally determined by the purely capitalist society towards which the actual process of development of capitalism pointed, the characterisation of the stages involves a procedure somewhat similar to the construction of Weber's ideal types. The proposition that Great Britain represented both the formative and the self-sustained growth stages of capitalist development, but that it only played the role of a passive counterpart of Germany in the declining stage of capitalist development cannot be deduced from the logic of the commodity-economy. That, however, does not mean, as Max Weber would have it, that the concept of the stages can be formed without presupposing the objective determinations of pure theory, but merely in the light of a 'one-sided emphasis' of our subject-ive 'viewpoints' leading to 'conceptual purity'. It is, moreover, impossible for the stages-theory, which is built on the study of economic policies, to claim for itself the 'conceptual purity' of economic theory, contrary to Weber's expectation. His error seems to derive from the unreasonable attempt to historically determ-ine capitalism without first grasping its inner logic. He apparently learned this erroneous lesson from Heinrich Rickert, the leading exponent of neo-Kantian philosophy at the time. For Rickert makes quite a few outlandish statements on economics.*

* Rickert, too, in his *Kulturwissenschaft und Naturwissenschaft* criticises the materialist conception of history while completely circumventing the economics of *Capital*. This conception, however, is essentially a socialist outlook on history. It is based on Marx's extensive knowledge, but it does not by itself constitute a science (or objective know-ledge). It must, therefore, be understood to be no more than an ideological hypothesis. Because Marx was aware of this, he subsequently devoted a number of years of study to economics so as to demonstrate the applicability of the hypothesis to capitalism. To ignore this truly great constituent of Marx's work and to criticise him as if he merely advanced an open-ended hypothesis of no use reveals the intellectual superficiality of the neo-Kantians, and the Weber-type socio-economic historians who uncritically fol-lowed them.

It is not my contention that *Capital*, as we know it, is, in any sense, theoretically perfect. Although I have learned virtually all of my economic theory from that book, it contains, for me at least, a large number of unsettled problems, which are left for us to work out. My *Principles of Political Economy* (1950–2) is an endeavour in that direction. Since Marx did not live to see the age of imperialism as the declining stage of capitalism, it is understandable that he failed to clearly distinguish the three levels of abstraction at which the study of economics must be undertaken. At present, however, we should know that the inner logic of capitalism can be rigorously comprehended only by pure economic theory as distinct from the stages-theory of capitalist development. It is, furthermore, my belief that only the logical theory of a purely capitalist society can demonstrate the (partial) credibility of the materialist conception of history, thus also grounding Marxist socialism generally on a scientific base.

Thus, the following study of economic policies under capitalism will probably not satisfy the reader who expects an immediately practical lesson. My purpose here, however, is to lay the foundation for the stages-theory of capitalist development by specifying the historical *types* of economic policies, as they necessarily occur in the process of the evolution of capitalism. To complete the stages-theory which is to mediate between the pure economic theory of capitalism and the concrete-historical analysis of real economic conditions, whether of one nation or of the world as a whole, one needs to further incorporate the knowledge of other specialised fields of economic studies as well as of law and politics. In closing the present Introduction, I wish to repeat once again that a concrete-historical study of current economic conditions, even when it is informed by a full-fledged stages-theory, does not immediately serve the purpose of any political practice. This view might appear to the impatient as being far too circuitous to be relevant, yet there is no shortcut to enlightenment so far as social-scientific inquiry is concerned.

PART I

Mercantilism

∵

Introduction to Part I

In their historical development, medieval societies, just as ancient societies before them, always tolerated a subsidiary operation of *the commodity-economy* on the periphery of their more prevalent mode of social relations, to which it was alien. Thus, not only commodities and money but also capital itself, in its early forms as merchant capital and money-lending capital, evolved from within the restricted sphere of the commodity-economy. Yet it was not long before the latter began to exert a disintegrating, if not a destructive, influence on the dominant feudal relations of medieval societies, upon the ruins of which capitalism was to emerge. The successful emergence of capitalism, however, required the sufficient infiltration by the commodity-economy into the material base which supported the then prevailing social relations. In other words, capitalism could not have arisen from the womb of traditional societies, unless and until the reproduction-process of material wealth, which constituted the ultimate base of their existence, had yielded to the sway of the commodity-economy. The essential condition for the latter was satisfied by the conversion of labour-power into a commodity.

This conversion, however, was not automatically realised, as the exchange of commodities grew inter-regionally, and even to some extent internationally, within medieval, feudal societies. As a matter of fact, these societies welcomed as well as resisted, in differing respects, the gradual encroachment by the commodity-economy, the operation of which diverged radically from the dictates of their prevalent economic mode. Thus, the European experience demonstrates that the conversion of labour-power into a commodity could not as easily be accomplished in Germany or France, where feudal societies had been more firmly entrenched, as in other countries which had actively participated in international trade since the fifteenth century. These latter countries, especially the Netherlands and England, acquired through their external contacts such manufacturing methods as had been slowly developing throughout the medieval age in various parts of Europe under feudal protection. In those countries, the commodity-economy could effectively penetrate to the root of the production-process, and separate manufacturing (especially textile manufacturing) from agriculture, the two occupations which had been naturally amalgamated in the peasant economy, and which together constituted the base of traditional societies. In England, in particular, which was abundantly supplied with the raw material for the manufacturing of wool, the conversion of labour-power into a commodity was consummated in the most definitive fashion.

From the beginning, this historical process presupposed, and was assisted by, the unfolding of international commodity trade, under the influence of which hitherto isolated local communities were drawn into the orbit of an integrated national economy. The economic catalyst of that process turned out to be *merchant capital*, as it was politically aided by the absolute monarchy of nascent modern nation-states. With the expulsion of the peasants from the land, their principal means of production, as the general premise, the nationwide conversion of labour-power into a commodity was systematically enforced, promptly realising the commodity-economic separation of manufacturing from agriculture. The much hailed advancement of national wealth, though generally understood to be synonymous with an increasing scale of society's productive activity, meant, in practice, the accumulation of capital in the hands of those who confronted the direct producers increasingly deprived of their traditional means of production. The accumulation of mercantile wealth, which proceeded even as the direct producers lost their own means of production, materialised, of course, no increase of wealth in their own hands. It was, on the contrary, their impoverishment which marked the 'primitive accumulation of capital' and which constituted the essential precondition of capitalism. Mercantilism was, thus, primarily the economic policy of merchant capital, as it enforced its primitive accumulation.

CHAPTER 1

The Formative Period of Capitalism

Merchant capital is the original formula for the operation of capital. As soon as commodity exchanges develop to some extent, the complex network of 'sales for purchase', $C-M-C'$ (where C represents commodities, M money and C' other commodities), invariably gives rise to 'purchases for sale', $M-C-M'$ (where M' means more money than M), which represent the characteristic activity of the merchant. The reason is that the circulation of commodities always entails a development in the function of money, from that of a mere medium of circulation to that of idle funds (or what Marx called 'money as money', the meaning of which is best conveyed by the Japanese word *shikin*, a step before *shihon* or capital), which enables the separation of the act of sale, $C-M$, from the act of purchase, $M-C$. Money that becomes free from commodity exchanges due to this separation can then be used as 'capital' with a view to profiting from price differentials, occurring spatially as well as over time, in the commodity-economy. Merchant capital, the first form of value augmentation, thus develops in the hands of the middleman, who typically does not question (and so stays aloof from) the social relations under which producers and consumers operate.

The profit, which merchant capital realises in the process of 'buying cheap and selling dear', has the inherent character of *expropriatory gain*. Yet there is another aspect to it as well. To the extent that the price differentials, prevailing among the products of more or less independent communities, reflect differences in their conditions of production, the action of the merchant, who turns their products into commodities, cannot remain entirely neutral. More likely than not, the contact with the merchant will teach each community to evaluate its own capacity relative to that of other communities, and will end in efforts to raise its productivity. This is not to deny the fact that the accumulation of mercantile wealth originates in the trade of surplus products, but trade can easily be extended to involve necessary products as well, which, at times, may even be encouraged by the feudal ruling classes. Nor do merchants refrain from speculative transactions. Thus, as merchant capital 'commodifies' certain products of the community, the latter's production-relations cannot escape erosion in one way or another. Yet, in general, the commodity-economy, which exercises this disintegrating effect on the existing relations of production, remained external to them. Because of its indifference to any particular mode of production-relations, the commodity-economy does not, for its part, intend to impose any definite alternative. Thus, the nature of the new mode of production-relations, when the old mode yields to the sway of the commodity-economy, will depend entirely on the specific nature of the productive powers that have already been cultivated in traditional society. Unlike ancient societies which simply wilted away upon contact with the commodity-economy, medieval societies followed a different course. Here the contact with the commodity-economy enabled them to raise their own productive powers, and thus to secure an extensive conversion of labour-power into a commodity on that basis.*

* In ancient societies, the growth of mercantile activity often intensified the exploitation of slaves, which impeded progress in their productivity, eventually entailing a decline, if not a collapse, of the existing social order. In medieval societies, in contrast, manufacturing productivity, stimulated by commerce, was not only preserved but was further developed in the hands of small handicraft producers. It can be said that this enhanced productivity in manufacturing provided the basis for the evolution of new (i.e. capitalist) production-relations, when the peasant economy disintegrated. This is not to suggest that merchant capitalists could be smoothly transformed into industrial capitalists. Yet it does explain why merchant capital (without as yet becoming industrial capital) could successfully infiltrate the production-process of commodities.

Indeed, the accelerated expansion of the world market from the fifteenth century onward made it possible for the merchants to establish capitalism in England. The merchants, who had long been excluded from the production-process by feudal restrictions, took advantage of the loosening application of these restrictions as medieval society disintegrated, and gradually found their way to the position of dictating to the producers. The so-called putting-out, or commission, system (which organised 'domestic industry') allowed capital to infiltrate the production-process, and to secure control over it, albeit in an indirect fashion. Under this system, small-scale individual producers were guided by the merchant in supplying commodities to meet a large-scale demand of the market. These small producers, though formally retaining their medieval independence from the merchant, but increasingly unable to reassert it effectively, were in the process of being integrated into capitalist production-relations. Small producers, who were separated from agriculture, and who could no longer return to it, were particularly vulnerable to this process. At the same time, 'manufactories', which incarnated Marx's manufacture division of labour, also made their appearance. This new method of production clearly implied a more advanced stage of the conversion of labour-power into a commodity, even though it never actually grew powerful enough to assume a dominant position, at least not to the extent of superseding the commission (putting-out) system that merchant capital operated. Since commodities were still largely supplied to international markets, the method of 'manufactory' production would have been inefficient, in any case, in adapting to unpredictable changes in distant demand. Rather it was to the advantage of capital to maintain the merchant method of procuring the outputs of formally independent small producers, who, as handicraft workers, were still in possession of some means of production of their own.

The separation of manufacturing from agriculture, either under the putting-out (or commission) system operated by merchant capital, or, even more so, under the 'manufactory' production of commodities, entailed the formation of extensive market relations within the country. As the 'home market' established itself, capital acquired the opportunity of directly descending to the root of the production-process. The home market, on the one hand, drew agriculture itself into commodity-economic relations, while, on the other, created an extensive population of direct producers in rural districts. These were the direct producers, who no longer retained a connection to the agricultural base, and who had thus been deprived of such means of production as raw materials, tools and workplaces one after another, and who, therefore, could no longer function as independent producers. The 'co-operation' of many workers in the manufactory did foreshadow the 'manufacture division of labour', which, under the capitalist method of production later, promoted an increase of relative surplus value. The productivity gain due to the manufacture division of labour was still limited, although, even under the commission (putting-out) system, the production-process was increasingly parcelled up and subdivided, as direct producers lost their own means of production. Thus, at this point, merchant capital derived an as yet relatively minor gain from the limited productivity effect of the manufacture division of labour, as compared with the overwhelming advantage it realised from the 'expropriation' of the direct producers. Indeed, merchant capital operating the putting-out system left the direct producers in their old occupation *in form*, and yet converted them *in substance* into wage-workers, not so different from the workers found in manufactories. It was in this manner that the accumulation of capital by the merchant prepared the ground for the subsequent development of the capitalist method of production.

Referring to this process of so-called primitive accumulation, Marx writes as follows:

> All revolutions are epoch-making that act as levers for the capitalist class in the course of formation; but, above all, those moments when

great masses of men are suddenly and forcibly torn from their means
of subsistence, and hurled as free and 'unattached' proletarians on the
labour-market. The expropriation of the agricultural producer, of the
peasants, from the soil, is the basis of the whole process. The history of
this expropriation, in different countries, assumes different aspects, and
runs through its various phases in different orders of succession, and at
different periods. In England alone, which we take as our example, has it
the classic form.[1]

He then refers to the 'prelude of the revolution that laid the foundation of
the capitalist mode of production' as it was 'played in the last third of the
15th and the first decade of the 16th century'.[2] This included 'the breaking-
up of the bands of feudal retainers',[3] and such early signs of enclosure as 'the
usurpation of the common lands'[4] and 'the transformation of arable land into
sheep-walks'[5] by the great feudal lords, as well as 'the colossal spoliation of the
church property'[6] that followed the Reformation. It was thus that a mass of
free proletarians was hurled on the labour market.[7] Whereas the capitalist class
in its formative period did indeed utilise such forcible and violent measures
as 'levers', these measures did not by themselves immediately establish the
capitalist production-relations. The severance of the direct producers from
their means of production by 'the expropriation of the agricultural producer,
of the peasants, from the soil' that constituted 'the basis of the whole process'
was accomplished *in concreto* by the establishment of the wool industry as
independent of, rather than directly subordinate to, agriculture. It was on this
basis that those 'epoch-making revolutions act[ed] as levers' for the formation
of the capitalist class. That the primitive accumulation of capital assumed, in
England alone, its classic form can also be explained by this fact.

1   Marx 1987, *Capital*, Vol. I, pp. 669–70.
2   Marx 1987, *Capital*, Vol. I, p. 672.
3   Ibid.
4   Ibid.
5   Ibid.
6   Marx 1987, *Capital*, Vol. I, p. 675.
7   Marx 1987, *Capital*, Vol. I, p. 672.

CHAPTER 2

The English Wool Industry as Representing Merchant Capital

The representative industrial activity of England during the seventeenth and eighteenth century was the manufacturing of wool, which occurred almost everywhere in the country, though Norwich in the East, Bristol in the West and Yorkshire in the North constituted the three major centres. The Eastern region specialised in the worsted industry which utilised longer wool fibres for the production of serge and similar fabrics. This area was also somewhat special in that skilled master combers controlled both the combing and the weaving of wool. In the West and the North, the woollen (as distinct from worsted) industry, which produced various types of short-fibre cloths, was more common. Moreover, these two regions, which exhibited a sharp contrast in their industrial evolution, furnished important insights into the capitalist development of the English wool industry. For example, the so-called 'clothiers' who dominated the domestic industry in the West were themselves wealthy merchants, actively involved, since early times, in the export of wool, whereas in the North traditional master craftsmen became 'working clothiers', who produced at their own risk and sold their output to merchants. In the meantime, manufactories (factories yet to be mechanised) which appeared after the sixteenth century mainly in the West and the South, though their precursors had reportedly been in operation as early as the fourteenth century, never really attained the scope capable of overpowering domestic handicraft industry.*

*The word 'manufacture' has come to be used in a special sense since Marx distinguished the three categories of 'co-operation', 'manufacture division of labour' and 'modern mechanised industry' as corresponding to the development of the specifically capitalist method of production. Marx also declared that 'the period, roughly speaking, extending from the middle of the 16th century to the last third of the 18th century' constituted the 'manufacturing period properly so-called', during which the manufacture division of labour was 'the prevalent characteristic form of the capitalist process of production'.[1] In view of this statement, Japanese Marxists have frequently sought instances of 'manufacture' in history as marking the genesis of the capitalist mode

---

1 Marx 1987, *Capital*, Vol. I, p. 318.

production. Western historians, in contrast, seem to generally hold the view that the manufactories did not necessarily embody the Marxian concept of 'manufacture' as an early characteristic form of capitalist production.

So far as Marx's above-quoted text is concerned, I cannot offer a definitive interpretation. However, I tend to believe that Marx's 'manufacturing period properly so-called' need not be interpreted in the same way as the epoch of 'modern mechanised (large-scale) industry' which established itself later. For Marx admits himself that 'during the manufacturing period proper, i.e., the period during which manufacture is the predominant form taken by capitalist production, many obstacles are opposed to the full development of the peculiar tendencies of manufacture'.[2] He also writes: 'At the same time manufacture was unable, either to seize upon the production of society to its full extent, or to revolutionise their production to its very core. It towered up as an economic work of art, on the broad foundation of the town handicrafts, and of the rural domestic industries. At a given stage of its development, the narrow technical basis on which manufacture rested, come into conflict with requirements of production that were created by manufacture itself'.[3] Thus, even though manufacture was 'the prevalent characteristic form of capitalist process of production', such that during the manufacturing period it (manufacture) was indeed 'the predominant form taken by capitalist production', this does not necessarily mean that manufacture was the leading method of production in the seventeenth and eighteenth century in England. The fact that it was not explains to me why merchant capital could continue to function as the dominant form of capital during that time.

The clothier of the Western region purchased raw wool with his capital, and then hired women of the rural districts at low wages to spin it into yarn. Subsequently, he handed out the yarn to weavers who then made fabrics out of it. However, since the fabrics that were returned to the clothier in exchange for wages needed some more finishing work, he most often operated a 'manufactory' of his own wherein to complete them as merchandise. The finished products were then either directly exported, or sent, in the first instance, to the London market, where they were consigned to a broker, called a 'factor', who circulated them. The clothier dictated specifications of the product; but he could not directly supervise the production-process. For his job consisted of providing the producers with materials to work on, and ensuring some quality control before buying up their products. He could oversee only the finishing stage of the cloth immediately prior to its sale. He was, therefore, not simply a merchant,

2 Marx 1987, *Capital*, Vol. I, p. 346.
3 Marx 1987, *Capital*, Vol. I, p. 347.

though not yet an industrial capitalist either. Indeed, his capital mainly consisted of funds for the purchase of materials and semi-products, yet with such capital he could indirectly employ a large number of workers. During the seventeenth century, a clothier was said to employ more than 500 workers at the rate of 40 persons per loom. In the eighteenth century, 150 to 200 weavers directly worked for a clothier; but the latter employed various other workers, including journeymen, so that his total employment often amounted to between 800 and 1,000 persons. One must understand, however, that the worker, for his/her part, did not always produce for one single clothier.

A wealthy clothier ordinarily purchased a one-year supply of raw wool directly from sheep-farmers, and arranged the processes of spinning, weaving and finishing at the lowest possible cost. In some cases, he also resold his surplus of raw wool to others at advantageous prices. There were brokers in raw wool as well, and some of them eventually became wealthy clothiers. In general, clothiers in the Western region were persons of means and operated like merchants.

Here as in other regions, the spinners of wool were almost always peasant women. Spinning was a sideline of their agricultural occupations during the winter time. Up to the sixteenth century, the producers of yarn had marketed their output themselves, before becoming reliant on clothiers during the seventeenth century. Clothiers operated extensively throughout a region, distributing materials and collecting yarn in many villages. The technique that the peasant women applied individually in their cottages was antiquated and unproductive, and their output was far from qualitatively uniform. Such a defect was only to be expected from the sideline production of yarn by peasant women, who were paid a pittance and whose work-hours had no definite limit. Neither could the pilfering of materials, a common risk to cottage industry of any sort, be easily avoided. The clothiers for their part, however, knew what to do under the circumstances. They depressed wages using one excuse or another when they collected the products, and they rigged the scale as they distributed materials. Sometimes, they also paid wages in goods that were exorbitantly priced. In short, they lived up to their reputation as swindlers in their operation of the commission system.

The weavers, to whom the clothier entrusted his yarn, worked with two or three looms at home as instructed by the clothier, so that what they received in exchange for their products was hardly different from piece wages. A master weaver often employed apprentices and journeymen along with his own family members. Their irregular workdays sometimes extended to fifteen or sixteen hours, especially when the master contracted with more than one clothier. At other times, however, they had little to do and were obliged to busy themselves with agriculture and kindred works, to which they were no longer accustomed. Under the circumstances, the traditional guild relation, binding the master and his hands, could not be strictly maintained. The term of apprenticeship was no longer observed, so that some apprentices who did not live with the master were simply paid money wages. Journeymen too were increasingly employed without a fixed term and for limited works, in which case they could, of course, not be trained to become masters. Thus, in the Western region, the commission system slowly formed three distinct classes: the clothiers, as merchant capitalists, who purchased raw wool and sold finished cloth; the weavers, who, despite their possession of looms and workplaces, were increasingly turning into wage-earners; and the apprentices and the journeymen, who worked for the master-weavers.

The situation was quite different in the Northern district around Yorkshire. The clothiers of Yorkshire, unlike their counterparts in the West, were weavers themselves, and so were called 'working clothiers'. They purchased their own materials to produce fabrics, but their scale of operation was quite small. They maintained businesses and earned their livelihoods by selling their output almost week by week, and did not possess more than two looms until early in the eighteenth century. Some were said to weave as a sideline, while being principally engaged in agriculture. However, in places like West Riding, which later was to flourish with the mechanised wool industry, agriculture had already been abandoned. In any case, the weaver of the North remained independent like the traditional guild masters until the beginning of the eighteenth century. Journeymen, too, were trained in all aspects of the trade from the buying of the materials, the dressing and colouring of wool, to the finishing of the fabric. Most apprentices lived with the master's family until they finished their training. After becoming journeymen, they either continued to work for their former master or for another working clothier. Although in most cases they worked in the master's shop, some operated at home and received piece-wages. The loom could be either their own property or the master's, but the master always provided them with materials. They were normally employed for the term of one year, and were hardly ever dismissed, even when the master clothier failed to sell their products. Since apprentices and journeymen themselves became masters eventually, the master-trainee relation was much more stable here than in the West.

In the latter half of the eighteenth century, however, this relation between the master and his trainees began to disintegrate. The traditional relation could not be maintained as the scale of the master-clothier's operation expanded. The practice of paying wages to apprentices became common, while journeymen resembled more and more the weavers of the West. By the end of the eighteenth century, the clothiers were hiring a large number of workers without apprenticeship backgrounds.

The conditions of production in the North, as described above, were also reflected in the marketing of the products. Unlike in the West, they were sold in regional markets, of which Wakefield in the seventeenth century and Leeds in the eighteenth century were the largest. At first, the market took place in the old-fashioned manner on particular streets at a given time; but, in the eighteenth century, a cloth hall was set up in several cities. Cloth halls increased in number and later housed sample fairs. However, since the products sold in those markets were not completely finished, the merchant purchasers took them to their manufactories for final processing. In this respect the working clothiers too remained under the control of the merchants.

In the latter half of the eighteenth century, however, an increasing number of Northern clothiers began to apply themselves to this final processing. Such clothiers were called 'opulent clothiers', as distinct from 'working clothiers'. At this point, they became capitalists in the same way as the clothiers of the West. By this time, the worsted industry had established itself in the North to the extent of outpacing Norwich, so that the previous practice of shipping long wool fibres to the Eastern district to be processed ceased. For such fibres could by then be competitively worked on at low wages in the North. Moreover, the worsted industry in this region was, from the beginning, developed by the new class of capitalist clothiers. They were the ones who built the foundation of the English wool industry in the North, which during the nineteenth century eclipsed its competitors in the East as well as in the West.

Of the handicraftsmen of the English wool industry at that time the wool-comber and the cloth-dresser occupied a special status. Wool-combing was a process similar to carding but required physical strength as well as skill. For that reason, the wool-combers had commanded relatively high wages and had faced the clothier with some importance and dignity, until the process was mech-anised later in the nineteenth century. The cloth-dresser, on the other hand, worked in a manufactory condition either for a clothier or for a master dresser, who had contracted with a clothier. The manufactory, as already mentioned, could be described as an imperfect concretisation of the manufacture division of labour, evolving as subsidiary to the commission system. However, it con-stituted the base from which merchant capital exercised its dominant control over the whole process of wool manufacturing, and was for that reason bitterly opposed by the craftsmen-masters in the dressing, dying and other trades.

The method of 'manufacture', which arises from the prior method of 'co-operation', or mere assembling of many workers in a factory, and which profits from the advancement of society's productive powers due to the division of labour, does indeed mark a stage of development of the capitalist method of production, as it prepares the ground for 'modern mechanised industry'. However, the experience of the wool industry, which represented the cradle era of English capitalism in the seventeenth and eighteenth centuries, does not support the view that this industry materialised an epoch of manufacture (division of labour). It is reported that already in the sixteenth century the famous manufactory of J. Winchcombe in Newberry employed 500 to 600 workers, including women and children, and that it operated all processes of wool-making from carding and spinning to dying, weaving and finishing, practising indeed a division of labour. It is also confirmed that equally large manufactories had been experimented with since the fifteenth century. None of these (proto-factories in) manufactures, however, appear to have survived long. Some say that these were organised expressly for the purpose of rescuing a group of peasants who had together lost their land. Others surmise that they were originally monasteries converted into rehabilitation centres. It seems that some such special and contingent circumstances motivated the launching of these 'manufactories'. Of course, I do not mean to say that the process of generating landless peasants as proletariat was a contingent matter. For instance, 'enclosure' was one of the ways in which the process of transforming arable land into pastures occurred. The circumstances under which that process resulted in the expulsion of a large number of peasant families at once must have constituted a rather special event. Even though each individual case in which that process was carried out involved all sorts of contingent factors, however, the whole process itself, which left a lasting mark in history, surely cannot be dismissed as a matter of accident. If, therefore, one evaluates the manufactories of the fifteenth and sixteenth century in this light, one can see why they neither played a leading role in the wool industry of the time, nor heralded the arrival of an era of the manufacture division of labour.

It is, therefore, not possible to consider manufactories as landmarks of the English wool industry in the process of the formation of capitalism. One must rather emphasise the fact that merchant capital gradually moulded capitalist production-relations from the seventeenth to the eighteenth century, by deskilling traditional handicraft workers, and converting them into wage-earners. The concrete manifestation of this process may, to some extent, be observed in the manufactories of merchant clothiers (since they often added the finishing touch to the products), and, particularly in those of the 'opulent' clothiers, which developed in the latter half of the eighteenth century in the North of England. The process, whereby the medieval specialisation in trades transformed itself into the manufacture division of labour in the capitalist factory, was grounded on the process whereby independent handicraft workers were gradually converted into unskilled partial operatives with hardly any professional training. History exhibits only the latter process with unmistakable clarity, without giving manufactories a chance to materialise a new method of production, capable of superseding the putting-out (commission) system, operated by merchant capital. The age of modern mechanised industry arrived before the 'manufacture division of labour' had had time to constitute a historical epoch of its own. Indeed, with a fairly limited number of workers under its command, manufactory production could not possibly have out-rivalled the accumulation of merchant capital.

In the above, I have mainly followed Lipson[4] in describing the concrete manner in which merchant capital dominated the manufacturing of wool in England, as its representative industry, in the seventeenth and eighteenth centuries. During that period, merchant capital did not stay clear of guild handicrafts as it did in the medieval age, nor did it undergo a qualitative transformation into commercial capital, under the influence and domination of industrial capital, as occurred at a much later stage of capitalist development. Merchant capital accumulated, by expropriating small producers, as was to be expected in this nascent period of capitalism. It subordinated both 'the town handicrafts and the rural domestic industries', which allegedly constituted the backbone of what Marx called 'the epoch of manufacture properly so-called'. The merchant capital that ushered capitalism into England was, moreover, always closely allied with the capital that was invested in foreign trade.

---

4   Lipson 1921, *The History of the Woollen and Worsted Industries*; Lipson 1931, *The Economic History of England*, Vol. II.

CHAPTER 3

The Economic Policies of Mercantilism

Marx wrote as follows:

> The discovery of gold and silver in America, the extirpation, enslavement
> and entombment in mines of the aboriginal population, the beginning
> of the conquest and looting of the East Indies, the turning of Africa into
> a warren for the commercial hunting of black-skins, signalised the rosy
> dawn of the era of capitalist production. These idyllic proceedings are
> the chief momenta of primitive accumulation. On their heels treads the
> commercial war of the European nations, with the globe for a theatre.
> It begins with the revolt of the Netherlands from Spain, assumes giant
> dimension in England's Anti-Jacobin War, and is still going on in the
> opium wars against China, &c.[1]

Indeed, capitalism found its foothold in those European nations, which realised their internal unity in the process of settling external conflicts with others.
On the world-historic scene, however, an intense competition for commercial
hegemony ended in the victory of England, where the 'momenta of primitive
accumulation' reached 'a systematic combination, embracing the colonies, the
national debt, the modern mode of taxation, and the protectionist system'.[2] Its
mercantilist policies throughout the seventeenth and eighteenth centuries created the groundwork for the birth of capitalism. As Marx observes, the same
momenta still lingered even in the nineteenth century outside Europe, and all
the more so in the more distant places.* Yet, they no longer appeared as the 'systematic combination' which earlier characterised the stage of mercantilism.

*Even mature capitalism, in which industrial capital became dominant, never
entirely outgrew its original characteristics shaped by the activity of merchant capital.
Thus, during the nineteenth century, even as the age of industrial capital established
itself, traits of mercantilism which had typified the economic policies of merchant capital in earlier centuries persisted, in international relations in particular. Capital must,
of course, assume its industrial form in order to impinge upon the economic base of

---

1 Marx 1987, *Capital*, Vol. 1, p. 703.
2 Ibid.

society. Yet, to regard industrial capital alone as the genuine form of capital is to over-look its essential character, thus making it difficult to appreciate the important fact that capital failed to govern a whole society before it developed its industrial form. Production did not belong to the original function of capital; for capital is not always an essential and indispensable form of social life. It is, moreover, for that reason that merchant capital remained the dominant form of capital during the formative stage of capitalism, and that even the subsequent dominance of industrial capital never completely obliterated the characteristics of merchant capital. The same fact also explains why the development of capitalist industry ended by generating the form of finance-capital at a later stage.

The formative period of capitalism corresponded with the world-historic process of transition from medieval, feudal societies to modern, bourgeois society. This transition was accelerated by the accumulation of merchant capital, which grew by resorting to the method of 'expropriation'. Merchant capital, however, was not vested with sufficient powers to enforce such a process by itself. Surviving in various pre-modern societies, yet remaining always external to them, merchants never entrenched themselves as a leading class in any one of them. For this reason 'the power of the state' which, in a 'hothouse fashion, hastened and shortened the transitional process'[3] played a significant role. Moreover, the state, too, was undergoing the transitional form of the absolute monarchy, which retained a considerable dose of feudalism, while being 'itself a product of bourgeois development'.[4] The world-historic significance of the royal policies, which expedited this transitional process, lay in the opening up of the national (or home) market for the commodity-economy, even though the latter had failed as yet to develop its own method of production.

The emerging nation-state in the form of the absolute monarchy assisted the development of capitalism by political and fiscal measures, as modernisation meant, in the first instance, the securing of the fiscal base of the nation. This was accomplished by the break-up of traditional political relations characteristic of feudal society, which obstructed the internal development of capitalism. Yet the methods of overcoming feudalism were themselves feudal, and often aimed at extending the scope of application of traditional practices to a nationwide scale. The policies that the state adopted to foster the enclosure movement, which, as remarked before, turned England's arable land into pastures, were typical. The flourishing of the Flemish wool industry in the fifteenth and six-

---

3   Ibid.
4   Marx 1987, *Capital*, Vol. I, p. 672.

teenth centuries prodded England to develop a competitive domestic industry in the same profitable field. Thus, feudal powers were frequently mobilised to assist enclosures, which, in consequence, destroyed traditional social relations to the advantage of the up-coming bourgeoisie. The seeming incongruity that 'feudal powers were applied to undermine the feudal regime itself' also reflected the transitional character of the absolute monarchy. Even as capitalism further developed in England, during the seventeenth and eighteenth centuries, and the economic policies of the state were thus made more systematically mercantilist, this incongruity was only partially overcome, since mercantilism constituted a stage of capitalism which was prior to the self-dependence of capital. Yet, the policies of the English monarchy in the preceding two centuries should be described as 'pre-mercantilist' in the sense that they only unconsciously prepared the ground for mercantilism, without which the future development of the capitalist method of production would not have been ensured. Thus, for example, 'the expropriation of the agricultural population from the land'[5] beginning in the fifteenth century was a process which the royal power, on the one hand, pressed forward, yet on the other, held back as the grim result appeared too frightening, although eventually it ended in the establishment of 'the discipline necessary for the wage system',[6] as was witnessed by the so-called 'bloody legislation against the expropriated'.[7] One may similarly characterise the 'compulsory laws for the extension of the working-day from the middle of the 14th to the end of the 17th century'[8] and the 'acts of Parliament forcing down wages' during approximately the same period.* In the seventeenth century, as capitalism finally emerged, such pre-mercantilist policies increasingly lost their meaning.**

* It is not possible to discuss fine points of the law in this connection. Yet all such measures are, to my mind, typical of legislation during the transitional period. For example, the Elizabethan Statute of Artificers of 1562 meticulously specifies the details of the working-hours for the 'labourers' as if they were handicraftsmen of the guild,[9] yet the real purpose was clearly an extension of their working-day. Thus, 'in practice, the conditions were much more favourable to the labourers than in the statute-book'.[10]

5   Marx 1987, *Capital*, Vol. I, p. 671.
6   Marx 1987, *Capital*, Vol. I, p. 688.
7   Marx 1987, *Capital*, Vol. I, p. 686.
8   Marx 1987, *Capital*, Vol. I, p. 252.
9   Bland, Brown and Tawney 1921, *English Economic History: Selected Documents*, pp. 327–8.
10   Marx 1987, *Capital*, Vol. I, p. 259.

** For example, in the newly formed wool industry of the late sixteenth and early seventeenth century, the wage-legislations of 1598 and 1604 even included measures to protect handicraft workers against capitalist spoliation, by stipulating minimum wages.[11]

Mercantilist policies were themselves classifiable into those belonging to the earlier period and those belonging to the later period. In the earlier period, mercantilist policies were primarily the policies of the monarch, and hence were direct and less systematic; in the later period they took, in Cunningham's terms, the 'parliamentary form', and aimed at more general results through indirect measures. The distinction corresponded with the period in which the strong resistance of the old social relations remained and thus required forceful measures to counter them, in contrast to the period in which new capitalist social relations existed in substance already. Yet, throughout both periods spanning the two centuries, which represent the formative stage of capitalism, political forces were mobilised, in one way or another, to expedite the transformation of small producers into modern wage-workers. The indispensability of political influences followed from the fact that merchant capital, which could not directly operate the reproduction-process of society, had to play a historically dominant role in the nascent stage of capitalism. The mercantilist policies of the earlier period could be represented by the system of royal charters to 'monopolies', which were direct and specific, and those of the later period by more general measures which promoted the nation's foreign trade. The Navigation Acts may be taken to have signalled the transition. Thus, I intend to summarise below what I consider to be the essential features of these policies, based on the following works of economic history: Cunningham's *Growth of English Industry and Commerce in Modern Times*, Part I; Lipson's *The Economic History of England*, Volumes II and III; and Brentano's *Eine Geschichte der Wirtshactslichen Entwicklung Englands*, Bd. II. I shall, however, avoid encumbering the reader with detailed references in the text.

1   The System of Royal Charters to Monopolies

This system according to which the king granted monopoly rights to domestic industries or to companies engaged in overseas trade, in return for the payment of licence fees, may be taken to define the period which preceded the establish-

---

11   Lipson 1931, Vol. III, p. 254; Bland, Brown and Tawney 1921, pp. 336–41, 342–3.

ment of the fiscal base of the modern nation-state. The licensing of industries was generally supposed to protect the use of new methods of production. In reality, however, it assured an important source of fiscal revenues to the king (the licensor), as well as guaranteeing the accrual of monopoly profits to capital (the licensee) over time, although the temporary guarantee of exclusive rights seems to have led to few capitalist successes. The high commodity prices thus artificially contrived were often equivalent to the imposition of excise taxes by the king. For example, Elizabeth issued monopoly charters for the production of numerous manufactured commodities, including salt, starch, acetic acid, glass, iron, tin, card and nitre, until she was forced to recognise excesses and was eventually led to cancel many. James I chose not to multiply industrial charters except with regard to some prominent company organisations; but his successor, Charles I, found himself compelled to extend such exceptions to supplement his internal revenues.*

*The licensing of the salt industry was a typical example. When a royal charter was granted to the manufacturing of salt in 1566, it was merely a patent of monopoly to the new method of production. However, its renewal in 1586, though restricted to a particular region, conferred the right of monopoly to the manufacturing as well as the sale of salt in that region, which led to a conspicuous rise in salt prices. Since this was protested by Parliament in 1601, Elizabeth was forced to revoke the licence. Although James I resisted the temptation to reintroduce control over the industry, Charles I issued a charter in 1636 to one company which monopolised the manufacturing and the sale of salt on the eastern seaboard of England. He prohibited the import of salt in return for a specified levy from this company. This licence was later revoked by the Long Parliament of 1640–60. When Cromwell achieved the economic integration of Scotland, the salt industry of England was dominated by its traditional competitor in Scotland, and the patent of monopoly lost its meaning altogether.

If industrial licences often directly benefited the king and his political repres-entatives, the charters granted to privileged merchants for foreign trade and the management of overseas colonies aimed at more general results, and also became the vital instruments of early mercantilist policies. In the latter half of the sixteenth century, Elizabeth chartered the Merchant Adventurers, who had been active in trade in the North-Sea area since the thirteenth and fourteenth centuries, together with The Eastland Company, The Russia Company, The Levant Company, and the like company. These were organisations empowered to trade exclusively with, respectively, Germany, Russia, Turkey, and the like company, and were mainly concerned with the export of English wool to these regions. Similar arrangements were soon extended to the East Indian, African and North American colonies. Thus, The East India Company* and several Africa companies (companies focused on Africa) were established early in the seventeenth century, followed by the inauguration of The Hudson's Bay Company in 1668. These companies were given a wide range of political powers and defended England's interests with armed forces *vis-à-vis* other powers in the region. Though they originally began as 'regulated companies', which like old guilds merely imposed certain collective rules on a group of independent merchants, they all developed into 'joint-stock companies', i.e. into more tightly organised concentrations of capital originating from diverse sources. The navigation technology of the time and the frequent need to deal with acts of piracy may have demanded not only a strict internal organisation but also the heavy armament of these companies, which were themselves highly prone to expropriatory forays. These companies manifestly combined political and military activities while furthering the economic aims of the merchants, and thus represented the policy of the state for the concentration of wealth by force. Such a character was particularly conspicuous in those colonial companies, which frequently had to defend English interests against the French and/or the Dutch. Their individual trading activities may not always have been gainful; but, overall, the companies realised enormous monopoly profits so much so that, in the end, so-called 'interlopers' from the home country could not be easily deterred. Indeed, with the development of international trade, such patents of monopoly eventually appeared antiquarian. Therefore, towards the end of the 1680s, The Eastland, The Levant and The Russia Companies lost their charters, and so did most Africa-focused companies. Not even the Merchant Adventurers could maintain a monopoly market for long, even though, together with The East India Company, they formally survived into the nineteenth century with some time-honoured privileges.

* The East India Company, which was to play a principal part in the later colonisation of India, occupied a special position. Established by Queen Elizabeth in 1600, it monopolised, for over two centuries, English trade with East India and the Orient. Because of its joint-stock system, the Company could assemble a large number of merchants experienced in overseas trade, such as those once associated with The Levant Company. In its first years (1601–13), The East India Company adopted the so-called separate voyage system whereby capital was assembled for each voyage and subsequently distributed its enormous profits to the contributors. Gradually, however, several voyages were financed by one single joint-stock. In 1633, the system was made more complex in order to allow the pursuit of five separate undertakings simultaneously. Only in 1657 did it evolve into a permanent joint-stock company. Yet the development of the Company was frequently hindered, on the one hand, by Dutch competition in the international

market, and, and, on the other, by internal criticisms of the Company's monopoly gains in trade, inasmuch as the Company contributed to significant outflows of precious metals from the country.

East India was not a good export market, which would directly promote the industrial development of England. It rather supplied cotton articles which competed with domestic textile products. Yet, the possibility of re-exporting the prized oriental commodities, such as silk and perfume, to Europe promised enormous commercial benefits, and justified political assistance to merchant capital which was concentrated under the joint-stock system. However, the Company had political enemies as well, particularly in the period extending from the Glorious Revolution to the early eighteenth century. Still, in 1709, Parliament granted new privileges to the Company, so that it could maintain its historical place until the beginning of the nineteenth century. It was after 1709 that the Company increasingly turned into the instrument of the British colonisation of India, countervailing the French ambition in that area.

2   The Navigation Acts

From the fourteenth century, England frequently asserted the preferential use of its own vessels in its foreign trade. The Navigation Acts of 1651 and 1660 established this old practice as a mercantilist policy. For instead of patronising individual vessels with monopoly licences in specific contexts, these Acts claimed once for all for the merchant fleet of England an exclusive right to carry goods to and from the English ports of trade. This meant that the development of her foreign trade already exceeded the old system of licensed monopolies, particularly so, when the trade with the American colonies gained in importance. Thus, the Act of 1651 stipulated that either English vessels or the vessels of the producing countries should carry European goods not only to England but also to its colonies, and that goods produced in colonies exported to England and to its other colonies be transported exclusively by English vessels. The Act of 1660 also required that important products of the colonies such as tobacco, cotton, sugar, dye and the like should be enumerated as special commodities, not to be exported elsewhere but only to England, and should be exclusively carried by English ships. The intention was obviously to exclude the Dutch fleet, which was then an important rival.* The Act also implied the characteristically mercantilist policy that colonial industries should be subordinated to mainland industries. However, with the approach of the eighteenth century, the original aim of the Navigation Acts faded, since France, in place of the Netherlands, emerged as a more direct threat to Britain's economic affairs. The Acts no longer retained the importance they held in the middle of the seventeenth century.

* Since the freight charged by Dutch ships was lower than that by English ships, this Act entailed higher import prices. The contemporary defence of the Act on the ground that England's long-run benefit outweighed the burden of extra freight charges to be borne may be viewed as manifesting a distinctly 'mercantilist' argument, given that England was unable to surpass the Dutch in colonial trade until the end of the seventeenth century.

3   Commercial Policies

England, which in the middle of the seventeenth century had contended with the Netherlands by way of the Navigation Acts, confronted France towards the end of the century with more general commercial policies. The tendency for England to run trade deficits with France was already a cause for concern, since by this time mercantilism, having outgrown the earlier 'monetary system', regarded the trade balance as a whole, rather than specifically specie flows, as a barometer of the nation's economic conditions. The aggressive policies of Colbert (1619–83) and others, especially as reflected in heavy French tariffs on English fabrics, aggravated the relation between the two countries. In the latter half of the seventeenth century, the commercial policies of England no longer directly served the king's interest, but were shaped by Parliament, which was under the influence of the wool manufacturers and merchants. Although commercial policies generally aimed at the protection of domestic industries, they also included radically mercantilist measures.

For example, England frequently prohibited the export of raw wool. This was originally meant to ensure that the domestic wool industry, the products of which had long been the most important export item of the country, should be adequately supplied with materials. In the latter half of the seventeenth century, however, the prohibition not only aimed at providing the domestic industry with cheaper materials but also at denying foreign competitors fair access to English raw wool. This unambiguously mercantilist measure was intended to achieve the monopoly of the English wool industry in the international market. Although the cheap price of raw wool in England made smuggling advantageous, and this could never be really controlled, the regulation lasted well into the nineteenth century, despite protests by the sheep-growers throughout the eighteenth century.

Retaliating against the French tariffs on English goods, England also prohibited in 1678 the import of some major French commodities including wine. Although, again, contraband could not be effectively prevented, the prohibition was not lifted until a century later. England concluded the Treaty of Methuen in 1703 with Portugal, hoping to recover in that country the market that it had lost in France. Portugal, too, had been in the process of developing its own wool industry, by stopping the import of wool products from England. It nevertheless relented to the English demand, in that year, on the condition that England imported Portuguese wine in preference to French wine. The English export of woollen products thus secured a foothold in Portugal. It was for that reason, according to historians, that a successful conclusion of a commercial treaty with France was aborted, even after the negotiations at Utrecht in 1713. According to them, the increase of English exports to Portugal during that period could be corroborated by a net inflow of Brazilian gold bullion into England.

As for the protection of the domestic wool industry, various measures were adopted against cotton goods from India, which were regarded as competitors of English woollen goods. Sometimes the import of Indian cotton products was forbidden outright, sometimes their use in England was prohibited and the use of English woollen goods instead was compelled, though none of these measures appeared to have been sufficiently effective. Yet the commercial policy, aimed at protecting the domestic wool industry, constituted the core of the system of economic policies in England since the second half of the seventeenth century and was continued throughout the rest of the mercantilist period. During this phase, the old export taxes, which had contributed solely to the securing of public revenues, were abolished, apart from a few minor exceptions. Rebates and export subsidies were extended, while import duties on industrial materials tended to be removed.

The Corn Laws are somewhat different in character from the mercantilist policies studied so far. Yet their importance as part of mercantilism in general can hardly be overlooked. Therefore, a brief account of them follows.

4   The Corn Laws

Since medieval times it had been a common practice for the state to ensure an adequate supply of food at home. This consideration led to regulations on the export of grains with a view to stabilising their prices. The policies of the Tudor kings, in this regard, were generally to set definite upward limits to grain prices, such that the export of grains was authorised only for so long as the prices stayed within those limits. Prior to the seventeenth century, however, grains were never important export items because of heavy transportation costs. Moreover, the limit prices were almost automatically raised as market prices rose. For example, in 1663, the limit price of wheat was raised to 48 shillings per quarter, which greatly exceeded the average of domestic wheat prices in the following several years, so that there remained in effect no real regulation against the export of grains. As if to confirm this trend, the act of 1670 abolished altogether the old regulation controlling the export of grains; but it introduced instead a new regulation on the import side, by imposing prohibitive duties on foreign grains until their prices reached certain levels. This had the effect of excluding foreign competition from the English grains market. As this effect continued until the end of the 1750s, the act of 1670 may be regarded as having opened a new epoch of English grains policy.

In the meantime, the same act also provided for the possibility of promoting the export of grains from England, enabling a new system of subsidies to be introduced during 1673–6. Furthermore, the act of 1689 stipulated a subsidy of 5 shillings per quarter of wheat, to whoever exported it at or below the price of 48 shillings per quarter, and also adopted like measures for other grains. Thus, from that time on, English grains, while continuing to be sheltered from foreign competition, gradually established themselves as export commodities as well. Although this led to higher ground rents at home because of a considerable increase in the profitability of grain production, high prices of grains could not always be sustained. Bumper crops in the first half of the eighteenth century explained part of this outcome, but perhaps the improved method of cultivation and the extension of arable land were more important factors. Yet the meaning of the grains policy was clear. It was to lend the resources of the state to guarantee benefits to the class of landowners. If England remained an exporter of grains until about the 1760s on account of this policy, that fact revealed an important aspect of mercantilism in that it required capital to concede to the interest of landed property. It must also be noted that the enclosures in the eighteenth century often aimed at an extension of arable land, whereas those in the fifteenth and sixteenth centuries signified the conversion of arable land into pastures. In both cases, the interests of capital and of landed property were in concert, one supporting the other.

Thus, the economic policies of mercantilism, which marked the formative period of capitalism in England, underwent several important changes over the course of two centuries. Yet they always aimed at assisting and promoting merchant capital, that is to say, at expediting the primitive accumulation of capital. Since merchants had by themselves no direct access to the political machinery of the state, they, sometimes, had to appeal to the fiscal greed of the kings, and, at other times, to make concessions to the interest of landed aristocracy. Merchant capital remained the dominant form of capital even in the eighteenth century, since industrial capital was yet to rise to social prominence. It was merchant capital, as the historically dominant form of capital, which set the pace and promoted the general trend of economic policies of the epoch. The mercantilist policies, which evolved from the system of royal charters to the Navigation Acts, and, from there, further on to more general commercial policies, were indeed the policies of merchant capital and not of industrial capital. The latter, for one thing, would never have sustained the century-long hostilities with France, merely for the protection of an 'infant' wool industry. The truculent rules that the absolute monarchy imposed over its colonies and the tendency of the state to abet the slave trade, which was said to have dealt with an average of 20,000 slaves a year, between the late seventeenth to the late eighteenth century, testified to the 'expropriatory' character of merchant capital, which dominated the English society of the time.

The economic policies of merchant capital, however, tended to undermine the ground upon which merchant capital itself stood, so that it was to lose its position of dominance eventually to industrial capital. The two centuries of mercantilist economic policies, during which the development of the commodity-economy in England dictated certain unavoidable changes, could be regarded as preparing the subsequent stage of industrial capitalism. Yet merchant capital itself was clearly unaware of what was to come. It was caught by surprise, when the age of industrial capital suddenly dawned. The capitalist method of production, once its foundation was secured, gained its own momentum and deprived merchant capital of its former significance. Its dominance understandably waned, as the now self-propelled growth of capitalism rejected the old mercantilist economic policies as its fetters. As stated in the Introduction, no economic policy under capitalism is conscious of its own objective necessity, and this indeed was the case with mercantilism as well. Indeed, those who 'prescribed' mercantilist policies, be they the kings or Parliament, remained just as in the dark as merchant capital itself about the historical significance of these policies, which, as it turned out, was no more than to expedite the process of primitive accumulation of capital.* They acted instinctively for immediate gain, and thus led history into the direction that they themselves had never imagined. The capitalist economy that they unconsciously helped to develop not only rearranged but also eventually rejected their myopic policy aims.

---

* A country like Japan, which joined the world-capitalist orbit as a latecomer, enforced somewhat different policies during its process of primitive accumulation for two compelling reasons. First, the process itself occurred in a wholly different context; and secondly, policies of more developed countries could frequently be imitated. Yet, in that case as well, the policymakers were just as much in the dark as to the historical significance of what they were doing. Nevertheless the take-off process of such a coun-

try can never be fully accounted for without first appreciating the historical meaning of mercantilist policies in England and the subsequent stages of development of capitalism that the advanced capitalist nations had already undergone.

PART II

Liberalism

∵

Introduction to Part II

It was the economy of Britain that most typically embodied the nascent stage of capitalism in the seventeenth and eighteenth centuries, overpowering the Netherlands in the first half of that period, and France in the latter half. The same country, Britain, also typified the second stage of development of capitalism, that of autonomous (or self-propelled) growth, after it went through the Industrial Revolution, which occurred there from about the end of the eighteenth to the early nineteenth century. In this second stage of the development of capitalism, it was industrial capital that manifested the dominant form of accumulation. It was under this form, moreover, that capitalism became a historical society, in the sense that its reproduction-process was primarily, if not wholly, regulated by the logic of capital. Industrial capital, in other words, accumulated by exploiting the surplus labour of wage-workers within society's reproduction-process itself, unlike merchant capital which, remaining outside that process, profited mainly from expropriations of existing wealth. By integrally adopting the relation of commodity exchanges as the principle to govern its reproduction-process, capitalism anchored the whole of society's economic life within the regularity and coherence dictated by the commodity-economy. Once the social relations were thus remoulded, the accumulation of capital no longer needed fraud, spoliation, or even an extensive reliance on the mercantile skill of buying cheap and selling dear. The coercive policies, which were needed at the birth and in the early formation of capitalism up to the end of the eighteenth century, now became not only dispensable but also repugnant to the newly emerging social order. The latter now stood by the religious enforcement of the principle of private property, and demanded the political regime of freedom and equality based upon law. In other words, it demanded the form of the 'legal state', which historically brought 'civil society' into being.

Indeed, the freedom and equality that civil society espoused were not just abstract ideological values, without contextual specifications. They stemmed from the separation of the direct producers from their means of production, and the consequent conversion of labour-power into a commodity. These were the processes which capitalism had achieved by force in its nascent period, and which it now presupposed, after having embraced the relation of commodity exchanges as the principle of governance of society's reproduction-process. Thus, the freedom of the workers to dispose of their own labour-power implied what Marx described as 'freedom in the double sense', that is to say, freedom not only from the feudal, master-servant bondage but also from the means of production with which to realise their labour. It did not imply the ability of the workers themselves to freely dispose of their own products, products that they had fashioned with their own means of production. As already repeated many times, the commodity-economy is never as natural, or intrinsic, a form of human society as to be able to realise an economic regime of independent commodity producers. The freedom and equality which the community of such small producers would ideologically aspire to were, in fact, achieved only in capitalist society, which came into being *after* the class of such independent, small producers had been dissolved and ruined. Hence, the freedom and equality that civil society proclaimed were, in fact, those of capital, and, in no sense, were freedom and equality universally applicable to all individuals.

The self-dependent character of industrial capital, which enabled capitalist society to develop of its own accord, rendered economic policies in principle unnecessary, as it outstripped such policies as had been adopted and implemented during the formative period of capitalism. Not only did it then tend to dismantle them, but it also prompted economics to theoretically repudiate their validity. Indeed, classical political economy, as propounded by Adam Smith, constituted a theoretical system, which denounced mercantilist policies as the incarnation of an economic fallacy. Liberalism, thus, appeared as the proper form of capitalism, i.e. as what capitalism ought to be, and that surely was correct in itself. Yet the significance of this fact would fail to be fully grasped were it forgotten that capitalism was itself a historical form of society. In order to control the process of production, capital had to secure, in one way or another, labour-power as a commodity, labour-power that it could not itself directly produce. During the age of mercantilism, merchant capital played its historical role of separating productive workers from their means of production, to which, in earlier feudal societies, they had been directly or indirectly tied. Industrial capital, which represented the age of liberalism, on the other hand, was already in possession and command of the mechanism whereby it could, unassisted by any external support, secure the conversion of labour-power into a commodity. Yet even that mechanism, as it turned out, was not free from the recurrence of periodic crises, a fatal flaw, as it were, which disqualified even liberalism from being a permanent economic order. That mechanism, therefore, had to undergo significant alterations with the further development of capitalism, until, in the end, finance-capital replaced industrial capital as the dominant form of accumulation in the final stage of capitalist development: imperialism.

Classical political economy, which failed to appraise liberalism in its historical context, viewed it as a natural economic order, and contrasted it to the artificial regime of mercantilism. This point of view differed from that of Marxian economics which, because of its socialist outlook, understood that not only liberalism but also capitalism itself was a historically transient social system. Indeed, Marx unambiguously taught that capitalism stood on the mechanism, whereby capital secured the conversion of labour-power into a commodity, even though, due to his inability to witness the full evolution of the age of imperialism in his own lifetime, he remained, at times, ambivalent concerning the future direction of capitalism. Nevertheless, the historical limitation of capitalism was clearly grasped by him, in the light of his scientific exposition of the class structure that underlay liberalism. By means of this theoretical exposition, Marx was able to see, behind the liberal euphoria over the promise of civil society, the laws of motion of capitalism operating as a self-contained logical system. In other words, his theorising penetrated to the economic base that supported the ideological superstructure of capitalist society, to use the idiom of his materialist conception of history, a conception that I take to be an ideological hypothesis. It was this separability, under capitalism, of the material base from the ideological superstructure that made the 'theory' (or systematic theorisation) of economics a feasible proposition.

Even though capitalism was a class society, in the sense of historical materialism, just as feudalism had earlier been, it was a generally more advanced society than its predecessor in that it did not outwardly exhibit its class structure. Capitalism, which adopted the liberal ideology as its fundamental social philosophy, was the limiting point, as it were, of all class societies, in that its unwritten class structure could be revealed only through a genuine economic analysis. Thus, Marx's insight, it must be repeated, offered the basis upon which pure economic theory was to be brought to completion. Nevertheless, liberalism, like capitalism itself, must be understood as a transient regime (and not as an eternal value), or more concretely, as a world-historic stage of the development of capitalism. This is so even though, unlike mercantilism or imperialism, liberalism was the form of social consciousness most congenial to the general nature of capital. In just the same way as economic theory may define a purely capitalist society, even though the latter did not factually evolve, but was merely conceivable as the limiting point of capitalism's existing tendencies, so is it warranted to conceive of liberalism, too, as a system of abstract values, which depicts what civil society ideally *ought to* be rather than what it actually turned out to be. The difference lies in that, unlike a purely capitalist society, in which the theoretical specifications are meant to work themselves out (even though, in the actual process of capitalist development, they are obstructed and distorted by many contingent factors), liberalism merely constituted a passing stage of capitalist development in real time, occupying as such the same status as mercantilism and imperialism. Precisely for that reason, liberalism *in concreto* can only be studied as a set of policies, or of anti-policies, aimed at undoing the outdated legacy of mercantilism.

The Period of the Self-Propelled Growth of Capitalism

As previously stated, capital is mercantile in its origin. It first arises in the circulation-process, or in the sphere of commodity exchanges, which is located outside society's reproduction-process, and only subsequently does it penetrate the sphere of production. It is then that capital gradually takes hold of society's reproduction-process. The vital condition for capital to be able to do so lies in the conversion of labour-power into a commodity. For in order to conquer society's reproduction-process, capital must, in the first place, enter the production-process, and, to do so, it must be able to purchase both the means of production and labour-power as commodities. In the act of purchasing commodities, capital, of course, retains its mercantile character. Although industrial capital takes the form M–C ... P ... C′–M′ (where '... P ...' represents the production-process), which is different from the form M–C–M′ of merchant capital, it still abides by the mercantile principle of buying cheap and selling dear in each individual operation, and, to that extent, the cost of production does not directly appear to it as the labour that society expends for the acquisition of the use-value in question. In other words, individual capital is not concerned with how much socially necessary labour went into the commodity, C′, which it sells, but only with how much more money it earns in it than it has paid to procure the elements of production, C. Thus, it buys C as cheaply as possible and sells C′ as dearly as possible, the difference constituting its profit, or the mark-up over the cost.

In capitalist society, however, in which labour-power is a commodity purchasable from the worker possessed of nothing else to sell, and in which means of production are capitalistically produced commodities, prices tend to settle to normal levels, corresponding to values. Though, in practice, some may still buy and sell at prices below or above normal, the chances of profiting only from circulation will gradually disappear. For example, if one capitalist buys his/her means of production from another for prices lower than normal, the latter capitalist loses his/her profit; and, if this condition persists, he/she will eventually relocate to a more profitable industry. Again, if labour-power is sold at a price below its reproduction-cost, though the worker is indeed frequently vulnerable to such exploitation, he/she will not, after a while, be able to reproduce it, and so to continue to sell it as a commodity. These considerations point to the fact that if a capitalistically produced commodity, c′, continues to be sold for a price dearer than its elements of production, c, it must be because labour-power has formed more value than its own in the production-process of capital. In other words, industrial capital earns its profits by producing surplus value. Society would not develop if human beings were not productive enough to be able to produce more than their own upkeep with their labour for the day. Ancient societies, which were based on slavery, and feudal societies, which rested on serfdom, were both class societies built on surplus labour. Capitalism is not different from them except that it realises surplus labour through commodity exchanges in the form of surplus value. Here, the mercantile principle of buying cheap and selling dear manifests itself in making use of labour-power's ability to produce more value than it itself possesses. Yet, due to the fact that the appropriation of surplus value is thus hidden behind the exchange of commodities at value (i.e. at normal prices), the class structure of capitalist society fails to be apparent to view.

At the same time, the principle of buying cheap and selling dear also undergoes subtle modifications. The practice of profiting from others' losses still remains in individual operations, and, indeed, provides the mercantile spirit of industrial capital with a strong motivation. Yet, when industrial capital governs the whole society and becomes the dominant form of accumulation, propelling capitalism in its self-expansionary phase, the *modus operandi* peculiar to industrial capital is established. It consists of raising the productive powers of society by reducing the hours of labour necessary for the reproduction of labour-power. The merit of the so-called 'production of relative surplus value' lies in that it can be pursued without limit. Capital, thus, satisfies its mercantile drive to buy what it needs as cheaply as possible, while promoting the productivity of society's reproduction-process. The same method enables capital to seek boundless value augmentation, even though it, in principle, cannot forever sell any commodity above the normal price, which reflects its value. Value augmentation is, in other words, the method of industrial capital, securely lodged in society's reproduction-process, unlike the simple buying cheap and selling dear of merchant capital, which tried to infiltrate pre-capitalist society from the outside and, in the process, undermined it. With industrial capital, therefore, the whole society becomes susceptible to rational organisation by its method of value augmentation. Capitalist society thus becomes endowed with an irresistible drive to pursue the advancement of the productive powers, entailing a constant improvement and progress in its methods of production, at a speed never dreamed of in previous societies.

Individual capitalists, however, do not seek such progress and improvement in the methods of production in the light of a general principle. They are motivated more directly by the special profit (sometimes called quasi-rent) that they can earn if they adopt a new method of producing the commodity with less input of labour, directly and indirectly, than others, who continue to operate in the same industry with conventional techniques. For the former (who have adopted an innovative technique) can then sell the commodity more cheaply than the latter (who continue to rely on conventional techniques). This extra profit due to innovation is earned whether or not the gain in productivity entails, in fact, a reduction in the value of labour-power. That kind of profit disappears in any case, as the new method is more and more widely adopted, but the same process often contributes, directly or indirectly, to the reduction of the value of labour-power, and, hence, to the production of more surplus value. This is the concrete manner in which Marx's so-called production of relative surplus value enforces itself. Although, in abstract-general terms, it can be said that the advancement of productive powers is that which provides human society with its material condition of progress, that aim is pursued automatically under capitalism through the commodity-economic mechanism just described. That, no doubt, shows the progressive aspect of capitalism.

Large-scale mechanised industry, which evolved after the Industrial Revolution, was an outcome of the manifestation of the above-mentioned driving force of capitalist development. The same driving force would also contribute towards the further development of mechanised industry. Yet all this was not achieved at once. For, as I mentioned in Part I, merchant capital had to divorce direct producers from their means of production first, in order to introduce the capitalist commodity-economy. In that early phase, however, capital's drive to enhance the productive powers of labour was still relegated to the background and remained latent as it were. It only gradually came to a head, as the separation of direct producers from the means of production proceeded. Indeed, that drive was occasionally seen in manufactories, in the first instance. Yet 'manufacture' (in the sense of production in manufactories) never displaced the dominance of merchant capital, nor did it easily grow out of the latter, so long as the workers were not yet rendered completely property-less. The room was still left there, in other words, for merchant capital to preserve its dominance.

The advent of machinery changed this situation. It was truly epoch-making in that it completed the separation of the direct producers from their means of production and the parallel divorce of industry from agriculture. Both processes had been initiated by merchant capital, though, ironically, its dominance lapsed once they gained momentum. When the advent of machinery took the form of the mechanisation of the cotton industry in England, it completed the divorce of industry from agriculture, which had already been progressing in the wool industry, operated by merchant capital. Of course, mechanisation did not consist of the invention of any particular machine, or its adoption in one particular industry or another. It lay in the revolutionary fact that the direct producers, who had been gradually deprived of their means of production, through a lengthy process over many years, were now irrevocably and massively turned into property-less workers. In 'manufacture' based on handicraft, it was still the labour-power of the workers that dictated the development of the method of production. It, therefore, remained ultimately dependent on human skills, no matter how minutely the production-process was split, by the division of labour, into partial (or segmented) operations. In large-scale modern industry, in contrast, the mechanisation of the means of labour, which liberated the work process itself from the individuality and idiosyncrasy of the workers, constituted the real point of departure. The workers were gradually de-skilled and reduced to the rank of proletarians. It was, as is often said, with the spinning machine that the Industrial Revolution of the eighteenth century in Britain began. It first opened up a new age for the key cotton industry, which, in turn, accelerated the mechanisation of other branches of industry. Even the transport system did not escape the same trend towards mechanisation.

Machines 'mechanise' the task which the workers used to perform with their own hand-tools. Machines separate these tools from the manual work of men and women, and make them their own parts. In this way, works are released from human constraints as machines develop. Indeed, a machine has the power to operate with many tools at a time, organising them into a co-ordinated operation of various different works. It can relate to other machines, and can progress further to an automated system almost entirely exclusive of human hand. Thus, in a mechanised factory, the workers find themselves subordinated to the machine rather than the other way round. All motions in the factory are regulated by the machine, and the workers must simply submit to its demands. Both the quality and the quantity of the product are defined by the machine, which is increasingly designed according to scientific knowledge beyond the grasp of the workers. All conditions for production are already laid out in the factory, in such a way as to ignore personal differences among workers. The machine now becomes the incarnation of capital. Rather than the workers running the machine, the latter exploits the former. The general character of the capitalist commodity-economy wherein things prevail over humans is thus realised in its crudest form in the capitalist factory.

A machine by itself is only a means of labour. Its development should, therefore, serve to save human labour in production. When it is capitalistically adopted, however, the relation is inverted in the sense that instead of lightening the toil of the direct workers, it serves to prolong the working hours and to intensify labour, so as to advance its efficiency for capital. It also opens up the factory to women and children, with the result that the household living expenses, which one able-bodied worker used to earn, must now be earned by the whole family. While anyone can now work in a mechanised factory, no one can be hired any longer as a worker elsewhere. Thus, the life of the working class becomes entirely dependent on wages.*

* Even under the putting-out system, and certainly under the manufacture division of labour, unskilled workers, i.e. ones without the skill-training of a journeyman, were employed. However, the capitalist factory, equipped with machines, made that kind of employment a standard, which, in many cases, entailed that members of the working-class family other than its head had to earn supplementary wages for the subsistence of the household. This did not necessarily lead to a proportionate reduction of the wages that the head of the family earned, as *Capital*, Vol. 1, explains.[1] In the earlier edition of this book, I simply reproduced Marx's argument; but I now think that there are more complex factors which contributed to the determination of wages. Marx, too, mentions, for one thing, that this tendency entailed a reduction of in-family labour and a corresponding increase in the family's money expenditure. This fact suggests to me an invasion into family life by the commodity-economy, an invasion that affected the real wages earned by the family, or its standard of living, in ways that could not be easily foreseen. How the value of labour-power expresses itself in wages is an involved problem fraught with many unsettled issues, some of which I discussed in an article, entitled 'The Theory of Crises', which is to be found in my book *Issues Related to Marxian Economics* [*Marukusu Keizaigaku no Shomondai*] (1969).

Not only does this change radically affect the worker's position in the factory, it also makes society's class relation irrevocable, as it has a bearing on the in-factory position of the workers. If, in this way, the capitalist use of the machine transforms the benefits of saving labour into a greater workload for the worker, it is because capital 'saves' the employment of the worker as a human being, by substituting machines for it. It is precisely for this reason that industrial capital was established in large-scale mechanised industry and assisted its further development. For although capital cannot use more labour-power than is made available by the natural growth of the working population, it can economise on the use of existing labour-power by means of this peculiar mechanism (of substituting machines for human labour).

1 See Marx 1987, *Capital*, Vol. 1, Chapter 13, Section 3, a: 'Appropriation of Supplementary Labour Power by Capital: The Employment of Women and Children'.

Generally speaking, a rise in productive powers under capitalism reduces the proportion of variable capital, which must be paid out as wages to the workers, relative to constant capital, which is devoted for the purchase of the means of production, and, thus, elevates what Marx calls the value composition of capital. In other words, the adoption of new machines, or improvement of existing machines, tends to reduce the number of workers employed per unit of capital. Therefore, what is generally called the 'rationalisation' of productive methods usually means reduced employment, and is bitterly contested by the workers themselves, a paradoxical fact inasmuch as better methods of production should, in principle, be deemed to benefit humankind. In any case, the fact is that an increase of capital brought about by its accumulation does not necessarily increase the number of employed workers proportionally. Of course, the number of workers does increase in absolute terms, as the scale of production expands and/or new businesses open up. Yet this increase will not be in proportion to the increased volume of capital.

The capitalist method of production internalises this peculiar relation governing the demand for, and the supply of, labour-power in its cyclical process of development (i.e. through business cycles). The increased demand for workers during the prosperity phase, as the scale of production expands, and as new businesses come into being, is met by the draining of the so-called 'industrial reserve army', which was formed by the adoption of new methods of production in the previous phase of depression. Then, as the accumulation of capital proceeds, absorbing more and more of the unemployed workers, (real) wages inevitably rise and the rate of profit falls, even though the absolute amount of profit may continue to increase. If, however, a greater advance of capital yields lesser profits, capital becomes excessive or superabundant. Further production of the means of production and articles of consumption will then become futile for capital, unless new methods of production are adopted in such a way as to raise the value composition of capital. Prior to this structural change, however, the need for it is signalled by the eruption of an industrial crisis. The latter occurs when capital accumulation suddenly ceases, as the declining profit-rate and the rising interest-rate, in combination, render capital insolvent, that is to say, as loan-capital prevails over industrial capital.*

* When the capitalist method of production begins to develop on its own, having taken hold of society's reproduction-process, at least in its broad outlines, the system is also given a chance to develop capitalistically. Banks concentrate idle money that arises in various parts of the reproduction-process, and offer it as loanable funds to those who can make use of them. Of course, not all loanable funds have their origin in money-capital, as it 'idles' in the reproduction-process of capital. Funds from all sources, if not

absorbed by industry, are lent to strictly mercantile operations as well. What makes the modern credit system capitalistically rational is that idle money, which one capitalist cannot use, is made available to other capitalists who can. By this capitalist-social sharing of idle money, more surplus value can be produced than in its absence, and loan-capital is established as the ultimate regulator of society's reproduction-process. Each individual capital sometimes offers its idle money for use by other capitals through banks, while it itself borrows funds from banks at other times for its own expansion. Its activity is always regulated by this mutual give-and-take of society's idle funds. No capital can be indifferent to the fluctuation of the rate of interest, even while pursuing its profit blindly. For example, industrial capital cannot by itself stop accumulating, even in the state of an excess of capital, that is to say, even if the marginal profitability of investment is no longer positive. It is only because the burden of the debt it holds has become intolerable, after loan-capital raises the rate of interest, that the indebted accumulator realises that his time is up. Although loan-capital constitutes a small proportion of the capital involved in the reproduction-process, it does function as 'capital's capital' because of its ability to temporarily leave and re-enter the reproduction-process. Modern commercial banks, as the agents of loan-capital, constitute the core of financial institutions under capitalism. In passing, the modern banking system established itself in England in the first half of the nineteenth century, when individually owned banks of olden times transformed themselves into joint-stock banks. The fact that the concrete-historical operation of the banking system did not always conform to theoretical expectations indicates, in no way, a weakness of the theory. For example, theory distinguishes clearly between 'merchant capital' and 'commercial capital', and yet, in reality, most better-known merchant houses are a hybrid of both.

Capital can then no longer sell its commodities, and the workers are thrown out of work. The intense competition among capitals in this phase of depression, which follows a crisis, goads them to adopt new methods of production which are labour-saving, and which will exacerbate unemployment, the exact opposite of what capital does in the phase of prosperity. For when workers are scarce and wages rise, capital tends to expand more, and thus make matters worse. This instability stems from the fact that in the era of large-scale mechanised industry, the means of labour involve fixed capital, and the method of production embodied therein delimits the period of business expansion, since capital remains profitable only for so long as the industrial reserve army is not yet exhausted. Capital has little motivation to pursue a gain in productivity by an innovation of its method of production for as long as it can continue to operate profitably. Only the intensified pressure of competition, during the depression period, forces it to consider that option. Thus, on the one hand, the accumulation of capital is, to some extent, freed from the absolute constraint imposed by the natural growth of the working population. Yet, on the other, it is still constrained by the present availability of the industrial reserve army, and must proceed cyclically through the alternate phases of prosperity and depression. All this stems from the fact that labour-power is a special commodity, which capital cannot produce. Yet capital also brings forth the peculiar mechanism whereby it controls labour-power as a commodity in the following manner. Capital first expands under the given production-relations, defined by the existing methods of production. Only when that becomes untenable does capital resort to innovations, which, by establishing new production-relations, enable and support its further expansion. This is how capitalism develops necessarily, while overcoming its fundamental contradiction that arises from the conversion of labour-power into a commodity, in concrete terms.

This specific mode of capitalist development, based on large-scale mechanised industry, also shapes the social relation, or class-relation, between labour and capital by means of the commodity-form. Capital maintains the commodity-form of labour-power, the supply of which it cannot increase beyond the natural growth of the working population. Although this constraint is circumvented, to some extent, by the mechanism described above, it cannot, however, be completely done away with. The survival of capital depends on its operating within this constraint, and this fact imposes upon it the need to live with fierce competition with other capitals. Just as the worker can lose his/her job, capital too can go bankrupt. This is what is expected, given the kind of freedom and equality that the commodity-economy pursues at the social level. Because of its origin in the circulation-process, capital does not take any direct interest in the use-value aspect of the production-process. Neither does labour-power take an interest in the same aspect because of its conversion into a commodity. Both capital and labour thus move freely from one sphere of production to another – though, in practice, only marginally in the process of accumulation – and are, in principle, not tied to a particular industry in the commodity-economy. This manner of mobilisation of capital and labour makes society itself radically commodity-economic, i.e. subject to the operation of abstract-general laws. Yet even such a society, in order to survive, must operate a reproduction-process involving use-values. This fact forces both capital and labour to abide by the same economic law that governs society. Although 'to achieve maximum gains with minimum costs' is the general economic norm, pursued, in one way or another, in all societies, this norm becomes a compelling law only in the radically commodity-economic capitalist society. For here, both labour and capital, while conceding to the blind and anarchic operation of the commodity-economy, unconsciously enforce the laws which secure the viability of that society. The capitalist ideology of freedom and equality, thus, cheerfully ignores the fact that surplus labour constitutes the source of profit, and treats the unemployment of labour as a failure of the same sort as the bankruptcy of capital, thus effacing from its consciousness all traces of the working of the laws of capitalist society.

In other words, unlike the accumulation of merchant capital, which thrived on the expropriation of small producers, the accumulation of industrial capital, based on the conversion of labour-power into a commodity, is propelled by a mechanism of its own creation. No longer dependent on political powers external to it, capitalism can now pursue its own end, by pauperising productive workers and by transforming means of production into capital. It is in this way that capitalism, as the economic system of a historically existing society, endures.

This economic regime, as already suggested, did not, however, evolve overnight; nor did it immediately impose its factory-type mechanisation on all productive spheres in society. It was by divorcing industry from agriculture, the sector that had occupied the productive centre of traditional societies, and by inserting commodity-economic relations between industry and agriculture, that the new system of capitalism gradually evolved, and, with it, the conversion of labour-power into a commodity became irrevocable. Capitalism in Great Britain had prepared the ground for this process in its wool industry during the seventeenth and eighteenth centuries, and completed it with its cotton industry in the nineteenth century. In the meantime, the commodity-economy increasingly penetrated agriculture as well. That process which had begun from the second half of the eighteenth century bore fruit in the nineteenth century, even though it was far from a simple matter. The evolution of capitalism in English agriculture was accelerated by the extraordinary circumstances that the cotton industry sought raw cotton in foreign (and not in domestic) agriculture, circumstances that critically affected both the cotton industry and agriculture. Capitalism in Great Britain, in other words, made full use of foreign commodity-economic development for its own perfection. This was by no means accidental, but was perfectly in keeping with the peculiar nature of the commodity-economy. As already stressed a number of times, the commodity-economy arose between independent communities. Its development was, therefore, necessarily inter-communal or international.* The British cotton industry, in effect, established Great Britain as the 'workshop of the world', by keeping other countries 'agricultural'. It is this international structure that defined the second world-historic stage of development of capitalism. It was this structure that fostered the evolution of capitalism in other countries, by means of international free trade between them and Great Britain.

*Since capitalism is a commodity-economy, its development has always had an intimate connection with international trade. Yet, in order for capitalism to be established as a purely economic mechanism that governs one whole historical society, albeit through transient commodity-forms, the theory which must mentally reproduce this mechanism cannot include foreign trade within itself. Capitalism, in principle, accepts and manages all commodities by means of its operative mechanism, without questioning the production-relations under which they have been produced. It, of course, makes no distinction between domestic and foreign commodities. The economic development of Britain after the Industrial Revolution made full use of external trade, and this contributed significantly to the evolution of capitalist production-relations at home. That is an empirical fact. Economic theory, however, looks at the evolution of capitalist production-relations from the inside, regardless of the impetus, which it may have received from the outside to accelerate its internal process. Foreign trade does not constitute the substance of this internal process. Nor did British capitalism care how its imported raw materials had been produced, provided that they were cheap and useful to its industry. The fallacy of misguided realism is best illustrated by the so-called theory of 'international values', which purports to constitute the foundation of international trade theory. In that context, it is clearly impossible to specify the substance of value, so that the concept of value, as distinct from price, becomes quite meaningless. It is for this reason that the question of foreign trade should, in my opinion, be discussed only at the levels of stages-theory and of historical analysis. Although this is not a proper place to elaborate on it, I nevertheless wish to draw attention to the fact that the international relations, which evolved under various mercantilist policies, and those which evolved during the liberal epoch were vastly different from each other. For instance, Britain's export industry during the mercantilist era was based on domestic wool, whereas the same in the second depended on imported cotton. This difference can never be explained at the level of abstract theory.

CHAPTER 5

The British Cotton Industry as Representing Industrial Capital

Up until the middle of the eighteenth century, the British cotton industry was not yet firmly established. Domestically, it remained a minor one relative to the wool industry; internationally, its products could not hope to compete with the fine cotton manufactures of East India. British products were confined to such coarser articles as fustians, velvets and the like, and it was widely believed that the imitation of such delicately hand-woven fine cotton cloths as India could supply remained well beyond British competence. However, it was the mechanisation of cotton spinning in the latter half of the eighteenth century that changed this whole perspective.

1   Mechanisation of Cotton Manufacturing

It is generally believed that the mechanisation of the spinning process responded to an increased demand for yarn, which was apparent already in the first half of the eighteenth century. It was about that time that the weaving operation was made more efficient, with the application of the fly-shuttle invented by John Kay. However, the subsequent inventions of the water-frame by R. Arkwright and of the 'spinning Jenny' by J. Hargreaves appear to have given a more decisive impetus towards the mechanisation of spinning. Water-frames mechanised all of the spinning operations that follow 'roving' with the application of the roller technology. This technology had been perfected through various experiments, before it reached a new level of excellence in 1775. It was called 'water-frame' since the plants, in which it was used, were powered by waterwheels. This invention enabled the substitution of cotton for linen, in the production of resilient warp at a sufficiently low cost. The spinning Jenny was a machine capable of turning many spindles simultaneously. This invention, too, was a synthesis of various earlier devices which had been tried over many years. At first, it could turn only eight spindles at once. Subsequently, however, the number of spindles increased to twenty, and eventually to one hundred and twenty. It then quickly displaced spinning wheels which had to be hand-driven. Unlike the water-frame, the Jenny did not require a large plant to operate in, so that it was already widely used by the time Hargreaves patented his invention in 1770. It produced threads that were finer and lighter than that which the water-frame could produce. They were, however, not strong enough to be used for warp but only for weft.

It was the 'mule', a spinning machine invented by S. Crompton, that combined these two earlier methods, and succeeded in twisting thin and strong threads, usable not only for weft but also for warp. As these were fit for muslin, British cotton products could at last compete with those of India, and thus rose to an international prominence that had previously been enjoyed only by woollen and linen products. The mule, unlike the water-frame, required sophisticated operations on the part of the workers; thus, the ones who supervised the operation of the machine exercised authority over other workers. The extended use of the mule consequently generated a group of working people, who were not so docile and obedient to capital. Confronted, thus, with repeated labour disputes, capital craved for an improved machine, which would circumvent the recalcitrance of the workers. The problem was solved, finally, by the self-acting mule, which R. Roberts completed in 1825, and by the throstle, which was but an improved version of the water-frame, even though these inventions did not spread immediately. Nor did the self-acting mule completely eliminate the need for skilled labour. Nevertheless, it is fair to say that the coming into being of these methods ensured the supremacy of capital over labour in the manufacturing of cotton.

By the late 1780s, the use of steam power was added to the above-mentioned mechanisation of the spinning process, so that productive capacity in spinning greatly exceeded the requirement by the weaving industry, which was yet to be mechanised. By this time the shortage of weavers became a serious problem, reversing the situation from that which prevailed earlier when the fly-shuttle was invented. High wages in weaving attracted all kind of workers to that occupation, so much so that the years between 1788 and 1803 were called the golden age of weavers. This state of affairs was short-lived, however. Already, towards the end of the eighteenth century, the weavers' wages began to fall because of the increased inflow of labour from other textile trades as well as agriculture. Due both to the fact that weaving techniques could often be relatively easily learned, and also to circumstances peculiar to contemporary English society, this section of the cotton industry was to depend on cheap labour for some time thereafter. That was one of the causes which delayed mechanisation in weaving, and which led to the extreme devastation of the handloom operators, when power-looms were finally introduced in the 1830s.*

---

* On this matter Marx writes as follows: 'History discloses no tragedy more horrible than the gradual extinction of the English hand-loom weavers, an extinction that was spread

over several decades, and finally sealed in 1838. Many of them died of starvation, many with families vegetated for a long time on 2½d. a day'.[1] 'The competition between hand-weaving and power-weaving in England, before the passing of the Poor Law of 1833, was prolonged by supplementing the wages, which had fallen considerably below the minimum, with parish relief'.[2] He then quotes the following passage from P. Gaskell's *The Manufacturing Population of England*: 'A family of four grown-up persons [as handloom weavers], with two children as winders, earned at the end of the last, and the beginning of the present century, by ten hours daily labour, £4 a week. If the work was very pressing, they could earn more. Before that, they had always suffered from a deficient supply of yarn'.[3]

The history of power-looms began with the invention by E. Cartwright in 1785. However, their practical use had to wait for the appearance of the dressing-machine in 1804, and its further improvement by H. Horrocks. Even then, it was slow in being adopted. According to Ellison,[4] there were only 2,400 power-looms in use in 1813, compared with the more than 200,000 handlooms at work. Yet the handloom weavers, who were probably in excess, were seriously threatened; so much so that, in 1813, riots broke out in many places and all new power-looms were destroyed. Only in 1822 was the possibility finally opened for the diffusion of power-looms because of a new improvement, which made them adaptable to the production of fustians and velvets. By 1832–3, the number of power-looms exceeded 100,000, though that number still remained lower than the number, about 250,000, of handlooms in operation. Power-looms were still primitive, and their operation had to be constantly supervised by the workers, which was one of the reasons why they failed to replace handlooms altogether. In 1841, a truly self-acting power-loom was completed. The mechanisation of the loom, unlike that of the spinning machine, created competition between male weavers who handloomed at home, and female workers who operated power-looms in factories. Its social effect was devastating, especially because of the difficulty of organising handloom weavers.

The mechanisation of the spinning and weaving processes naturally entailed the mechanisation of related operations. That was the case with scotching, carding, bleaching and dyeing. As the productivity of the cotton industry consequently made remarkable progress, the prices of its products also fell con-

---

1   Marx 1987, *Capital*, Vol. i, p. 406.
2   Marx 1987, *Capital*, Vol. i, p. 406n.
3   Marx 1987, *Capital*, Vol. i, p. 418n.
4   Ellison 1886, p. 35.

spicuously. According to Ellison,* the average annual output of yarn per worker was 968 lbs. in 1819–21, 1,547 lbs. in 1829–31, and 2,754 lbs. in 1844–6.⁵ The annual output of power-loomed cotton cloth, too, increased similarly, from 342 lbs. to 521 lbs. and further to 1,681 lbs., during the same periods. In the meantime, the price of yarn kept falling, even though the trend was sometimes counteracted by the price of raw cotton and by fluctuating exchange rates. Specifically, one pound of yarn (40 hanks), which was priced at 7s.6d. in 1799, became 2s.6d. in 1812, and 1s.6½d. in 1830. In the case of cotton cloths, the average price of printing cloth (chintz) which was 28s. apiece in 1815, was 8s.9d. in 1830, and 6s. in 1845. As for calico, which was sold for 13d. per yard in 1815, it could be bought for 2½d. per yard in 1856.

* Ellison also gives an interesting table, reproduced below, in which he estimates the selling price of a pound of cotton yarn (40 hanks), together with the cost of the material (18 oz. of raw cotton) and outlay on labour and capital.

TABLE N-1   *Make-up of cost of yarn (40 hanks to the lb)*

	1779	1784	1799	1812	1830	1860	1882
Selling price	16s.0d.	10s.11d.	7s.6d.	2s.6d.	1s.2½d.	11½d.	10½d.
Cost of cotton (18 oz.)	2s.0d.	2s.0d.	3s.4d.	1s.6d.	7¾d.	6⅞d.	7⅛d.
Labour and capital	14s.0d.	8s.11d.	4s.2d.	1s.0d.	6¾d.	4⅝d.	3⅜d.

2   The Development of the Cotton Industry

As described above, the cotton spinning process was mechanised over the 15 years following the Napoleonic War, i.e. from 1815 to 1830, and the process of cotton weaving over the twenty to thirty years between the 1820s and the 1840s. The mechanisation of the cotton industry, in other words, did not occur overnight. Yet it firmly established the mode of mechanised factory production within a relatively short span of time. This is in contrast to the mode of 'manufactory' production, which, after two centuries of gradual progress, never really became a dominant form of business enterprise. Mechanised cotton manufacturing formed the core of British industry. It was concentrated in the three North-

5   Ellison 1886, pp. 68–9. With regard to the prices, see p. 61 of this book.

ern districts, especially in Lancashire, centring around Manchester, the area north of Lancashire (the Glasgow region), and the area to its south (the Nottingham region). Such a formation of regional centres makes a striking contrast to the case of the wool industry, which largely remained dispersed nationwide, and focused primarily on domestic production during the seventeenth and eighteenth century, even though there were regions which produced relatively more than others. (Only with its later mechanisation did Yorkshire and West Riding achieve relative prominence in wool production). In the three cotton-producing Northern districts, the population increased explosively. In Lancashire, it increased from 670,000 to 1,330,000 during the thirty years ending in 1831. The spectacular growth of the cotton industry, in the meantime, can be confirmed in Table 1 and Chart 1 below.

At first, the production of cotton cloth followed that of cotton yarn with some delay, but caught up during the 1850s and the 1860s, and subsequently increased just as vigorously. Cotton cloth also became increasingly dependent on exports, and the ratio of export to production gradually rose. The reason why the export of yarn was not quite as pronounced may be explained by the development of the spinning industry abroad. Since spinning could be more easily mechanised than weaving, international competition may have been severer in yarn. In any case, there is little doubt that the primacy of the British cotton industry, which began in the 1830s and 1840s, came to an end in the 1860s and 1870s. During that interval, the position of this industry in Britain underwent an important change. First, it replaced the wool industry which had been the leading manufacturing activity. The following table on British exports makes this point apparent (Table 2). The values in the table contain the price fluctuations under the influence of the Napoleonic war, and, hence, do not directly indicate the trend in export volumes. They are nevertheless good enough to demonstrate the position that the cotton industry had achieved in Britain prior to the 1820s. The dominant position did not change, even in 1845, when the export of cotton goods amounted to £26.1 million in the total export of £60.1 million, as compared to the export of woollen goods of £8.8 million, and that of iron and steel products of £3.5 million.[6]

---

6   Cole 1932, p. 58.

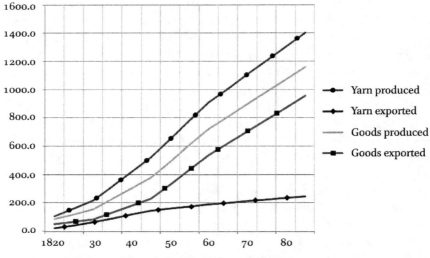

CHART 1   *Cotton yarn and goods in millions of pounds (lbs.)*

TABLE 1   *Cotton yarn and goods in millions of pounds (lbs.)*[7]

	Average of the three years indicated				
	1819–21	1829–31	1844–6	1859–61	1880–2
Cotton consumed	119.6	243.2	588.0	1,022.5	1,424.6
Yarn produced	106.5	216.5	523.3	910.0	1,324.9
Yarn exported	20.9	63.3	145.2	189.1	236.4
Goods produced	85.6	153.2	378.1	720.9	1,088.5
Goods exported	50.0	82.6	228.5	536.0	888.0
Home consumption	35.6	70.6	149.6	148.9	200.5

Chart 1 shows four curves plotting the figures given by Ellison in Table 1 above.

---

7   Ellison 1886, pp. 58–9.

TABLE 2   *Certain of the principal British exports at current prices in 1796–8, 1815 and 1820*[8]

	(average)		
	1706–98	1815	1820
Woollen goods	8,459	9,338	5,583
Cotton goods	4,175	20,621	16,516
Total of principal textiles	16,159	33,355	24,504
Brasses and copper manufactures	1,042	731	723
Iron and steel manufactures	2,167	1,093	947
Total of principal metal goods	3,876	4,740	3,138
Glass and earthenware	540	1,386	811
Coal	368	115	109
Total of the above classes	20,943	39,596	28,562
Total of British exports	31,273	51,603	36,425

However, the growth of the cotton industry did not follow a monotonic path of increase year after year. Business cycles, which characterise capitalist production, made their appearance in precisely that period, and involved the industry in a cyclical process of expansion and contraction. More accurately, the cyclical process itself was decisively influenced by the growth of the cotton industry. Although the phenomenon of economic cycles was observed a number of times beginning in the seventeenth and eighteenth century, it was not until 1825 that a typically capitalist crisis occurred. This was the form of crisis that regularly punctuated the decennial cycles of prosperity and depression at their mid-point during the liberal era. Earlier crises occurred for contingent reasons, such as the bursting of commercial or speculative bubbles, fiscal failures, and so on, and did not originate in the core of society's reproduction-process. They

---

8   Adapted from Cole 1932, p. 58.

were triggered by disruptions in financial relations, which operated in a sphere largely disjoined from the reproduction-process, yet caused widespread economic disturbances. In contrast, the crises which occurred after the 1820s were clearly due to a failure of the reproduction-process itself. By this time, even financial relations were broadly determined by society's reproduction-process, which now embodied the core functioning of capitalist society. I say 'broadly' because, to some extent, financial relations remained, even then, under the control of merchant capital, the accumulation process of which still followed the old tradition. That was especially the case with foreign trade. Thus, business cycles were frequently influenced by conditions in the external market. It would, therefore, be correct to say that industrial crises were caused by combinations of such external factors and disruptions originating in the domestic reproduction-process. Yet the extreme regularity of the cyclical process, after 1825, makes it hard to believe that external factors were the primary determinants of capitalist crises. The following table (Table 3) shows the volume of raw cotton consumed side by side with the money value of cotton goods exported. Both series indicate slowdowns or setbacks during periods of crisis followed by depression, and recoveries in subsequent periods, yet on the whole maintaining the general trend upward. The years of crisis were 1825, 1836, 1847 and 1857.

TABLE 3   *The volume of raw cotton consumed and the value of cotton goods exported*[9]
A = Consumption of Raw Cotton in Britain, in millions of lbs.
B = Total value of Piece Goods (all kinds) exported from Britain, in millions of £s.

	A	B		A	B		A	B		A	B
1821	129.0	16.09	1831	262.7	17.26	1841	438.1	23.50	1851	658.9	30.09
1822	145.5	17.22	1832	276.9	17.40	1842	435.1	21.68	1852	739.6	29.88
1823	154.1	16.33	1833	287.0	18.49	1843	517.8	23.45	1853	760.9	32.71
1824	165.2	18.45	1834	303.4	20.51	1844	544.0	25.81	1854	776.1	31.75
1825	166.8	18.36	1835	318.1	22.13	1845	606.0	26.12	1855	839.1	34.78
1826	150.2	14.09	1836	347.4	2463	1846	614.3	25.60	1856	891.4	38.23
1827	187.2	17.64	1837	365.7	20.60	1847	441.4	23.33	1857	826.0	39.07
1828	217.9	17.24	1838	416.7	24.15	1848	576.6	22.68	1858	905.6	43.0
1829	219.2	17.54	1839	381.7	24.55	1849	629.9	26.77	1859	976.6	48.2
1830	247.6	19.43	1840	458.9	24.67	1850	588.2	28.26	1860	1,083.6	52.01

---

9   Based on Ellison 1886, pp. 58–9, Tables 1 and 2.

The development of the cotton industry in Britain during this period is also corroborated by the increase in the number of machines and workers, as one might expect (Table 4). In weaving, as already mentioned, power-looms were introduced during the 1830s. The switchover from handloom operators to power-loom operators is graphically apparent in Table 5. The total number of persons directly employed by the cotton industry, including the bleachers, printers, dye-workers in addition to the weavers and spinning workers, was about 445,000 in 1819–21; 515,000 in 1829–31; 540,000 in 1844–6; 646,000 in 1859–61; and 686,000 in 1880–2. It is hard to find out how these workers were distributed to separate factories, but Table 6 gives us some indication of the state of affairs between 1850 and 1878.

TABLE 4   *Evolution of the cotton industry in Britain (1)*[10]

| | Cotton Yarn | | Cotton Goods | |
	Spindles at work (millions)	Hands employed (thousands)	Looms at work (thousands)	Hands employed (thousands)
1819–21	7.0	110	255	250
1829–31	10.0	140	305	275
1844–6	19.5	190	282	210
1859–61	30.4	248	400	203
1880–2	42.0	240	550	246

TABLE 5   *The number of workers in cotton weaving*[11]

	Operatives in weaving mills	Handloom weavers
1819–21	10,000	240,000
1829–31	50,000	225,000
1844–6	150,000	60,000
1859–61	203,000	–
1880–2	246,000	–

---

10   Ellison 1886, pp. 68–9.
11   Ellison 1886, p. 66.

Some of the factories surveyed in Table 6 were specialised in spinning, others in weaving. There were also ones that combined both spinning and weaving. In such cases, the number of workers per plant was large. For example, there were 573 such factories in 1850, and each employed 332 workers on average; in 1878, there were 597 such factories and each employed 354 workers on average. These factories also operated a relatively large number of spindles and looms. It is also noteworthy that women and children occupied an important proportion of the workers in these factories. In 1850, the proportion of female workers was 55.6 percent, and that of male workers was 39.9 percent, and the remaining, 4.5 percent were children younger than 13. In 1878, the proportion of children rose to 12.8 percent, and that of adult workers declined (although their absolute number did increase). The increase of child labour reflected the progressive mechanisation of the industry, which was particularly conspicuous in factories specialised in weaving.*

TABLE 6　　　*Evolution of the cotton industry in Britain* (2)[12]

	1850	1878
Number of mills	1,932	2,674
Number of spindles (per mill)	20,977,000 (10,857)	44,207,000 (16,532)
Number of looms (per mill)	249,627 (128)	514,911 (192)
Hands employed (per mill)	330,924 (171)	482,903 (180)

*The following passage from Engels seems to describe the state of affairs with a fair degree of accuracy: 'And if at the moment of highest activity of the market, the agricultural districts, Ireland, and the branches least affected by the general prosperity temporarily supply to manufacture a number of workers, these are a mere minority, and these too belong to the reserve army, with the single difference that the prosperity of the moment was required to reveal their connection with it. When they enter upon the more active branches of work, their former employers draw in somewhat, in order to feel the loss less, work longer hours, employ women and younger workers, and when wanderers discharged at the beginning of the crisis return, they find their places filled and themselves superfluous – at least in the majority of cases'.[13]

12　　　Ellison 1886, p. 72.
13　　　Engels 1952, p. 85.

3   The British Cotton Industry and International Trade

As it mechanised itself, the British cotton industry immediately gained a position of international leadership, outdistancing all others. After the 1820s, it
even exported to India, from which Britain used to import cotton goods. France
became cotton manufacturer second only to Britain in the world; but its output, early in the nineteenth century, was only one-quarter that of England.
Furthermore, despite the prohibition, which France continued even after the
Napoleonic war, a large quantity of yarn was smuggled into that nation from
England. The contraband occurred because of the wide gap in the cost of production.* The United States too became a producer of cotton goods early in the
nineteenth century, and, by the 1830s, operated over one million spindles in 800
factories. However, the American products were much inferior to the British in
quality; and prices were relatively higher because of unfavourable conditions of
production.** The manufacturing of cotton was developing gradually in other
countries as well, though their output was still too small to matter in the international market.

* E. Baines lists the following disadvantages of the French cotton industry: (1) the
weavers and even many of the spinners could not be induced to work in factories the
year round; (2) iron and coal were comparatively scarce; (3) manufacturing establish-
ments were small and scattered over many parts of the country, which made the mass
production of cotton goods unprofitable; (4) roads and inland navigation were inferior
and defective; (5) the importation of raw materials was costly; and (6) interest rates
were high. For these reasons, the prices of French cotton goods were higher than those
of English goods by as much as thirty to forty percent, according to Baines. He also
mentions that the French labour cost was substantially higher than the English, owing
to inferior labour productivity, even though daily wages were lower in France than in
England.[14]

** In 1809, there were 62 mills with 31,000 spindles. Subsequently, the number of spindles were said to be 80,000 in 1811 and 500,000 in 1815.[15] The US cotton industry, according to Baines, had several disadvantages relative to the British. For example, the cost
of mules (spinning machines) in the United States ranged from 13s. to 14s. per spindle,
while in Britain they were no more than 5s. per spindle. Yet the price of raw cotton was
more or less the same, given that the freight charge between New Orleans and Boston
was only ¼d. lower than that between New Orleans and Liverpool per lb. of cotton.[16]

14   Baines 1835, pp. 512–15, 520, 523.
15   Taussig 1923, pp. 28 ff.
16   Baines 1835, pp. 508–9.

The export of British cotton goods expanded greatly, as the industry established itself. Changes in the destination of the exports were significant too.
As shown in Table 7, the export of cotton cloth to Europe first rose until
1840, remained stagnant thereafter until 1860, then resumed expansion. Ellison
attributes this peculiarity to the export of spinning machines during the 1840s,
and to the normalisation of Anglo-French trade relations in 1860. With regard
to the United States, the export of cotton goods from Britain continued to rise
until 1860, but stagnated thereafter, due in part to changes in the US trade policy.
Overall, export to these developing capitalist countries was bound to reach a
limit, regardless of their trade policies. For they would eventually overtake Britain as major cotton manufacturers. While cotton cloth gradually found markets in Asia and other less developed countries, Europe continued to absorb
almost 50 percent of British export even in 1870. Britain preserved this strength
in Europe because of fine yarn, in the production of which it excelled. In any
case, whereas the export of cotton yarn remained about 20 to 30 percent of its
total production, the ratio in the case of cotton cloth was more than 50 percent from the beginning, and went up to 70 to 80 percent during the 1860s
and afterwards. This shows that Britain was truly an export-oriented industrial
power.

In order to ensure that position, Britain imported a growing volume of raw
cotton from abroad. Thus, by importing raw materials and exporting manufactured goods, Britain played a proper international role as the nation in
which capitalism developed first. It forged a typically complementary relation with the United States in particular. The United States experimented with
the cultivation of 'sea-island cotton' towards the end of the eighteenth century, in response to the emergent cotton industry in Britain. This high quality
cotton, however, failed to grow in quantity because of unfavourable natural
conditions. It was the invention of the 'saw-gin' device that finally mechanised the process of ginning 'upland cotton', which grew in abundance, thus
making American cotton an international commodity. The Southern states
made use of slavery to expand the production of cotton for export so that
by the middle of the nineteenth century cotton replaced tobacco as the top
export commodity of that country. As the British importation of American
cotton increased in the meantime, a complementary relationship between
the two countries – the one industrial and the other agricultural – emerged,
and was maintained until at least 1860. Indeed, as Table 9 indicates, American cotton occupied 70 to 80 percent of British cotton imports after the decade of the 1830s. It replaced cotton from the British West Indies, which occupied 70 percent of British imports at the end of the eighteenth century, but
which declined quickly thereafter. Towards the end of the 1860s, because of the

TABLE 7   *British export of cotton goods to the principal districts of the world, in millions of yards*[17]

	Europe (exc. Turkey)	Turkey Egypt & Africa	Americas (exc. USA)	USA	British India	China & Japan, etc.	All others	Total
1820	127.7	9.5	56.0	23.8		14.2	19.7	250.9
1830	137.4	40.0	140.8	49.3		56.9	20.2	444.6
1840	200.4	74.6	278.6	32.1	145.1	29.9	29.9	790.6
1850	222.1	193.9	360.4	104.2	314.4	104.3	58.9	1,358.2
1860	200.5	357.8	527.1	226.8	825.1	324.2	214.7	2,676.2
1870	294.6	670.5	594.5	103.3	923.3	478.2	188.4	3,252.8
1880	365.1	588.6	651.6	77.9	1,813.4	632.0	367.7	4,496.3

The same in percentage terms

	Europe (exc. Turkey)	Turkey Egypt & Africa	Americas (exc. USA)	USA	British India	China & Japan, etc.	All others	Total
1820	50.90	3.79	22.32	9.48		5.66	7.85	100
1830	30.94	8.99	31.66	11.68		12.79	4.54	100
1840	25.35	9.43	35.24	4.07	18.35	3.78	3.78	100
1850	16.35	14.27	26.53	7.68	23.15	7.68	4.34	100
1860	7.49	13.37	19.70	8.48	30.83	12.11	8.02	100
1870	9.06	20.61	18.28	3.18	28.38	14.70	5.79	100
1880	8.12	13.09	14.49	1.73	40.33	14.81	8.18	100

Civil War, the importation of cotton from Brazil and India greatly expanded, but that was only a temporary phenomenon.

17   Ellison 1886, pp. 63–4.

TABLE 8   *British exports of cotton yarn to principal districts of the world, in millions of pounds*
           (lbs.)[18]

	Europe (exc. Turkey)	Turkey Egypt & Africa	British East Indies	China & Japan Java, etc	All others	Total
1820	22.0	0.5	–	–	0.5	23.0
1830	56.0	1.5	–	4.9	2.2	64.6
1840	91.9	3.3	16.1	1.8	5.4	118.5
1850	90.7	4.7	21.0	3.1	11.9	131.4
1860	116.0	19.6	30.7	8.8	22.2	197.3
1870	93.7	14.2	31.0	20.8	28.0	187.7
1880	95.1	12.4	47.1	46.4	14.7	215.7

The same in percentage terms

	Europe (exc. Turkey)	Turkey Egypt & Africa	British East Indies	China & Japan Java, etc	All others	Total
1820	95.66	2.17	–	–	2.17	100
1830	86.69	2.32	–	7.58	3.41	100
1840	77.55	2.78	13.58	1.52	4.56	100
1850	69.03	3.58	15.98	2.36	9.05	100
1860	58.79	9.94	15.56	4.46	11.25	100
1870	49.93	17.56	16.51	11.08	14.92	100
1880	44.09	5.79	21.84	21.51	6.81	100

18   Ibid.

TABLE 9   *Imports to Britain of raw cotton from various sources in bales of uniform weight of 400 lbs.*[19]

	USA	Brazil	British West Indies	Mediterranean	East Indies etc.	Sundries	Total
1786–90	100	5,000	45,000	13,000	500	–	63,600
1796–00	22,480	10,670	32,890	17,250	8,310	1,770	93,370
1806–10	107,500	32,500	32,830	2,590	25,870	1,000	202,290
1816–20	166,310	55,760	23,800	1,030	93,710	10,970	351,580
1826–30	433,800	60,850	12,940	16,100	55,720	2,860	582,270
1836–40	920,580	52,330	3,480	19,360	145,940	10,300	1,151,990
1846–50	1,247,230	57,860	1,910	31,310	196,140	2,870	1,537,320
1856–60	2,172,820	55,060	1,960	89,840	480,020	22,430	2,822,230
1866–70	1,410,860	190,700	7,570	363,950	1,218,370	73,600	3,265,050
1876–80	2,589,070	85,330	1,670	402,190	510,800	51,710	3,640,770

The above in percentage terms

	USA	Brazil	British West Indies	Mediterranean	East Indies etc.	Sundries	Total
1786–90	0.16	7.87	70.75	20.44	0.78	–	100
1796–00	24.08	11.43	35.23	18.47	8.90	1.89	100
1806–10	53.14	16.07	16.23	1.28	12.79	0.49	100
1816–20	47.31	15.86	6.77	0.29	26.65	3.12	100
1826–30	74.50	10.45	2.33	2.76	9.57	0.49	100
1836–40	79.91	4.54	0.31	1.68	12.67	0.89	100
1846–50	81.13	3.76	0.12	2.04	12.76	0.19	100
1856–60	77.00	1.95	0.07	3.19	17.01	0.78	100
1866–70	43.23	5.83	0.24	11.15	37.32	2.23	100
1876–80	71.11	2.33	0.05	11.04	14.04	1.43	100

---

19   Ellison 1886, p. 86.

TABLE 10   *Production and distribution of US cotton (in 1,000 bales)*[20]

	Total supply (total crop plus stock at start of season)	Exported	Consumed (Britain)	Consumed (USA)
1830–1	1,060	773	619	168
1840–1	1,698	1,313	859	297
1850–1	2,583	1,989	1,418	464
1860–1	4,054	3,128	2,175	839
1870–1	4,412	3,167	2,376	1,135
1880–1	6,731	4,596	2,844	1,915

Table 10 above exhibits the fact that Great Britain was by far the most important purchaser of American cotton. The United States exported over 70 percent of its cotton production until the 1870s. The share of Britain in US exports of cotton was also over 70 percent, and sometimes as high as 80 percent. It was only in the 1870s and afterwards that the domestic consumption of US cotton exceeded 30 percent, save for the brief period immediately following the Civil War. On the other hand, the United States also provided an important export market for British manufactures. According to Leone Levi,[21] out of the total British export of £38.27 million, £6.13 million went to the United States in 1830. That increased to £10.57 million in 1835 out of the total of £47.37 million, the proportion now becoming 22 percent. The close relation between the two countries, forged by trade, was no longer of the nature of the colony-metropolis connection, which had existed in the eighteenth century. It was now part of the network of world trade that industrial capital, as it grew with the cotton industry, brought into being. The Anglo-American relation was a relation between an industrial and an agricultural nation.* This relation, unlike the old colony-to-metropolis relation, did not handicap the development of capitalism in the United States. As Britain moved towards international free trade, the United States, too, was drawn to it as an agricultural exporter, its emphasis resting, of course, on the export of raw cotton to Britain. As will be studied later, there was agitation for tariff protection in the United States from early on; but this remained quite ineffectual until the Civil War, which

20   Based on Ellison 1886, p. 86, Table 3.
21   Levi 1880, p. 255.

suggests that international trade had not, up to that time, impeded the development of capitalism in that country.

* As shown in Table N-2, it was only after the Civil War that either the proportion of raw materials exports to total exports, or that of manufactured goods imports to total imports, fell under 50 percent.

TABLE N-2[22]   A = Crude materials as percent of
total exports of u.s. merchandise
B = Finished manufactures as percent of
total u.s. imports

	A	B		A	B
1821	60.62	56.86	1851–60	61.67	50.74
1830	62.65	56.97	1861–70	38.80	40.98
1840	67.83	45.09	1871–80	38.59	33.01
1850	62.36	54.93	1881–1890	35.96	30.74
			1891–1900	29.89	25.80

The unfolding of such trade relations in the world market resonated with business cycles in Britain, in which the cotton industry embodied industrial capital, the dominant form of capital during that stage of capitalist development.* Pivotal to this connection was the fact that funds accumulated through the development of British capitalism were lent as credit to merchant capital engaged in foreign trade. 'Practically speaking ... England gives long credits upon her exports, while imports are paid for in ready money'.[23] This combination of credit sales and cash purchases was typical in trade relations between an industrial and an agricultural country. Because of the availability of such credit, commodity production during the phase of prosperity expanded to its technical limit, which, in turn, made the disruptions at the time of crisis all the more painful. For, both industrial and agricultural products, which could not be sold, then became 'superabundant'. Foreign trade stimulated the development of capitalism, but it also intensified its instability.**

---

22   *Statistical Abstract of the United States*, 1848, p. 858.

23   *The Economist*, 11 January 1851, p. 30, as quoted from Marx's *Capital*, Vol. III, Chapter 35: 'Precious Metal and Rate of Exchange', section: 'England's Balance of Trade', p. 591.

*The British export trade, during its expansion process, manifested the characteristic fluctuation, especially as the cotton industry developed from the 1820s to the 1840s.

TABLE N-3   *The trend of British exports, in values of £ million*[24]

1821	36.7	1831	37.2	1841	51.6	1851	74.4	1861	125.1
1822	37.0	1832	36.5	1842	47.4	1852	78.0	1862	124.0
1823	35.5	1833	39.7	1843	52.3	1853	98.9	1863	146.6
1824	38.4	1834	41.6	1844	58.6	1854	97.2	1864	160.4
1825	38.9	1835	47.4	1845	60.1	1855	95.7	1865	165.8
1826	31.5	1836	53.4	1846	57.8	1856	115.8	1866	188.9
1827	37.2	1837	42.1	1847	58.8	1857	122.1	1867	181.0
1828	36.8	1838	50.1	1848	52.8	1858	116.6	1868	179.7
1829	35.8	1839	53.2	1849	63.6	1859	130.4	1869	190.0
1830	38.3	1840	51.4	1850	71.0	1860	135.9	1870	199.6

Exports peaked at £38.9 million in the crisis year of 1825, after which they fell and remained stationary during the period of depression. In 1833, they surpassed the previous peak, and, in 1836, they recorded a new peak, which was surpassed again in 1844. The effect on exports of a crisis and of the depression that followed was not so clear with regard to the crises of 1847, 1857 and 1866. However, in general, exports reached a peak in the year of the crisis and then declined until they once again expanded after the recovery of business in the next prosperity phase.

Cole has examined the relation between business cycles and overseas investment. Up to 1825, Britain lent to the Continent. From the end of the 1820s through the 1830s, Britain exported capital mainly to the United States. From the late 1830s through the 1840s, investment in railways was the prominent feature. In the 1850s and 1860s, overseas investment was active generally, according to Cole. Yet he also states that such foreign investment could not be said to have been mainly responsible for the tremendous expansion of overseas trade during this entire period from the 1820s to the 1860s.[25] The precise figure for Britain's foreign investment in this period is not available, though it was apparently not as overwhelming as during and after the decades of the 1870s and the 1880s. In any case, however, it cannot be denied that, to some extent, overseas trade and investment grew interactively.

---

24   Cole 1932, pp. 57, 76.
25   Cole 1932, pp. 62–4.

** The following explanation of the 1847 crisis by Engels makes it clear that the previous expansion of the export trade greatly contributed to the intensity of the crisis, even though the latter was also influenced by such special circumstances as the railway speculation of the 1840s and the crop failure of 1846. I venture to quote from it at some length:

> At the close of 1842 the pressure which English industry suffered almost uninter-
> ruptedly since 1837 began to lift. During the following two years foreign demand
> for English manufactured goods increased still more; 1845 and 1846 marked a
> period of great prosperity. In 1843 the Opium War had opened China to Eng-
> lish commerce. The new market gave a new impetus to the further expansion
> of an expanding industry, particularly the cotton industry. 'How can we ever
> produce too much? We have to clothe 300 million people', a Manchester manu-
> facturer said to this writer at the time. But all the newly erected factory buildings,
> steam-engines, and spinning and weaving machines did not suffice to absorb the
> surplus-value pouring in from Lancashire. With the same zeal as was shown in
> expanding production, people engaged in building railways. The thirst for spec-
> ulation of manufacturers and merchants at first found gratification in this field,
> and as early as in the summer of 1844. Stock was fully underwritten, i.e., so far as
> there was money to cover the initial payments. As for the rest, time would show!
> But when further payments were due – Question 1059, C.D.1848/57, indicates that
> the capital invested in railways in 1846–47 amounted to £75 million – recourse
> had to be taken to credit, and in most cases the basic enterprises of the firm had
> also to bleed.
>
> And in most cases these basic enterprises were already overburdened. The
> enticingly high profits had led to far more extensive operations than justified by
> the available liquid resources. Yet there was credit, easy to obtain and cheap. The
> bank discount rate stood low: 1¾ to 2¾ % in 1844, less than 3% until October
> 1845, rising to 5% for a while (February 1846), then dropping again to 3¼ % in
> December 1946. The Bank of England had an unheard-of supply of gold in its
> vaults. All inland quotations were higher than ever before. Why not go in for
> all one was worth? Why not send all one could manufacture to foreign markets
> which pined for English goods? And why should not the manufacturer himself
> pocket the double gain arising from selling yarn and fabrics in the far East, and
> return cargo in England?
>
> Thus arose the system of mass consignments to India and China against
> advance payments, and this soon developed into a system of consignments
> purely for the sake of getting advances, as described in greater detail in the fol-
> lowing notes, which led inevitably to overflooding the markets and a crash.
>
> The crash was precipitated by the crop failure of 1846. England, and particu-

larly Ireland, required enormous imports of foodstuffs, notably corn and pota-
toes. But the countries which supplied them could be paid with the products
of English industry only to a very limited extent. Precious metals had to be
given out. Gold worth at least nine million was sent abroad. Of this amount
no less than seven and a half million came from the treasury of the Bank of
England, whose freedom of action on the money market was thereby considerably impaired. Other banks, whose reserves were deposited with the Bank of
England and were practically identical with those of that Bank, were thus also
compelled to curtail accommodation of money. The rapid and easy flow of payments was obstructed, first here and there, then generally. The banking discount
rate, still 3 to 3½ % in January 1847, rose to 7% in April, when the first panic
broke out. The situation eased somewhat in the summer (6½ %, 6%), but when
the new crop failed as well panic broke out afresh and even more violently. The
official minimum bank discount rose in October to 7 and in November to 10%;
i.e., the overwhelming mass of bills of exchange was discountable only at outrageous rates of interest, or no longer discountable at all. The general cessation
of payments caused the failure of several leading and very many medium-sized
and small firms. The Bank itself was in danger due to the limitations imposed
by the artful Bank Act of 1844. The government yielded to the general clamour
and suspended the Bank Act on October 25, thereby eliminating the absurd legal
fetters imposed on the Bank. Now it could throw its supply of bank-notes into
circulation without hindrance. The credit of these bank-notes being in practice
guaranteed by the credit of the nation, and thus unimpaired, the money strin-
gency was thus instantly and decisively relieved. Naturally, quite a number of
hopelessly enmeshed large and small firms failed nevertheless, but the peak of
the crisis was overcome, the banking discount dropped to 5% in December, and
in the course of 1848 a new wave of business activity began which took the edge
off the revolutionary movements on the continent in 1849, and which inaugurated in the fifties an unprecedented industrial prosperity, but then ended again –
in the crash of 1857. F.E.[26]

It goes without saying that each economic crisis is different, as it reflects the special
circumstances of the time. Even in Great Britain between the 1820s and the 1860s,
when capitalism most closely approximated its ideal image, it is not possible to find
one industrial crisis undisturbed by such contingent factors as 'railways speculation
and crop failure', which occur by chance. In the present context of economic policies,
in which stage-theoretic determinations matter, however, the vital influence of inter-

---

26   Engels in Marx 1987, *Capital*, Vol. III, pp. 407–8.

national trade on economic crises must be distinguished from the contingencies or 'special circumstances of the time'. A 'crop failure', which depends on weather, is always a contingent factor, even though 'railway speculation' will assume more significance later. In all stages of capitalist development, international trade forms an integral part of the stage-theoretic argument, as I stress in the text. In passing, let me remark that the Peel Act, which restricted the notes issue of the Bank of England, was not itself a cause of the crisis. It was only an element that exacerbated the crisis unnecessarily, while benefiting the Bank. It is true that the suspension of the Act mitigated the severity of the crisis, but we must also take note of the fact that, by that time, the worst moment of the crisis had already been passed.

The period between the 1820s and the 1860s in Great Britain constituted the epoch in which industrial capital established itself, based upon the capitalistic development of the cotton industry. The latter became the dominant industry which entailed in its wake the similar capitalistic development of other industries, including iron and steel. Industrial capital, of course, does not in reality bring into being a purely capitalist society, such as the one that must be presupposed in theory. Yet its development in real time tended to realise such a society composed of the three basic classes of the capitalists, the wage-workers and the landlords. In the same process, moreover, the relation of international trade played a crucial role, which suggests that British capitalism would not have tended to realise a purely capitalist society if it had developed in isolation. Yet, it is an undeniable fact, first of all, that capitalism centring around the cotton industry, simplified productive labour as far as possible and, by eliminating the occupational restrictions which had divided medieval workers, generated a single class of wage-workers in service of the capitalist method of production. Secondly, capitalism managed to generate a relative surplus population, by way of improvements in its method of production, and thereby averted, to some extent at least, the constraint of the natural growth of the working population, thus giving capital some latitude in the purchase of labour-power which it could not produce. The adoption of machines as instruments of labour, needless to say, imposed the management of fixed capital, such that the expansion of output did not always presuppose a steady improvement in the method of production, nor did the latter become mandatory for as long as capital earned adequate profits. In other words, even though the accumulation of capital was never free from the restriction of labour-power as a special commodity, that restriction did not absolutely obstruct capital accumulation either. It was these circumstances that caused the repetition of business cycles, peculiar to the capitalist mode of production, and that also led to the centralisation of capital, even as free competition prevailed among capitals. Industrial capital, which established itself in the British cotton industry, thus completed the separation of industry from agriculture, and paved the way for the diffusion of its method of production to all other branches of industry. Particularly noteworthy, in this connection, were the circumstances in which the cotton industry sought the agricultural supplier of its raw material abroad rather than at home. By thus avoiding a confrontation with domestic agriculture, industrial capital tightened its grips successfully on manufacturing production.

Economic Policies of Liberalism

Great Britain was the nation-state which, through its application of mercant-ilist policies, had most typically represented the epoch of the birth of capit-alism. Subsequently, however, i.e. from the late eighteenth century onward, it underwent the Industrial Revolution, by virtue of which it was enabled to lay the foundation of capitalism as a world-historic economic regime. Once firmly established, capitalism in Britain no longer required the assistance of external forces, but only its own internal resources, for its survival and further devel-opment. Thus, the Elizabethan Statutes of Artificers,* the Navigation Acts,** and the Royal Charters for monopolies*** gradually lost their significance, and could be abolished with relative ease from the late eighteenth to the early nineteenth century. Somewhat different in nature were the Corn Laws and the attendant system of tariff duties.**** They did not necessarily become obsolete with the development of capitalism. That is why, instead of fading out, as a mat-ter of course, their repeal became the main thrust of the economic policies of liberalism. As stated previously, and as the term by itself connotes, 'liberal' eco-nomic policies were not destined to be implemented quite as aggressively as the 'mercantilist' policies had previously been. They rather defensively aimed at the removal of mercantilist policies, as the latter had outlived their useful-ness. Yet the abolition of existing policies meant, as always, the repudiation of the privileges which had long been enjoyed by protected sectional interests. As it turned out, this could be enforced with the least resistance as a spin-off of the Free Trade Movement, which was gaining increasing public support both domestically and internationally. As will be noted later, this movement was resisted only by infant-industry protectionism, the call for which arose, in due course, among late-developing capitalist countries; but their campaign for pro-tectionism never grew so powerful as to block the international spread of the Free Trade Movement, which emanated from Great Britain, the then centre of capitalism in the world.

* The development of the English wool industry under merchant capital in the seven-teenth and the eighteenth century no longer permitted the survival of the old system of apprenticeship in the guild, as already noted. The Statute of Artificers, which was already losing ground, was formally abolished in 1814.[1]

---

1 Cunningham 1903, Part II, pp. 658–60.

** The Navigation Acts, too, which were originally intended to block the Netherlands' rivalry with England in overseas trade, by privileging the latter's intercourse with its colonies, fell into desuetude with the subsequent evolution of British foreign trade as a whole. Since some colonies proved increasingly refractory to the main country's will, the acts began to be abandoned during the late eighteenth century. In 1796, the transport of American goods on US ships to British ports had to be conceded. The same privileges had to be granted to the Portuguese possessions in South America and elsewhere in 1808.[2]

*** The royal charters granted to companies specialised in overseas trade with distant areas of the world also lost much of their meaning during the eighteenth century. Only the East India Company and the Hudson's Bay Company retained their monopoly power well into the nineteenth century. Yet the exclusive privileges of the former were confined to the China trade, after the 1813 renewal of its charter; and the latter, too, maintained little of its erstwhile glory after the British appropriation of Canada in 1763.[3]

**** As will be noted later, the substance of the Corn Laws had changed by the nineteenth century and had become devices to protect landed interests in Britain. Yet the removal of customs duties on corn, timber, and the like, would significantly affect not only the economic interest but also the political position of both the British landowners and the colonial exporters. Thus, the intervention of both power and money made the repeal of the entrenched protective devices a particularly difficult process.

1   Free Trade Movement in Britain

By the end of the eighteenth century, Great Britain had already begun to occupy a far more important position in the international market than earlier. That was due, on the one hand, to its rapidly developing cotton industry, and, on the other, to the iron industry in which, in particular, technical progress permitted the use of coal for energy. On account of these industrial advantages, Britain no longer needed to reciprocate French antagonism in matters of commerce, a practice which had been religiously observed since the seventeenth century; and, with the Treaty of 1786,* Britain could begin to undo its prohibitive mercantilist policies, which had been aimed especially at France. This treaty, it is said, did not immediately gain general support in either of the two countries; yet it marked an opening in the international scene to the extent that it sub-

---

2   Levi 1880, p. 160.
3   Cunningham 1903, pp. 818–21.

sequently entailed the conclusion of similar treaties between France and Russia, between the United States and Prussia, between Russia and Austria, and so on.[4] After the 1780s, a new trend in British trade appeared. Though exports were at a low ebb in the beginning of the decade, due mainly to Britain's troubles with its American colonies, they soon recovered and registered conspicuous annual gains, and this development was also matched by a rise in imports. This new trend, however, was to be interrupted by the French Revolution and the following wars on and with the Continent.** Britain clearly was in no position, during the war, to review its customs policies, as it had to address, with greater urgency, matters of foreign policy and of war finance. In the meantime, moreover, radical advances were occurring in methods of production within the cotton industry. Thus, on the morrow of the peace of 1815, Britain found itself saddled with an outdated commercial policy based on a schedule of high tariff-rates and an increasingly protectionist Corn Law, on the one hand, and with a rapidly growing cotton industry, on the other. The need for imported raw materials had now to be counterbalanced by an increase in the export of manufactured products.

* Earlier, England signed the Methuen Treaty of 1703 with a view to securing favourable terms in trade with Portugal to the exclusion of France. By 1786, however, as Portuguese trade no longer appeared promising, and as Britain became more confident of its industrial prowess, it concluded the Eden Treaty so as to gain direct access to the vast French market. By this treaty, Britain extended the most favoured-nation treatment to French wines, lifted its bans on French farm products and on some specialised industrial products such as glasses, and, in return, gained access to the French market for its own products, both sides agreeing to stipulate the maximum levels to which either country could raise their tariffs on imported cotton goods, iron goods, and others.[5] In consequence, British exports to France, which had not exceeded £100,000 in 1783, and remained at £600,000 even in 1785 and 1786, grew to a remarkable £1,300,000 in 1789. On the other hand, the imports from France, which were only £87,000 in 1783, became £717,000 in 1792 as compared to the exports to France of £1,200,000, even though this was a revolutionary period.[6]
** The following table shows trends in British foreign trade after 1760. The figures are in terms of official prices, so that they, in effect, indicate roughly the trends in the volume of trade. It may be stated here in passing that, during the French Revolution (1789–

4   Levi 1880, p. 56.
5   Levi 1880, pp. 55–6.
6   Cole 1932, p. 41.

95), British trade with South America expanded significantly, so that Britain seemed to
suffer setbacks in its trade only during the period of the Napoleonic war (1806–15).

TABLE N-1   *The value of British imports and exports (£ millions)*[7]

	Imports	Exports		Imports	Exports[‡]	Re-exports
1760	10.7	15.8	1801	31.8	24.9	10.3
1765	11.8	15.8	1802	29.8	25.6	121.7
1770	13.4	16.0	1803	26.6	20.5	8.0
1775	14.8	16.3	1804	27.8	22.7	8.9
1780	11.7	13.7	1805	28.6	23.4	7.6
1785	16.3	16.1	1806	26.9	25.9	7.7
1790	19.1	20.1	1807	26.7	23.5	7.6
1795	22.7	27.1	1808	26.8	24.6	5.8
1800	30.6	43.2	1809	31.8	33.5	12.8
			1810	39.3	34.1	9.4
			1815	33.0	42.9	15.7

[‡] After 1801 'Exports' excludes re-exports

The resumption of foreign trade after the war put off, if temporarily, the need
for reviewing long-run perspectives on commercial policy, so that it was only
in 1819, as the postwar boom ended in a downturn, that the matter was taken
up in earnest. In 1820 a group of London merchants presented a petition to the
House of Commons, advocating the abolition of customs duties other than the
ones needed for revenue purposes. This petition was drafted by Thomas Tooke
(1774–1858), the author of *A History of Prices*, and it reaffirmed the doctrine of
free trade, espoused by the classical political economists since Adam Smith,
the gist of which could be summarised as follows.

1. Every nation should produce the commodities for which it is best adapted. It
   should sell them where they fetch the highest price, while obtaining foreign
   commodities it requires where they can be purchased at the lowest price.
   Yet, the system of customs duties hampers international trade, by obstructing the formation of rational prices, while working against the industries of
   all nations.

---

7   Cole 1932, pp. 44, 57.

2. It is wrongly believed that the import of foreign products narrows the outlet for domestic products. Yet, no country can keep importing endlessly, without exporting a corresponding amount. The import of foreign products merely curbs unfit production, while expanding fit production in any country.
3. The system of tariff duties benefits sectional interests, but harms the general interest of the nation. Moreover, once customs duties are imposed, their perpetuation tends to be insisted upon by sectional interests both at home and abroad, often ending in unnecessary international conflicts.
4. The distresses that Britain suffered at the beginning of the nineteenth century were greatly exacerbated by the existing system of tariff duties. Many such distresses could be allayed by a prompt removal of the tariffs. If, moreover, Britain took the initiative in moving in that direction, other countries would follow suit and international free trade would be realised for the benefit of all nations.

The petition, in short, maintained that the wisest economic policy consisted of pursuing free trade, and it became the accredited message of the movement.[8]

This document undoubtedly embodied the point of view of the capitalist, though, of course, there was no clear awareness of that fact at the time. For it unmistakably reflected the evolution of Great Britain to the international position of the exporter of manufactured products and the importer of industrial materials and foods. Since British society was beginning to be attuned to that position, the response to the call for free trade almost instantly reverberated throughout the country. The Free Trade movement gathered strength, as similar petitions were presented in Glasgow, Manchester, Liverpool and other cities.[9] Even Parliament, in which the landed interest had always been well entrenched and influential, was moved to set up a commission of inquiry in each of its two houses, so as to examine the possibilities of implementing measures that might lead to the improvement and expansion of British foreign trade. The reports of the commissions were said to have brought to light a great many instances of restriction that were hampering the nation's foreign trade, which they recommended be speedily removed. The tenor of the reports was unambiguously 'liberal'. Though not asking for immediate changes, the reports strongly demanded gradual improvements in trade practices, beginning with amendments to the Navigation Act, and continuing with changes in the regulations pertaining to colonial trades, and an improvement in the ware-

---

8   Tooke and Newmarch 1928, *History of Prices, 1792–1856*, Vol. VI, pp. 332–5.
9   Page 1919, p. 53.

housing of bonded articles for re-export, among others, and ending with the
revamping of other old-fashioned regulations on timber, raw silk, wine and the
like.[10]

Thus, in the first instance, efforts intended to bring about the amendment
of the Navigation Act began in 1822,[11] as the postwar business slowdown finally
took a turn towards a full-scale recovery, and as there appeared signs of vigorous
recovery in trade with America. However, the Navigation Acts, which had long
been in place for the promotion and development of transoceanic shipping and
British colonial trade, could not be gotten rid of so easily. They had to undergo
gradual adjustments, as already remarked, over a due span of time, so as to
peacefully reconcile conflicting interests. First, the Spanish-speaking countries
(including Spain's former territories) were allowed to carry their products for
export to Britain on their own ships, as similar rights had already been granted
to the United States and the Portuguese possessions earlier. The exclusive
privilege which British vessels had enjoyed under the Acts was thus gradually
eliminated, as its scope was reduced in stages. Similarly, the former stipulation
of the Acts that European goods for export to Britain had to be carried by
British ships or ships of their producing country was gradually abandoned. For
its original intent had been merely to block the intervention of the Dutch, at
the time when they were formidable rivals of the British on the seas. Even in
relation to trade between British colonies and European countries, the Acts
now conceded to the direct export of colonial products to Continental Europe
by ships of the producing colonies. As far as the import of European goods
to British colonies was concerned, even the last stipulation that they should
be carried exclusively by British vessels was renounced in the end. As for the
indirect import of Asian, African and American products to Britain, the ban was
lifted, so long as they arrived at Britain aboard British ships. In short, Britain
no longer needed the Navigation Acts either to curb Dutch competition in
international shipping or to secure a monopoly over its colonial trade. Thus,
in the following year, 1823, Britain also voluntarily revised its system of bonded
warehousing, so that a wide range of commodities could be re-exported from
Britain without having to pay to it import customs in the first instance.* Thus,
Great Britain took a new policy stance for promoting foreign trade based
upon the principle of reciprocity, by renewing, with many of its trade partners,
the commercial treaties that had been left ineffectual during the Napoleonic
War.**

---

10   Levi 1880, pp. 156–8; Page 1919, pp. 55–6.
11   Levi 1880, pp. 159–66; Page 1919, pp. 58–61.

* Britain's bonded warehouse system is said to have begun in 1714, with the stipulation that tobacco, rum, rice and imported sugar could be held in special warehouses in British ports for a limited period of time, without the imposition of import duties. Up to 1820, the number of ports where such facilities were offered and the kind of goods to which such exemption was extended were both stringently limited. The 1823 revision greatly expanded the scope of application of this system.

** Britain concluded new commercial treaties with Denmark, the Hanseatic Cities, Prussia and Sweden in 1824, with France in 1826, with the United States and Brazil in 1827, and with Austria in 1829.

On the other hand, tariff reforms involved more complications. For not only had the existing tariffs already generated a tight web of vested interests, but tariff revenues were also still quite important from the fiscal point of view. During the 1823–4 period, customs duties on several commodities were lightened. The import tax on wool was reduced, while the ban on its export was lifted. The duties on raw silk and silk twist were also lessened. At the same time, the subsidies on whaling and other forms of fishing were not renewed, when their validity expired. The export subsidy on linen, too, was revoked. In 1825 and 1826, a more general reform on tariffs was carried out, and the import ban on silk cloth was replaced by an import duty of 30 percent. For cotton goods, the import tax of 50 percent stipulated in 1819 was reduced to 10 percent. The next largest reduction of import tax was granted on woollen manufactures. Other items such as various dyestuffs for textiles, medicinal products, flax, hemp, leather, iron and other metals were similarly liberalised with considerable tariff reductions.* All these measures were put in place by William Huskisson, the serving Minister of Commerce, whose policies were based on the following principles: (1) Import duties on materials should be reduced, so as not to impede the development of British industries; (2) The export of manufactures must be left as free as possible from domestic and foreign intervention; (3) Import duties on foreign products, even on those with which British industry cannot compete, must not exceed 30 percent; for, beyond that limit, they merely encourage contraband imports in any case.** The above-mentioned silk duties reflected this thought, implying that prohibitive restrictions on trade, which had for long been in practice, merely stunted sound industrial development. It was at this point in time that the tariff schedule which Pitt had compiled, and which had become highly complex with a series of modifications imposed during the Napoleonic War, was simplified and consolidated into just eleven acts of Parliament.***

* Levi produced the following table for comparison.

TABLE N-2 *Comparison of the tariff schedules of 1787, 1819 and 1825*[12]

Manufactures	Mr. Pitt's tariff of 1787			Rates of duties, 1819			Mr. Huskisson's tariff of 1825		
	£.	s.	d.	£.	s.	d.	£.	s.	d.
Cotton manufactures,	44	0	0	50	0	0	10	0	0
Woollen	prohibited			50	0	0	15	0	0
Linen	44	0	0	50	0	0	25 to 30 percent		
Silk	prohibited			prohibited			25	0	0
Leather	prohibited			75	0	0	30	0	0
Earthenware	45	0	0	75	0	0	15	0	0
Iron, manufactured bar, per ton	2	16	2	6	10	0	1	10	0
Olive oil, per tun (252 gallons)	8	8	10¾	18	15	7	4	4	0
Sugar	2	5	6	4	6	8	3	3	0

In this Table, the duties on iron and olive are specific and are shown in so many pounds per ton or per tun (of 252 gallons), respectively, while the duties on all other items are ad valorem, and are shown in percentages.[13]

** Huskisson was aware that reduced or lightened tariffs would increase the quantity of imported foreign commodities, but he claimed that it was not a significant cause for worry since, as can be judged from the effects of the Treaty of 1786, the import of superior foreign products served to remove the defects of British industry. Moreover, according to him, even when Britain lowered its tariffs unilaterally, without stating so in treaties, British industries were already strong enough to withstand the effects, and the state budget no longer depended much on revenue tariffs.[14]

*** Given the fact that a complicated system of tariffs often impeded the development of free trade, the simplification of the schedule under Huskisson at that time could no doubt be demonstrated to have had a highly significant effect on the subsequent development of international trade.

The tariff reform of 1823–4 can, no doubt, be said to have been an offshoot of the Free Trade Movement. Yet many commodities still remained subject to import duties. Moreover, the crux of the old system did not reside in the

---

12   Levi 1880, p. 168.

13   Ibid.

14   The Speeches of the Right Honourable William Huskisson 1881, Vol. II, pp. 327–54.

taxation of manufactured goods or of industrial materials. As already suggested, Britain instituted a new Corn Law after the war with the Continent, intending to maintain the high levels of rent in correspondence with the high prices of grains, which had prevailed during the hostilities. Contrary to the Corn Laws of the seventeenth and eighteenth centuries, however, the new law did not benefit grain producers at large, but only a small number of large landowners. From the point of view of the newly emerging capitalist interest, such a law backed only by the reactionary interest, would have to be repealed in due course. Indeed, that law was put forward by very powerful political forces, which represented the survival into the nineteenth century of the old patronage system. As previously stated, British farmland had undergone a radical change during the eighteenth century. At its beginning, enclosures occurred mainly to enlarge the scale of farmland for cultivation.* Yet that did not suffice to ensure self-sufficiency in grain production in the British Isles, and so, in the latter half of the eighteenth century, Britain became an importer of foreign grains.** Even though the first reaction to this turn of events in 1773 was to adopt the policy of relaxing restrictions on grains imports, the authorities later renewed these restrictions, ignoring the fact that the country now had to import increasing quantities of grains. Their prices thus rose intermittently throughout the period of the French Revolution and the Napoleonic War, due not only to the reduced scale of foreign trade and the inflation of prices in general, but also to frequent crop failures. Underlying the enactment of the new Corn Law was the hardly concealed self-interest of the landed class, which benefited abundantly by stemming the import of cheap foreign grains.***

* The following figures[15] will enable us to surmise the extent and nature of the enclosures that occurred in the eighteenth century:

Under the reign of	No. of acts	Total no. of acres	Average of acres per act
Anne (1702–14)	2	1,438	719
George I (1714–24)	16	17,660	1,103
George II (1724–50)	226	318,778	1,410
George III (1760–1820)	3,554	5,348,524	1,504

15   Taken from Tooke and Newmarch 1928, Vol. VI, p. 448.

It is estimated at the end of 1854 that 9 million acres of land in England and Wales had been enclosed after 1709, which came to one third of the total of cultivated land in England and Wales.[16] Whether or not these enclosures reflected, as did the Corn Laws, the official policy for extended cultivation of grains is not certain. Nevertheless, they undoubtedly caused the dissolution of the commons and the concentration of landed property, and thereby exerted a powerful influence on the decomposition of traditional rural life in Britain. These enclosures destroyed the yeomanry and other traditional segments of the agricultural population in Britain, and replaced them with tenant farmers and agricultural workers who introduced a new way of managing the farm. With it the landlords became large and few, and many tended to become absentee lords.[17]

** Contrary to the first half of the eighteenth century, the prices of grains tended to rise after the 1760s, and their importation increased. The price of wheat per quarter and the volume of its importation (including flour and similar products) moved as shown in the following tables.

TABLE N-3   *Average prices of*
             wheat, 1661–1770[18]

1661–70	44s.	9(1/10) d.
1671–80	46s.	5d.
1681–90	35s.	9(8/10)d.
1691–1700	52s.	(3/5)d.
1701–10	39s.	6(7/10)d.
1711–20	41s.	1(1/2)d.
1721–30	38s.	4(9/10)d.
1731–40	34s.	9/10d.
1741–50	30s.	11(1/5)d.
1751–60	38s.	10(1/2)d.
1761–70	43s.	9(9/10)d.

For the period 1691–1700, the average price was rather high due to the exceptional weather conditions mentioned by the author on p. 261. The volumes of wheat exports and imports were roughly as follows, in 1,000 quarters:

16   Tooke and Newmarch 1928, Vol. VI, p. 449.
17   Hasbach 1966, pp. 112–14.
18   Calculated from Ernle 1922, Appendix III.

TABLE N-3'[19]

	1697–1731	1732–66	1767–1801
Exports	3,592	11,540	3,064
Imports	124	292	10,541

*** That tendency can be observed from the following table, which indicates the movement of the average wheat price per quarter from the 1770s to the nineteenth century.

TABLE N-4 *Average prices of wheat, 1775–1824*[20]

1775–84	43s.
1785–94	47s.
1795–1804	75s.
1805–14	93s.
1815–24	68s.

Marx, too, stressed the fact that rent and profits increased at the expense of wages during this period: 'Various circumstances such as the depreciation of money and the manipulation of the Poor Laws in the agricultural districts, had made this operation possible at a time when the incomes of the tenants were enormously increasing and the landlords were amassing fabulous riches. Indeed, one of the main arguments of both tenants and landlords for the introduction of duties on corn was that it was physically impossible to depress farm-labourers' wages any lower'.[21]

Thus, the Corn Law of 1815 first set the price of wheat at 80 shillings per quarter, taking as a norm the high price of grains under wartime inflation, and prohibited the import of wheat at a lower price. Then the export subsidy on grains, which had long remained in place even after it had long outlived its usefulness, was abolished. The average price of wheat, which was still over 100 shillings per quarter in 1812 and 1813, dropped to 74s.7d. in 1814 and further down to 65s.7d.

---

19   Ernle 1922, p. 500.
20   Ernle 1922, p. 264.
21   Marx 1987, *Capital*, Vol. III, p. 627.

in 1815. Observing the continuous price fall which began in the autumn of 1813, the agricultural interests demanded a revision of the policy on grains, indicating to the parliamentary committee in charge a level of prices which would be necessary for maintaining the extended acreage under cultivation, and which had been agreed upon during the war in order to ensure Great Britain's self-sufficiency in grains. The law of 1815, in effect, upheld their demand, when it passed in the Parliament by a clear majority, despite the presence of vociferous opposition. The price of wheat rose in 1816 since its import still remained negligible, but went up to the neighbourhood of 100 shillings per quarter in 1817. The large import of grains which it then entailed, however, depressed the price after 1819; and the price then gradually fell to below 50 shillings per quarter by 1822. All of this was indicative of the fact that the Corn Law of 1815 had proven itself to be wholly ineffective, within ten years of its enactment, in achieving its intended result.*

* The following table shows the evolution of the average price and imported volume of wheat between 1810 and 1822.

TABLE N-5   *Average prices and volumes imported of wheat, 1810–22*[22]
A = Average price of wheat per quarter (s. d.)
B = Volume of wheat imported (1,000 qrs.)

	A	B		A	B
1810	106s. 5d.	1,439	1817	96s. 11d	1,064
1811	95s. 3d.	188	1818	86s. 3d.	1,593
1812	126s. 6d.	131	1819	74s. 6d.	472
1813	109s. 9d.	340	1820	67s. 10d.	585
1814	74s. 4d.	623	1821	56s. 1d.	129
1815	65s. 7d.	191	1822	44s. 7d.	43
1816	78s. 6d.	209			

In other words, the law, even with small amendments in 1822, 1825 and 1826, for its less imperative application, did not, in any case, serve to maintain grain prices stable at a desired level. Thus, in 1828, a sliding scale method such as the following was introduced into the new tariff schedule: If the price of wheat

22   McCulloch 1859, p. 438.

per quarter went above: 66s., 67s., 68s., 69s., 70s., 71s., 72s., 73s., then the duty, respectively, of 20s.8d., 18s.8d., 16s.8d., 13s.8d., 10s.8d., 6s.8d., 2s.8d., 1s.0d., would be imposed. However, if the price of wheat per quarter fell below 66s.0d., the tariff duty of 1 more shilling would be charged per each shortfall by 1 shilling of the wheat price on top of 20s.8d. [Thus, for instance, if the wheat price fell to 64s. per quarter, then the total duty of 2s. + 20s.8d. = 22s.8d. would be imposed upon it]. This revision was more attuned to the purpose of the law than the original version of 1815; but, as a general rule, it was observed that the import of wheat increased rather suddenly only when its price rose significantly, so that the burden of the additional duty became less onerous. This meant, considering the still limited ability to transport grains from distant places at the time, that the effect of the sliding scale was felt, for the most part, by the neighbouring countries where the condition of the crop was not all that different from that in Britain. [In other words, by the time Britain imported German wheat, its price was already close to the British price anyway, even though that of American wheat which Britain could not import easily may have remained significantly lower]. Such circumstances were clearly not helpful in stabilising the price of grain in Britain. Instead, it varied rather violently between 36 shillings and 73 shillings per quarter. Indeed, the average price of wheat, which went up to 66s.4d. in 1831, fell to 39s.4d. in 1835, then rose to 64s.7d. in 1838 and further to above 70s. in 1839.*

* The following table shows the variation in the average wheat price after 1823, side by side with its imported volume.[23]

TABLE N-6   *Average prices and volumes imported of wheat, 1823–47*[24]
           A = Average price of wheat per quarter (s.d.)
           B = Volumes of wheat imported (1,000 qrs.)

	A	B		A	B		A	B
1823	53s. 4d.	15	1832	58s. 8d.	447	1841	64s. 4d.	2,770
1824	63s. 22d.	82	1833	52s. 11d.	297	1842	57s. 3d.	3,040
1825	68s. 6d.	384	1834	46s. 2d.	176	1843	50s. 1d.	1,064
1826	58s. 8d.	576	1835	39s. 4d.	66	1844	51s. 3d.	1,379

23   On the price movement during this period, see Tooke and Newmarch 1928, Vol. III, Chapter 1. Marshall, too, in his 1923 *Industry and Trade*, Appendix E, makes comments on this development in some detail.

24   McCulloch 1859, p. 438.

(cont.)

	A	B		A	B		A	B
1827	8s. 6d.	304	1836	48s. 6d.	241	1845	50s. 10d.	1,141
1828	60s. 5d.	741	1837	55s. 10d.	559	1846	54s. 8d.	2,344
1829	66s. 3d.	1,663	1838	64s. 7d.	1,371	1847	69s. 9d.	4,64
1830	64s. 3d.	1,661	1839	70s. 8d.	2,875			
1831	66s. 4d.	2,303	1840	66s. 4d.	2,432			

Thus, the 1828 revision of the law only made grain prices even more speculative. Moreover, it was customary that the cultivators had to sell before the price rose, and the consumers to buy after it did. Therefore, it gradually became apparent that the law worked to the disadvantage not only of workers in general, but also of cultivators, especially of small peasants. Soon the antipathy against the law spread even amongst the leaseholders in rural districts. In August 1838, while the retail price of wheat rose to 73s.8d., the first Anti-Corn Law Association was formed in Manchester, to which Richard Cobden (1804–65) lent his support. As branches of the Association were created one after another in many other cities, it became a national movement, reorganised under the name of the Anti-Corn Law League, and it seemed poised to win the eventual repeal of the act. Cobden led the movement with persistence, sometimes (as in 1842) even allying himself with the Chartists, whose aim often diverged from his own, and sometimes (as in 1843) appealing directly to the tenant farmers in the agricultural districts, who had long been seduced into believing in the virtue of the law. The movement thus increasingly appeared to represent the battle that the newly emerging capitalist class waged against the reactionary landed class which clung to the old privileges.*

* Commenting on the circumstances of the time, Marx wrote as follows: 'The time just before the repeal of the Corn Laws threw new light on the condition of the agricultural labourers. On the one hand, it was to the interest of the middle-class agitators to prove how little the Corn Law protected the actual producers of the corn. On the other hand, the industrial bourgeoisie foamed with sullen rage at the denunciations of the factory system by the landed aristocracy, at the pretended sympathy with the woes of the factory operatives, of those utterly corrupt, heartless, and genteel loafers, and at their "diplomatic zeal" for factory legislation. It is an old English proverb that "when thieves fall out, honest men come by their own", and, in fact, the noisy, passionate

quarrel between the two factions of the ruling class about the question, which of the two exploited the labourers the more shamefully, was on each hand the midwife of the truth'.[25]

The implementation of the Factory Acts and the more or less simultaneous repeal of the Corn Laws brought to fruition the ascendancy of the capitalist method of production. This, of course, does not mean the coming-into-being in real time of the purely capitalist society, which the theory of capitalism must presuppose. It merely signified the decisive entry of real capitalism into a mode which would inspire such a theoretical idealisation of capitalist society.

It is sometimes said that Britain underwent a revolution in agriculture after the 1830s, as innovation occurred in all its aspects. However, for small capitalist tenant farmers, it was not a mere innovation. The repeal of the Corn Laws expedited the development of capitalist agriculture.[26]

The anti-Corn Law Movement constituted the background of the tariff reform of the early 1840s. The Parliament set up a committee for the investigation of the existing system, and found that even then the principle of compulsory tariff remained in force, which required the imposition of various specified tariff rates on as many as 1,150 items, with the reservation that still more items were potentially subject to some unspecified tariff protection. This was the case, even though such measures were not justified for revenue purposes, since, in 1839 for instance, 94 percent of customs revenues were derived from the tariffs imposed on only 17 commodities. The report of this committee, coinciding with the flare-up of Chartism and the strain of the economic slump, greatly contributed to bringing the issue of the Anti-Corn Law Movement onto the agenda for parliamentary debates. So the government of Sir Robert Peel (1788–1850) contrived to circumvent a potential political crisis by way of a fairly radical tariff reform, so as to be able to deal rather perfunctorily with the issue of the Corn Law with a mere token of its revision. In other words, he conceded to the principle of free trade with his tariff reform, which entailed the adoption of the policy of imposing only nominal duties on industrial materials, reducing duties on semi-finished goods, and exposing finished manufactures to free foreign competition. The result was that he reduced tariffs on 750 of the 1,200 items listed on the existing tariff schedule, with the understanding that the maximum tariff on materials, semi-finished goods and fully manufactured products should not exceed, respectively, 5 percent, 12 percent, and 20 percent. As for

---

25   Marx 1987, *Capital*, Vol. III, p. 632.
26   Hasbach 1966, 242–4.

the loss of fiscal revenues owing to the adoption of these measures, it was to be covered by an income tax and other domestic impositions.[27]

However, by 1843, the economic conditions that had long been depressed began to pick up, and, in 1844, vigorous activities returned to both the domestic and international market. Under the circumstances, the impetus to engage in parliamentary debates on the anti-Corn Law issue was beginning to wane, which enabled Peel to circumvent it by merely continuing his tariff reform of 1842 into 1843. However, in 1845, this option was no longer available to him, as crop failures coincided with a spread of the potato disease. The price of wheat, which was 45 shillings per quarter in March, shot up to above 60 shillings in November. Peel at first tried to temporarily suspend the Corn Law to meet the crisis, but disagreements in the cabinet led to his resignation. When he returned to office, however, he announced the uniform tariff of one shilling per quarter of imported grains to be put in force as of 1849, and aimed to make do, up until then, with a revised sliding scale at reduced rates. He was accused of reneging on his word by his friends in Parliament, but his bill passed.[28] Thus, industrial capital won its victory after years of struggle. The Corn Laws that merchant capital once adopted as part of its mercantilist policy, in the spirit of concession to the old landed aristocracy, had by then turned into the last bastion of those who had outlived their usefulness, and were destined to be stamped out of existence. With the abolition of the Corn Laws, the tariff policy of Britain too lost its stronghold.

Peel continued his style of tariff reform in 1845, and abolished existing duties on 423 commodities, which were either industrial or supplementary materials such as raw silk, flax, hemp, furniture wood, various oils, metal ores and dyestuffs, and which were insignificant as revenue tariffs. The tariff on raw cotton too was abolished. Export duties on a few commodities (woollen fabrics, silk and linen, iron-wares) had been removed since 1842, but those on remaining items were abolished at this time. In undertaking this reform, Peel believed that an expansion of foreign trade would bring not only increased fiscal revenues but also more employment of labour. With the same hopes in mind he extended its scope in 1846, and reduced tariffs on lumber and animal fat, which were the only remaining materials still dutiable. He also reduced the 20 percent tariffs on hemp, woollen and cotton products to 10 percent, and the 20 percent tariff on silk products to 15 percent. Thus, the average tariff rate of 20 percent on foreign manufactures was lowered to 10 percent. Many tariffs on farm products and livestock were also alleviated on the ground that they worked against domestic agriculture. As for the tariff on sugar, the discriminatory differential between foreign and colonial products was lessened. Thus, overall, the tariffs were considerably lightened in their rates and in the number of applicable items. The trend towards liberalisation thus became unmistakable.

As mentioned above, the Navigation Acts were relatively easily adapted to new developments in British foreign trade, and their partial amendments did not meet strong resistance; but they could not be wholly abandoned because of the well-entrenched privileges remaining, especially in connection with trade with the colonies. Thus, the preferential treatment of such colonial products as timber, sugar, and so on, still remained in force, so that a carcass of the Navigation Acts remained long after they had ceased to be of any significance, either to the mother country or to the colonies. Only in 1848 did the government finally propose its abolition in Parliament, and the proposal was passed despite still considerable opposition in 1849.*

* This bill actually passed the Parliament subject to the condition that the British ships (whether built in Britain or not) would retain their privileged access to fishing and transportation of cargo along the British coast.[29]

Thus, with the final repeal of the Corn Laws and the abolition of the Navigation Acts which closely followed it, together with the tariff reforms that it undertook at frequent intervals, Great Britain managed in the end to realise the regime of free trade. This, however, did not entail the economic ruin of either the old landed aristocracy, or the mercantile lords of transoceanic shipping and of colonial exploitation, nor did they diminish in their political influence. They merely had to adapt to the new relationships of capitalist society. Furthermore, the untrammelled development of these capitalist-social relationships was not realised only within the boundary of the British nation. As already repeated, this development occurred in an international context, in which Britain was to occupy the position of the 'Workshop of the World', which would maintain the appropriate commercial relationships with less developed 'agricultural nations'. The success of the Free Trade Movement in Britain implied the wish that other countries would follow suit. For only in that way could the international regime of free trade be brought to fruition.

---

29   See Page 1919, p. 173.

2   Internationalisation of the Free Trade Movement as a Sequel to Its
      Success in Britain

Even after the 1850s, Great Britain continued its tariff reforms; but they were
motivated more readily by the need to secure fiscal revenues rather than to
affirm a new policy stance. The liberalisation of trade having been already
accepted as the norm, the reform was implemented as, and to the extent
that, fiscal conditions permitted it. That was the case with the tariff reforms
of 1853 and of 1860, adopted by W.E. Gladstone (1809–98), which were then
viewed as completing the process of liberalisation of foreign trade in Britain.
Yet the reform of 1853 only partially achieved its intended aim, which was to
abolish the import duties altogether on semi-finished goods (such as industrial
materials), and to lighten them on manufactured goods to below 10 percent.
The duties on lumber remained untouched, and those on silk goods continued
to be applied at 15 percent. Though the tariffs on cotton, hemp, wool, and so on,
were reduced from 10 to 5 percent, and preferential treatment of the colonies
was abandoned, the tariffs on handicrafts were generally retained. Overall, 146
items were exempted from duties and those on 242 items were reduced by this
reform; but the fiscal loss which resulted was no more than £50,000, which had
been collected on 123 of the first cited 146 items and 133 of the second cited 242
items. This reform also aimed at switching duties from ad valorem to specific,
and at simplifying import procedures. These measures were adopted expressly
to promote free trade.* Yet the tariff reform of 1853 fell short of being thorough
and systematic, and the remedy for such defects had to await the reform of 1860
which came after the Crimean War. This reform of 1860 finally reduced *all* tariffs
on manufactured (finished) goods to below 10 percent, and abolished them
entirely on luxury items, food items, and items of daily convenience such as
candles, soap, glass, and so on, as well as on industrial materials such as animal
fat. The result was that only 48 items remained on the tariff schedule of the
country. Of these 48 items, 15 were retained mainly as revenue tariffs; and of
the 29 remaining, 5 paid duties merely to complement domestic consumption
taxes, and 24 did so because they closely resembled the above-mentioned 15.**
Britain thus emerged as a genuine free-trading nation with virtually no vestige
left of the former protective or preferential tariffs.

* The collection of specific tariffs is procedurally simpler, but, in this case, higher priced
items of superior quality tended to be lightly taxed. Moreover, when the price fell due
to an improved method of production, the existing tariff could become needlessly
oppressive. Ad valorem tariffs avoid these defects. Yet, their collection requires prior
evaluation of the fair price upon which the duty is imposed. Thus, the two types of

tariff had their merits and demerits. Yet, in the policy process of trade liberalisation, it was always the reduction or abolition of specific tariffs that played the leading part.
** Gladstone, who occupied the post of the Chancellor of the Exchequer in three successive cabinets between 1852 and 1866, refers to these points in some details in his parliamentary speeches.[30] The 15 items in question included spirits, sugar tea, tobacco and wine in the first category which yielded the revenue of £1–6 million; coffee, corn, currants and timber in the second category, which yielded the revenue of £0.2–1 million; as well as chicory, figs and fig-cake, hops, pepper, raisins and rice which constituted the third category, yielding the revenue of £0.02–0.2 million. These 15 items were retained on the list for revenue purposes. Of these, however, only timber stood somewhat apart from the others in that it may have benefited from its former preferential treatment.

The achievement of the free trade regime in Britain also paralleled the culmination of liberalism as the ideological exaltation of freedom. It was, of course, not the exaltation of freedom as such in the abstract, but of freedom congenial to capitalism. Neither was capitalism, which industrial capital achieved at that time in history, in its pure form such as the one that theory must presuppose in the abstract. Yet liberalism, as the ideological apotheosis of freedom, can be said to have acquired its material grounding in that industrial capital then gained a dynamic of its own which tended to realise a society entirely governed by the logic of capital.* Thus, as expected, capitalism in Britain after the 1850s was to exhibit, for some time, the most stable phase of its historical development *in concreto*.

* The stipulation of the Factory Acts for the protection of women and children is frequently regarded as foreshadowing *sozialpolitik* (social welfare policies). However, the meaning of the latter will be obscured if it is understood in so wide a sense. For *sozialpolitik*, properly speaking, was advanced as systematic measures of welfare assistance to the victims of industrial crises and unemployment, who would necessarily emerge in a capitalist society. In opposition to socialism, *sozialpolitik* sought to rescue affected parties within the capitalist framework, even though it recognised the fact that capitalism, based on the logic of the conversion of labour-power into a commodity, automatically tended to abuse the labour of women and children. The Factory Acts, in contrast, regarded such abuse and its excesses, which would detract from the sound operation of capitalist industry, as being controllable by simply prohibiting them by law. They expected that the free play of capital's logic [within a state under the

---

30   *Gladstone's Financial Statements* 1863, p. 179.

rule of law] would by itself suffice to deal with the labour problem, without requiring any direct intervention of the state by way of a systematic labour policy. In this
sense, the spirit of the Factory Acts embodied a liberal ideology which *sozialpolitik* did
not.

During the 1850s, even though the Crimean War and a series of other external
events in Asia (in India and China especially) engaged more public attention,
the development of capitalism in Great Britain took a new turn. The economic
and political difficulties of the previous decade receded, and foreign trade, both
on the export and the import side, made remarkable progress. To some extent,
this was due to such contingent factors as the discovery of new gold mines
overseas and improvement in the means of transportation, which enabled
Britain to forge closer ties with Australia and Asia. Yet, more fundamentally,
it reflected the coming of age of the capitalist method of production inside the
country, together with the development of the capitalist commodity-economy
in Continental Europe and North America, which it induced. The nations in
these two areas were still largely 'agricultural' in contrast to 'industrial' Britain,
even though they were not to remain so forever. They, too, were motivated
to begin their industrialisation. It is this fact that provided the basis for the
internationalisation of the Free Trade Movement.

Towards the end of the 1850s, Britain concluded new commercial treaties
with China, Japan and Siam, thus significantly expanding its network of modern trade relations into the so-far little tapped Oriental market. Meanwhile,
Richard Cobden, who travelled to France in 1859, succeeded in persuading the
French authorities to conclude the Anglo-French Commercial Pact of 1860,
thus initiating the Free Trade Movement on the Continent. In this pact, the
French agreed to generally revoke all prohibitions related to merchandise trade
with Britain, and to permit the import of many British goods, including cotton and wool products, at a tariff-rate not exceeding 30 percent. Britain, in
return, agreed to grant the duty-free importation of a number of French goods,
including silk, and reduced the tariff on French wine. On coal, in particular,
the two countries agreed not to resort to an export ban on it. The conclusion
of this trade pact prodded France, which had long been a strongly protective
nation, to depart dramatically from its past practice; and that meant, for Britain, the opportunity to quickly universalise the principle of free trade, which
it espoused. The new departure resided in the adoption of 'the most-favoured-
nation clause' in this pact. This clause required that any trade concession that
one of the two signatories had already granted to a third country would automatically be granted to the other party.* As France then adopted this clause
in concluding commercial treaties with a number of other European coun-

tries, Britain could benefit from the best deal that France had offered to any of them. It was thus that the trend towards freer trade promptly spread through Europe.**

* The most-favoured-nation clause is either 'unconditional' or 'conditional'. The network of commercial treaties that emerged in Europe subsequent to the Anglo-French Pact invariably contained the unconditional version (or the European clause), as opposed to the conditional version (or the American clause), such that any benefit (by way of tariff reduction) that either France or Britain granted to a third country, whether gratis or in return for some specific concession, would automatically be shared by Britain and France. The unconditionality was perfectly adapted to the needs of Britain as the champion of free trade. Yet, for many countries of Continental Europe, which had thus far heavily depended on tariffs, it was a major effort to accept it. Thus, Cobden's success in persuading the French to adopt the unconditional version of the clause in the original pact contributed enormously to the early realisation of the age of free trade in the world.[31]

** In 1861, France negotiated a new commercial treaty with Belgium, and, in return for its concessions, especially on wine, silk and leather products, granted the same favourable treatment for Belgian products as for the British ones by way of treaty tariffs that were applicable under the existing pact. They also agreed to further reductions of tariffs on flax and leather products, which, through the most-favoured-nation clause, ended by benefiting Britain as well. In 1862, France concluded a similar treaty with the German Customs Union, with a reduction of tariffs on wine, cloth and a few other products. In much the same way, France renewed its commercial relations with Italy in 1863, with Switzerland in 1864, with Sweden, Norway, the Hanseatic Cities, Spain and the Netherlands in 1865, with Austria in 1866 and with Portugal in 1867.[32]

After the conclusion of the epoch-making pact of 1860 with France, Great Britain entered into commercial negotiations with Belgium so as to benefit from, among other things, the latter's concessions to France on equal terms, and won, by 1862, the equivalent of a 50 percent reduction of the Belgian tariffs on British exports overall. Most of this was due to the effect of the most-favoured-nation treatment which the two countries guaranteed to each other. In much the same way, the 1863 treaty with Italy brought to British trade and shipping far greater benefits than could have been obtained from their reciprocal tariff concessions alone, by virtue of the principle of the most-favoured-nation clause

---

31   Gregory 1921, pp. 450–61.
32   P. Ashley 1920, pp. 299–300.

to which the two nations committed themselves.[33] In 1865 as well, Britain won from the German Customs Union concessions equal to that which it had previously granted to France, which included the abolition and reduction of many of the union's export duties on goods destined for Britain, including pulp, as well as the abolition of duties on the union's import of British industrial materials and wool products along with the reduction of the union's import duties on all British manufactured goods. The adoption of these measures meant that the North and the East of Germany secured the British market for their grains, while, in cotton weaving, Germany still depended on imports of British yarn.* In any case, what Britain gave in return for all these huge benefits amounted to the mere repeal of the ban, and the guarantee not to tax, on its exports of coal to the German Customs Union. In this treaty, as in that with Belgium, Britain guaranteed to this negotiating partner more or less the same benefits whether they arose from its colonies or from the mother country. Towards the end of 1865, Great Britain also negotiated a trade treaty with Austria. As with France originally, Britain started with a reciprocal tariff pact (without the most-favoured-nations clause) with Austria, and agreed that the latter's ad valorem tariffs on the import of British goods would not exceed 25 percent (later reduced to 20 percent). Moreover, when Austria concluded a treaty with the German Customs Union in 1868 and revised it in 1869, Britain became a beneficiary of the most-favoured-nation treatment, and obtained the same concessions from Austria that it granted to the German Customs Union. It was in this way that Britain succeeded in bringing most major countries of Continental Europe, except Spain and Portugal,** into the orbit of free trading nations, thus radically alleviating the protectionist tendencies which had prevailed in the 1840s and 50s. Since most of the above-mentioned treaties were valid for over ten years, the decade of 1860s became literally the golden age of international free trade.

* The German Customs Union, which was in formation since the 1830s, constituted a step towards the economic unification of Germany that culminated in the Prussian Empire in 1871. In the beginning, however, it consisted of a number of small principalities, the political and economic interests of which were diverse and not easily reconcilable. The contrast between the largely agricultural region, clustering around Prussia and the Hanseatic Cities in the North and the East, and the region in the South and the West in which industrial development was beginning to appear, was quite striking until the late 1860s. In particular, the industrialising region could not easily countenance the

---

33   Page 1919, pp. 234–5.

free trade stance adopted by the agricultural region. Thus, although the German Economic Conference of 1858, led by J. Prince-Smith (1809–74), who was born in England, constituted the centre of the free trade movement in Germany during those years, it exerted little influence in the newly industrialising region of the South and the West. Yet the accelerated development of German capitalism in the 1860s and 1870s radically changed the situation. As the economy quickly grew out of its 'infant-industry' stage and became distinctly export-oriented, the protectionism of the 1840s and 1850s began to fade way, and the customs union in the 1860s became increasingly 'liberal'. It was then that the customs union concluded new commercial treaties with a number of European powers. It is sometimes said that this move of the union reflected Prussia's political interest in gaining ascendancy over Austria, since the latter remained outside of the union. In any case, Austria and Hungary were then beginning to fall behind the economic development of Central Europe.[34]

** It was by the Treaty of Methuen at the beginning of the eighteenth century that Britain secured privileged access to the market in Portugal, while renouncing the French market, after having charged a heavy duty on French wine. Now in the 1860s, the situation was reversed, inasmuch as the lowering of the tariff on French wine made it difficult for Britain to come to amicable commercial terms with Spain and Portugal. However, the development of capitalism in Britain, in the meantime, no longer permitted it to sacrifice the vast French market (together with whatever might lie behind it through the most-favoured-nation clause) for British products.

The values of Britain's exports and imports grew virtually uninterrupted until the early 1870s, except in the years affected by industrial crises. This no doubt reflected the significant expansion of new commodity markets in Asia and Africa. A similar trend could also be observed in the German and French markets in Europe. A conspicuous increase in the value of British exports to France after 1861, and to Germany after 1867, can easily be confirmed in Table 1 on the following page, not only in comparison with the figures for America and India, but also in comparison with the figures representing the total value of British exports. However, not all of the expansion of trade on the European front can be explained by the beneficial effect of the new commercial treaties. For it was more likely due to the accelerated development of the capitalist commodity-economy in those countries. That, in turn, was no doubt stimulated by the advance of Britain as the 'workshop of the world', which entailed the formation of a vast world market.*

---

34   P. Ashley 1920, Chapters 2 and 3.

TABLE 1   *Principal markets for British exports, 1854–73 (£ millions)*[35]

	Germany	France	USA	India	Total
1854	8.5	3.2	21.4	9.1	97.2
1855	9.8	6.0	17.3	9.9	95.7
1856	12.1	6.5	21.9	10.5	115.8
1857	14.0	6.2	19.0	11.7	122.1
1858	12.6	4.9	14.5	16.8	116.6
1859	11.7	4.8	22.6	19.8	130.4
1860	13.4	5.3	21.7	17.0	135.9
1861	13.0	8.9	9.1	16.4	125.1
1862	12.7	9.3	14.3	14.6	124.0
1863	13.4	8.7	15.3	20.0	146.6
1864	15.4	8.2	16.7	20.0	160.4
1865	17.8	9.1	21.2	18.3	165.8
1866	15.7	11.7	28.5	20.0	188.9
1867	20.5	12.1	21.8	21.8	181.0
1868	22.8	10.7	21.4	21.3	179.7
1869	22.8	11.5	24.6	17.6	190.0
1870	20.4	11.8	28.3	19.3	199.6
1871	27.4	18.3	34.2	18.1	223.0
1872	31.6	17.4	40.7	18.5	256.3
1873	27.3	17.4	33.6	21.4	255.2

*Levi's table N7 below, which shows the evolution of British exports in percentage terms by the regions of their destination, may indeed give the impression that, in the 1860s and 1870s, the increase in the exports bound for the European nations was particularly pronounced. The other table by Cole N8 shows that the remarkable increase in the total value of Britain's exports was accompanied by a corresponding increase in the total value of its imports.

---

35   Cole 1932, pp. 66, 76.

TABLE N-7   *Relative position of the different parts in the export trade of the United Kingdom (%)[36]*

	1840	1850	1860	1870	1878
Europe	41	37	36	40	43
Asia	13	15	19	18	19
Africa	5	5	7	8	6
America	37	40	30	29	22
Australia	4	3	8	5	10
	100	100	100	100	100

TABLE N-8   *British exports and imports (£ millions)[37]*

	Exports	Imports
1855	96	123
1860	136	182
1865	166	218
1870	200	259
1875	223	314

One must, of course, not overlook the fact that this advent of Britain on the international scene as the 'workshop of the world', in the mid-nineteenth century, went *pari passu* with the coming-of-age in that country of new capitalist social relations. These social relations were shaped by the autonomous forces that drove the capitalist method of production after the Industrial Revolution. Prior to that Revolution, Britain had had to undergo the nascent period of capitalism in the seventeenth and eighteenth centuries. During that time, the chrematistics of merchant capital had to be assisted by the mercantilist

---

36   Levi 1880, p. 564.
37   Cole 1932, pp. 76, 99.

policies of the state, with a view to disintegrating the well-entrenched, old (i.e. pre-capitalist) social relations. In contrast, the new process of the implantation of capitalism in the hitherto agricultural countries, through international trade with Britain, though also the process of the formation in those countries of the capitalist-social relations, was expedited by the spread of the commodity-economy, together with the introduction of already established modern mechanised industry. Thus, in these newly emerging capitalist nations, the process of disintegration of the old social relations, consisting of the coalescence between merchant capital and the state's mercantilist policies, as formerly witnessed in England, could be dispensed with. Even though primitive accumulation in such late-starter countries was assisted by protective tariffs, the latter implied in no sense a revival of mercantilist policies. The infant-industry protection (by means of the so-called *Erziehungszoll*) should, therefore, be regarded as constituting an integral part of liberal (and not mercantilist) economic policies.

3   Tariff Protectionism in the United States

Though originally European colonies, the United States could, after independence, make a fresh start as a modern nation with virtually no negative carry-over of traditional social relations. This very clearly distinguished America from other powers, such as France and Germany, in which capitalism developed relatively late. As a newly developing capitalist state in the nineteenth century, the United States, too, could dispense with the lengthy and painful process of primitive accumulation, which was experienced earlier by Great Britain. In common with other similar countries, the United States was spared from mercantilist policies and could instead adopt the policy of tariff protection appropriate to the context of the liberal age. Moreover, as the country which had already possessed, by the end of the eighteenth century, a leading 'theory' of infant industry protection,* the United States demonstrated the most typical example, among the late-starting capitalist nations, of economic development assisted by protective tariffs.

* Alexander Hamilton (1755–1804), reputed theorist of protectionism, espoused a doctrine of national self-sufficiency first in 1791, when he was the Secretary of the Treasury.[38] He argued that even though a policy of protection might, in the first instance, tend to raise prices, the subsequent development of domestic industries, which would

---

38   P. Ashley 1920, pp. 136–8.

increase employment, would eventually end by depressing them. Moreover, it would encourage competition within the country and would contribute to the elimination of monopoly interests, while assuring rational profits to capital. Thus, a temporary rise in prices would be compensated for later by their permanent fall. In the meantime, domestic agriculture, too, would secure more home markets in response to the development of industry within the country. Yet his advocacy of protection applied only to the industries, the sound development of which would be deterred by foreign competition. This argument was later adopted by Friedrich List of Germany, who reformulated it as the so-called principle of productivity, which was inspired by his historical studies. However, in both the American and the German version, these arguments did not amount to an 'economic theory' properly speaking. They were at most practical claims of the capitalists of the then newly industrialising countries. Furthermore, even in a practical context, they were never pushed to their logical end.

The United States adopted a policy of tariff protection soon after its independence.[39] By that time, however, material conditions in the country had not yet evolved to a level which would have justified industrial protection. Thus, indeed, the tariffs stipulated in 1789, which were mostly at levels between 10 and 15 percent in ad valorem terms, could not be thought to be effective as devices to protect its industries. Clearly, their main purpose was to secure fiscal revenues for the federal government, the protection of industry being only a matter of secondary consideration. Thereafter, several tariff reforms were put into place and they prevailed until 1816, but there was no change to this general background. In the meantime, the Napoleonic wars in Continental Europe, culminating in the blockade of Britain, powerfully sheltered American industries from foreign competition, and that to a degree far greater than any deliberate policy of tariff protection would have managed to achieve. These circumstances precipitated a vigorous capitalist development in America, notably in such core industries as cotton, wool and iron.

Thus, in order to counteract the inflow of British products, which was expected after the war, newly emerging American capitalists demanded, in 1812, a *pro tem* strengthening of protective measures, with the result that the tariffs adopted in 1816 assumed a mildly protectionist colour. Specifically, the tariffs on cotton and woollen goods were raised to 25 percent, though it was agreed that they were to be reduced to 20 percent in 1819. However, not only did the economic crisis of 1818 and 1819 change that perspective, but also the mech-

---

39   The following description on American protectionist movement owes much to Taussig's *The Tariff History of the United States* (1923).

anisation of the textile industry, then being introduced, provided the impetus for renewed calls for a more strongly protective commercial policy. Thus, the 1819 reduction of the 25 percent tariffs to 20 percent, previously agreed to in 1816, was put off to 1826 in the revised agreement of 1818. The tariff reform of 1824, which then followed, was significant in that it was adopted in the background of the political turmoil, which sharply divided the free-trading interests of the Southern states, where the livelihood of many depended on the export of raw cotton, and the quite different economic interests of other federated states. Indeed, this reform raised the tariffs on cotton and woollen goods at the same time as it raised them on such raw materials as hemp and raw wool, the latter part being clearly in response to the demands by the capitalists belonging to the central and western states. The fact that both finished manufactured goods and industrial raw materials were subject to tariff protection constituted an outstanding feature of this tariff reform, which clearly defied the theory of Hamilton. The circumstances under which tariff policy was actually implemented were such that infant-industry protection could be put into practice only by being coupled with agricultural protection.

The tariff reform of 1828 reinforced the same tendency, although the principal force behind it was the demand for protection of domestic woollen manufacturers against the inflow of more competitive British products.* The method adopted for the purpose was that of 'minimum duties', which did not fully satisfy the domestic producers.** Only in 1832 did either the abolition or the reduction of duties on raw materials become possible, together with the replacement of the minimum duties on woollen products by an ad valorem tariff of 50 percent. This was meant to roughly preserve the degree of protection which was in force in 1824. However, the Southern states were diametrically opposed to it; hence, in the end, a compromise was struck in the form of a supplementary clause stipulating that it would be gradually reduced to the general tariff-rate of 20 percent by 1842. Industrial development in the United States, though it had already produced a situation requiring a policy of tariff protection in the 1820s, did not follow a path which might normally be expected of it. The international trade position of the United States vis-à-vis the powerful industrial nation of Great Britain prevented the former from immediately shedding its role of an agricultural nation. The same problem manifested itself, within the country, as the opposition of the North and the South, with the latter preserving the dominant role based on agriculture for a long time.

* The development of the cotton industry, as is well known, was in the background of the Free Trade movement in Britain. In contrast, it was the wool industry that constituted the anchor of the American movement for tariff protection. This was a

rather interesting feature, given that wool was an older form of textile industry than cotton in the history of capitalism. Moreover, the American movement was backed up by a strong nationalist demand for the protection of all industries that could be developed within the country. In 1827, a large gathering in favour of the movement for tariff protection took place in Harrisburg. This gathering was inspired and organised by manufacturers, led by the producers of woollen goods. Yet, even there, agitations for tariff protection of agricultural produce were not absent. Friedrich List, who later became a leading theorist of protective tariffs, was in the United States at the time; and it is said that he was deeply moved by the dynamism of this movement.

** The wool manufacturers first demanded the application of the method of 'minimum duties' (already in force since 1816 with regard to cotton) to their products. This involved dividing imported wool products into five categories according to whether their price ranged from (1) below $0.50; (2) from $0.50 to $2.50; (3) from $2.50 to $4.00; (4) from $4.00 to $6.00; and (5) above $6.00, per yard, and charging a duty of 40 to 50 percent for each category. However, the fact that all products belonging to category (2) were to be evaluated as being worth $2.50 was questioned, and the division of the wool products was changed against the wishes of the wool producers into the following five categories, i.e. (1') below $0.50; (2') from $0.50 to $1.00; (3') from $1.00 to $2.50; (4') from $2.50 to $4.00; (5') above $4.00, per yard, and the tariff rate applicable to each category was amended to 45 percent of the maximum price. At first sight, the 'minimum duties' appear to be ad valorem tariffs of 45 percent, but, in fact, they are specific tariffs which are assigned as if each commodity in the group were priced at the maximum price of the category. For instance, a wool product priced at less than $0.50 per yard is judged as being worth $0.50 per yard regardless of its price, and is charged 45 percent duty of 22.5 cents. Thus, the cheaper the price, the heavier the duty. [If the price is $0.30, the tariff applicable of 22.5 cents comes in fact to an equivalent of a 75 percent ad valorem tariff]. This method understandably displeased the producers of woollen goods. For those who produced woollen goods at a price above $0.50 but below $1.00 [i.e. those who belonged to group (2') in the list] and who suffered most intensely the competition of imported British goods, could be protected by at most $0.45 [or 45 percent of $1.00], and not by $1.125 [or 45 percent of $2.50] as previously, before the categorial amendment. In the meantime, the grievance of the woollen goods producers did not make the anti-protectionist Southern states any happier, given that tariffs on raw materials such as iron, etc., including raw wool, remained unchanged. Thus, the result of the 1828 tariff reform, having failed to satisfy both the supporters and the opponents of protection, was dubbed the Tariff of Abomination.

The economic slump of the late 1830s and the attendant fiscal difficulties were responsible for the return of a mildly protectionist tendency in 1842 which sought a degree of protection roughly equivalent to that which prevailed in

1832. The 1846 tariff reform hearkened back to the tariffs introduced in the 1830s. All imported commodities were classed into four groups labelled A, B, C and D, to which the fixed tariff rates of 100, 40, 30 and 25 percent, respectively, were assigned. Most of the important commodities (such as iron and other metals, together with goods made thereof, wool and woollen goods, leather goods, paper, glass, lumber, etc.) were classed in C, and cotton goods were classed in D. These tariff rates were maintained until 1857, when the duty on cotton goods, as well as that of the goods formerly classed in group C, was reduced to 24 percent. At the same time, several raw materials became duty-free. Thus, the years between 1846 and 1860 could be characterised as constituting the era of free trade for the United States, *qua* protective nation. Certainly the meaning of 'free trade' to the United States differed from that of Britain. It was the free trade of an agricultural country in which capitalism developed late, in the specific sense that the economic interest of the Southern states as agricultural exporters predominated. This twist was also indicative of the important fact that the protective commercial policy that accompanied the growth of capitalism in the late-developing countries, in the liberal era, did not provide any theoretical insight into the logic of capital as such.* It was indeed in this era of international free trade that the United States achieved its most vigorous capitalist development.**

* List's theory of the *Erziehungszoll* (infant-industry tariff) based on the so-called principle of productivity indicates no understanding of the fact that the development of industry, if successful (tariff-assisted or not), must entail the formation of capitalist social relations. Nor does it bring to light the fact that when the late developing capitalist nation can import large-scale mechanised industry ready-made, it need not necessarily reproduce the grim political process that accompanied the dissolution of the old social relations as it was experienced in England during the period of primitive accumulation. Surely, one cannot regard the formative period of capitalism in the United States and Germany in the same way as we do that in Britain.

** The industrialisation of the United States during the 1840s and 1850s was accompanied by the rapid expansion of railroad construction and the discovery of gold mines in California. During this period, the United States accepted a large population of immigrants from the European continent, many of whom were Irish and German. Statistics show that 599,000 immigrants arrived in the 1830s, followed by 1,713,000 in the 1840s, and 2,598,000 in the 1850s. In the 1840s, there were 789,000 Irishmen and 434,000 Germans, whereas in the 1850s there were 914,000 Irishmen and 950,000 Germans.[40] Such

----

40   *Statistical Abstracts of the United States* 1934, pp. 92, 98.

a large inflow of immigrant workers from Europe was one of the features that characterised the development of capitalism in the United States.

However, as soon as the tariffs of 1857 were put into effect, criticisms arose
against their liberal tendency, as the climate of an oncoming economic crisis
then made itself felt. Of course, no phase of a business cycle, be it a crisis, a
downturn or an upswing, could be directly caused by an economic policy. Yet
commercial policy was routinely either defended or criticised for being presumed to have caused such effects. This unreasonable association of cause and
effect, which no doubt underlies the popular idea of 'policy recommendation
by the knowledgeable', revealed a lack of scientific discretion. Even so, it was
often cunningly used, given the prevailing fiscal exigencies. In 1861, the Mor-
rill Tariff was adopted, which, in principle, aimed to return to the degree of
protection of the 1846 tariff regime. However, when the ad valorem tariffs of
1846 on many important commodities were switched to specific tariffs of presumed equivalence in 1861, the degree of protection, in fact, became heavier.
That was especially the case with iron, wool and their products. Moreover, the
spirit of the 1861 reform was reinforced, soon afterwards, with the outbreak of
the Civil War, which, of course, called for more fiscal revenue. The call for the
protection of industry, which had long been suppressed by the opposition of
the Southern states, was then at last given the first chance to be heard loud and
clear. Ironically, however, American industries had by then already grown out
of their formative stage, during which they needed infant-industry tariffs for
their protection.

   After 1866, many domestic taxes that had proliferated during the war were
abolished, but the reduction of the tariff burden was delayed under strong
protectionist pressures. It was generally believed then that those industries,
which had developed under tariff protection, would not survive if such support
were removed. The reform of 1867 intended to reduce tariff rates to what was
then perceived to be the rationally required level of protection after the war;
but, in reality, it so happened that the wartime policy of extra protection was
reinforced even further. In the following reform of 1870, the only meaningful
tariff cut was that on pig iron, since the other cuts implemented by the reform
were only on such commodities as tea, coffee, wine, sugar and pepper, for which
there existed no competitive domestic supplier. Moreover, the reduction of the
tariff on pig iron represented merely a removal of the extra charge imposed
in 1864 in order to compensate for the domestic tax, which would cease to
apply after 1866. This reform, which also included an elevation of the tariff on
steel rails, could thus in no way be regarded as representing a retreat of the
hitherto protective commercial policy. At the time of the 1872 reform, tariff

reductions were again on the agenda because of the fiscal surplus, and also because of the support for them among the farmers of the Western states; but the protectionists cunningly circumvented them, by accepting the Senate proposal to limit the reduction to a uniform 10 percent. That, moreover, became a dead letter in 1875, when fiscal revenue tended to fall short, as the climate of depression deepened.

During the decade of the 1880s, the question of tariff reform arose first in 1883 in connection with the problem of fiscal surplus; but, contrary to the expectation, this reform failed to achieve any reduction of tariffs overall. For example, tariffs were, in fact, raised on the kinds of woollen and cotton goods that were most likely to be imported, and, similarly, on steel and its products. On some items, such as copper products, tariffs were indeed reduced. In this particular case, however, the effect turned out to be negligible since their prices fell. In this period, American capitalism was already introducing monopoly organisations of capital; and so tariffs were clearly no longer sought for the protection of 'infant industries'. During the election of 1888, the two major parties confronted each other on tariff issues;* but the Republican victory ended by endorsing the party's protectionist stance. The McKinley Tariff of 1890 confirmed it, as it strengthened the measure of protection overall, though especially with regard to agricultural goods. This reform introduced complicated methods of tariff evaluation, applied new rules of commodity classification, adroitly combined ad valorem and specific tariffs, simultaneously raising and reducing many tariffs, and, in the welter of all such complexities, achieved *de facto* a substantial increase in the degree of protection. Yet none of its measures could be justified as genuinely protective of an infant industry. Even in the case of steel rails, on which it was lowered, the tariff still remained prohibitive, revealing the fact that the McKinley Tariff was nothing other than an instrument for strengthening the monopoly power of capital within the United States.**

* Towards the end of 1887, President Cleveland, in his address to the nation, indicated his opposition to protective tariffs and called not only for a general reduction of import tariffs but also for the abolition of tariffs on raw materials altogether. This then became the primary election issue in the following year. Taussig, too, points out the fact that the contrasting position of the two main parties in the United States never became as radically opposed as on this occasion after the Civil War.[41]

** On the question of the 1883 tariff on steel rails, Taussig has the following to say: 'The duty on steel rails showed a considerable reduction. The old rate had been $28

41   Taussig 1923, p. 253.

a ton; the new one was $17. If this change had been made four or five years earlier, it would have been of much practical importance; but when made, it had no effect whatever. It had already been said that, after the enormous profits made by the steel-rail makers in 1879–1881, the production in this country was greatly increased. At the same time, the demand from the railroads fell off, and the huge quantities which the mills were able to turn out, could be disposed of, if at all, only at prices greatly reduced. The consequence was that the price of rails, which in 1880 was higher than the English price by the full extent of the duty of $28, fell rapidly after 1881, and brought the American price of 1885 to a point but little above the English. The new duty of 1883 was under these circumstances still prohibitory. In 1887, when a revival of railway building set in, the price of rails again went up. It is probable that at this time, when there was an active demand for rails, the decline of the duty to $17 was of real effect, preventing the American price from rising as high as it would have gone if the old duty had been retained. But the demand fell off quickly after 1887; the American price fell correspondingly, and soon became higher than the English price by an amount much less than the duty of $17. With the possible exception of the year 1887, the duty of $17 was as much a prohibitory one as the old duty of $28 had been, and the reduction on the whole was as much nominal as those in other parts of the iron schedule'.[42]

By around 1890, the US steel industry had already achieved a degree of development that permitted its cost of production to fall to a sufficiently low level. Since the industry had become fully competitive internationally, the tariff on steel was then used merely for the maintenance of a cartel price within the United States.

So long as free competition prevails within a country, an increased tariff need not raise the domestic price provided that the domestic industry remains a low-cost producer. However, in a country like the United States endowed with a vast market, at a time when the cost of inland transport was not negligible, local production could, to some extent, be naturally shielded from foreign competition. Such natural conditions were consciously utilised by large capitalist firms with monopoly power for the establishment and maintenance of cartel (monopoly) prices. It may not be justified to attribute the general trend towards the elevation of tariffs after the 1860s in the United States wholly to the advent of such firms, and their pursuit of monopoly profits. Yet it cannot be denied either that such firms took much advantage of the contemporary strengthening of tariff protection. Even the partial alleviation of tariffs, under such circumstances, was perfectly compatible with the formation and maintenance of cartel prices, so long as the domestic production cost fell, which indeed was then the case.

---

42   Taussig 1923, pp. 244–5.

4   Free Trade and Tariff Protection

The maturation of large-scale capitalist industry in Britain demanded the elimination of tariffs, while nascent industrial capital in the United States called for
a tariff protection of its inchoate industry. Both reflected the demand of industrial capital, but at different levels of development. The policy of free trade,
however, remained powerless to resolve the problems of persistently recurring economic crises and of the unemployment of labour which they entailed,
both being necessary attendants of the operation of fully developed industry.
In much the same way, neither could protective commercial policy in the late-
starting capitalist nations halt the ruin of old-style small producers as the process of industrialisation progressed. The latter steadily exacerbated the situation. If temporary mitigation of this tragic trend intervened, it was no more
than a momentary respite before a more devastating storm returned. Unlike
Britain, which could adopt a policy of free trade, and leave the dissolution of
small producers in the face of mechanised large-scale capitalist industry to the
process of 'natural selection', the late-starter nations had to make use of tariff
policies as political expedients, pretending, thereby, to protect the interests of
the small producers. Yet the idea of 'infant-industry protection' was opportune
only for so long as it allowed time for small producers to transform themselves
into capitalist ones. By the end of the nineteenth century, however, when the
imperialist state enforced its new tariff policy (for the benefit of finance-capital
and not for that of industrial capital), the meaning of 'protection' had completely changed, and its justification as a social policy had been undermined.
The economic policy of industrial capital, whether in the form of free trade
or in that of tariff protection, always aimed at the dissolution and liquidation
of small producers, as residues of the old social system, in the face of capitalist
industrialisation. In either case, what it sought was to install and entrench capitalist social relations. The form of free trade was appropriate when large-scale
capitalist industry was already in place and operated autonomously, whereas
that of protective tariffs was called for, and was more appropriate, in the process of implanting and fostering industrial capital.

The tariff protection of infant industry, as a policy of industrial capital, did
not seek to repudiate free trade and competition. Its theory called for discretion
in the imposition of tariffs, and tolerated them only within certain limits and
for a definite span of time. They were not meant to exclude foreign competition
altogether, but instead were aimed at counteracting the infestation of foreign
goods to the extent that they imperilled the formation of a sound capitalist
industry within the country. Protective tariffs were, therefore, intended to be
removed when domestic capitalist producers had grown to the point that they

were able to compete fairly with foreign capitalist producers. The industry to be protected was usually not yet large enough to supply the whole of the domestic market; and so a tariff that would equalise the price of the domestic good and that of a comparable imported good was justified, so long as the domestic industry could continue to expose itself to competition. Should a heavier tariff be imposed, the domestic industry would miss the chance of ever growing out of its infancy, and would never become internationally competitive, which would clearly contradict the spirit of protection as a policy of industrial capital. On the other hand, the proper tariff, so adjusted as to keep domestic industry exposed to reasonable competition, would (and should) disappear when it had served its purpose, that is to say, when the industry had become internationally fully competitive.

This thesis, generally known as the doctrine of 'infant-industry protection', has, since List, been widely propagated among economists in all developing countries; but, as already remarked several times, it did not for that reason constitute a dependable economic theory, which could be substituted for classical political economy. It was, in fact, no more than a theory-like formulation of the practical demand put forward by the emerging industrial capitalists in developing countries. The economists who subscribe to this doctrine are usually not aware of the fact that the implementation of commercial policy inspired thereby did not fail to end in a full development of capitalist social relations within the country in question, even though this immutable fact may have remained hidden behind the two following 'complicating factors'. First, contrary to the conventional expectation, the representatives of the agricultural interest, specifically the landed class, rooted in the old (pre-capitalist) social relations, were now converted into free traders and opponents of the protective policy. Second, the dissolution of the old social relations could now be accomplished by industrial capital alone, and no longer required the alliance of capital with landed property, since the method of large-scale mechanised industry could now be imported (introduced) ready-made from abroad. These complicating factors notwithstanding, the fact remains that the doctrine (of infant-industry protection) was primarily a pragmatic guide for the emerging national capitalist in the late developing countries, in the liberal stage of capitalist development; and, as such, it contained no 'rational' or 'theoretical' arguments comparable to those embodied in classical economics.

Because of such considerations, the commercial policy inspired by that doctrine was never put into practice consistently or with full conviction. In the United States, for example, the policy of protective tariffs was first introduced in the 1820s; yet it was a long time before it came to fruition in the 1860s. By that time, however, it was no longer certain to what extent the existing tariffs were consistent with the original intention, inasmuch as they were already beginning to be taken advantage of by monopoly capital. The latter had nothing to do with infant industry, its objective being altogether different from that of early industrial capital. Yet any tariff, once introduced, could not so easily be eliminated. That was especially so as falling prices in periods of business slump were bound to rekindle the fear that its abolition or its lightening would expose domestic industry to predatory acts of foreign competitors. The fact that each industrial sector had its own specific economics and technical conditions made inter-industry relations complex, as they became entangled with many conflicts of interests; and this paralysed the progress of tariff reforms, delaying forever the elimination of outdated custom duties.

Thus, the doctrine of infant-industry protection, even though it was not a fallacy in itself, could in no way be elevated to the status of a scientific economic theory, since it completely failed to recognise its own economic and historical significance. To some extent, it acquired its wide support and influence precisely because of its lack of awareness of its own historical role. It was the doctrine which aimed at the development of capitalism at the time when, in Great Britain, it was already in full bloom, and, all the more, when it was becoming obvious that capitalism was not necessarily the best method of production. Indeed, the fundamental contradictions of this method of production had already manifested themselves in the form of periodically recurring industrial crises. (Capitalism was then no longer pictured as an ideal method of production as it was at the time when classical political economy was being formulated). If the development of capitalism was, nevertheless, to be pursued, the doctrine that supports such a doubtful aim could not stay perfectly truthful, nor could it expose a true theory capable of being defended scientifically. List's criticism of Adam Smith brought out such circumstances inadvertently. Thus, the policy of protective tariffs adopted in developing countries must be studied, not as part of the economic theory of capitalism as such, but as the practical device whereby the emergent industrial capitalists wished to achieve their aim. It was a commercial policy of industrial capital, different from the mercantilist policy of merchant capital during the earlier world-historic stage of development of capitalism. It was also different from the tariff policy of finance-capital in the subsequent world-historic stage of imperialism, which will be studied in the next part.

PART III

Imperialism

..

Introduction to Part III

The world-historic development of capitalism, up until the decade of 1860s, was centred on Great Britain, as already remarked a number of times. It was indeed the only industrial power capable of playing the role of the 'factory of the world', since it alone enjoyed a 'monopoly in industry', as Engels described it.[1] It thus realised the typical pattern of capitalist development in that era, while the other European countries, as well as the United States, still remained largely agricultural in their economic occupation. However, as its liberal policies signified, the 'monopoly in industry' that Britain then achieved was quite different in character from that which it pursued earlier in the mercantilist age. In the liberal age, Britain no longer prevented agricultural nations from evolving their own (industrial) capitalism, especially insofar as they could assist, through the enhancement of international trade, a further development of British industry. In such agricultural countries, protective tariffs and other measures were adopted so as to encourage the advance of an indigenous capitalism, which, whether or not on account of these policy measures, gradually took shape in any case. It would, however, not be reasonable to expect that these countries would follow the same path of capitalist development as Great Britain had done earlier, in the seventeenth and eighteenth century, in the absence of any plausible rivals. Indeed, they could not, and did not, reproduce the same pattern. Rather it was their industrial capital that accomplished its own primitive accumulation by way of 'importing' the fully mechanised clothing industry from Britain. For that enabled these countries to almost instantly generate a massive population of property-less workers. Despite the strident calls for protective tariffs, the latter were not as effective as they pretended to be, nor did they need to be so. For even the determined 'liberal' opposition to such tariffs by the agricultural interests of these countries could not block the operation of mechanised, large-scale industry from carrying out its own primitive accumulation far more speedily and efficiently than merchant capital in Britain could have done during the previous era. The newly industrialising countries were then primarily France, the United States and Germany; but it was Germany, in which 'finance-capital' evolved as the newly dominant form of capital, that most typically represented the post-liberal evolution of capitalism.

In the 1830s and 1840s, Germany was still divided into the old feudalistic territories, and the capitalist development of the time could not immediately

---

1 Marx 1987, *Capital*, Vol. III, Chapter 30, p. 489n8.

facilitate the emergence of a unified single nation. Yet, once a customs union was formed in 1834, the gradual trend towards a modern nation-state soon became apparent. Not surprisingly the clothing industry, and cotton manufacturing in particular, which operated with imported machines, led the way in the evolution of capitalism in Germany. The building of railways also played an important part from the second half of the 1830s on. Furthermore, joint-stock companies with limited liability, which were still exceptional in manufacturing during the 1840s, began to proliferate in the 1850s and 1860s. For Germany, which was not yet industrially advanced, the form of the joint-stock company proved to be a highly effective method of introducing mechanised cotton manufacturing. It was even more useful as a method of financing and managing large-scale enterprises in such industries as iron and coal, which were soon to develop hand in hand with the railways. Responding to such trends, banks too assumed the pattern characteristic of the 'industrial banks' of the so-called continental-type.[2]

Thus, from the time it first emerged to challenge British hegemony, German capitalism already possessed features which, in the 1870s and onward, increasingly distinguished it from its rivals and which were, indeed, indicative of a new world-historic stage of capitalist development. This stage was characterised by the widespread adoption of the form of joint-stock company by capitalist enterprises, as it proved useful not only for the inauguration of such light industries as textile and clothing but also for the launching of firms in heavy industries (such as iron-and-steel and chemical). Furthermore, larger banks succeeded in establishing new relationships with industry, such that they directly participated in the operation of industrial enterprises. They, thus, became 'continental-style' industrial banks which, going well beyond the traditional practice of the English commercial banks, directly involved themselves with business-industrial management. Innovations in steel-making such as the Bessemer process introduced in 1855, the Siemens-Martin process which appeared in 1865, and, especially, the technique developed jointly by S.G. Thomas and P.C. Gilchrist in 1875 to improve upon the above two processes, allowed the German

---

2   For a survey of Germany's capitalist development in this period, see the concise account by Riesser in *Die Deutschen Grossbanken, Abschnitt II* (Riesser 1912). Here Riesser attributes the fact that the German *Kreditbank* showed greater business resilience than the French *credit mobilier*, though they were similar institutions in principle, to the vastly superior management skills of the former. In my view, however, mere skills in bank management do not adequately explain the difference. One must examine factors which were present in Germany's capitalist development but absent in France's, and which were favourable to the kind of banking business that a *Kreditbank* operated.

steel industry to make a giant stride forward.* Great Britain, which had formerly been the leading producer in the field, was consequently outstripped, first by the United States and then by Germany, in the last decade of the nineteenth century. Unlike the United States, Germany did not possess an abundance of iron ores with low phosphorous content, so that it was only after the advent of the Thomas-Gilchrist method that the German iron-and-steel industry accelerated its development and became the industry that underpinned the new era of finance-capital.**

* The Bessemer process, which initiated a new steel-making technique, consisted of directly producing steel out of molten pig iron by blowing air onto it, and thus burning off carbon and other impurities. The Siemens-Martin process, on the other hand, mixed pig iron and scrap iron at a high temperature in a reverberatory furnace. The former was also called the 'revolving furnace' method and the latter the 'open-hearth furnace' one. However, neither could use pig iron (and hence iron ore) containing much phosphorous. Only with the adoption of the Thomas-Gilchrist technique, which made possible easy separation of phosphorous from iron, could these two types of furnaces, produce steel without relying on high-quality iron ores. There were presumably merits and demerits specific to the two types of furnaces as both were used side by side. The source of my information comes from Kuni-Ichi Tawara, *Iron and Steel*, a rather old but valuable book.

** About the industrial progress in Germany and the contrasting eclipse in Britain, Alfred Marshall points out, first of all, that the German educational system was far better prepared than that in rival countries to meet the human resources requirement of the new age. He states, in the second place, that Britain's reserves of iron ore were rapidly depleting, while Germany had easy access to the rich deposits of Lorraine, Luxembourg and elsewhere in the vicinity – this advantage becoming decisive after the adoption of the Thomas-Gilchrist technique. Most importantly, however, he concludes that the management style in the British iron-and-steel industry had become obsolete, while Germany pioneered the fostering of 'organised monopolies' that integrated industry and banking.[3] In an earlier edition of the present book, I stated that British steel industry developed more slowly than its German counterpart, even though all the new techniques came to fruition first in Britain. Makoto Itoh questioned the factual validity of this statement by arguing that Britain did maintain the dominance in the world steel market, during both the age of the Bessemer process and the preceding one of the puddling furnace. No doubt, I overemphasised the speed with which the German industry overtook the British; however, I cannot help noti-

---

3   Marshall 1923, pp. 556–9.

cing that, even according to statistical references in Mr. Itoh's work, Britain was outstripped in steel production during the 1890s, first by the United States and then by
Germany.[4] Since Itoh's essay focuses on the period of the Great Depression, he may
be justified in reaching conclusions different from mine, with regard to the relative
strength of the German and British steel industries. However, for the stage theory of
imperialism, what matters crucially is the coming-into-being of finance-capital. From
my own perspective, the Great Depression in Britain should be studied at the level
of economic history (rather than as part of the stage theory). As far as the formation of finance-capital in Britain is concerned, I will later treat that matter in some
detail.

In the era of liberalism, the development of the cotton industry proved most
compatible with the operation of individually owned industrial capitals. The
latter reproduced pretty much the same pattern of accumulation that one
would visualise in studying the behaviour of individual capitalists in pure theory. In contrast to this, in the era of imperialism, heavy industries such as
iron-and-steel, which required a massive investment in plants and equipment,
and which, in consequence, entailed the pooling of capital from a large number of small individual owners, became the norm. This was particularly the
case in a country such as Germany, where capitalism started late, and where
such conditions as just described gave rise to a new form of capital known as
'finance-capital'. This form of capital no longer enforced the rule of free competition among individual capitalists, but rather sought to reap 'monopoly profits'
by deftly organising the industry already dominated by large firms. This does
not imply that free competition, which stemmed from the logic of capital, was
summarily discarded. Since monopoly remains always partial or relative, no
capitalist organisation could be entirely spared from competition and attain
a comprehensive control of society. Often, a monopoly was broken up from
within by the re-emergence of conflict among the hitherto allied capitalists.
Yet, unlike free competition in the marketplace, which constantly replaced
mediocre performers with shrewder ones, through a process akin to 'natural
selection', competition in the age of monopolies intensified the domination
of more concentrated capitals. These were the type of capitals that survived
after a given period of mergers and acquisitions, by concluding among themselves business pacts, which sometimes even transcended national boundaries,
these pacts granting them, however, only a temporary respite from ruinous and
internecine trade wars.

---

4   See Kôichirô Suzuki 1971, p. 75.

It is apparent, from what has been said above, that these features did not follow straightforwardly from the routine capitalist development which the pure theory of capitalism would lead one to surmise, since they even repudiate, to some extent, the free competition that capitalism, as a system, must presuppose in principle. Unlike the regime of industrial capital, which possessed an economic mechanism of resolving its systemic contradiction, the subsequent regime of finance-capital had to expose such a contradiction outwardly.* In the freely competitive market, the fundamental contradiction of capitalism, which stems from the commodification of labour-power, manifested itself straightforwardly in the form of periodic crises. In this case, the contradiction inherent in society's reproduction-process, due to the conflict between capital and wage-labour, was quite apparent as the fault of the system. Under the regime of finance-capital, in contrast, since it partially controlled the market and thus distorted the pattern of business cycles, the same contradiction assumed legal, political and various other ideological (superstructural) dimensions, rather than simply economic.** Accordingly, there arose the illusion that the social conflicts could be resolved with an appropriate blend of government policies, although the policies that the state then undertook merely shifted the problem from one sphere to another, without really addressing it. Nevertheless, what characterised the era of imperialism could be said to reside in the fact that capitalism, in its over-ripening (foreshadowing its decay), could no longer subsist without some periodic interventions in the form of makeshift state policies.

* It goes without saying that, even during the age of industrial capital, economic crises did not occur exactly as pure theory would lead us to expect, due to the omnipresence of extraneous and contingent factors. As was shown in Part II of this book, industrial crises in the liberal era often appeared under the influence of foreign trade, in the first place. British industrial capital, which was then based on the manufacturing of cotton, imported its raw materials and exported much of its product. Therefore, it cannot be said to have put into practice the self-contained capitalist society that pure theory envisages. Moreover, the development of the cotton industry, which represented the age of industrial capital in concrete terms, had undergone a lengthy process of maturation as mechanisation first begun in spinning spread only gradually to weaving with the long tradition of handicraft. Theory cannot explain all such historical details of industrial evolution. Even while the establishment of industrial capital in the cotton industry exerted a powerful influence on other industries, not all of the latter necessarily operated capitalistically in a fashion akin to the cotton industry. Rather industrial capital in its development had to depend heavily on related sectors that persistently remained part of the old handicraft industry. Theory, which intends to expose the inner mechanism of the capitalist commodity-economy, must nevertheless presuppose an ideal form

of its operation, quite distinct from the concrete historical process leading towards it. This, of course, does not mean that we may resort to arbitrary abstractions, which 'idealise' the object of study from the outside (i.e. subjectively). It is in the development of the commodity-economy itself that the objective tendencies towards its theoretical ideal must be located. For that, to my mind, grounds the materialism to which Marxian philosophy subscribes. Difficulties arise, however, when these tendencies are thwarted and rendered ineffective under imperialism, so that capitalism no longer tends towards its ideal image but rather diverges from that trajectory. Perhaps it is for this reason that many Marxists underestimate the methodological foundation of Marxian economic theory. The diversity of empirical phenomena that characterises the stage of imperialism must, however, not be allowed to divert our attention from the true significance of economic theory; for, in its absence, the specifications of the three stages of capitalist development (mercantilist, liberal and imperialist) would become quite meaningless. Capitalist crises, for example, must be properly defined and explained in the context of pure theory first, before their specific appearance in different stages of development may be studied in detail.

** It is not possible to infer the theoretical specifications of capitalist crises from mere observations of the crisis-phenomena in the age of finance-capital. For the operation of this type of capital presupposes a distortion of the normal interaction of the real and the monetary aspect of the capitalist commodity-economy. Thus, not only is loan-capital deprived of its power to regulate the accumulation of industrial capital, but the concentration of capital, under the form of joint-stock company, also obscures the fact that the excess of capital is to be overcome by the periodic formation of a relative surplus population, following a cluster of technical innovations. In the regime of finance-capital, some innovations can occur at any time, so that the necessity derived from pure theory that they should occur primarily in a depression period is obfuscated. It is frequently thought that financial conditions in the stock market are responsible for causing or relieving capitalist crises – all the more so because an increasing number of ordinary persons in society involve themselves with their stakes in the stock market. Moreover, the proliferation of economic 'policies' in the age of finance-capital tends to give the false impression that economic theory is there merely to serve policymakers. The policies in question are no longer quite as naïve and simple as at the time of Friedrich List, when Germany was still underdeveloped. The great pretence of *sozialpolitik* to cover up its not-entirely-blameless motives seems to attest to the fact that economic power, directly and indirectly, translates itself into political power. This also puts the law at the service of politics. All this represents the ideological confusion of the age. This confusion becomes all the more obvious after the coming-into-being of the so-called socialist countries. Even though the development of socialism in those countries was originally guided by Marxism, with its claim to 'scientific' socialism, their slow progress seems to abet this confusion even further.

Another example of this confusion may be the word 'ideology', which now means nothing other than Marxist ideology in ordinary parlance. This distorted usage also derives from the fact that Marxism has become 'ideologised' by those who resort to the authority of Marx and Lenin for the endorsement of Marxism's scientific content, instead of examining the latter objectively and establishing it rationally. All this stems from the confusing nature of the imperialist age, which, under the form of finance-capital, blinds the observer to the inner truth of capitalism.

Capitalism in Its Decline

1   The Concentration of Capital and the Bulking Large of Fixed Capital

The development of heavy industries, especially iron-and-steel, in the second half of the nineteenth century, entailed an enormous increase in the average size of capital required for their business management. First, the extensive construction of railways stimulated the demand for iron-and-steel products; then, the advent of the new steel-making technology gave further impetus to their even more extensive use. That stimulated the construction of ever-larger blast furnaces as well as steel-making furnaces, the sustained operation of which undoubtedly increased the magnitude of capital. That was not all. Technical and economic rationality frequently demanded that one unit of an iron-works should operate several blast furnaces side by side, and that the production of pig iron should be integrated, not only with steel-making and the lamination of steel products downstream, but also with the utilisation of chemical by-products together with the various upstream operations, such as the production of coke, the mining of iron-ore and of coal, and the like. Thus, not only did the capital needed to run each individual enterprise bulk large, but the formation of monopoly organisations in the industry* also called for a truly extended scale of the mobilisation of available capital. The combination of many enterprises in one organisation promoted not only a large-scale mechanisation of the plant, but a large-scale business management as well. These tendencies could not be adequately explained by reference to the theoretical concepts of 'the concentration and centralisation of capital', since they clearly exceeded what could be expected of ordinary capitalist development. In other words, industrial capital based on cotton manufacturing would never have required such a bulk of fixed capital at one time. Although the iron-and-steel industry would not have developed without the prior stage characterised by cotton manufacturing, the former (the iron-and-steel), once it passed a certain level of maturation, could no longer be viewed as a simple extension of the latter (the cotton industry). There was a qualitative difference in the size and weight of fixed capital, which the new industry required, whether in the form of the means of labour or in that of raw materials. Thus, the single most important distinguishing feature of the new stage of capitalist development must, first of all, be found in the bulkiness of fixed capital in the iron-and-steel industry, which now emerged in the forefront of other manufacturing activities.

* The combination of firms, related to the production of iron-and-steel goods, started early due to freight costs involved in the transportation of raw materials. Later, various technical improvements such as the one that made possible the large-scale utilisation of exhaust gas from coke-ovens and blast furnaces called for the further combination of related works. There arose, in consequence, the so-called 'mixed works' [*gemischte Werke*]. Such a combination of works, however, was not restricted to the iron-and-steel industry nor was it found invariably everywhere in that industry. Still, as Marshall especially emphasised,[1] the emergence of 'mixed works' confirmed their superiority in large-scale business management, in such industries as iron-and-steel, in which a large volume of fixed capital had to be tied down and managed.

Because of the bulkiness of fixed capital, the iron-and-steel industry cannot easily respond to fluctuations of demand, caused, for example, by business cycles, by resorting to the setting up of new plants or the extension of the existing ones. The same is true, to some extent, even with cotton manufacturing, as soon as mechanisation makes it dependent on fixed capital. The free inter-industry mobility of capital is always restricted, to a greater or lesser extent, under capitalism. Yet, in the liberal age, in which light industries predominated, the problem could be overcome relatively more easily. For in the expansion phase of business cycles, an additional investment of capital could be allocated to any industry which faced an increased demand for its product that was more intense than elsewhere. Even with regard to the destruction of capital that was due to declining demand occurring in the depression phase of business cycles, the fixed capital to be abandoned had already been more or less used up during the preceding phase of prosperity, with only a small portion of it left un-depreciated. These attenuating considerations, which applied to cotton manufacturing, do not apply to the iron-and-steel industry, which plays the key role in the age of imperialism. The expansion of this type of industry requires massive funds to build its fixed capital. Even when new facilities are put in place, it often takes several years before they are made ready for actual operation. Once the capacity is expanded, however, a sudden rise in output may, in some instances, even cause a shortage of raw materials, which will elevate their prices. By the time the supply increases, the boom may have passed and the firm may then be stuck with overcapacity throughout the subsequent

---

1 Marshall 1923, pp. 218–21.

period of depression. Thus, the destruction of capital in this phase is no longer quite as mild a blow as in the age of industrial capital. For example, the cost of reactivating a blast furnace that has been out of operation can be staggering. A closed-down plant must either be scrapped or be disposed of for a paltry sum. Hence, it is as difficult to cut back production during the depression when demand is low, as to step it up during the prosperity phase when demand is high. Such conditions can impose a concatenation of unbearable excesses and shortfalls of supply capacity on individual capitals.*

* G.H. Heymann summarises this point concisely, and says that 'mixed operation firms' developed in the iron-and-steel industry for this reason even before the advent of cartels.[2] The shortages and high prices of raw materials in the prosperity phase of business cycles encouraged either the setting-up of new enterprises or the buying-out of old ones that produced raw materials for iron-and-steel product makers. On the other hand, the excess supply and low prices of raw materials in a given depression phase made it easier for the producers of iron-and-steel products to expand at the expense of raw materials producers. Clearly their combination or mutual accommodation would relieve them both from the stressful conditions of the market.

The existence of fixed capital is a decisive factor in what Marx calls the rising composition of capital. Theoretically, and in the age of industrial capital represented by cotton manufacturing (since this age illustrates the theory most closely in concrete terms), capitalist enterprises tend to realise an average profit, even as the general rate of profit falls secularly. However, the large bulk of fixed capital in heavy industries tends to obstruct, as already suggested, the process of averaging profits. When the price of a particular product rises in the prosperity phase, its production cannot necessarily be expanded, in which case surplus profits must continue, for some time, to accrue to that branch of production. Yet, when the accumulated surplus profits induce a large expansion of productive facilities, it is almost certain that the same branch will suffer a severe fall in rates of returns in the following depression period. In this way, the ordinary movement of profit-rates through business cycles will be significantly impaired. Fixed capital then fails to be cyclically renewed to launch a new phase of prosperity, as innovations do not necessarily occur towards the end of the depression phase. Thus the regularity of business cycles that pure theory explains, as consequent upon the capitalist method of production being adopted, can no longer be widely observed. The iron-and-steel industry frequently

---

2   G.H. Heyman 1904, pp. 220–3.

resorts to a major expansion towards the end of the prosperity phase, prompted by the enormous profit that tends to be earned during that phase. This expansion is not timed in such a way as to gradually absorb the industrial reserve army available at the beginning of the prosperity phase. Nor does it generate unemployment of labour-power proportional to the increased productivity embodied in the newly introduced facilities. A sharp fall in profit-rates (so-called profit squeeze) reflecting a prior elevation of wages, which explains the ultimate cause of the crisis, thus tends to be buried in a decline of profit-rates due simply to the 'overproduction of commodities'. It is, of course, not merely the glut of commodities that has caused the trouble. It is rather the excess of productive capacity embodied in the bulk of newly built fixed capital, but becoming useless as circumstances change. The business cycles, which formerly regulated the growth of capitalist production, are, thus, seriously deformed by the hypertrophy of fixed capital in heavy industries.

There are, however, two sides to the same trend. First of all, those industries which do not suffer from the bulkiness of fixed capital expand easily, while those which do are slow to expand. Thus, the increases in the prices of the products of the former are easily held in check, while the inflation in the prices of the latter's products will remain unrestrained. The predictable result is that the former industries lose much of their profits to the latter industries in the prosperity phase. Secondly, the other side of the same story is that, even in these latter industries, there are relatively small enterprises which are engaged in a restricted range of production, or which have been in trouble because of high production costs. These enterprises, when they expand or are reactivated in a prosperity phase, will endeavour to keep their prices low in order to compete with larger ones in the same industry. Whereas those in the former industries (which do not suffer from the bulkiness of fixed capital) benefit, to some extent, from the drastic fall in the prices of the means of production in the depression phase, the smaller enterprises in the latter industries (which do suffer from the bulkiness of fixed capital) are often ruined in the same phase because they are unable to withstand the strain as resiliently as larger firms can do in the same sort of industry. Thus, the process of centralisation of capital, which occurs during the depression phase, can, as a consequence, eliminate smaller firms in those industries, which are saddled with the bulkiness of fixed capital.

As a general rule, the capitalist method of production evolves when industry separates itself from agriculture. Industry then divides itself into a number of specialised branches and sub-branches. If profit-rates become unequal in different branches or sub-branches of the industry, for whatever reason, capital, which seeks nothing but profit, will automatically move from the less profitable to the more profitable operations. Though that is the case in principle, some part of capital is always fixed and so fails to move easily from one branch of industry to another. Therefore, the equalisation of profit-rates cannot be achieved all at once. If unequal profit-rates arise, due to inter-industry differences either in the value composition or in the turnover frequency of capital, that problem is, of course, dealt with in pure theory by (what has come to be known as) the transformation of values into production-prices.* The description above applies to inequalities in profit-rates that remain even after that transformation has been effected. Capital overcomes the delay in the profit-rate equalisation process by a method appropriate to the social regulation of anarchic production, namely by enabling the market to signal which are the branches and sub-branches of industry where new investment should take place, and by inducing banks to allocate the idle funds, which capital automatically generates in its motion, to the more profitable spheres of investment. However, when the above-mentioned hypertrophy of fixed capital occurs in specific industries, and, particularly, when a small number of large firms operate in them, the process of equalising profit-rates which the inner logic of capitalism requires, is faced with a major obstacle. As heavy industries centred around the iron-and-steel industry become important, even the gradual working of the mechanism, which might otherwise correct the uneven growth of the economy – the mechanism which was available to industrial capital in the liberal era – can no longer be counted on. As the form of the joint-stock company becomes more and more widely adopted in manufacturing industries, the tendency for this mechanism to be undermined is bound to be reinforced. The law of average profit, one of the most fundamental laws of capitalism, thus suffers a serious distortion.

---

* The so-called transformation of values into production-prices is the peculiar method whereby capital brings about an equalisation of profit-rates generally. It implies the mechanism whereby capital allocates productive labour for the provision of socially necessary products. It, in other words, refers to capital's peculiar mode of enforcement of the law of value. If capital buys and sells its products for production-prices, that does not change the values of these products. Capital trades commodities, sometimes above and sometimes below their values, because it cannot otherwise satisfy the social demand for them. In the theory of commodity exchanges, it is often customary to assume that equilibrium prices are proportional to values. Marx's *Capital*, too, followed this well-established convention of classical political economy. Thus, when Marx eventually introduced production-prices that diverge from values in Volume III of *Capital*, he was blamed for contradicting himself. However, this kind of criticism derives from a fundamental misunderstanding of the meaning of the law of value. In the first

place, as has already been stated, the transformation of values into production-prices by no means affects or alters the determination of commodity values. Value continues to be determined by the amount of socially necessary labour for the production of the commodity, i.e. by the amount embodied in it. However, for capital, which is not a direct producer, and which is solely guided by profits in its investment decisions, the exchange of commodities at production-prices is the only way to ensure the satisfaction of the social demand for all commodities. In other words, only in the light of production-prices can capital socially allocate itself, and, hence, labour along with it, to all branches of industry appropriately. By far the most important point, which must not be overlooked in this connection, is that labour-power, as a commodity, differs from other commodities, in that its production-price does not diverge from its value. Even if articles of subsistence are sold to the worker at production-prices diverging from values, he/she receives a wage which enables him/her to buy his/her subsistence. Whatever his/her wages are, he/she, in the final analysis, buys back the articles of subsistence which he/she him-/herself produced, directly or indirectly, with his/her necessary labour. The failure to understand this point has led to a series of fruitless debates. It is also worth paying attention to the fact that, if society lets the commodity-economy regulate its basic human relations, it is obliged to buy and sell commodities at production-prices diverging from values. What this means is that a commodity-economic society becomes historically viable only as capitalist society; and, hence, it must accept capital's peculiar method of enforcing the law of value through the formation of production-prices.

2 The Functioning of the Joint-Stock Company

The joint-stock company, as a form of business enterprise, had existed far back in the nascent period of capitalism, though it was not until the 1860s that it made significant inroads into the industrial sector, even in Great Britain. Since that took place some considerable time after the evolution of individually owned capitalist enterprises, however, the new form of business did not, at once, alter the old conception of the firm as property belonging to an individual.* As will be examined later, this fact may have been responsible for significantly delaying the formation of finance-capital in Britain. In contrast, a less developed capitalist nation such as Germany, as already pointed out, witnessed a comparatively early diffusion of the joint-stock ownership in industrial enterprises.** As these enterprises could accelerate massive investment in fixed capital, it was a country such as Germany that exemplified, in the most typical fashion, the ascendancy of finance-capital, which distinguished this new stage of the development of capitalism.

* I shall elaborate on this point later, when I come to the formation of finance-capital in England.

** In Germany as well, it was only after the 1850s that the form of joint-stock company became widespread. So far as this timing is concerned, there is no major difference from the case in England. Yet in Germany, capitalist development itself began in the 1840s and 1850s, so that restrictive practices of a mercantilist nature (such as monopoly charter) survived well into the 1860s and 1870s. Thus, the conditions in Germany were quite different from those in England.[3]

A   *The Capital of a Joint-Stock Company*

Although the equity of a joint-stock company consists of the money originally paid in by the founders, the moment it is paid in, there occurs, so to speak, a doubling of capital.* On the one hand, as the capital of the company, it undergoes the circular motion $M-C \ldots P \ldots C'-M'$ as would any industrial capital. Yet, at the same time, capital acquires a separate existence as shares, apparently quite independent of its motion as real capital – 'shares' being the titles to periodic sharing in the profit of the firm in the form of dividends. The profit of the firm is earned as a result of the real motion of capital, while its other form, capital as shares, can be bought and sold in the securities market independently of its real motion.

* Marx wrote as follows: 'The stocks of railways, mines, navigation companies, and the like represent actual capital, namely, the capital invested and functioning in such enterprises, or the amount of money advanced by the stock holders for the purpose of being used as capital in such enterprises. This does not preclude the possibility that these may represent pure swindle. But this capital does not exist twice, once as the real capital-value of titles of ownership (stocks) on the one hand and on the other hand as the actual capital invested, or to be invested, in those enterprises. It exists only in the latter form, and a share of stock is merely a title of ownership to a corresponding portion of the surplus value to be realised by it'.[4] Obviously, the 'share of stock' is only a 'title of ownership to surplus value', and not by itself independent capital. Yet share-capital implies a little more than a mere claim to an income stream. As will be explained below, shareholders themselves are divided into two classes, and this division has to do with the 'twofold existence' of capital, which cannot be as lightly dismissed as in the

---

3   For the diffusion of joint-stock companies after the 1870s, see Riesser 1912, pp. 105–9. For more details on the German Companies Act, see the article under the entry *'Aktiengesellschaften'* in *Handwörterbuch der Staatswissenschaften,* fourth edition. For additional information on joint-stock companies in Britain, see the article on 'Joint-Stock Company' in Palgrave 1963.

4   Marx 1987, *Capital,* Vol. III, Chapter 29, p. 466.

above-quoted passage. I would rather say the following: Although share-capital exists
in the final analysis only 'in the actual capital invested in those ventures', it also exists
as 'commodified capital' subject to transactions, which not only transfer 'the title to
surplus value' (in which alone small capitalists are interested), but also 'the control
of the real company' (in which large capitalists are mainly interested) based on the
ownership of capital. Capital acquires the twofold existence in this sense. If this point
is de-emphasised, 'shares or equity' become mere fictitious capital in the same way
as 'bonds and debentures', and one can only conclude that 'the capital value of such
papers is wholly illusory'.[5] It is important to bear in mind, however, that the transaction
in shares, unlike that in bonds and debentures, does transfer, from time to time, the
control of the company from one party to another. This fact is anything but 'illusory'.

In the original sense, capital is a self-augmenting motion of value, which takes
on and off the forms of commodities, money, means of production and labour-
power, yet it is none of these considered separately. Even when it takes on
the form of commodities, it does not itself become a commodity. It only temporarily assumes that form, pending the sale of the commodities for money.
Neither does capital itself become money, which is also only a form it temporarily assumes. One talks of the means of production and labour-power as capital
in the same sense, i.e. only as passing phases in the motion of capital. That
is why, for example, one does not buy capital by purchasing its products. One
only buys commodities for their specific use-values. Though capital also sells
its commodities, it does not sell itself. At any one time, capital exists, in part, as
money and, in part, as commodities; but it is mostly found in the form of 'productive capital'. As it changes its form, capital augments value that remains, at
all times, in the hands of its owner.

   This fundamental fact is not altered merely because capital assumes the
form of a joint-stock company. Real capital remains in the hands of the company. Capital-as-shares differs from real capital in that the former is a commodification of the latter. In the form of shares, capital as value-augmenting
motion can be bought and sold in bits and pieces. Of course, it is always possible to buy and sell the whole enterprise, in which case it is traded for its 'value
as capital', as distinct from the commodity value of the assets belonging to it –
its 'value as capital' being 'expressed in the profit which is derived from the
productive or mercantile employment of its assets'.[6] So long as such operations
remain exceptional, there is no need for the enterprise to necessarily take the

5   Ibid.
6   Marx 1987, *Capital*, Vol. III, p. 419.

form of a joint-stock company: an adequate development of the credit system suffices to finance them. However, the conversion of an ongoing enterprise into a commodity, in the form of shares, enables the buying and selling of real capital in its value-augmenting motion, in whole or in part, to occur as a common and routine practice, and introduces a new capitalist mechanism in concrete terms. It is this mechanism that has a profound impact on the imperialist stage of capitalist development.

Capital-as-shares is, in general, of a different money-value from paid-in capital. The former is the present value, capitalised by the prevailing rate of interest, of the shares' entitlement to a periodic series of dividend revenues, expected in the light of present credit conditions. For instance, if I invest $50 in shares with the expected dividend-rate of 12.5 percent p.a., then I am entitled to the annual revenue of $6.25. If the prevailing rate of interest is 5 percent p.a., the present value of the shares which I purchased for $50, capitalised at this rate, is $6.25 / 0.05 = $125. Thus, 'capital-as-shares' does not reflect the value of 'real capital' – the former being only 'fictitious capital' which, when possessed, will automatically bear interest. Even though money is paid in to acquire a share in real capital which, when it performs, yields expected profits and dividends, these considerations determine only the annual revenue. The present value of that revenue depends on the rate of interest, which can fluctuate for completely extraneous reasons. The founder of the company, who paid in $50, can now realise the profit of $75, if he does sell his shares for $125 in the market. This is what Hilferding called *Gründungsgewinn* or the profit of the founder (original investor). Of course, there are many more volatile factors to consider, such as the expected performance of the enterprise, which is the subject of stock market speculation. For example, the dividend rate expected at the outset may have to be radically revised downward; in which case, the subsequent selling of shares in a later period may not even recover the original investment. If the shareholder sells off his equity, he will not remain a capitalist. Even when he retains his shares, the money value that he owns as capital may be different from what he had paid in. He merely owns fictitious capital, which has a money value that must be determined in the stock market.

It is this fundamental fact that explains the ease with which the form of the joint-stock company spread over many industries, especially those that required a large contingent of fixed capital. Those who invest in shares transform their funds directly into capital, which can be retrieved in cash at any moment, often with some capital gain. From the point of view of the enterprise, this form of ownership enables it to raise capital needed for its operation, without the limitation of individual accumulation. In other words, it can mobilise socially available funds and can transform them into capital at short notice.

It, therefore, becomes relatively easy to launch a large project that requires a massive advance of capital, so long as it promises to be sufficiently profitable. The same considerations apply if an increase of capital is required for an existing enterprise. Unlike the individually owned firm, which is necessarily constrained by individual and contingent conditions, this form of enterprise can readily respond to the calls of rational management because of its ability to raise capital when necessary. Moreover, as far as the original paid-in capital is concerned, it cannot be pulled out by individual shareholders. Even if they sold their shares and personally withdrew from the business, others have bought the same shares with the result that the company's real capital continues its motion, undisturbed by the transfer of ownership titles, from which the function of capital is independent. This fact lies at the root of the separation of ownership and management.

The management of even a joint-stock company devolves on its capitalist owners who, in this case, are the shareholders. However, since their participation in the enterprise is proportional to the number of shares they hold, and they are often numerous, management ends up in the hands of the so-called 'large shareholders' who possess the majority of shares. A small number of shareholders can, by virtue of their majority holdings, wrest control of the company by prevailing in the shareholders' meetings. Ordinary shareholders have little choice but to delegate the management of the company to the 'large capitalists', now called the directors, and must content themselves with merely receiving dividends. The ownership form of a joint-stock company thus often creates two types of capitalists whose interests diverge sharply: one type is directly involved in the management of the enterprise, while the other is concerned only with dividend incomes or share-price fluctuations. What the latter group loses by virtue of the fact that they are no longer industrial capitalists, the former gains by being able to control much more capital than they themselves have invested. Thus, neither do the latter remain 'industrial capitalists' simply speaking. Those in control have now acquired the right to do what they like with the total capital invested in the company, as if it wholly belonged to them. Even though their own contribution is, in fact, only a relatively modest part of the total, they need not, and do not, consider the rest as the debt of the company. The leverage they thus acquire is obvious. However, the differentiation of the capitalists into such powerful ones, on the one hand, and inactive ones, on the other, does not arise merely from the legal form of the joint-stock company. There are substantive reasons as well, and these relate to the evolution of 'industrial' enterprises. From this perspective, individual entrepreneurship lost ground in the imperialist period for two reasons. On the one hand, the operation of a large-scale enterprise, which required massive investment in fixed capital, could not have raised funds in the necessary volumes, had it retained the form of individual ownership. On the other, the extreme mechanisation of the production-process demanded managerial organisations far exceeding the limitations of individual entrepreneurship. Ordinary shareholders, for their part, invested in the enterprise in a manner not very different from simply lending funds to it. However, they expected better returns than what would have been available from simple lending, due to the proportionally greater risks that they assumed by committing themselves to the firm.

In the formative period of capitalism, 'bubble companies' were set up by those who had funds but no capitalist skill; and even in the subsequent period of capitalism, speculative investments were often made in railway construction. The evolution of the joint-stock company after the 1870s was, however, quite different in nature. It generally established the 'capitalist-social' mechanism, whereby society's monetary savings could be mobilised, as the need arose, to provide industrial enterprises with the necessary capital. It is true that these new joint-stock enterprises, too, were not wholly unaffected by speculative factors, which called to mind the 'bubble companies' of olden times and the railways construction of the early nineteenth century. Yet, what made the crucial difference was that, speculatively or otherwise, capitalist enterprises could now mobilise idle funds formed in society at large as their own capital. By this time, indeed, individually owned enterprises were no longer competitive with 'capitalist-socialised' enterprises in the same industry. Marx, therefore, had sound reasons for observing that: 'This result of the ultimate development of capitalist production is a necessary transitional phase towards the re-conversion of capital into the property of producers, although no longer as the private property of the individual producers, but rather as the property of associated producers, as outright social property'.[7] If one takes a long view, one may indeed describe the joint-stock company as 'a necessary transitional phase towards the re-conversion of capital into the social property of producers'. However, capitalism evolved the widespread joint-stock company system as a 'capitalist-social', and not an outright 'social', form in its highest stage of development. This it did, moreover, in order to be able to adequately manage large-scale enterprises, requiring a high concentration of capital. The joint-stock company system of investment is 'capitalist-social' but not genuinely social, an important distinction that is frequently overlooked. This fact is evidenced by the differentiation of the capitalists into two types. This cap-

---

7   Marx 1987, *Capital*, Vol. III, p. 437.

italist 'socialisation' of commodity production, while partially overcoming its anarchy, does also manifest the tendency to magnify and reinforce the same anarchy.

Capitalism always endeavours to mobilise socially available funds for the production of surplus value. The commercial banking system achieves this purpose to some extent by means of loan-capital. The joint-stock company, however, enables its 'large shareholders' to lay hands on the same socially available funds, not through loan-capital but directly as investment capital, that is to say, as capital that they can use as if it were their own. For this reason, a joint-stock company must make its operation public, at least form-ally. Modern large-scale industry, because of its mechanisation makes such 'open' management, to some extent, possible. That is yet another reason why the joint-stock company system spread so quickly during the stage of imperial-ism.*

* The form of joint-stock company (or corporation) is nowadays adopted even by small enterprises in Japan because it has tax advantages. I do not deal with such matters at present.

B   *Joint-Stock Companies and Banks*
The characteristics of the joint-stock company examined above brought about an important change in the relationship between banks and industrial enter-prises, especially the large ones that are organised in that form. In this respect too, Germany differed significantly from Great Britain and the United States, and it was the conditions in Germany that illustrated this relationship in the most typical fashion.*

* In reference to this point, Marshall writes as follows: 'Thus the movement towards the consolidation of industry under high financial control is strong in many countries. It will suffice to consider three: Britain where the movement is opposed by tradition and perhaps by national character and where therefore it is not very prominent; Ger-many, where its development is perhaps most typical and uniform; and the United States, where the movement has been irregular, but has gone very far in several great departments of industry'.[8] Britain's 'national character' suggests a rather peculiar inter-pretation on Marshall's part. It would be more appropriate, it seems to me, to explain this 'national character' as deriving from the traditions of capitalism in Britain.

---

8   Marshall 1923, p. 338.

Originally, commercial banks in England represented the most typical form of the modern banking institution. This form allowed all capitalists to share in the use of idle funds which were necessarily generated in the process of the metamorphosis of capital. This gave rise to loan-capital and a general rate of interest that was formed in the money market. In that context, however, banks remained external to industrial enterprises and simply mediated the latter's utilisation of society's idle funds. Once the form of the joint-stock company was adopted by industrial firms, the majority of the shareholder capitalists were petty savers who opted to use their savings for investment in equities rather than merely lending them for interest, while always retaining the right to retrieve their funds at will by selling off their shares. This procedure was secured as stock exchanges developed as the core of the securities market. The latter then constituted the 'capital market' operating in close connection with the 'money markets', in which banks played the leading role in mediating the capitalist-social utilisation of idle funds. In other words, investments in the capital market depended directly on rates of interest already formed in the money market. Even though each investment was primarily guided by the profit rate of the enterprise, other factors such as the firm's dividend policy were taken into consideration before the expected annual return was estimated. The latter was then capitalised with the prevailing rate of interest to determine the money value of the firm, which then played a decisive role in the allocation of socially available funds among different firms and industries. Simultaneously, the same funds moved between the loan market and the equity market, regulating the demand and supply of both loans and investments. This situation was quite unlike the earlier one in which individual capitalists made use only of the money market for their business finance.

With the development of joint-stock companies in industry, banks not only enlarged their traditional operations in business finance (i.e. those of transforming idle money-capitals in the hands of individual firms into socially available funds), but they also began to forge closer relations with industrial firms, their relations becoming more systematic and less personal, in view of the fact that the organised management of large-scale enterprises tended to require more public exposure of their business accounts. Banks became involved with such new operations as the underwriting of shares and the payment of dividends; in short, they were entrusted with the financial administration of the firm. What used to be a personal connection between the banker and the manager of the business firm was gradually superseded by a quantitatively enlarged and qualitatively integrated network of relations based on objective requirements. In fact, funds concentrated in banks contained a large proportion that could, at any moment, be converted into the equity of a joint-stock enterprise.

Even if funds lent by the bank were sunk in the company's incremental fixed capital, the bank could always earn more than enough for having involved itself in the process of issuing the company's new shares. In fact, German banks did frequently lend a large amount of funds to finance the customer firm's fixed investment with the proviso that when the bank therewith opened an account subject to overdraft [*Kontokorrentverkehr*], it could closely scrutinise the company's internal management in return. Thus, banks no longer restricted themselves to short-term lending for the purpose of facilitating the circulation of commodities, as had been the case with the business finance of an individually owned firm; they responded to a much broader range of credit requirements, which also rebounded to the great advantage of the joint-stock company.

Thus, the bank willingly began to take part in the business of issuing new shares. The business of issuing and underwriting shares as well as bonds and debentures did indeed become an extremely important function of German banks. By this time the relationship of banks to joint-stock companies was no longer external or 'at arm's length' as it had previously been, when enterprises were individually owned and operated. For the banks, which looked after the overall credit needs of the enterprise, had to hold its newly issued shares at least for some period of time. Nor could such banks exclusively depend on deposits to finance such a burden; hence they needed to increase their own capital. This increase in capital was made possible, in part, by sharing in the founder's profit [*Gründungsgewinn*] of their client firms and, in part, by the commissions that banks earned from the business of issuing and underwriting new issues.* In other words, the activity of bank-capital extended from a mediating role in the buying and selling of funds as commodities, to the selling of capital as a commodity. In the former activity, banks earned the interest differential between the rates on loans and the rates on deposits as profit on their own capital, though the money value so earned was extremely small relative to that of either the loan or the deposits. In the latter activity, banks went beyond mediation in the buying and selling of funds, and sought the founder's profit [*Gründungsgewinn*], which both required and entailed a considerable commitment of their own capital. As a matter of fact, if banks merely contented themselves with lending, they would not easily have realised an average profit. If they merely earned commissions for mediating the issue of securities, the increase of their own capital would still have been limited. However, the service of underwriting new shares was more than simply offering the mediator's service to a large number of investors who had limited knowledge of the enterprise. Banks invested on their behalf because they were privy to 'insider knowledge'. Not only when they assisted a company already well known to them in the process of increasing their capital, but also when they promoted the founding of a new company, there too they took the long view of their future association with that firm, rather than merely focusing on a consideration of the immediate return. Banks, thus, gradually evolved enduring relations with specific industrial firms.** For example, those companies that expanded during the prosperity phase with the assistance of a particular bank became totally dependent on it in the ensuing depression phase, when they needed to contract their business. Nor could the bank leave them to their own devices. Thus, the relation between a particular bank and its client companies had to become significantly closer. Thus, to quote from Jeidels, 'The banks must become bedfellows of the industrial enterprises from their birth to their death, i.e., from their inauguration to their dissolution. The banks must look after both the day-to-day and the emergency finance of these enterprises, throughout their lives and on all occasions, while sharing in their business profits'.[9] It, thus, became a routine practice for banks to send directors to their affiliated companies, the duty of which it was to supervise their managerial policies.***

* In England, this kind of mediation was undertaken by specialised financial houses rather than ordinary commercial banks. In Germany, however, banks, especially large ones, underwrote the issuing of shares as well as of public bonds from early times. This was a significant difference between the two countries. However, the reason that German banks tied up their funds for the period between the acceptance and the sale to the public of shares was not simply to wait strategically for a more favourable market or to attempt to monopolise the founder's gain. German law prohibited the release of shares in the stock exchange for one year subsequent to the conversion of an individually owned enterprise into a joint-stock company.[10]

** The relation between banks and business enterprises was certainly not a temporary one, whereby banks profited by offering the service of financial mediation or monopolised the founder's gain, once and for all. To see the matter in that way is to miss the fundamental character of finance-capital. The latter would not have come into being if banking and industry benefited from each other only from time to time, without forging an enduring relationship between themselves. The conditions in Germany differed from those in the United States, where individual financiers and promoters played prominent roles, in that the connection between banks and business companies proved much more cohesive and permanent. It was for this reason that even though the general direction of economic development was the same in both countries, finance-capital established itself more typically in Germany.

9   Jeidels 1913, p. 50.
10   See Hilferding 1981, p. 128n25.

*** On this point, see Hilferding 1981, p. 121. In some instances, directors were sent from industrial firms to banks rather than the other way round. However, such directors did not seem to have exerted the same degree of power and influence as the ones who were sent to industrial enterprises by the banks.[11]

The banks did not form such close connections with a single business enterprise at random; they did so with many firms belonging to a variety of related industries or to a given region. Thus, a bank may have, by tradition, dealt with a group of firms in a particular line of business clustering around it. In such a case, the competition among the firms of the group became subject to regulation by the bank. A bank which was capable of organising a group of industrial and commercial firms under its wing was bound to be one of those few leading banks that had the capacity to mobilise a substantial amount of capital. Hence, its influence on the firms of the group was likely to become overwhelming, and could often lead to the formation of a cartel-like organisation, which excluded competition among its members. The bank did not benefit from cutthroat competition among the firms under its own control, since, regardless of the outcome, such rivalries typically squandered resources. The directors sent by the bank to the firms of the group played an important role in at least restraining unnecessary competition even if they fell short of actively guiding the future goals of the firms.

The form of joint-stock company enabled business firms to achieve a very large size. Correspondingly, banks too were obliged to grow in size, normally by amalgamation, a tendency which became decisive as banks became progressively more involved with industrial finance. The close ties between large banks and large business enterprises generated benefits which small regional banks and firms could not enjoy, so that the smaller entities, in each case, tended to be eliminated. Therefore, eventually a few large banks, with main offices located near financial centres tended to dominate the whole nation with their networks of branches. These large banks often syndicated themselves in such businesses as the issuing of shares. Their co-operation became even more conspicuous in international banking, which developed together with overseas investment.[12] Banks, which dealt in financial services, were not constrained by any specific use-value as were industrial firms, which made them less prone to competition and more attuned to mutual accommodation. Hence, more often than not, they worked together in pursuit of monopoly profits.* That is the

---

11   See Riesser 1912, p. 303.
12   Jeidels 1913, pp. 97–80.

reason why banks played a crucial role in the unfolding of this new stage of capitalism. As already mentioned, however, it was industrial development, especially in those heavy industries which required a massive investment of fixed
capital, that gave banking this new role. As the form of the joint-stock company
spread in manufacturing, banks found lucrative opportunities in industrial finance, and grew into finance-capital. All this, in the final analysis, came from the
need on the part of industrial companies to concentrate resources.

*On this point Hilferding writes as follows: 'Competition on the money market, how-
ever, is essentially different from that on the commodity market. The most important
difference is that on the money market capital has always the form of money, whereas
on the commodity market it must first be converted from commodity capital into
money capital, and this implies that the conversion may miscarry, that the commodity capital may decline in value, resulting in a loss rather than a profit. In commodity
competition it is a matter of realising capital, not only of realising value. In the competition of money capital the capital itself is secure and it is only a matter of the level of
value it attains, the level of interest. But interest is determined in such a way as to leave
the individual competitors very little room for manoeuvre. It is primarily the discount
policy of the central financial institutions which determines the situation for everyone
else and sets rather narrow limits to their freedom of action'.[13] So far as I can see, this
explanation fails completely to clarify the real situation. What is traded in the money
market is 'funds as commodities', and not capital. These funds are by no means certain to become capital. When funds are traded as commodities, the rates of interest, or
their prices, fluctuate accordingly. Interest rates fall if the supply of funds exceeds the
demand for them. Even the discount policy of the central monetary authority cannot
ignore this fact. It is certainly not the central bank that sets the level of interest. One
must first of all understand that funds as commodities are not produced in response
to the demand for their peculiar use-value, but are generated from the circular motion
of capital, as its by-product, regardless of the demand for funds. Even in more contingent cases, in which idle money originating elsewhere in society is commodified in the
old-fashioned way by money-lending capital, funds will still remain special commodities, the supply of which cannot be adjusted to the intensity of demand. Therefore,
their prices, or the rates of interest, fluctuate according to the vagaries of the market, in
each of its differentiated sections, i.e. depending on conditions specific to the particular
periods and ratings of credit. Secondly, what is bought and sold in the capital market,
which emerges beside, and in close connection with, the money market, is 'capital as a
commodity', be it in the form of shares or of bonds. These securities are not producible

13   Hilferding 1981, pp. 178–9.

use-values, nor are their prices simply rates of interest, as in the case of loans (loanable funds), which are dependent on the prevailing conditions of the money market. Bonds and shares are traded in the capital market according to their fictitious values, i.e. the capitalised values of incomes as they reflect the rate of interest already formed in the money market. In this way, the capital market differs from either the commodity or the money market. The capital market competes with the money market for available funds, since the issue of securities will be the easier the more funds can be drawn into investment-capital rather than remaining as loan-capital. Now, according to Hilferding: 'In industry, it is necessary to distinguish between the technical and the economic aspects of competition, but in the case of the banks, technical differences play a minor part and banks of the same type use the same technical methods ... Here there is only an economic, purely quantitative, difference which involves simply the size of their competing capitals'.[14] In this passage again, Hilferding does not clearly distinguish between 'funds' and 'capital', nor does he comprehend that the 'technical aspect of competition' has to do with the nature of the real commodities traded. He, therefore, sees no distinction between the 'money market' and the 'capital market'.

Hilferding follows Marx in not distinguishing these two markets. That, however, makes it impossible for him to understand why the banks' own capital increases along with the increase of their activities in issuing and underwriting shares. The distinction is also important in clarifying the relationship between the rate of interest, which is determined in the money market, and the banks' part in the issuing of industrial shares in the capital market. This is the relation that Hilferding tries unsuccessfully to explain.[15]

C   *The Joint-Stock Company as Means of Concentrating Managerial Control*

As mentioned earlier, the shareholders of a joint-stock firm divide themselves into those who merely aim at receiving dividends periodically and those who dictate the management of the enterprise permanently. This tendency reinforces itself as the enterprise increasingly makes use of society's investment funds concentrated in the hands of banks. Ordinary shareholders tend to occupy a position similar to that of loan-capitalists, by simply buying shares at market prices from the banks which underwrite them. Large shareholders, in contrast, not only speak for the company but also exert increasing control over an enormous concentration of capital in the company, even though they themselves have invested a relatively small proportion of it. The so-called

---

14   Hilferding 1981, p. 179.
15   Hilferding 1981, pp. 177–8.

'democratisation' of capital, which refers to the mobilisation of investible funds even from the smallest of their savers is, in fact, nothing more than the cunning device of capital to achieve, in the first instance, the separation of 'the control' from 'the ownership' of society's investible funds concentrated under the name of the company. Not that 'the concentration of control' in the hands of the large shareholders does not presuppose 'some concentration of private wealth (which enables them to hold a majority of shares)'; for the latter always remains the natural goal of the capitalist. Yet, instead of achieving that goal directly, capital intends to achieve it through the 'concentration of control'. This circuitous route, which enables capital to control more than it owns, proves to be the more efficient way for capital to self-augment.

Large shareholders, who are in control, enforce the company's policy of dividend distribution, often at the expense of ordinary shareholders, as the firm retains its net earnings instead of paying them out as dividends. The joint-stock company thus aims at accumulating as much of its retained earnings as possible by way of 'the concentration of control', since their more 'democratic' dispersion in the form of dividends to all shareholders may not result in as much concentrated savings immediately convertible into the firm's investment (accumulation of capital).* Even in the near term, while the amount of retained earnings still remains insufficient for immediate investment, the policy of withholding its earnings in a liquid form makes the joint-stock company quite resistant to the vagaries of business fluctuations. Not only can the firm turn this feature to its advantage in competition, but it can also fall back on the same feature when its operation earns little or no profit for an extended period of time. For instance, the ordinary shareholders can be made to bear a major part of the burden, when the company undergoes adjustments and reorganisation to prepare for future competition. Of course, the large shareholders too must bear their share of that cost, it is true; but, as those who are permanently in charge of the running of the firm, they escape with much less hardship than what they would sustain were they the mere individual proprietors of the firm. Needless to say, the banks which assist the firm in this process are allied with the large shareholders, with whom they share the same destiny.

* As a joint-stock company accumulates its own capital, it tends to convert its equity into debentures. In other words, it takes advantage of debt-financing. That occurs, of course, only up to a certain point, since, for a joint-stock company, debt finance is always a subsidiary method. A joint-stock company is quite different from a state enterprise, which may depend totally on public bond financing. It operates basically on its own capital, the control of which has been delegated by many investing owners to a small number of controlling owners. The recent trend for state enterprises to multiply

and to exhibit tendencies dissimilar to what is normally expected of finance-capital is an interesting theme to consider. It may perhaps even clarify an economic aspect of Nazism. The relation between finance-capital and Nazism is, of course, not simple. About so-called 'state-monopoly capitalism', I shall state my strictly tentative view in the appendix to this book.

In actual practice, the diffusion of the joint-stock system goes hand in hand with the enlargement in size of each individual company, and with the reinforcement of the tendency towards the separation of ordinary from large shareholders. It, furthermore, enables one company to own shares of another (subsidiary) company, which then owns shares of yet another and so on, until one powerful company achieves dominance over many subsidiaries by means of holding the majority shares of the latter. Thus, the separation of management from ownership soon becomes both systematic and irrevocable. A small number of very large capitalists manage and control not only the company in which they have their own stakes, but also other companies in which that company owns a majority of shares as the parent company [*Beteiligung*]. Alternatively, they may form and rule over a co-ordinated group of companies [*Interessenge-meinshaften*], by letting these companies mutually hold shares of one another. The development of such complex structures makes it possible for a small number of large capitalists, with a relatively small original investment, to control an enormous sum of capital. They thus systematically concentrate the control of businesses in their hands, while a large number of ordinary shareholders sink to the status of mere dividend receivers. The management of the company now belongs quasi-permanently to the large capitalists, and this also has effects on the managerial organisation of the company. For, more often than not, a class of (hired) professional managers emerges in service of the large shareholders, since the latter, with extensive interests, cannot in practice supervise the whole operation, which is theoretically under their personal command. They, therefore, require the assistance of skilled professionals.

In this way, what used to be the task of individual entrepreneurs, who, in the age of industrial capitalism, guided society's reproduction-process, has now become the function of business organisations placed under the command of 'large capitalists'. The class of capitalists is divided into a larger group of ordinary shareholders, who no longer act as real capitalists, and who differ but little from the holders of deposits with a bank, and those few large capitalists who ultimately control the companies with the assistance of the professional managers whom they hire. This tendency sometimes appears to support the half-truth that the control of a company is now divorced from the ownership of its capital. It is, indeed, true that the control is not in direct proportion to the ownership of capital, inasmuch as the large shareholders, with a relatively small investment of capital, control an enormous sum of it, whether they manage the company themselves or delegate that operation to hired professionals. All of this results, however, from the 'concentration of the controlling power' amongst the shareholders; it does not imply the 'independence of control from ownership'. Furthermore, the evolution of such a complex structure itself originates in the radically altered conditions of the direct production-process; and the latter in turn accelerated the course of centralisation, in which large capitals devoured small. The evolution of capitalist control in management merely reflects changes in the capitalist reproduction-process, to the extent that the latter still presupposes the capitalist form of ownership. I will show later that such things as the evolution of *cartels* and *syndicates* in Germany, the spread and strengthening of *trusts* in the United States, and the like, are all but specific instances of the concentration of controlling-power over the capitalist reproduction-process, which was made possible by the form of the joint-stock company.

It is important to stress, however, that concentration of the controlling-power over the capitalist reproduction-process did not evolve in all industries uniformly, but impacted specifically on such heavy industries as iron-and-steel, in which the method of managing the finance of production required enlarged capitalist organisations. It was this characteristic that defined the new stage of capitalism. Indeed, in such heavy industries, the traditional method of production-finance, which earlier depended on loan-capital (i.e. on the method of securing a capitalist-social utilisation of the idle funds that the motion of industrial capital by itself generated), proved inadequate. In the new stage of capitalism, all of society's monetary savings (investible funds) had to be mobilised, partly as equity capital for use by large firms in heavy industries, and partly as loan-capital for use by smaller firms in other more traditional industries. The new credit system which then evolved embodied a hierarchical structure, in which monopoly organisations dominated small firms, and in which a small number of large capitalists had privileged access to these funds. They were the ones who controlled that new system, positioning themselves more and more distantly from the direct process of production. The so-called *Konzern** (or combine) represented, concretely, this type of social structure within a group of firms in different industries.

---

* The word 'Konzern' has been in wide use since the meteoric rise of the Stinnes Konzern during the inflationary period in post-WWI Germany. It did not originally refer to a proper monopoly organisation such as a trust or cartel. The Stinnes family, which had started in the riparian transportation business along the Rhine in the

nineteenth century, branched out into coal, iron and steel, and, by the time of the post-war inflation, possessed controlling interests in virtually all industries. It formed an alliance with Siemens and Schuckert to establish an organisation called the Siemens-Rheinelbe-Schuckert Union, which then dominated German industry. Although the Stinnes Konzern, through its member firms, exerted a powerful influence over cartels and other monopoly organisations, its real character lay in its control of major firms in virtually all fields, from heavy industry to transportation and communication, from banking to newspapers, and so on. Because of its fame and its background, which was specific to the German economic conditions of that time, it was thought that Konzern was a form of monopoly organisation that would necessarily accompany the development of the joint-stock company system. The Stinnes Konzern itself, however, collapsed when the postwar inflation was brought under control, as its success presumably owed much to inflationary conditions. Yet the term Konzern, in the broader sense of a 'centrally controlled group of firms operating in a number of different industries', can probably be applied to the Japanese *zaibatsu*, and to such American financial conglomerates as the Morgan group and others.

The issue here, however, is not merely that industrial enterprises assumed the joint-stock (or corporate) form. For one joint-stock company can be controlled by another joint-stock company, which can then be controlled by yet another, in a process that not only extends the managerial control of the firm at the top, but also accords to it an increasing financial leverage. Thus, the power centre tends to distance itself more and more from the down-to-earth level of real reproduction-process, such that it appears as if the control of the direct production-process had become quite remote from the ownership of capital. As pointed out earlier, however, the full control of the management of industry is never achieved under the capitalist form of the joint-stock company. This form only gives rise to *finance-capital*, the type of capital which becomes dominant at a definite stage of development of capitalism, and which exemplifies a historically particular mode of accumulation, in the same way as merchant capital and industrial capital did in their respective stages. Finance-capital must, therefore, be understood as the historically dominant form of capital in the age of heavy industries and monopoly organisations, i.e. in the final stage of development of capitalism. One must not conceive of it as, in any sense, transcending capitalism, even though overindulgence in the legal formalisms of the joint-stock system might induce one to do so.

3   The Mode of Accumulation of Finance-Capital

The accumulation of merchant capital, which represented the mercantilist age, stood on the formation and centralisation of capital, based largely on the expropriation of small producers, while the accumulation of industrial capital, which subsequently represented the liberal era, stood rather on the concentration of capital consequent upon the growth of individual capitalist firms, based on what Marx called the 'exploitation of wage-workers' in the direct production-process. The difference was that the former had to enforce the commodification of labour-power by primitive means, whereas the latter could count on the same to be ensured within the autonomous operation of the capitalist reproduction-process itself. Yet capitalism, in its later development, required fixed capital in great bulk in order to produce required commodities, particularly in heavy industries, and that entailed a new mode of accumulation that was predicated upon the ability of capital to centralise (mobilise and polarise) investment funds in large amounts from the very outset. Needless to say, even the accumulation of industrial capital (in the liberal era) occasionally resorted to centralisation (by way of annexation and amalgamation of unsuccessful firms), but this typically occurred during the depression phase of business cycles. In contrast, finance-capital rather enforced its accumulation, after having mobilised dispersed investment funds in society within the joint-stock firms under its control. It, in other words, did not work from the outside of the direct reproduction-process, as merchant capital had done before. It rather combined its accumulation with the centralisation of investible funds which had arisen within society's reproduction-process. This, in effect, indicated the fact that with the advent of heavy industries which required a massive advance of fixed capital, the mode of accumulation of capital (and the conversion of labour-power into a commodity which constitutes its reverse side) had to undergo a definitive mutation, thus marking a new stage of development of capitalism, distinct from either the mercantilist or the liberal stage.

Capitalist enterprises now tended to produce on a large-scale especially in such heavy industries as required massive investment of fixed capital. In so doing, moreover, they also took advantage of the form of the joint-stock company. Under these circumstances, the generation of relative surplus population, consequent upon the sharp rise in the organic composition of capital, was greatly enhanced. The fact that production on a large-scale, involving a heavy investment of fixed capital, could be relatively easily realised by the mobilisation (centralisation) of investible funds that had been formed in widely dispersed sections of society implies, in the first instance, that the expanded reproduction was no longer constrained by the accumulation of individual capitalists. That was not all. Neither was the adoption of a technically improved method of production constrained by the existing fixed capital, as it would have been with the individually owned capitalist enterprises. For, in principle, a new company could always be started up, which would already be equipped with the new technical method. Of course, no capital could wholly escape the general trend towards 'rationalisation' in periods of depression; but if there were a good enough business prospect, it need not, in principle, be deterred from adopting a new technique at any time by way of establishing a separate company. The uninterrupted improvement in technical methods of production, to which capitalism always aspires, could thus become reality once capital had been freed from the constraints to which individually owned enterprises were subject. The latter could expand their production only within the capacity of their existing fixed capital, and only to the extent that they had saved their own accumulation funds for its renovation, although these could, in some cases, be supplemented by the circulation-credit made available capitalist-socially to industrial firms. It was mainly in the depression period of business cycles that such firms could renovate their plants and equipment, and thereby raise the value composition of capital. However, finance-capital transcended these limitations because it was always capable of adopting a new technique and of incessantly raising the organic composition of capital. Yet, if that were indeed the case, a chronic tendency for the working population to be in excess supply would also arise, unless capital grew at an even speedier pace to absorb it.

The tendency just explained has another aspect to it as well. For the adoption of a new method of production by progressive firms does not always lead to the downfall of lagging firms. Nor does such decisive improvement or progress in industrial technology occur all the time.* As producing firms tend to operate on a large-scale, they can adopt a new method in only part of their operation; and if they have a monopoly power in the market, they can so price their product as to enable them to continue to exploit the older method alongside the new one. They can even delay the adoption of the new method by protecting it with a patent for their exclusive use. Even without relying on such a stratagem, they can exert a monopoly or competitive power, as the case may be, with a view to manipulating the market to their advantage. In all cases, they may insist upon utilising their old plants and equipment for so long as they can profitably do so. At the same time, the increased production of these large firms can lead to the employment of more workers, even though the firm has adopted a new, labour-saving method of production in one segment of its operations. In such a case, the firm in question does not necessarily contribute to create an excess supply of the working population.

* Capital does not itself explore or develop a new technique or method of production. Even if it is invented or discovered in a research centre or institute owned by capital, it is still adopting that which emerged outside its own capitalist activity. There should be no confusion about this point.

Thus, there are two opposite aspects to the situation: on the one hand, large firms intend to constantly improve upon their method of production, as part of their drive for the 'rationalisation' of their operation; and, on the other, they also wish to utilise their present plants and equipment for as long a time as possible. The one aspect prevails over the other, depending on the state of affairs in which they find themselves currently, and also on the way in which the operations of the firm are allocated to different branches of industry. In the final analysis, however, the determining factor may be said to hinge upon the interests of the banks involved there. For capitalist society derives its maximum benefit when the banks, which have extensively mobilised idle (investible) funds from all segments of society, pursue the most lucrative utilisation of these funds as capital. In this regard, the 'capital market', as it is closely linked with the 'money market', plays the central role in co-ordinating the relationships among individual enterprises and among different industries, by letting them compete intensely with one another. This co-ordination in the capital market is accomplished, and is supported, by the constant tendency for labour-power to be supplied in excess, which allows capital to employ it on the most advantageous terms. Here again, the allocation of capital is not fully regulated or comprehensively controlled in society. Yet, unlike industrial capital, which accumulates in an essentially autonomous way, and lets its pace of expansion and contraction in each industry be regulated externally (and *ex post facto*) by loan-capital, finance-capital interferes directly (and *ex ante facto*) in the allocation of the funds to be invested as capital in different branches of industry. This co-ordination, or social allocation, of capital does not, of course, occur independently of the money market; and, thus, it cannot be said to be directly regulated by society. In other words, even in the capitalist-social co-ordination, capital cannot ultimately transcend its roots in private property, which persist not only in its relation with wage-labour but also in the interrelation amongst its own individual units. What distinguishes this new system from the practice of the age of industrial capital is that the money market and the capital market are closely connected in such a way as to share the same funds with each other – so much so that fictitious capital becomes directly comparable to loan-capital. This fact greatly affects the phenomenon of industrial crisis in the imperialist age. For the typical process observed in the age of industrial capital, in which the money market foretold the onset of the excess of capital with a sharp rise in the rate of interest, is now no longer applicable.

It goes without saying, and that should be obvious from what has been said, that industrial crises do not disappear in the age of imperialism. For there is always a limit to the ability of specific industries and individual firms to mobilise unemployed workers, even though their collective action has created the so-called industrial reserve army. At the society-wide level, firms are often saddled with excessive commodity outputs, whether in the form of means of production or of articles of consumption, which they cannot transform into capital. The chronic problem for industries and firms, which, rather than being alleviated, may be indeed exacerbated by virtue of the fact that they are financially regulated, resides in the difficulty of finding reliable outlets for their products. They are caught here in the double-bind of an overpopulation of workers, on the one hand, and an over-production of commodities, on the other. Yet, if an external factor, such as the opening up of a new market, complicates this state of affairs, a speculative boom, entailing the start-up of new firms, may suddenly flare up in the capital market, igniting a frenzy that is far more furious than anything seen in the age of industrial capital. Even in the absence of an external disturbance, if the prospect for profit suddenly wanes for whatever contingent reason, a collapse in share prices will follow as the money market draws funds away from the capital market. Such circumstances do not fail to disrupt the periodicity of economic crises, which was more clearly observable in the age of industrial capital. The expansion of output by industrial firms, constituted as joint-stock companies, is no longer strictly constrained by the periodic adoption of new techniques in the depression phase of business cycles, and this alone is sufficient to account for the disappearance of the periodicity in the occurrence of industrial crises. However, for the same reason, the explanation of prosperity, too, must often be sought in contingent factors, which are external to the actual process of capital accumulation. Moreover, since the source of idle (investible) funds, which the money market regulates no longer necessarily springs from the motion of industrial capital, finance-capital, rather than loan-capital, now regulates finance, with the inevitable consequence that the dynamics of capitalist development too must depend upon the initiatives of finance-capital.

The development of industrial firms as joint-stock companies thus necessarily entailed the switchover of the dominant type of capital from industrial to finance-capital in the imperialist era. This transfer, however, did not occur expeditiously in a country like Britain, in which industrial capital had earlier established its undisputed sway, as has already been pointed out. In Britain, as will be detailed later, the investment of capital abroad was already beginning to play an important role during the heyday of industrial capital. Moreover, the accumulation of capital by individual entrepreneurs in industry retained lasting importance there. These circumstances retarded the adoption of the form of joint-stock company until quite late in the nineteenth century; and, even then, its adoption was not pursued as thoroughly and vigorously as in Germany. The fact that investment in a joint-stock company hinges on the mobilisation of idle funds arising in the hands of all social strata, and not specifically on the behaviour of accumulating industrialists suggests that its surge would tend to be restrained, in one way or another, in a country already attuned to overseas investment. In contrast, Germany's process of capitalist development involved extensive mechanisation of the factory even in the initial phase of implanting light industries and, within two or three decades, shifted its focus to heavy industries which required a massive investment of fixed capital. The adoption of the form of the joint-stock company was, in this context, quite natural. Germany, as a latecomer to capitalism, could utilise that form extensively even in its early capitalist development. Although it commenced its overseas investment much later than Great Britain and other advanced nations, Germany caught up with them very rapidly, once finance-capital established itself there.

These circumstances also suggested some important social factors peculiar to Germany. So far as Britain was concerned, because it had undergone primitive accumulation in the age of merchant capital, it could, in the end, realise the most typical development of industrial capital, under the regime of which the whole society tended towards a purely capitalist society. Capitalism could then penetrate even agriculture, while the members of society divided themselves, more or less neatly, into the three major classes of capitalists, workers and landlords. Germany, where capitalism started late, did not reproduce this pattern. For the very process of separating industry from agriculture could be expedited by the powerful operation of mechanised modern industry, which enabled capital to acquire a large enough population of wage-workers without depending on mercantilist policies. Neither did the dissolution of the old social relations have to be as radical as in Britain in order to launch modern industry. Not even the mild policy of the kind espoused by List was really necessary, since an adequate number of industrial workers could easily be generated without eradicating traditional agriculture. Thus from early on, the accelerated development in Germany relied on the presence of firms organised as joint-stock companies which strengthened its industrial foundations, enabling that nation to promptly shift its focus from light to heavy works, and that, in the process, gave birth to finance-capital. Under this dominant form of capital, a surplus population was always retained in agriculture or in petty industrial operations, which were then plagued with so-called 'disguised unemployment'. A *dual eco-*

nomy thus emerged, in which a highly modernised industrial sector coexisted alongside the remnants of the past. This does not imply, however, that Britain was always free from such residues from the past. On the contrary, once industrial capital began to be overpowered by finance-capital, whether due to its expansion in overseas market or not, the erstwhile tendency of capitalism to rid itself of contingent impurities in its development had to be reversed even in Britain. Under finance-capital, capitalism no longer tended towards a purely capitalist society.*

* As pointed out in the introduction of this book, the reversal of the tendency towards a purely capitalist society reflects the fact that capitalism is by no means a permanent form of society, but instead a historical one beginning at a given time and coming to an end at another. Capitalism never actually realises its own ideal image; it most certainly does not do so in its early and late stage of development. Even in its most adequate middle stage, the approach of real capitalism to its ideal image cannot realistically be expected to consummate itself. Indeed, the stage of the typical development of industrial capital occurred only in Britain, when that nation became the 'factory of the world' and was surrounded by other countries which remained predominantly agricultural. This means that the ideal image described by theory was only approximately played out by the capitalism of that time. On the other hand, as has been explained in the text, the advent of finance-capital does not completely suspend the features typical of the age of industrial capital. Even as the liberal tendencies of that age were reversed, much of their imprints remained and could not be completely eliminated. The complexity of the historical process must be taken fully into account; it must not be mechanically oversimplified.

Thus, the pursuit of monopoly profit by finance-capital cannot be reduced to the simple case of any capital with monopoly power seeking a maximum profit. It stands on very particular historical and social circumstances, the characteristics of which consist of securing the conversion of labour-power into a commodity against the background of the constantly present relative surplus population. Finance-capital can enforce an intensification of labour* in the factories under its control, because agriculture and petty industrial operations are always suffused with surplus population; it can also wrest the profit accruing to these surviving traditional sectors by resorting to monopoly pricing of one sort or another. It can, as well, expropriate all industrial firms unprotected by a monopoly power, especially the outsiders without strong connections to its monopoly organisations. It goes without saying, however, that there always exists a limit to the practice of profiting by expropriation, be that due to the monopoly pricing of commodities or to the intensification of labour; for even a monopoly cannot overcome receding demand and falling efficiency. The maximum of the monopoly gain that a firm can expect to earn can sometimes be known to it in advance, though not to all firms, nor to society as a whole. Thus, competition intensifies even among the largest firms, or groups of firms, possessed of strong monopoly power. It is due to this fact that the centralisation of capital (resulting from the stronger capital gobbling up the weaker ones) persists even at this stage of the development of capitalism.

*Against the monopoly power of large enterprises, the workers themselves set up an organised movement, which without question succeeded in restricting monopoly profits to some extent. At the same time, the so-called *sozialpolitik* may have intervened between capital and the working class by playing a mediating role. Incidentally, the term 'monopoly capital' is rather frequently applied to the 'big businesses' in recent times. The word is used politically with a view to mobilising the middle classes against it rather than strictly as a technical term in economics. One has to be careful, however, in the use of such a subtle term. If, for example, the goal of the socialist movement is narrowly focused on criticising the unfair profiteering of monopoly capital, there is a danger that the movement will lose sight of its original aim, namely the abolition of capitalism itself. The leadership of the movement may then be shifted away from the proletariat to all sorts of non-descript, anti-monopoly groups in society.

There is another important aspect of the development of finance-capital to consider. It not only reverses the one-way tendency to dissolve traditional (pre-capitalist) social relations, which prevailed in the age of industrial capital; but it also tends to conceal the social relations actually in place among different interest-groups, burying them underneath the vicissitudes of the securities market. This is due to the fact that finance-capital, in the course of its accumulation, creates a mass of salaried workers and other similarly dependent social strata, while pumping their idle funds into its own hands in order to control them as if they were its own. The strident condemnation of finance-capital for its outrageous profiteering, whether through the questionable management of companies or through the doubtful machinations in the securities market, obscures reality even further. In the end, a fantasy is generated to the effect that, if restrained and held within proper bounds, finance-capital could represent the interest of the nation or of the state. Thus, just as in the age of mercantilism, when political power easily turned into economic power, the age of imperialism may be viewed as standing on a social ground which is likely to turn economic power directly into political power.

CHAPTER 8

Multiple Faces of Finance-Capital

Just as merchant capital, which guided the era of mercantilist policies, found its most concrete expression in the woollen industry of early-modern Britain, so did industrial capital, which defined the general trend of the liberal age, leave its mark most decisively on the British cotton industry of the mid-nineteenth century. In a similar manner, it can be said that finance-capital, which drove the age of imperialism, proved to be most at home in the German heavy industries at the turn of the century. Yet, it so happens that, whereas the world-historic stages of both mercantilism and liberalism could most typically be represented by Britain alone, that of imperialism required several players, as indeed has been pointed out, since Germany and the United States, which had emerged as late-starters in capitalism, confronted Britain as its vigorously competing powers on the international scene. Conflicts among the capitalist states thus became an essential feature of imperialism, with Germany in particular going on the offensive, while Britain adopted a more defensive posture. Accordingly, in this chapter, I cannot exclusively privilege the heavy industries of Germany as the sole context in which finance-capital exhibited its stage-typical operation. Recall that finance-capital, as the most developed and, hence, the dominant form of capital in the imperialist age, was still fundamentally characterised by its readiness to control the capitalist reproduction-process upon which it was based, while yet disengaging itself to some extent therefrom.* Thus, if the connection of finance and production can most clearly be illustrated in the development of the German heavy industries, that fact does not in any way exclude the possibility that finance-capital might manifest itself differently in Britain, operating in a space somewhat dissociated from its national productive base. In the United States, on the other hand, because of its historical and geographic peculiarities, the development of capitalism does not provide as sharply delineated a picture of the stage-theoretic features of imperialism as do the cases of Germany and Britain. Yet, the American case is of enough importance that it cannot be summarily dismissed. Therefore, in what follows, I must outline, if briefly, the multiple faces of finance-capital. I will first describe the central role played by German finance-capital, as it developed *monopoly organisations* mainly in heavy industries, and then the subsidiary role played by finance-capital of Great Britain with its highly distinctive features will follow. Finally, I will not neglect to pay due attention to the finance-capital of America, as it developed its endemic monopoly institutions.

*In theory, merchant-capital (M–C–M′) presents itself as the first form of capital, which is followed by money-lending capital (M ... M′), and subsequently by industrial capital (M–C ... P ... C′–M′). Capitalism begins, however, only as industrial capital commences its action, at which point the other two forms of capital become subsidiary to it as commercial capital (M–C–M′) and loan-capital (M ... M′). From a historical perspective, however, it was merchant capital (M–C–M′) that first emerged as the dominant form of accumulation in the early stage of capitalist development, then came industrial capital (M–C ... P ... C′–M′) in the middle stage, and, finally, finance-capital (M ... M′) in the declining stage. This historical sequence does not correspond with the theoretical (logical) one, nor do commercial and loan-capital in theory have any direct bearing on merchant capital and finance-capital in history. Yet finance-capital may nevertheless be viewed in some sense as a concrete-historical manifestation of what I call in theory 'automatically interest-bearing capital', which is, by far, the most sophisticated (or synthetic) form of capital, having itself become a commodity in the form of an automatically interest-bearing asset (which appears to be the furthest away from the production-process), in much the same way as land, once commodified, may be regarded to be an asset that automatically bears rent.[1] Thus, this relationship between interest-bearing capital and finance-capital can be understood in parallel with the relationship between merchant capital *in theory* and merchant capital *in history* (and with the relationship between industrial capital *in theory* and industrial capital *in history*). The fact that merchant, industrial and finance-capital appeared successively in history as the dominant types of capital, however, cannot be logically explained. It was the real historical conditions that assigned to each of the three theoretical capital-forms the concrete-specific ways in which to play the dominant role in the three historical stages of capitalist development. From this point of view, Hilferding's statement – 'Bank capital was the negation of usurer's capital and is itself negated by finance-capital'[2] – cannot be supported at all. Usurer capital does not, by its own logic, turn into bank capital, nor does the latter turn into finance-capital. Finance-capital appears only when the capitalist production of use-values physically develops into a new stage. The correct way to understand its emergence is that finance-capital replaced industrial capital when industrial supremacy passed from lighter industries, centred on cotton, to heavier ones, centred on iron-and-steel.

Thus, the issue here is whether industrial capital, which we claim forms the theoretical basis of capitalism in general, has the capacity within itself to logically develop into finance-capital. Actually, not even the theoretical concept of automatically interest-bearing capital possesses such a virtue, even though, once in existence, finance-capital

1   See Uno 1980, pp. 115 f.
2   Hilferding 1981, p. 226.

may be said to have its theoretical base in that concept. This is what is meant by my claim that finance-capital can be interpreted as a stage-theoretic manifestation of automatically interest-bearing capital. The same considerations should apply to both merchant and industrial capital as the stage-theoretically dominant forms of capital accumulation. It is not justified to simply confound the historical and the logical process, nor is it meaningful to 'unify history and theory' directly without explicating how they are related to each other. History, too, in some instances, exhibits abstract-theoretical features, so that not all historical processes can be adequately described by concrete-specific details alone. To me, however, it is not possible to explicate dialectically the relationship of the three (historically) dominant forms of capital, for each of these capitals confronts a different type of 'real' production-process (involving different types of use-values). There cannot be any abstract logic relating merchant, industrial and finance-capital with one another as stage-theoretically dominant forms of capital.

1   The Development of Monopoly Organisations in and around the Heavy Industries in Germany

Most of the monopoly organisations in Germany developed in the second half of the 1870s and thereafter, as the exceptional boom of the early 1870s suddenly collapsed into a slump with the crisis of 1873. It is often said that iron-makers had established a cartel as early as in the 1850s, and the producers of alum even earlier in the 1830s and 1840s. Yet many such early cartels, which operated before the 1860s, were apparently formed due to circumstances specific to the individual member-firms involved, and were generally small and local in their operation.[3] After the late 1870s, however, what used to be short-lived cartels were extended repeatedly, gaining organisational strength at every renewal of the contract. The number of cartels, too, increased as they spread well beyond the mining sector, in which they may have had the power of natural monopoly, into a wide range of important (manufacturing) industries, particularly into heavier ones.* Most cartels were at first devised to overcome adversities in periods of depression; but, in the late 1880s and in the second half of the 1890s, they were adopted even in periods of prosperity.** Furthermore, the contents of the cartel agreement also changed, from a mere price accord or simple market sharing agreement to co-ordinated restrictions of production and then, further on, to the setting-up of organisations such as 'syndicates' in order to co-ordinate

---

3   Liefmann 1927, p. 29.

the sale of the product of all of its members.*** The development of cartels was, of course, by no means uniform in all industries; but once a cartel was formed in the materials industries, the semi-finished products industries were also compelled to launch a cartel in order to shift the burden to the finished-goods industries. Thus, from the end of the nineteenth century to the early twentieth century, Germany saw a veritable proliferation of cartel agreements of diverse contents in virtually all of its main industrial fields; and these agreements were, as a general rule, more strictly binding in the up-stream range of production and more loosely so in its down-stream range of operations. A 1905 study of the German government confirmed the presence of 385 cartels.

* Kuczynski provided the following table to show the increase in the number of cartels.[4] As he himself admits, these numbers are not all accurate, which is understandable because some agreements are necessarily short-lived, and certain industries such as the chemical industry had to conclude multiple agreements with regard to their diverse products. Moreover, many agreements were informal and could not be detected easily from the outside. With all such reservations, however, the spectacular increase in the number of cartels in the late 1880s and the late 1890s can hardly be doubted.

TABLE N-1   *Increase in the number of cartels*

Year	Number	Sources
1865	4	Liefmann
1870	6	same
1975	8	same
1979	14	same
1884	54	Schoenlank
1885	90	Liefmann
1887	70	Verein für Sozialpolitik
1888	75	same
1889	90	Zeitschrift für Industrie
1889	106	Verein für Sozialpolitik
1890	117	Philippovich
1890	137	Verein für Sozialpolitik
1890	210	Liefmann
1896	250	Philippovich

4   Kuczynski 1952, pp. 85–6.

Year	Number	Sources
1896	260	Liefmann
1897	230–50	Liefmann
1900	300	Centralverband
1905	385	Deutcher Industrieller Amtliche Enquete
1911	550–600	Tschierschky

Kuczynski's book also shows the breakdown by industries of the 385 cartels confirmed by the German government in its 1905 study as follows.

TABLE N-2   *Industry breakdowns*

Industry	Number	Industry	Number
Coal	19	Glass	10
Iron	62	Bricks	132
Metal (ex-Iron)	11	Quarry	27
Chemical	46	Pottery	4
Textile	31	Food and Beverage	17
Leather and Rubber	6	Electrical Machinery	2
Lumber	5	Other	7
Paper	6		

Here, too, Kuczynski expresses doubt, referring to the unusually large number of cartels in the bricks industry and also to the absence of any in the beer producing sector. Liefmann says that the number for the chemical industry must be far more than just 46.[5] As stated above, the number of cartels tends to increase if the number of products in the same industry is large. This is due to the fact that a cartel is an item-by-item agreement, so that one company, as it grows, may have to belong to an increasing number of cartels.

** Liefmann refers to cartels that are formed in the period of prosperity, when prices tend to rise due to increased demand.[6] Since free competition, to some extent, militates

---

5   Liefmann 1927, p. 32.
6   Liefmann 1927, p. 31.

against this price rise, and prevents the producers from profiting from it, they may wish to protect their interest by forming cartels in various sectors.

***The general practice so far has been to place cartels in several classes according to the content of the agreements entered into. Liefmann, however, regards the following three types to be the fundamental ones: (1) agreements regarding the division of the market for the product; (2) those having to do with the setting of its price; and (3) those aimed at controlling its production, all others being either subsidiary or derivative forms.[7] For example, the so-called cartel governing the 'terms of sale', which agreed on how the charges on packing were to be borne by the member-firms or how the date for settlement of account was to be decided, was, in his view, a subsidiary form of (2), the agreement pertaining to the setting of the price.[8] A cartel, which regulated the distribution of profit amongst the member-firms, was likewise viewed by him as a developed form of (2) the price cartel. For that sort of agreement involved a pooling in common of the difference between the basic price (which is more or less the cost of production) and the minimum sales price agreed upon, in the first instance, and to make an appropriate distribution of benefits to each member-firm afterwards. Needless to say, the purpose of this scheme was to ensure that the commodity was not sold at a price lower than the minimum price agreed upon, so that it was, in fact, a price agreement.[9] On the other hand, a cartel which allotted to the member-firms the orders for the product was equivalent to (1), an agreement regarding the market share, of which the most developed form was the syndicate [*Syndikat*]. Similarly, a cartel that apportioned the quantum of shipment amongst the member-firms amounted to (3), an agreement regarding how reduced production was shared. The so-called *Submissions-kartell*, which required one of the member-firms to sell at the minimum price (cartel price), while other member-firms might sell at apparently higher prices, stood, according to Liefmann, half way between (1) the agreement on the allotment of an order, and (3) the agreement pertaining to the apportioning of shipment.[10]

In the older edition of this book I made reference to Eiji Ohno, 'The Structural Characteristics of German Finance-Capital'[11] as the most up-to-date pertinent work in this country. However, Professor Ohno's view is somewhat different from mine; therefore, I now wish to recommend instead Mr. Shirô Tohara's more recent book: *The Advent of Finance-Capital in Germany* [*Doitsu Kin-yûshihon no Seiritsu Katei*], and from

---

7   Liefmann 1927, pp. 41–3.

8   Liefmann 1927, p. 47.

9   Liefmann 1927, p. 45.

10   Liefmann 1927, pp. 44–5.

11   *Keizai-Ronsô*, vol. 67, no. 6 and vol. 71, no. 1.

which I have been able to learn more. My purpose, in any case, is to formulate the stage-theoretic determinations of finance-capital, and I have found Mr. Tohara's book useful in providing me with concrete examples on which to base my understanding.

It goes without saying that the resilience of a cartel depends on the degree to which the industry is concentrated. For if there are many firms in the industry, a price agreement can easily be broken, as soon as more of the commodity is produced than is demanded, so that competition among the supplying firms intensifies. An agreement on production is then introduced, which may be stated in the form of a restriction on the operating hours of the plant, of the mothballing of some of the existing facilities or of the allotment of quotas in the light of past performance. Regardless of how it is stipulated, however, such an agreement cannot eliminate the tendency towards excess capacity in the industry, which is the root cause of overproduction. Besides, whatever may be the benefit accruing to the members of the cartel, there are always new entrants to the industry, which do not subscribe to the cartel. In such an industry, a cartel periodically makes use of the common funds set up in advance by the members in order to confront these new competitors, or outsiders, who insist on not taking part in it, by radically underselling them for some time, until they are either forced out of the market or, alternatively, are forced to join the cartel. In some cases, the cartel may buy out the outsider's factory, or any other inefficient one in the market, so as to suspend their operation. Yet there are always limits to the funds available for such purposes. In any case, unless the scale of operation of the industry becomes extensive, and the massiveness of fixed capital in it becomes forbidding to new entrants, a cartel organisation cannot always assert its staying power. In the meantime, as cartels are formed in many industries, firms belonging to a number of cartels of varying types tend to trade their commodities with one another. Here again, the relative strength of their commitment to the organisation plays an important role. Cartel-members, in this context, can put pressure on the buyers of their own commodity as well. For instance, they may refuse to sell, or sell only at an exorbitant price, in order to deter their customers from purchasing from a non-member firm. They may also force the sellers of the raw materials that they need not to sell to their competitors under the threat of boycotting the incompliant sellers. That strategy, however, may not work quite so easily, if the other party belongs to another powerful cartel. In that case, negotiations across cartels may have to occur. Under all circumstances, the advantage accrues, of course, to the one equipped with the strongest monopoly power. In any case, in order to ensure that the participating firms abide by the rules of the cartel, it must enforce significant penalties on the violators. Still, the effectiveness of all these measures depends on the degree of concentration of the industry, which facilitates the barring of outsiders.*

*This condition, however, does not apply exclusively to a produce of the land that may enjoy the power of 'natural monopoly'. Of course, in mining in particular, one observes numerous instances of strong cartel organisations from early on. However, a natural monopoly does not always guarantee a successful cartel. Liefmann gives cement and potash as examples of industries possessed of natural monopoly power. In the cement industry, it was not easy to maintain a cartel for any length of time, since new enterprises appeared quite easily as soon as the cost of production fell. In the potassium industry, though there were only a few firms at the beginning, there soon emerged a great many. The government, at first, compelled all producers to join one cartel, but that only induced a further increase in the number of new entrants. Thus, it eventually had to take such measures as to bring about more concentration in the industry.[12]

As Kuczynski recounts, the heavy industries surrounding iron constituted the core in the process of development of German monopoly organisations. These industries, as already stated, swiftly expanded the scale of their operation and pushed the process of their concentration, until the colossal investment in fixed capital by a small number of large firms lent support to the increasing strength of monopoly organisations. These organisations, however, evolved gradually as periods of rivalry and agreement alternated among competing capitals. First, they emerged separately in each of the three related sectors of iron, coal and steel; then, with the subsequent development of so-called 'mixed enterprises', complex networks of interest groups stretched across all the three key sectors. In the meantime, large banks also actively took part in the generation and formation of such networks, co-ordinating the varying interests of industrial firms, until powerful 'syndicates' appeared in each of these sectors.

The iron-makers of Germany first secured protection from external competition by the customs law of 1879. It is true that this law resulted from the petition of the iron-makers particularly concerned with foreign competition; but they did not necessarily envisage it as a first step towards a cartel. In any case, it is not justified to regard cartels as having originated in a customs policy. Although earlier, at the time of the crisis of 1873, the producers of pig-iron in the Rhineland-Westphalia region were said to have already formed a council, in which they mutually exchanged information concerning their production, sales, in-house consumption, stocks, and the like, it was not until the end of

---

12   Liefmann 1927, pp. 78–82.

the 1870s that a price agreement on cast iron and wrought iron emerged, frail and short-lived though it was. This event was more likely to have marked the beginning of a cartel in Germany. At about the same time, a syndicate in pig-iron was formed in Lothringen (Lorraine). In Siegerland, as well, a short-lived cartel agreement arose, in the same product, in 1882, which was transformed a while later into a syndicate of 1886. In Rhineland-Westphalia, a central council was inaugurated in the same year to co-ordinate the sale of various pig-iron products. Thus, in the three leading industrial regions of Western Germany, cartels multiplied increasingly from the end of the 1870s and throughout the 1880s. From the end of the 1880s to the 1890s, moreover, these regional cartels tended to gradually interlock themselves. In 1899, the syndicate in pig-iron of Rhineland-Westphalia, which had come into being in 1897, entered into an accord with the council of price agreements, already in existence in Siegerland, to form a larger organisation. This organisation then concluded a treaty with the syndicate of Lothringen for co-ordinated sales in pig-iron produced by the Thomas-method. However, this grand monopoly organisation of pig-iron makers was still somewhat fragile due to the fact that some leading mixed enterprises did not join it. Even inside it, conflicts of interest between mixed and specialised firms persisted. Furthermore, in the maritime districts of the North, there remained iron-makers who operated with imported raw materials. All this led to the dissolution of the organisation during the crisis of 1900. Yet, in 1901–2, an even more comprehensive organisation for the marketing of pig-iron (called *Roheisenverband, G.m.b.H.*) was established in Essen, which brought together not only the West German iron-makers but also the Silesian and other producers, who had, up to that time, operated separately. This organisation completed the iron-producers' drive for monopoly in that it integrated the three key sectors of iron, coal and steel for the first time.[13]

In coal-mining as well, the first cartel is said to have appeared as early as 1877 in the Rhineland-Westphalia region with agreements to co-ordinate production;* but it was of small scale and broke up in no time. Later, in 1880, 1885 and 1887, there emerged short-lived agreements among coal-mining firms one after another, until, in 1893, a major organisation called *Rheinisch-Westfälisches Kohlensyndikat* was finally established.** This one was built on a regional federation of councils set up earlier during the depression years of the 1880s in Dortmund, Bochum, Essen and Mülheim and soon grew into a powerful and

---

13   About the formation of cartel in the iron industry, see Kuczynski's brief but lucid exposition (1952, pp. 119–22). See also Seiichi Kojima 1928, *The Development of Iron and Steel Industry* [*Tekkôgyô Hattatsushiron*], Part III, Chapter 22 (Section 2: A Brief History of Cartels by Iron-Producers).

comprehensive cartel of coal-miners in Western Germany. It brought together
the coal-mines, which together counted for roughly ninety percent of the output of the Rhineland-Westphalia region, and facilitated the setting up of a syndicate in the form of a separate company to handle the co-ordinated selling of
their product. The terms of the cartel accord, whether relating to the conditions
of sale, the regulation of production or the determination of the sales price,
were no longer negotiated with individual member-firms, but were applied systematically by the directorate of the syndicate, to which the member-firms were
bound. This syndicate was to last, in the first instance, for ten years. During
these ten years, however, an extremely important change occurred. At its inception in 1893, the syndicate was an organisation exclusive to the coal-mining sector, and was not much involved with mixed enterprises, which both mined coal
and produced iron. The syndicate excluded them, since most of the coal that
was mined by these mixed enterprises was destined for in-house consumption
and not for sale; moreover, their interest differed from that of the specialised
coal-mining firms. However, the moment it began its operation, the syndicate
was forced to realise that it could not afford to ignore them, since, as it turned
out, the mixed firms expanded very quickly and soon were impeding its marketing of coal. At the same time, some leading firms within the syndicate moved
into the production of iron as mixed enterprises. Thus, in the 1903 revision of
the syndicate's covenant, the exclusion of mixed enterprises could no longer
be insisted upon. Needless to say, mixed enterprises used most of the coal that
they mined as materials for their own iron- and/or steel-making, and sold only
the surplus in the market. They, therefore, enjoyed a substantial advantage relative to those specialised iron-and-steel makers, which had to purchase coal
from the syndicate. Moreover, such mixed firms were usually operated by large
capitals with intimate connections with large banks, so that their admission
to the syndicate amounted to its integration into the rule of such great capitals. Nor did banks remain passive in the operation of the syndicate. Instead of
taking part, as before, in the monopoly organisation specific either to the iron-
and-steel industry or to coal-mining, they now actively involved themselves in
the inter-industry business of the syndicate.***

* It may be stated in passing that in 1877 coal-mining firms in Bochum and Gelsenkirchen concluded a treaty relating to the export of coal. Kirdorf, one of the architects
of this treaty, was later to play a leading role in the foundation of the powerful syndicate,
which emerged in this field.[14]

---

14   Kuczynski 1952, pp. 123–4.

** As for the development of the coal syndicate for the Rhineland-Westphalia region up to that time, see once again the concise description by Kuczynski.[15] Available, also, is an extremely detailed account of the agreements concluded at the time relating to the organisation and administration of the syndicate in Kinpei Matsuoka, 'German Coal Syndicate', in *Kokka-Gakkai Zasshi*, vol. 27. Marshall too describes the syndicate, which he considers to be 'the strongest cartel in the world', providing us with information on its organisational structure and pricing policy in his *Industry and Trade*,[16] which may well be the most noteworthy document from which to learn the nature of this type of monopoly organisation. Below, I will borrow much from Matsuoka's paper to summarise the main feature of this organisation.

First of all, this organisation, known as the 'syndicate', was a business enterprise which sold coal, endowed with the legal status of an independent joint-stock company, and its equity was owned by the coal-mining firms belonging to the cartel (which was known as the 'syndicate'). Each of the member-firms had to sell all of the output, previously allotted to it in quantitative terms, to this company and was not permitted to sell coal elsewhere, the company being the sole agent authorised to sell the coal produced by the member-firms. To the extent that the market was under its control, the syndicate sold coal at the cartel price, calculated appropriately from the prices at which it was bought from the members. Where it did not exercise control, the syndicate might sell coal at the market price, which could result in profits or losses for the syndicate. Its status as a profit-seeking company was, however, strictly nominal in the sense that its operating cost was charged, case by case, to the member-firms, and any surplus accruing to the company was quickly returned to them. In other words, the syndicate did not seek profit for its own sake, even though, as a joint-stock company, it had a board of directors and auditors. The management team of this company (the syndicate) administered the cartel, by determining its selling price and regulating the transactions between itself and the member-firms. The latter's operation it also generally supervised. The equity of the company was owned exclusively by the member-firms in the fixed proportion agreed upon at the time of its inauguration, or, in other words, in proportion to their allotted output quota, in the light of their performance in that base year. Thus, the member-firms retained the exclusive decision-making power in the stockholders' meetings, and in the monthly council meetings of the elected executives with regard to all important issues, such as the determination of the mode of regulating outputs by the members, the pricing of different coal products and the mode of calculating and settling accounts between the members and the company, as well as approving or disapproving any changes in the previously agreed

---

15   Kuczynski 1952, pp. 122–9.
16   Marshall 1923, p. 552.

upon assessment of each member's part in the cartel. In other words, the syndicate company was an executive organ of all the firms participating in the cartel, and they could vote according to the number of the company's shares that they held.

Now let us examine the administrative side of the syndicate. As for the regulation of production, it was decided upon by the shareholders' meeting in the light of the information on the prevailing state of the market received from the council which reported once every one to three months. As a result of these reports, a greater quantity of certain coal products might be produced by some firms than was normally assigned to them, and less of certain other coal products might be produced by certain other firms than was anticipated originally. Then, the syndicate would levy charges on the firms which produced more than normally, while compensating those which produced less than normally. As for the pricing of the products, the syndicate sold them at varying market prices in the competitive markets such as Hamburg and Bremen, where British coal was readily imported; but in other markets under its control, it sold them at the fixed cartel prices, which were so calculated as to assure profits to the member-firms. These prices were fixed for one year, since the contractual terms of coal supply were usually for that duration. As was often the case with cartels involving raw materials for the production of iron, the coal cartel too had to worry about the price of coal, as it impacted on the export of Germany's iron products. Since a high price for coal would clearly militate against the export of German iron-products at low prices, the syndicate co-ordinated with cartels in pig-iron, from the end of the 1890s onward, to pay together the equivalent of an export subsidy to the German exporters of iron products. A similar step was taken with respect to the export of sheet-glass and mirror-glass products. The syndicate sold over 60 million tons of coal in a year, directly to bulk-order customers such as the railways, gas providers, producers of iron and steel, and, indirectly to small-order customers via retailing coal-dealers. The syndicate restrained its customers, large and small, from buying coal from outsiders in the Ruhr district, especially for the purpose of reselling it. If a bulk-order customer ever resorted to the practice of resale, the syndicate imposed a penalty charge on the whole of its contract supply. In all cases, the freight had to be paid by the customer, and the payment for the delivery was to be settled on the fifteenth day of the following month. Anyone mediating a transaction between the syndicate and the customer had to pay the security money to the former. Moreover, the region under the control of the syndicate was divided into 29 districts, and the region outside it, including foreign markets, into two districts. The syndicate recognised only one dealer for each of the coal products in each district, and demanded that all such dealers join together in one company of which it owned an important part. In this way, the syndicate ensured that its rules would be implemented in strict detail by all concerned.

Finally, we should examine the relationship between the syndicate and mixed firms. In the beginning, both the coal used by the miners themselves and that used by small

consumers near the mine were excluded from the dealings of the syndicate, and so also was the in-house consumption of coal by mixed firms, since these seemed to be of largely the same nature. It turned out, however, that the latter was of a wholly different nature from the former. The syndicate's original exclusion of the mixed firms would have been defensible, had they continued to market only a small proportion of coal that they produced; but, as mentioned in the text, the development of 'mixed firms' did not permit the syndicate to ignore them for long. Thus, the 1903 revision of the agreement included them. It was nevertheless left to the discretion of the mixed firms themselves to decide on the amount of coal that they intended to consume in-house, the syndicate supervising only the amount that they marketed. Now, under that arrangement, the mixed firms would use, in years of boom, more of its output for in-house consumption, cutting back on its allotted market supply, while cheerfully paying penalties on the shortfall. Since that caused troubles for the syndicate's planning, the agreement had to be revised further in 1909, in such a way that the amount of in-house consumption, too, was made subject to the syndicate's control. This, however, did not iron out all the differences between the mixed firms and the specialised coal-miners. For instance, it goes without saying that cutbacks in production affected the latter more severely than the former. Matsuoka apparently regards this as an indication of the weakness of the coal syndicate. However, this point, it seems to me, indicates rather that the syndicate, though starting humbly in the coal sector, grew over the years into an unchallenged monopoly organisation dominating all the core sectors of German heavy industries (involving coal, iron and steel) by astutely embracing mixed enterprises. Indeed, of the 70 member-firms belonging to the syndicate, 14 were mixed firms, including those whose allotted supply exceeded one million tons in 1910. At least five of them consumed more than a million tons of coal in-house (by the definition of 1909). As for the ones that produced more than a million tons for marketing and for in-house consumption combined, there were three firms. For example, Kirdorf's Gelsenkirchen, previously mentioned, prided itself on supplying the maximum allotted amount of 1.70 million tons. In contrast, the allotted quantity for Krupp was 0.70 million tons, but its approved in-house consumption amounted to 2.67 million tons. The total of the allotted coal supply, which the syndicate handled, was 78 million tons, of which the mixed firms provided 21 million, while the in-house consumption was 17 million.
*** At the time the covenant of the coal syndicate was reviewed in 1903, large banks and enterprises in heavy industries were, according to Jeidels, interrelated in the following manner: Später and the Schaaffhausen Bank Group represented the iron industry, as Thyssen and the Dresdner Bank did the coal-mining, while Stinnes dealt with both banks.[17] It is not easy to appraise the relationship between the large banks and the

---

17   Jeidels 1913, p. 264.

leading industrialists because of extreme complications in the manner in which they either opposed one another or allied themselves together in coalitions.[18] It is, however, an incontrovertible fact that the large banks very actively involved themselves in the formation, as well as the administration, of the cartels in this period. Thyssen, which figures here, was a leading steel-maker with its allotted sale of coal to the syndicate and its in-house consumption of coal both exceeding one million tons, while Später was a merchant house of Koblenz, which dominated the steel industry in Lothringen and Luxemburg.

It is, therefore, clear that the syndicate that developed in this manner in the Rhineland-Westphalia region was not just another monopoly organisation serving only the coal-mining firms. It rather marked the real foundation upon which the whole system of organised monopoly was built to serve the German heavy industries, with its fulcrum in the iron-and-steel industry. Within this key industry as well, different groups of large capitalists stood at loggerheads with one another, due to the complicated entanglements of their conflicts of interest. The large banks, too, with their own somewhat different interests, also played their part at arm's length from the industrialists. The Steel-Makers' Association [*Stahlwerksverband*] in Düsseldorf, which came into existence in 1904, typified the monopoly organisation that could arise in a heavy industry. Because of the extensive variety of its products, the steel-makers could not generate as comprehensive a cartel as coal-miners; but after assimilating the members of the previously existing Union of Steel-Makers (constituted in Upper Silesia in 1887 as the first brotherhood of the profession), this new Association of steel-makers in Western Germany became *de facto* the nationwide monopoly organisation, with its strong base established by the co-operative ties among these producers. As Kuczynski describes, this association counted 31 member-firms in 1905, of which 17 were engaged in coal-mining, 25 in iron-ore mining and 27 in the production of pig-iron, which indicated that many of them were indeed mixed enterprises. Although there were some fully specialised firms as well, their participation was relatively passive, since they could not otherwise survive than by belonging to the association and abiding by its rules. Actually, the greatest part of the allotted production was supplied by six or seven of the largest member-firms, and those few which were really powerful in the coal syndicate were also quite important in this association. Just as the coal syndicate was fostered by the large banks closely allied with steel-makers, so too was this association cordially bolstered by the same banks with the same steel connections.*

---

18   Riesser 1912, pp. 599–604.

*On the development up to a more recent date of monopoly organisations in the steel industry, I refer again to Kuczynski.[19] Kojima's above-quoted work also helped me with details in the history of the steel industry.[20] As this latter reference states, the Schaffhausen Bank Group prevailed upon Phönix Steelworks (A.G. für Bergbau und Hütten Betrieb Phönix in Saar) to join the Steel-Makers' Association of Düsseldorf at its inception, since, as Jeidels states, Phönix 'would have been a dangerous outsider since it has been the greatest user of unfinished goods up to the present'.[21]

It is said that, as of 1913, the six largest capitals 'accounted roughly for some 45 percent of the heavy steel products supplied by the members of the Steel-Makers' Association, 25 percent of the pig-iron products handled by the leading iron syndicate, and 22 percent of all allotted production under the coal syndicate'.* These capitals all made their fortune within ten to twenty years, spanning from the late nineteenth century up to the early twentieth century, by operating mixed enterprises, which either spread to coal-mining from their origins in the iron-and-steel industry, or, conversely, started in coal-mining and later spreading into the iron-and-steel industry. The process of their concentration, as Riesser points out, was accelerated by the service of underwriting the shares which the large banks provided them with, and this process, in turn, accelerated the concentration of these banks themselves.** The ever closer ties that large enterprises forged between themselves and with the large banks can be seen in the practice, then prevalent, of a bank sending directors to several enterprises, and of an enterprise receiving directors from several banks.*** Needless to say, iron and coal were just the two most typical examples of the heavy-industrial sectors that witnessed the development in the manner described above of the monopoly organisations of capital in Germany. In chemical products, electricity and other important sectors as well, industrial firms made full use of the form of the joint-stock company, forging a variety of alliances with banks, in order to develop an organised monopoly, suitable to their particular circumstances. In all cases, the banks acted not simply as bank-capital but as finance-capital, which was singularly in tune with the evolution of heavy industries.

*The six companies Kuczynski mentions are: Gelsenkirchen, Deutsch-Luxemburgische Bergwerks-und-Hütten A.G., Phönix, Krupp, Thyssen, and Vereinigte Burbach.[22]

---

19   Kuczynski 1952, pp. 129–33.
20   Kojima 1928, pp. 574–84.
21   Jeidels 1913, p. 256.
22   Kuczynski 1952, pp. 133–4.

** In this connection, Riesser mentions, in particular, the adoption in the 1880s of the Thomas method in the production of pig-iron.[23]

*** In an appendix to Riesser's book, one finds a table that shows the number of auditors sent by the six leading banks to joint-stock industrial enterprises. The six banks are the following: Bank für Handel und Industrie, Berliner Handelsgesellschaft, Deutche Bank, Diosconto-Gesellschaft, Dresdner Bank, and the Schaaffhausen Bank Group.

2   Britain's Overseas Investment

By the 1860s, capitalism in Britain had evolved into 'the factory of the world', a feature most eloquently testified to by the rapid growth of its foreign trade, especially in the 1850s and 1860s. This process was, however, accompanied by an expansion from early on of overseas investment, which gained in importance as time passed. The fact that London superseded Amsterdam, after the Napoleonic War, as the centre of international finance, doubtless laid a solid foundation for the development of Britain's capitalism by providing it with highly sophisticated facilities indispensable to both international trade and investment. The growth of foreign trade naturally entailed the shipping of goods, an area where Britain traditionally prided itself in its comparative advantage. At the same time, the enormous wealth accumulated over and above that which was needed by British industry and trade soon responded to the call for capital from overseas. Thus, already in the first half of the nineteenth century, Britain became the principal exporter of capital to the Americas and continental Europe, supplying them with an important chunk of funds for investment in businesses as well as subscribing to public debts in huge amounts. The building of the railways in the newly developing regions of the world also owed much to the supply of British capital. Past the middle of the nineteenth century, the regions in which British funds were invested expanded further to the Pacific coast of the United States and Australia, especially after the discovery of gold mines in those areas, to which was soon added the building of railways in India as the principal magnet of British foreign investment.[24] Needless to say, these investments expanded the market for British commodities, and that, in turn, also confirmed the ascendancy of Britain as the leading provider of capital

---

23   Riesser 1912, p. 305.

24   C.K. Hobson 1914, Chapters 4, 5, 6. Incidentally, this book has recently been translated into Japanese by Katsumi Yanai under the title of *Shihon Yushutsu Ron* (Tokyo: Nihon Hyôronsha, 1968).

overseas. Statistically, as shown below in Table 1, this country's foreign trade after the mid-1850s showed a conspicuous increase in the excess of imports over exports. Part of this trade deficit was, of course, covered by incomes on freight and service items, though no direct data is available for the period which would permit us to see the manner of this coverage in detail. However, in 1903, the Board of Trade estimated such service incomes at £90 million, so that the remaining deficit, if any, must have been covered by the interest incomes on the capital previously invested abroad, even though some portion of such incomes might have been ploughed back into further investment abroad.

TABLE 1   *British trade in annual average over the five years (in £ millions)*[25]

	Imports	Exports	Trade deficit
1855–9	146	116	30
1860–4	193	138	55
1865–9	237	181	56
1870–4	391	235	56
1875–9	320	202	118
1880–4	344	234	110
1885–9	318	226	92
1890–4	357	234	123
1895–9	393	238	155
1900–4	466	281	185

According to Bowley, Britain made the foreign investment of about the same amount as its interest earnings from abroad in 1873, when the trade deficit was £60 million, and in 1886, when it was £70 million, respectively, whereas the amount of its foreign investment exceeded its interest earnings from abroad in 1859, when its excess of imports over exports was only £23.5 million, and similarly in 1872, when the same was merely £40 million. Thus, one may safely say that the trade deficit (apart from freight incomes) was, in the main, covered by interest earnings on capital invested abroad. Bowley illustrates how the trade deficit of £125 million in 1880 was covered as follows. First, the freight incomes of £70 million and other service revenues would leave roughly £45

---

25   Adapted from Bowley 1906, p. 156.

million to be covered by the interest earnings on overseas investment. However, the total stock of British investment abroad then amounted to £1,500 million, which, due to the prevailing interest rate of five percent, should have yielded £75 million. Therefore, after covering the current deficit, Britain was still left with a surplus of £30 million or so available to be applied for further investment abroad.[26]*

*It appears that no direct data of sufficient reliability are available on the amount of British foreign investment, though some estimates have been attempted. In any case, from the annual data, which shows consistent trade deficits, we can easily surmise its general trend.

Here is an overall picture that we can learn from Bowley. Britain, which had already invested £550 million in foreign public debts, railway and other equities by 1854, exported, thereafter, capital of about £30 million annually, so that the stock of its exported capital amounted to £750 million in 1860. During the period of the so-called 'cotton famine' following the Civil War in the United States, Britain's export of capital slowed down somewhat. However, in the 1870–5 period, owing to the business boom triggered by the Franco-Prussian War, the annual export of capital from Britain recovered to £55 million and the stock of capital invested abroad amounted to £1,400 million. Though, in reaction, there came setbacks in the following three years, Britain's foreign investment recovered once again to the annual average of £60 million from 1881 to 1890, with its accumulated balance going up to £2,000 million. There was no sign of decline during the depression years of 1886–8, and that also explains why the amount of foreign trade then suffered but a small loss. It must be borne in mind, however, that the outlet for British foreign investment was not limited to Britain's colonies; it made its way to practically everywhere, including Russia, Germany, the Americas, Turkey and Greece. In the case of Turkey and Greece, these countries ended by defaulting after having contracted an excessive volume of loans from Britain; but the exorbitant interest which the latter earned over several years easily compensated for its loss. India too was sometimes pushed into a state of affairs in which it had to borrow further to pay off the interest. Such instances occurred, of course, in exceptional circumstances. The general rule was that British colonies at first imported capital from Britain to pay for their trade deficit (stage one); but as they gradually restored their own trade balance (stage two), they eventually returned to a state in which

---

26   Bowley 1906, pp. 75–6.

they could pay off their past debt with their export surplus (stage three). South Africa was still in the first stage at the beginning of the twentieth century, while both Australia and India were already in the second stage, and Canada in the third. South America was also in the third stage, and so were the United States, Germany, Russia, France, Holland, Belgium and the like in relation to Britain. Of course, Britain need not have settled its trade relation with each of these countries separately. For instance, as Britain's exports to the United States declined, the former paid for part of its American imports with its positive balances vis-à-vis India and China. In the meantime, the United States always remained an important area for British foreign investment.[27]

Such an outburst of foreign investment, however, could not help exerting a profound influence on the financial markets in Britain. The general rule would have it that only at a certain stage of development did industry need to depend on idle funds capitalist-socially mobilised by the mechanism of the joint-stock company. In Britain, however, idle funds had been available in abundance even at the earlier stage of industrial capital and these found profitable outlets in foreign investment. Such idle funds available for long-term investment were then traded in the capital market of a very peculiar kind. It developed side by side with the money market, which conducted the business of financing short-term credit needs of domestic industry. While the ordinary joint-stock banks satisfied the needs of industrial firms for circulation-credit, the old financiers known as 'merchant bankers' and others who specialised in investment banking, along with colonial and foreign banks, partook of the services of financial intermediation on behalf of the investors in overseas assets.* The fact that the securities market in London was originally involved with investments in foreign public bonds and private debentures, railway stocks and the like, acted against the normal development of a capital market that would have focused on domestic industrial finance as its main area of business, even while such a market grew at a spectacular speed in Germany, the United States and elsewhere in the late nineteenth century.**

* The British banking system, which constituted the core of the nation's financial markets, clustered round the Bank of England, the central bank which had the authority to issue notes. Deposit banks took the forms of joint-stock banks or private banks; but the

---

27 Bowley 1906, pp. 76–8, 93–4. It may be noted that other experts give lower estimates than Bowley's. Thus, G.D.H. Cole after a comparative study concludes that it must have stood roughly at £1,200 million in 1875, £2,000 million in 1900 and £3,000 million in 1907 (Cole 1932, pp. 63, 109).

former soon overwhelmed the latter, and, after a process of absorption and amalgamation, the Big Five (Midland, Lloyds, Barclays, Westminster and National Provincial)
emerged as representative commercial banks. The old financiers were then converted into so-called merchant bankers (such as Baring, Rothschild, Goschen, etc.), which
specialised in the acceptance of foreign trade bills as well as in underwriting national
debts and foreign securities. These were not proper banks entitled to create demand
deposits. Around them, a group of specialists engaged in the dealing of diverse sorts of
securities sprang up, whether as 'acceptance houses', 'discount houses', 'bill brokers' or
'stockbrokers'. Assisting them were the 'issue houses' and the 'investment trusts', etc. In
their minute specialisation, they dealt with foreign securities of various kinds. These
were joined by the so-called 'colonial banks' of Australia, Canada, South Africa and the
like, all of which maintained a head office or a principal branch in the City of London.
These were active in colonial trade and investment, financing trade bills, underwriting
securities and in managing accounts on behalf of their clients. There were also similar
banks from India and the Far East, as well as 'foreign banks', each of which typically
maintained a branch in London, to deal with foreign exchanges and the trade finance
for their respective countries, as well as the marketing of the respective nation's public
and private securities in the City of London. Thus, the City grew into the centre not
only of British finance, but of international finance as well.

** In this regard, there remain a variety of interesting and unresolved issues needing
more in-depth study. The work of C.W. von Wieser, *Der finanzielle Aufbau der eng-
lishchen Industrie*, on the formation of joint-stock companies in Britain since the turn of
the century, is an especially useful and remarkable work.[28] In this country, Mr. Ikukawa
Eiji has been dealing with this issue, though his conclusions are rather different from
mine.[29]

Needless to say, the money market and the capital market, though specialised
in different fields of finance, do not remain independent of, nor do they stand
in opposition to, each other, as I have mentioned already. In fact, foreign investment is often closely related with trade finance; and for that reason, industrial
finance within the country cannot remain immune to the mobilisation of funds
for foreign investment. One of the reasons why industrial firms in Britain were

---

28   Wieser 1919.
29   See Ikukawa's papers 'On the Appearance of Industrial Finance', in *Management Research*,
      no. 8, Faculty of Commerce, Osaka City University; 'Industrial Finance under the Form-
      ation of Monopoly' and 'Deposit Banks and Industrial Finance', *Bulletin of Economics*,
      vol. 27, no. 4–5, Society for Economic Research, Osaka City University. These studies are
      now assembled in his book *Formation of Financial Capital in Britain* [*Igirisu Kin'yû-shihon
      no Seiritsu*] (Tokyo: Yuhikaku).

slow to adopt the form of the joint-stock company for their reorganisation may thus be explained in this light. In Britain, the accumulation of industrial capital had, in fact, been quite adequate on the basis of the solid foundation of private enterprises, so that its enterprises were used to count on the financial market almost exclusively for short-term circulation-credit. The financial market, which had evolved under such circumstances, remained biased, for its part, against offering such services as the underwriting of shares for domestic industrial firms, even when such a practice became the preponderant business of the capital markets in Germany and the United States. This did not mean that, in Britain, large banks were not generated by amalgamation, or that large business firms did not emerge in various branches of heavy industry; in fact, on the eve of the First World War, both banking and industrial organisation had been profoundly transformed even in that country. Yet, the large banks in Britain, unlike the ones in Germany, did not involve themselves actively in the issue of industrial shares, nor did large British firms develop monopoly organisations with the assistance and involvement of the large banks. Some industrial firms did indeed finance the construction of their new plants and equipment by means of massive bank loans; and once the construction was finished, repaid the loans by issuing securities. However, even in such cases, banks played little substantial role in their operations. The relationship between bank and industry remained strictly that of the lender and the borrower, without developing further into a permanent and systematic fusion of the two parties, as was witnessed in Germany.*

*Von Wieser's work, mentioned above, in comparing the British case with that of Germany, notes the following. It is not that British banks were unwilling to come to the rescue of industrial firms in predicament during a depression phase; but 'they insisted on being paid back to the extent that the borrower could bear'. He stresses the fact that this had little to do with the amount of the funds loaned, and more to do with the quality of the relationship between the lending bank and the borrowing enterprise. Finally, the author strongly refutes the thesis, often held by German economists like Vogelstein, to the effect that the British banks did not make very large loans to industrial firms.

A trend towards the centralisation of firms into monopolies was not entirely absent even in Great Britain at the dawn of the twentieth century. Yet, a cursory glance at this trend in heavy industries reveals, first of all, that coal mining remained completely dispersed, and showed little sign of forging closer ties with the iron-and-steel industry, while, in the latter, any movement towards monopolisation, if at all, was led by industrial capitalists, whose operations continued under the management of private enterprises.* Even when the form of the joint-stock company was made use of, it did not generate as systematic a development such as was witnessed in Germany, since the relationship between banks and industrial firms always remained at arm's length, given the fact that the scope for utilisation of idle funds in the capital market was severely limited, as stated above. This fact was particularly apparent in the circumstances in which the mobilisation of capital had to be carried out by means of 'preferred stocks', for which a fixed dividend was to be paid prior to any payout to common stocks, or by means of 'cumulative preferred stocks', for which an additional payment had to be guaranteed at the end of the following term,** if the distribution of profits in the current term did not reach the expected rate. The difficulty lay in that even when funds were to be assembled in small lots, as by means of £1 shares (1,000 DM stocks in the case of Germany), that operation had to be carried out by the old financiers, to whom the handling of foreign securities, public bonds and corporate debentures, and so on, were far more lucrative, since these financiers always earned handsome fees as mediators in the latter process. Thus, as is often popularly believed, the financial and industrial interests competed, and were at times at odds with each other. Of course, the British steel industry, in which capital was concentrated in the hands of monopolies under the form of the joint-stock company, could no longer be viewed as being operated by industrial capital. Yet movements for the amalgamation of capital, without direct connection with large banks, could not be viewed either as realising the kind of organised monopoly specific to finance-capital. Britain never generated monopoly organisations in as systematic a fashion as in Germany, in which large firms in the three key branches of heavy industry (coal, pig-iron and steel) formed interlocking cartels and syndicates, with the unfailing collusion and connivance of the great banks.

* As mentioned before, there were German capitalist families such as Thiessen, Krupp, Kirdorf and the like, whose names became prominent in heavy industries; but they attained and maintained their fame by systematically forging a monopoly organisation in close co-operation with large banks. In Britain, too, it is true that prominent names (such as Bell Brothers, Dorman-Long, Bockow-Vaughan, Sir Christopher Furness, Sir W.G. Armstrong, Vickers, and so on) emerged in the iron-and-steel industry in the process of concentration or amalgamation of capital (for example, of Bell Brothers with Dorman-Long). Yet their relation with banks or financial companies still remained largely external (for example, as between commercial banks and their client firms), without realising a monopoly organisation, in which the industry and its financial allies were systematically fused. Such circumstances also account for the fact that British

industrialists retained the stamp of individual enterprises even as they adopted, and made use of, the form of the joint-stock company. The same features applied to industries other than iron-and-steel.

** Wieser cites many examples to show that it was not easy for British firms to issue additional shares at their own cost and risk, even in unfavourable times, and that they frequently increased their capital by sustaining rather disadvantageous conditions.[30] Preferred shares were then used as means for ensuring success in the issuing of new shares. It is said that this constituted the peculiar feature of the share market in Britain, where the marketability of industrial shares was limited, which also raised, to a high level, the brokerage fees of the mediating agents.[31]

Surely, it is not possible to claim that the case of Britain at the turn of the century, in which cartels and syndicates did not emerge as they did in Germany but merely trust-like large firms, did not typify the development of finance-capital because their monopoly power was comparatively weak. For, on the contrary, a trust in which one single firm acted as a monopoly frequently imposed a stronger commanding power on the market than a cartel. The point is rather that the emergence of these trust-like large firms in Britain emerged without presupposing a monopoly organisation based on a systematic fusion of banking and industry. This, I believe, was due to the fact that even when capitalism reached the stage centred on heavy industries, Britain's financial markets continued to be dominated by foreign investment (i.e. by the exporters of capital). Yet, for all that, it cannot be said that finance-capital did not become ascendant in the British capitalism of that time. Rather, one should say that the latter realised the dominance of finance-capital specifically in the sphere of foreign investment, while leaving domestic industry largely to its own devices. Britain, in other words, was already becoming a *rentier* state, as the productive base that its finance-capital sought to dominate was to be found abroad, its domestic industry being largely sidestepped. This striking contrast explains the difference between British and German imperialist policies.*

* The fact that large enterprises evolved in Britain, without the form of the joint-stock companies being fully made use of, illustrates the peculiar way in which finance-capital came into being in that country. Indeed, it may even be said that the emergence of finance-capital does not necessarily presuppose the formation of monopoly organisations in industry. Clearly, capitalism in Britain towards the end of the nineteenth

30   Wieser 1919, Chapter 7.
31   Wieser 1919, pp. 387–93.

century no longer remained at the stage of industrial capital. It was, instead, mater-
ialising the stage of finance-capital to the extent that British investments in foreign
portfolios were gaining in importance, investments which forged a long-term capital
commitment to foreign productive activities. No doubt the German case, in which
finance-capital emerged as the embodiment of an organised monopoly in domestic
heavy industry, was more typical. Yet, to seek to apply that pattern mechanically to Britain would fail to shed light on the versatility of finance-capital, which can assume the
British, as well as the German, pattern. By contrasting the two limiting cases, one can
learn more about the nature of finance-capital.

Furthermore, the importance of foreign investment in Britain comes out strikingly
in the following table, which compares the proportion of domestic and foreign securities in the nation's investment portfolio. The table suggests that an important change
occurred after the First World War, though the precise nature of that change can only
be a matter of conjecture.

TABLE N-3   *Britain's portfolio investment*[32]

Year	Domestic securities	Foreign securities
1907–11	21%	79%
1912	21	79
1913	24	76
1914	21	79
1922	75	25

Moreover, even in Germany the export of capital (foreign investment) was
by no means wholly absent. Investment in securities (portfolio investment)
could be made, whether at home or abroad, so long as it was viewed as safe
and secure. Thus, Germany, too, increased its foreign investment rapidly after
the 1880s, but at a scale incomparably lesser than what Britain undertook.*
Clearly, Germany's priority was in the development of capitalism at home.
As stated earlier, Britain invested overseas something like £150–60 million a
year, including the reinvestment of its interest income. In 1914, the stock of its
overseas investment was estimated to be at £4,000 million, on which it earned
the interest of no less than £200 million.

32   Ernest Davies, 'Foreign Investment', in Cole 1935, p. 228.

* As suggested above, an accurate estimation of the extent of foreign investment in the nineteenth century is hard to come by. We can quote, however, from Cole's work the following table, which compares the stock of foreign investment of the three major European countries.

TABLE N-4   *Foreign investment by three major European powers*[33]

Year	Britain	France	Germany
1870		500	
1875	1,200		
1880		600	
1883			250
1885	1,300		
1898			500–600
1900	2,000	1,120	
1905			750–900
1907	3,000		
1914	4,000	1,800	1,100–1,200
			(in £ million)

3   The Trust Movement in the United States

In the United States as well, it was after the 1860s or 1870s that the form of the joint-stock company (or the corporate form) began to be generally adopted by business enterprises. Those who previously invested their funds, often speculatively, in railroad securities and public bonds of all sorts, now turned to industrial finance through the new method of 'investment banking'. As distinct from both Germany and Britain, the United States underwent the formative period of finance-capital with a strong speculative tendency. The penetration of industry by investment bankers,* or American-style merchant bankers, such as J.P. Morgan, as well as the creation of monopoly capital, based solely on one (for example, the oil) industry, by an individual such as John D. Rockefeller, both occurred in America against the background of

---

33   Cole 1932, pp. 109–10.

extensive activities in the securities market.** In order to concentrate the funds of the 'investing public' many investment media,*** such as commercial banks, trust companies and insurance companies, were mobilised, and a great variety of investment instruments, whether in the form of equity or of debt, were utilised.**** All manner of manipulative practices were resorted to so as to swindle innocent investors.† This process, therefore, possessed the aspect that truly deserves the appellation of 'securities capitalism' as it was assigned by G.W. Edwards following the example of R. Liefmann.††

* Investment bankers were originally financiers comparable to the British merchant bankers. Until the 1860s and 1870s, they concentrated in mediating imports payable in foreign currency, but with the dawn of the new era, they shifted to domestic industrial finance.[34]

** Between 1870 and 1910, the number of issues listed in the New York Stock Exchange rose from 143 to 426 for stocks, and from 200 to 1,013 for bonds and debentures. In addition to New York, stock exchanges were active in Baltimore, Boston, Chicago, Philadelphia and San Francisco. The volume of transactions in one day in New York increased from 700,000 shares on 28 November 1879, a high point in those days, to an enormous 3,281,226 shares on 30 April 1913.[35]

*** Since the function of the investment bankers was to guarantee the issues of the securities which will be the ones held as 'investments' by commercial banks, trust companies and insurance companies, they endeavoured to maintain and increase the control over these institutional investors which in effect manage the funds that ultimately belonged to the depositors, the owners of trust-money and/or the insured. J.P. Morgan, for example, became a director of the National Bank of Commerce, which was closely allied with the First National Bank, which in turn maintained relationships with such banks as Chase, Liberty, Hanover, Astor, National, and the like through the ownership of shares and/or exchange of directors. At the same time, Morgan & Co. sent directors to such trust companies as Union, Commercial, Fidelity and the like, while, by setting up the Bankers' Trust Company, it remained in close touch with the Manhattan Trust Company and the Guaranty Trust Company. In the meantime, the First National Bank launched the First Securities Company in 1908. Among the insurance companies allied with Morgan were the Mutual Life Insurance, the New York Life Insurance and Equitable Life Assurance Companies.[36]

---

34   See Edwards 1938, pp. 157, 169–71.
35   Edwards 1938, p. 167.
36   Edwards 1938, pp. 170–1.

**** For details concerning equities, debts and other types of securities, see Masuchi Yôjirô, *Kabushikigaisha Zaimuron* [*Treatise on Corporate Finance*], and other texts. Here, it is crucial to focus on the mechanism whereby funds of small amounts are funnelled into large sums, which are ultimately made use of for the empowerment of corporate magnates. Incidentally, even in America, the use of such varieties as 'non-voting stocks' and 'no-par-value stocks' became noticeable only after the First World War.

† This has to do with what has been referred to as *overcapitalisation*, due fundamentally to an over-valuation of the corporate property. When a company issues new securities at a precipitous pace, their quality naturally tends to deteriorate. For, in effect, it resorts to unwarrantable 'over-issues'. That was especially the case with the railways; but the same tendency was also observed with many industrial securities, especially when *trusts* were formed in pursuit of windfall profits around the turn of the century. In addition to bonds and preferred stocks that had already been issued in excess of the actual property value, common stocks were often issued and allotted as bonuses to the promoters and the original owners. In the case of railroad securities, for example, superannuated rails and cars, which were no longer in use, were not infrequently pledged as security for new issues. Needless to say, the losses were incurred by general investors, as the price of the securities inevitably declined.[37]

†† Liefmann calls this recent capitalist development 'securities capitalism' [*Effecten-kapitalismus*], having in mind that securities, as mere representation of claims to profit, vested capital with the properties of fungibility [*Vertretbarkeit*] and impersonalisa-tion.[38] Largely in line with this view, Edwards uses the term 'securities capitalism' in contradistinction to individual capitalism. These scholars cannot be said to have gone beyond Marx in the scientific conceptualisation of capital; consequently, they are not successful in clearly identifying the recent development of capitalism as belonging to a historically specific stage. Perhaps they intended rather to dispute the link between 'imperialism' and finance-capital. For instance, in the case of Edwards, while admitting the immensity of the political and economic power which the holders of foreign secur-ities in Britain exerted, he denies their connection with imperialism, on the grounds that they scarcely ever acted to mobilise military forces to prevail upon the defaulting countries.[39] It cannot, of course, be denied that finance-capital sometimes displays an aspect, which may be conveniently described with such a name as 'security capitalism'. Yet an emphasis on that aspect cannot supplant the definition of finance-capital as such. What is more important is to understand the specific reasons why finance-capital

---

37   Edwards 1938, pp. 186–7.
38   Liefmann 1923, Chapter 1.
39   Edwards 1938, pp. 28–9.

in Britain or in America failed to realise the combination of industrial monopolies and large banks which financed them, as appeared in its typical form in Germany. In the United States, the process of concentration of capital was driven forward, often fraudulently by swindles, in the securities market in which a very extensive 'investing public' participated. One should, of course, not be content to merely criticise this process as immoral; but it should not be reduced either to its formal aspect such as the 'impersonalisation of capital', which the extensive use of securities made possible in America. In either case, the real import of finance-capital fails to be grasped. An excessive reliance on the concept of securities capitalism, to which Edwards so frequently returns, tends to obscure the historical significance of finance-capital, as it represents the terminal and decadent form of capital, whether or not it actually resorted to the intemperance and fraudulence that characterised its American manifestation.

The swift growth of American industry within the corporate form was made possible by the mobilisation of widely held idle funds in the vast domestic market relatively sheltered from foreign competition. These conditions, in turn, made it easy to practice methods of monopolisation, which were attuned to the working of the securities market. In the United States, the cartels involving agreements on prices, on regulated production and on the division of sales territories, and so on, developed first under the name of 'pools'; but legal barriers prevented this particular form from growing systematically into a full-fledged monopoly organisation there. In its place, the form of *trust* developed not only because it was legal, but also because it was more suited to machinations in the securities market, and, thus, more congenial to the American way of concentrating capital. John D. Rockefeller of the Standard Oil Company was said to control a number of oil companies in the late 1870s already. In 1882, he succeeded in making a 'trust agreement' with the shareholders of some forty companies, an agreement whereby they handed their shares to a nine-member board of trustees, in exchange for 'trust certificates'. On behalf of the original shareholders, the board of trustees was to control the management of the oil companies that altogether accounted for 90 to 95 percent of the nation's oil refineries. The shareholders of each company now held a stake not only in their respective companies but also in the overall operation of the group, the unified management of which was the responsibility of the trustees. The latter, however, were also the owners of the majority of the trust certificates; hence, the control of the 'trust' system, in effect, fell into the hands of the very small Rockefeller coterie. Thus, although, in form, each company was managed independently, in effect, it functioned as a plant belonging to the trust. As a matter of fact, a plant which could not operate profitably could be closed, and a new one opened elsewhere, the shareholders of the individual member-firm having, by then, been reduced to simple recipients of dividends paid out of the profit from the entire operation of the group. Moreover, the trust contract was to last until the end of the twenty-first year, after the death of the last surviving signatory, so that it created no obstacle to unified management, despite its appearance of non-permanency. The trust could even purchase shares of any company operating outside the group, buying it out with accumulated, undistributed earnings, thus considerably strengthening the monopoly power of the trust which could act as a single firm.[40]

This ingenious method, invented by the refiners, was immediately copied in other industries, giving birth to The American Cotton Oil Trust in 1884, the National Linseed Oil Trust in 1885, the Distillers' and Cattle Feeders' Trust (commonly known as the Whiskey Trust) in 1887, and the Sugar Refineries Co., a trust which was formed around the sugar refiner which held a 78 percent share of all the sugar refining companies. However, the proliferation of trusts soon aroused political opposition to monopolies in various states, which led to legislations against them. Some were even indicted as illegal. In 1890, the u.s. Congress enacted an anti-trust law known as the Sherman Act; and, in the end, the Standard Oil Trust was, along with other trusts, ordered dissolved in 1892. Yet, in substance, their monopoly power remained. If the form of trust was declared illegal, the member companies sometimes merged directly to form a single company, as in the case of the sugar trust. Alternatively, they set up a holding company to replace the form of trust and stayed together, as in the case of the Cotton Oil Trust. The holding company, whether it was originally one of the member firms in the trust or newly set up, now acted as one unifying entity, owning the controlling shares of the affiliated companies. It could, therefore, maintain the same strong monopoly power as the original trust itself. As New Jersey took the initiative of chartering such a holding company in 1889, it soon became a favoured new instrument of monopolisation. However, the number of trusts adopting the form of the holding company was relatively small until the late 1890s. The Standard Oil Company of New Jersey, which was set up in 1898, was then regarded as a conspicuous exception to the rule.[41]*

*Jones also shows the following statistical table pertaining to the consolidation of firms. This table was compiled by Luther Conant.[42] Jones notes that it sometimes

40   Jones 1922, pp. 19–22.
41   Jones 1922, pp. 27–40.
42   Jones 1922, p. 39.

counts one trust several times over and that some of them cannot be regarded as indicating a trend towards monopoly.

TABLE N-5   *Consolidation of firms*

Year	Number of consolidations	Total resources (stock and debentures) in thousand dollars
1887	8	216,226
1888	3	23,600
1889	12	152,179
1890	13	155,156
1891	17	166,200
1892	10	193,412
1893	6	239,015
1894	2	30,400
1895	6	107,255
1896	5	49,850
1897	4	81,000
subtotal (1887–97)	86	1,414,293
1898	20	708,600
1899	87	2,243,995
1900	42	831,415
subtotal (1898–1900)	149	3,784,010
Total (1887–1900)	235	5,198,303

From 1900 to 1904, holding companies spread fairly widely in a variety of industries, including steel, tobacco, explosives, whiskey and meat-packing. In other manufacturing industries (such as harvesters, cans and glucose), amalgamations and mergers were more common. The trust in explosives, which first switched to the expedient of a holding company, later dispensed with it by merging the affiliated firms into a single company. Thus, the holding company was not necessarily the most dominant form of monopolisation; but it had the advantage of achieving a unified management of the member-firms at a relatively lower cost than in the case of an outright amalgamation or merger. This advantage was made use of by the United States Steel Corporation, which, when it was established in 1901, was the largest holding company. However, the depression of 1903–4 blunted the momentum of the trust movement, and the celebrated case of *Northern Securities versus the United States* of 1904 outlawed the holding company. The legality of the Oil Trust was challenged in 1911, and could not escape the court order for its dissolution and subsequent division into eleven independent companies. Yet the individuals who were in control of the holding company continued to dictate over the newly formed independent companies, so that no substantive change occurred to that monopolised group. By and large, the American trust movement may be said to have reached its peak in the years between 1900 and 1904, and subsequently lost its momentum by the First World War. The reason may be that the room for stock-market manipulation, which had always constituted the central drive of that movement, reached a point of saturation by that time, industrially as well as financially.[43]

As briefly outlined above, the trust movement in the United States spread its tentacles into a broad spectrum of industries around the turn of the century. As I repeatedly emphasised, the mainstay of this movement was always in the pursuit of monopoly profits by means of manipulation in the stock market. This, presumably, was due to the circumstances specific to the United States, for example, that the nation possessed an unusually vast territory and an abundant supply of funds available for investment in the stock market. It is, in any case, certain that the investors were motivated by the promise of an immense profit, accruing to the founder of a firm with monopoly power [*Grundungsgewinn*]. For example, the above-mentioned Steel Trust was organised in 1901, by consolidating eight firms, which had already exerted considerable monopoly power, in order to further enhance their monopoly profits. The promoters of this reorganisation were then rewarded with astronomical benefits. Those who promoted the original eight firms had already acquired $63 million in stocks; but, with the formation of the trust, the syndicate of promoters received 1,299,975 stocks (half of which were in common, and the rest in preferred, shares) valued at roughly $130 million. It is said that this, in effect, amounted to a net profit of $62.5 million, after allowing for the $28 million that they spent to buy up the shares of the original eight companies. One fifth of the profit of $62.5

---

43   For an overview of the trust movement in this period, see Jones 1922, pp. 42–5. See also Koga Hidemasa 1952, *Shihaishûchû-Ron* [*Concentration of the Control of the Firm*]. In Chapter 3, Section 2 of this book, entitled 'Highly Promoted Concentration of Control in Trusts', Koga deals with the concentration of capital based on detailed data on the American trust movement.

million went to Morgan & Company as the manager of the syndicate of promoters, and the remainder, amounting to $50 million, was distributed among the syndicate-members, including Morgan & Company once again.* The profit accruing to the promoters with a view to enhancing the monopoly power of the trust was, needless to say, the founders' gain [*Grundungsgewinn*], realised when they sold the newly issued shares to the public. As a matter of fact, the Steel Trust controlled three-fifths of the industry, so that even the companies beyond its control had to follow its lead in such matters as the determination of prices, which, of course, secured handsome monopoly profits for it. Admittedly, even this trust could not forever maintain its dominant position, which it wielded at its inception. Indeed, its share of the market, which was 66.3 percent in steel ingots and cast iron in 1901, declined to 54.7 percent in 1910. Though the trust increased its production, its competitors grew even more. Yet, the trust easily retained its monopoly power, since it produced ten times more than its largest competitor.[44]* This trust was organised, in the first place, when large steel-makers, which had come into being during the prosperity period in the last part of the 1890s, suddenly faced difficulties in the crisis of 1900. The competition among them intensified, as some firms which had been specialised in half-finished products began to produce finished ones, while others, which had supplied only finished products, now wanted to produce semi-finished ones as well. Under the circumstances, the industrial interests led by Carnegie allied themselves with Morgan's financial power to form the trust. Industry and finance thus accommodated each other for their mutual prosperity. The funds were, in effect, made available gratuitously at the inception of the trust, since the latter collected them in return for shares with no other backing than the expectation of a subsequent monopoly profit (i.e. what was to become the founders' profit), to be substantiated as the share price later proved its strength in the market (when the operation of the trust actually began to earn monopoly profits). The long-term profitable operation of the trust was thus secured by this financial machination at the outset.*** Here we see a striking example, which reveals the true nature of American finance-capital.

* Jones explains the remunerations paid to the promoters of the Steel Trust, by using the data available in regard to eight out of the ten large companies which constituted the trust. Apparently, Carnegie's company did not use promoters for their reorganisation before the establishment of the Steel Trust. The description in the text is owed to Jones.[45]

---

44   Jones 1922, pp. 215–16.
45   Jones 1922, pp. 286–9.

**Jones further deals with the ways in which the leading giant trusts in oil, sugar, tobacco, shoes, copper and farm machinery (harvester) were formed in respective chapters of the book, to which I draw the reader's attention.

***The capital structure of the Steel Trust, including the new company that joined in August 1901, can be seen from the table below.[46]

TABLE N-6 *Capital structure of the steel trust*

Debenture	$362,541,657
Borrowing	21,872,023
Preferred Stock	510,201,743
Common Stock	508.227.394
Total	1,402,846,817

Note that the 'real' value of the Trust's total capital was estimated to be in the order of $600 to $700 million. Thus, in the table, nearly all of the common stocks must have been grossly overvalued, and so were part (perhaps one-fifth or two-fifths) of the preferred stocks, an astonishing over-capitalisation indeed! Yet they were nevertheless made good by the Trust's subsequent earning of monopoly profit.

The trust movement in the United States constituted the operation of finance-capital, which concentrated capital by astutely making use of the corporate form of business enterprises. As the case of the United States Steel Corporation most strikingly shows, the monopoly-seeking combination was jointly fashioned by the financial interest led by Morgan and the industrial interest represented by Carnegie. The combination was, of course, intent upon pursuing a spectacular gain realisable only by stock-market operations. However, to the extent that these operations (or manipulations) played the principal role, it must be concluded that finance-capital made use of the monopoly power of the industry from the outside as it were, and, thus in effect, failed to penetrate it by means of a systematic monopoly organisation of the kind that was formed in Germany. In other words, finance-capital expropriated funds invested in stocks by the general public, often by fraud and swindles in the process of promoting industrial monopoly. This indeed turned out to be the peculiarly American feature of finance-capital in the stage of imperialism.*

---

46   Quoted from Jones 1922, p. 207. See also Koga Hidemasa 1952, pp. 269–71.

*I do not believe that such stock-market manipulations, often involving fraud and swindles, which we observed in connection with its American variant, should constitute the essential part of the definition of finance-capital as a stage-theoretic type. Since its ultimate goal is to pursue monopoly profits, finance-capital may quite naturally resort to expropriation, circumstances permitting; and expropriation by means of stock-market manipulations may be viewed as reflecting the exercise of its monopoly power. Yet one should not magnify that aspect out of proportion, lest one arrive at an incorrect idea of finance-capital. The latter accumulates by means of its monopoly power in industry, which it uses, for example, to intensify the labour of the wage-workers, peasants and small entrepreneurs. Stock-market manipulation, which was frequently used to expropriate idle funds from the masses of the investing public, was the surface phenomenon that tended to submerge that aspect of reality. Of course, due attention must be paid to the special feature of the American economy, which led to the prominence of that form of expropriation – all the more so because, in many nations in the age of finance-capital, an expropriation of small funds proved to be the prevalent feature. Nevertheless, the theoretical specification of finance-capital must not be confused with its concrete manifestations in different circumstances.

CHAPTER 9

Economic Policies of Imperialism

Monopoly firms, as the agents of finance-capital, especially as they were grouped together in an organised monopoly, regulated their own production and dictated the prices at which their products were to be sold in the domestic market; at the same time, they aggressively promoted the export of their commodities at competitive prices well below the domestic ones, and/or undertook the export of capital with no less determination. Some may thus regard them as having adopted their own economic policies, inasmuch as the systematic enforcement of these moves may well have given the impression that the whole economy and society were now effectively organised under the control of capital. It goes without saying, however, that capital cannot by itself achieve a truly comprehensive organisation of the whole society without negating itself. As is only to be expected, capital's own control over the organisation of its production and sales within the framework of the commodity-economy must always remain partial and can never fully engulf the whole control of society. During the stage of imperialism, as previously mentioned, it was also the case that the working of the capitalist law of population tended to be distorted, as the adoption of new productive methods and the consequent creation of relative surplus population did not occur in the regular process of business cycles, as had been typical in the previous stage. At the same time, the lender-borrower relationship between banks and firms, which used to stall periodically in key industries and to burst into a panic and a crisis, was now transformed into a co-ordinated investment policy of a small number of monopoly firms and large banks combined in an organic fusion. These circumstances may also nurture the false impression that the anarchy of the capitalist economy was finally overcome within a new capitalist regime; but that impression, though partially true on the surface of it, does not warrant a prospect of a fully planned economy. On the contrary, the partial organisation of the economy by monopoly capital only aggravated its unevenness inside the nation, which, in turn, translated itself into an increased pressure for imperialism of the nation's external policies. Referring to Kautsky's idea of a so-called 'ultra-imperialism', V.I. Lenin scornfully commented thus: 'It encourages ... that profoundly mistaken idea, which only brings grist to the mill of the apologists of imperialism, i.e., that the rule of finance-capital lessens the unevenness and contradictions inherent in the world economy, whereas in reality it *increases* them'.[1]* Lenin correctly affirms

---

1 Lenin 1971, p. 237.

here that the imperialist policies, far from mitigating the 'unevenness and contradictions' in the development of capitalism, actually render their resolution
even more difficult. The imperialist policies certainly do not serve to restrain
the development of capitalism; they, on the contrary, add to its violence.

* On Kautsky's theory of ultra-imperialism, Lenin comments further as follows:
'"From the purely economic point of view", writes Kautsky, "it is not impossible that
capitalism will yet go through a new phase, that of the extension of the policy of the
cartels to foreign policy, the phase of ultra-imperialism", i.e., of a super-imperialism,
of a union of the imperialisms of the whole world and not struggles among them, a
phase when wars shall cease under capitalism, a phase of "the joint exploitation of
the world by internationally united finance-capital" ... If "the purely economic point
of view" is meant to be a *pure* abstraction, then all that can be said may be reduced
to the following proposition: development is proceeding towards monopolies, hence,
towards a single world monopoly, towards a single world trust. This is indisputable,
but it is also ... meaningless ...'.[2] It is not absolutely clear to me what Lenin implies
by the phrase 'if "the purely economic point of view" is meant to be a pure abstraction', but he may mean by 'pure abstraction' something akin to what I call 'purely
theoretical determination'. If so, a very interesting and important problem of methodology arises here. In the context of pure theory, which must surely abstract from
international relations, how can one possibly infer such propositions as 'development
is proceeding towards monopolies, hence towards a single world monopoly, towards
a single world trust', and conclude that 'this is indisputable, but ... meaningless'? The
real question is rather how such things as the state and international economy can be
treated in the context of 'purely theoretical determinations' such as are developed in
Marx's *Capital*. It is surely the failure to bring to light this sort of problem that led to
Kautsky's 'lifeless abstraction of ultra-imperialism'.[3] Does not Lenin's conclusion that
'the best reply [to such empty abstractions] is to contrast them with the concrete economic realities of the present-day world economy' become more convincing, when the
levels of abstraction appropriate to the 'purely theoretical' and to the 'stages-theoretic'
determinations are distinguished more clearly? Of course, these 'concrete economic
realities' cannot be stages-theoretically determined in full, by a study of economic
policies alone. They must, no doubt, be jointly studied, in concrete terms, from the
point of view not only of economics but also of law and politics. That, however, does
not prevent us from 'discussing the purely economic conditions of the epoch of finance-
capital as a historically concrete epoch which began at the turn of the twentieth cen-

2   Lenin 1971, pp. 236–7.
3   Lenin 1971, p. 237.

tury',[4] though in a manner different from Kautsky's. It is the failure to distinguish between the stages-theory and the pure theory of capitalism that poses the danger of dissolving the theory of imperialism into mere political discussions.

The economic policies of imperialism came into being as capitalism matured to its final developmental stage, in which monopoly enterprises, as manifestations of finance-capital, sought to extend the sphere exclusively reserved for their action. The accelerated development of capitalism during the 1870s on the European Continent, and especially in Germany, was to mark a new epoch with the arrival of a slump in the latter half of that decade. Yet, no clear policy perspective existed at the outset. On the one hand, somewhat 'nationalistic' policies of protective tariffs were adopted by Germany and others with a view, in the main, to counterbalancing the aggressive internationalisation of the free-trade movement, led by Britain in the preceding decade. On the other hand, the United Kingdom, for its part, led the expansionist policy, aimed at a world-wide pursuit of colonies and spheres of influence. It could not be denied that these external policies were inspired by a new mode of capital accumulation, yet what that new mode was about to be was not as yet unequivocally clear on either side. It only became apparent in the beginning of the 1880s, and over the following several decades, that these were the policies of finance-capital, which aimed to repudiate, and supplant, the liberal policies of industrial capital that had unquestionably prevailed in the previous era.

These new policies, whether geared to tariff protection or more obviously to territorial expansion, were quite distinct, in nature, from the policies practised earlier in the mercantilist and the liberal ages. For, in the final analysis, they represented the drive of finance-capital as it struggled to extend its spheres of influence, by way of the division and re-division of the globe's surface. These policies also reflected the limitations of monopoly capital in that they never sought a rational organisation of the world economy, nor did they, as the mercantilist policies of the past, prepare the ground upon which liberalism was to be brought to fruition. The tariff policies of monopoly capital, as previously mentioned, were quite unlike the ones advocated earlier by Friedrich List, which aimed to provide temporary protection to an infant industry that would eventually take part in liberalised trade. They aimed at the protection of domestic cartels by setting up tariff walls, with the hardly disguised intent to subsequently 'dump' domestically unsold commodities in the world market, so as to carve out an ever increasing section of it as an exclusive territory for

---

4   Ibid.

the nation's finance-capital. The export of capital added further impetus to the same intent. The consequent 'division and re-division of the world' into spheres of influence eventually led to the polarisation of two imperialist coalitions, one led by Germany and the other by the United Kingdom, until they inevitably clashed in the First World War.

1   Customs Policy and Dumping

In the United States, customs policy took a new turn as early as the 1860s as the Civil War ended with the ascendancy of the northern states. As far as Germany was concerned, it consummated its free trade between 1873 and 1877, as its capitalist development accelerated in the early 1870s consequent upon the birth of the Empire, which, for its part, entailed a spectacular economic boom. Since the United States was isolated from the other capitalist states, and endowed with such peculiar conditions as has already been pointed out, it was destined to follow a unique path, both in the formation of finance-capital and in the customs policy which it put into practice. In contrast, Germany, which was located in close proximity not only to the United Kingdom, a far more advanced capitalist rival, but also to several other late-starters following close on its heels, needed to catch up with and quickly outpace its arch rival in capitalist production, by proving its prowess in a systematic and efficient organisation of the economy. German tariff policies, which closely echoed the needs of finance-capital coming of age in that country, could thus exhibit the most typical pattern of capitalist policies appropriate to the imperialist stage of development.

The German customs union, prior to the advent of the Empire, could not be said to have aimed single-mindedly at a unified goal, since it was difficult to co-ordinate the dissenting interests of the constituent states. On the whole, however, it tended to support the trend towards free trade, under the leadership of Prussia, a leadership which achieved the unification of Germany in 1870. Soon after that date, the tariff system was revised and simplified, in such a way that the duty on iron-goods was reduced, while chemicals and many other goods were made exempt from duties. In 1873, protective tariffs were generally lightened or abolished in the spirit of free trade, the remaining duties being meant only to serve the purposes of national revenue. In 1877, pig-iron and half-finished iron-goods became duty-free, and, in regard to other commodities, only a few finished goods remained dutiable. These measures, however, were not so enthusiastically supported by iron-makers and those who had stakes in the cotton industry. Indeed, the Southern states of the empire, where these industries were mainly located, took a position against the liberal revisions of the tariff schedule; but the traditional liberal policy of Prussia, strongly backed by its agrarian interests, still held sway over the policy decisions of the Empire.[5]

However, in the latter half of the 1870s, economic conditions had changed so radically that they would not permit the continuation of such a policy any further. The recession of 1873 and the improvement in the means of transportation, which eventually led to the massive import of foreign grains, especially from Russia and the United States, impacted severely on German agriculture, while bringing into prominence large capitalist industries, which abruptly surfaced during the wild economic boom following recovery from the crisis. German agriculture, represented especially by the Prussian landlords, now had reasons to demand a switch from free trade to a protectionist commercial policy.* It appeared as though the need for a radical policy switch arose at precisely the moment when Germany was about to achieve its ideal of free trade. Thus, the conversion could not occur smoothly as a matter of course. Moreover, as the swift expansion of public expenditure, which the newly formed German Empire required, had to depend increasingly on indirect taxes, Bismarck naturally counted on increased customs revenue, rather than on raising the member states' dues to the imperial coffers, which would risk being translated into heavier direct taxation within the states. That strategy, he felt, was opportune, given that France and other countries around Germany had, by this time, resorted to the elevation of numerous tariffs. Thus, by 1879, Germany had returned to protectionism, with the express intent of shielding domestic industries from foreign competition within its national market. Yet the tariff policy of 1879, adopted under these special circumstances, could not be categorised immediately as belonging to the new, imperialist economic policies, enforced by the coalition of monopoly capital and landed property. For one thing, the tariff rates were still quite modest, such as one mark for one hundred kilograms of wheat, rye and oat, one mark for one hundred kilograms of pig-iron, and a 15–30 percent ad valorem on textile goods. The merchandise classified as raw materials (such as cotton, flax, hemp, wool, hides, coal, and the like), remained duty-free. This new tariff policy, though novel in appearance, was only the outcome of a compromise achieved among different competing interests. Yet the fact that tariffs on iron goods and grains were both there, side by side, marked a fresh beginning for German tariff policy.

---

5   On the evolution of German customs policy, see P. Ashley 1920, on which my descriptions in this paragraph depends.

*The following table shows the evolution of grain prices in Prussia. They reached a peak in 1871–80 and then declined. On entering the twentieth century, however, they rose again, which is worthy of note, quite apart from the comparison of these with other prices.

TABLE N-1   *Grain prices in Prussia (in marks per 100 kg)*[6]

Period	Wheat	Rye
1861–70	20.46	15.46
1871–80	22.32	17.28
1881–90	18.15	15.15
1891–1900	16.32	14.17
1901–13	18.74	15.80

This 1879 revision of duties gave agricultural countries, which exported farm products to Germany, and imported industrial goods therefrom, such as Austria, Russia and so on, grounds for strengthening their own tariff policies. They were, in particular, provoked by the German grains tariff. However, since that tariff did not stop grain prices from falling further in Germany, the latter raised the duty on wheat and rye to 3 marks per one hundred kilograms in 1885, and then to 5 marks in 1888. With all that Germany still managed to maintain, in its commercial treaties throughout the decade of 1880s, the most-favoured-nation clause with its trade partners, except Russia. Only the development of German capitalism during the boom years of the late 1880s, coupled with the rise of grain prices consequent upon the bad harvests of 1890 and 1891, brought into being a situation requiring a new departure in the thus far haphazard tariff policy of the Empire. The retirement of Bismarck, followed by the instatement of the Caprivi cabinet, marked a veritable turning point for the German tariff policy.

As a matter of fact, the countries which maintained commercial treaties with Germany, containing the most-favoured-nation clause, had announced their intention to revise them. At this point, in order to secure the export of manufactured goods, the newly installed German government tried to conclude fresh treaties with Austria, Russia, Italy and others, offering to reduce duties on agricultural products, and with Belgium, Switzerland, and others, offering

---

6   *Handwörterbuch der Staatswissenschaften*, IV. Aufl., IV. Bd., p. 899.

to reduce duties on industrial products. Thus, Germany was successful in concluding new treaties at the end of 1891, first with Austria-Hungary, and then with Italy, Belgium and Switzerland. In these treaties, Germany reduced duties on agricultural products below the level of 1888 to roughly that of 1885. As for industrial products, it reduced duties on glass, paper, textile goods, iron-and-steel goods among others. In return, Germany obtained general tariff reductions from its trade partners. These treaties, which granted the most-favoured-nation treatment on reciprocal terms, were to remain effective until the end of 1903. However, inside the country, most of those with stakes in industry were not happy with these treaties, while the agriculturalists felt that they had been duped into making undue concessions. That was not all. With such countries as Serbia, Rumania and Russia, which had a vital stake in German agricultural tariffs, the treaties remained yet to be revised. Russia and Rumania, in particular, were important for Germany as traditional exporters of agricultural goods to Germany while being dependable importers of German industrial goods to their markets.*

* Rumania's share in the German import of wheat was only 5 percent in 1889, but increased to 20.4 percent in 1893. Rumania had a greater share in the German import of rye. On the other hand, Russia imported £10.3 million from Germany, but exported to it £270 million in 1890. About half of the German imports of grains came from Russia in 1891, which constituted one sixth of Russia's exports of grains. Germany not only exported her own manufactured goods to Russia, but also mediated Russia's importation of raw cotton and wool, thus competing with Britain.[7]

During the 1880s, Russia was a high-tariff nation. However, when, in the early 1890s, Germany concluded new treaties with Austria and several other countries, Russia found that its exports to Germany were blocked by unusually high tariff walls, and so it undertook to demand concessions. The negotiations between the two countries did not progress smoothly, and, in August 1893, the celebrated tariff war broke out, such that, as soon as one party raised a tariff on any item, the other retaliated to it by stepping up discriminatory treatment of one sort or another. Such a war, needless to say, imposed damages on both sides, so that, as early as September of the same year, a new round of negotiations began, and finally bore fruit, in February 1894, in the form of a new treaty. By this new treaty, Russia obtained most-favoured-nation treatment on its exports of grains, on which Germany no longer applied a discriminatory tariff. At the

7   P. Ashley 1920, pp. 68–9.

same time, Germany obtained from Russia concessions in reduced tariffs on 120 items. The two countries also agreed not to raise tariffs on a limited number of commodities for ten years. Meanwhile, Germany waged tariff wars with Spain and Canada as well. With Spain, however, Germany managed, in the end, to conclude a new treaty with a most-favoured-nation clause in 1899. On the other hand, when Canada granted preferential treatment to the United Kingdom in 1897, Germany objected to it on the grounds that it violated the treaty of 1865 between Germany and the United Kingdom. Thereupon a tariff war broke out between Germany and Canada, such that Germany levied statutory tariffs on Canadian goods, to which Canada responded by charging a surtax amounting to one third of the ongoing duties on all German goods. All this seemed to indicate that, in treaty negotiations, the new German policy amounted to a continuation of protectionism, which was achieved by first threatening the other party with high statutory tariffs on its goods, but then relenting to lower them to treaty tariffs, only when the maximum concessions had been obtained from the other party.

However, such a policy in treaty negotiations faced stringent opposition from the agricultural interest at home, an opposition which intensified further as Hohenlohe replaced Caprivi as head of the government, shortly after the conclusion of the treaty with Russia. Germany was then clearly drifting towards stronger protectionism. How far in that direction the German policy of treaty negotiations proceeded remains unknown; but it is quite certain that German industries had, by that time, made a giant stride forward, with its iron-and-steel industry on the verge of surpassing its British rival, while its overseas trade generally expanded with vigour in the background. At the same time, it was from about that time that the so-called 'agricultural problem' began to surface and attract increasing attention, so much so that by the end of the 1890s, politicians and scholars had embarked upon heated debates on it in preparation for a new customs act in 1903, since the current treaties were expected to be revised in that year.* The tariff bill, proposed by the government in the summer of 1901, was enacted after an intense debate towards the end of the following year. The act's central feature was the strengthening of agricultural tariffs. Indeed it raised tariffs on staple grains, such as wheat and rye. It also introduced the statutory maximum and minimum of tariff rates, stipulating the rule that no treaty could adopt a tariff rate below the minimum. The tariff rate on wheat and rye had been raised from the 1885-level of 3 marks per 100 kilograms to 5 marks in 1888, but this was lowered by a subsequent treaty to 3.5 marks. The new customs act now stipulated the maximum rate on wheat and rye, respectively, at 7.5 and 7 marks and the minimum rate at 5.5 and 5 marks per 100 kilograms. The duties on oats and malting barley were similarly raised. At the same time, duties on manufactured articles, such as iron goods, cotton and woollen goods, silk manufactures, and so on, were raised. As regards raw materials, however, duties were either reduced or abolished, unless the old rates were maintained. The general tendency was to subdivide merchandise into minute classes so as to circumvent the application of the most-favoured-nation clause, and to provide retaliatory tariffs to be applied against any discriminatory treatment that the trading partner might take recourse to in future. The new customs act of Germany thus offered a typical example of imperialist tariff policy.

* The leading German economists of the time, representing more or less the stand-point of the school of *socialpolitik* expressed various opinions on this customs act. As P. Ashley recounts, Adolf Wagner led the right wing which called for the intensifica-tion of protection, while Gustav Schmoller led the moderates and Lujo Brentano the left wing that demanded free trade. Their debates, however, exposed in broad daylight the emptiness of the so-called 'policy recommendations' so stridently argued by prac-tically minded economists. By the way, the academic association for studies on social policy [*Verein für Sozialpolitik*] adopted 'tariff policy' as the theme for its 1901 annual convention.

With this customs act in hand, Germany negotiated and concluded a new com-mercial treaty first with Russia, which was still at war with Japan, in 1905, and with almost all of its other trade partners, offering to grant the most-favoured-nation treatment on reciprocal terms. As most of them came to the negotiating table, prepared to take a stiff stance to counter Germany's drift towards pro-tectionism, the latter did not, on this occasion, necessarily obtain the most advantageous terms. That was in fact only to be expected, given the circum-stances in which its foreign trade, in both exports and imports, increased by leaps and bounds, along with the accelerated advance of its domestic produc-tion. What characterised Germany's policy stance at this juncture was the fact that with such industrial dynamism in the background, the nation was also compelled to introduce high tariffs on grains so as to protect its agriculture, which had lost its competitive edge in the international market. In other words, Germany had to protect practically all products simultaneously, with agricul-tural goods on one side and iron-and-steel goods on the other, the need for protection arising for different reasons at each end of the spectrum. In neither case, however, were these new tariffs still intended to provide infant-industry protection; the tariffs levied on the products of heavy industries were unmis-takably 'cartel tariffs'. What is remarkable was that these cartel tariffs came into being together with, and in the background of, the high tariffs on grains, which attracted much more heated debate politically. It is also worth noting that the tariff rates on industrial goods were not uniformly elevated. There were items for which the tariff rate was reduced somewhat and there were ones, such as wool, cotton and leather goods, for which it was elevated significantly. As for the tariff on pig-iron, it remained at the same level as in 1878, i.e. at 1 mark per 100 kilograms, which, of course, does not necessarily disqualify it as a *cartel tariff*. For the latter must be understood as any tariff that safeguards the existing price dictated by a domestic cartel. Given that iron-and-steel industry had, by that time, progressed to a level so far ahead of where it had stood in the 1870s, the same tariff of 1 mark per 100 kilograms was expected to have a much stronger protective effect. On the other hand, a high tariff rate did not always permit the cartel to raise its domestic price to the full extent of the protected margin, nor to appropriate the whole of the price differential between the home and international market as its monopoly profit. For a strong cartel in raw materials and half-finished goods could, by exercising its own monopoly power, always charge monopoly rents on its products so as to expropriate part of that which might otherwise have accrued to the cartel in finished goods. As Hilferding described, cartels were empowered to appropriate the monopoly profit that the protective tariff secures, which amounted to charging and collecting an indirect tax on the domestic population.[8]

The development of the German tariff policy since the late nineteenth century, which has just been summarised, entailed yet another very important factor. When that factor surfaced, it forced the United Kingdom, the stronghold of free trade throughout the nineteenth century, to also confront the problem of trade afresh in the context of this new era. When the tariff policy of the state changed direction in the latter half of the 1870s, German industries no longer needed the infant-industry protection of the sort that List had espoused. They had outgrown that phase and had become industries characterised by large-scale production, with much at stake in the export of their products. The protection of the domestic market with tariffs meant, for many important industries, the protection of the cartels that had emerged within the country, and contained, from the beginning, elements that contradicted the idea of the promotion of exports. The contradiction was magnified as surrounding countries gradually strengthened their tendency to protect their respective domestic markets, in response to the German promotion of exports. Cartels sought to raise the domestic prices of their products, while selling them abroad at prices significantly below them. Heavy industries requiring a massive investment of fixed capital could not easily cut back on their production, even when

8   Hilferding 1981, p. 308.

demand in the domestic market declined, not only because it was technically difficult to do so but also because of the accompanying increase in the unit cost of the product. Therefore, the products supplied over and above the amount that could be sold domestically had to be sold abroad even at drastically lower, giveaway prices.* During the depression years of the late 1870s, German industries protested loudly against the sacrifice sales of British commodities in the German market. Yet, as cartelisation subsequently progressed in Germany, it was the British who now complained, quite as vociferously, of German 'dumping'. This dumping carried out systematically by cartels was quite unlike the bargain sales occasionally resorted to by individual firms; and to that extent, it caused several serious problems, even within the German domestic market. For in order to promote the export of its products, a cartel was obliged to compensate its affiliated firms for their products which had to be sold abroad at reduced prices, the compensation then becoming like an export subsidy. The domestic purchasers of the cartel's products could, however, become high-cost producers and exporters of their own goods in the international markets, if they, as non-members, failed to be compensated by the cartel for the extra burden of the cost that they had to bear.

*The relation between the production and the estimated domestic consumption of pig-iron in Germany from 1897 to 1902 were as shown in the following table. It shows that the quantity of pig-iron which had to be exported increased enormously in 1901 and 1902.

TABLE N-2 *Production and domestic consumption of pig iron in Germany (1000 tons)*[9]

Year	Production	Consumption
1897	6,881	6,053
1898	7,312	6,210
1899	8,143	7,473
1900	8,520	7,955
1901	7,880	5,933
1902	8,402	5,362

9 W. Ashley 1920, p. 121.

It is generally accepted that Germany resorted to the dumping of coal in the early 1880s. Then the practice spread to iron in 1891, and became distinctly more systematic after 1897. In 1902, the syndicates in coal and iron established a joint clearing office, which recorded all exports of these commodities by the affiliated members of the syndicates, so as to pay compensation according to the prevailing rates, which were revised quarterly.[10]* For instance, the iron bars which were sold for 95 marks in the domestic market were exported at 80 marks or at 75 marks, as the case may be. As the rolling mills in Britain and Belgium used iron goods imported from Germany, the international price of rolled wire fell. The German wire industries, which exported almost 60 per cent of their products and had to purchase their materials at high domestic prices, were then clearly disadvantaged relative to the foreign wire producers.[11] Moreover, the German wire makers were not the only ones to suffer from the deleterious effect of dumping. It also affected British industries as well. During the depression years of 1901 and 1902, the United Kingdom massively increased its import of iron-and-steel goods, most of which were dumped in the international market by Germany** at the expense of British competitors. That then gave new impetus to the movement, which had been growing in Britain since the 1880s and 1890s, demanding a revision of free trade policy.

* Already, in 1897, German heavy industry products which were exported were compensated at the rate of 15 marks per ton by the syndicates operating in coal, raw iron, and half-finished iron-goods, depending on the quantities of the raw material bought from them (sometimes, exported coke also received the same treatment by the syndicate operating in the product). Still, during the prosperity phase of 1898–9, as the world market price of heavy industry goods rose to a level above the domestic cartel price, this scheme became superfluous. Consequently, a more systematic scheme was adopted, in 1902, to confront the new depression. On 1 April 1902, the following rates became effective: 1.5 marks per ton of coal and coke (where coal was reckoned to be equal to 70 percent of coke) used to produce goods that were exported; as for iron goods, 2.5 marks per ton of raw iron were added to the compensation rates on coal; 10 marks were paid for each ton of half-finished iron goods exported, and likewise for goods to be used in bridge construction which were exported, including the compensations on coal and raw iron.[12]

---

10   W. Ashley 1920, pp. 121–3.

11   W. Ashley 1920, pp. 128–9.

12   W. Ashley 1920, pp. 122–3.

** The following two tables show the jump in the quantity of iron imported to the United Kingdom from 1901 to 1902.[13]

TABLE N-3   *Basic iron goods imported to UK (in tons)*

Year	Iron bar, etc.	Unwrought steel	Total
1901	98,100	182,649	280,749
1902	171,754	280,945	452,699

TABLE N-3'   *Manufactured iron wares imported to UK from Germany, Holland and Belgium (chiefly German goods)*

Year	(in tons)
1901	171,849
1902	269,759

The whole period extending from the second half of the 1870s to the late 1890s is known as the age of the Great Depression in Great Britain. There were signs of recovery in the early 1880s, in 1888 and again in 1890; but the turnaround did not last long. It was, thus, not until 1890 that the volume of British exports exceeded the level of 1872–3. Even when Britain's major industries managed to increase production, they could not find sufficient outlets in the market. More or less similar situations prevailed in other industrial nations as well, which induced them, and especially Germany, to strengthen their respective policies of protectionism. This trend affected the United Kingdom in a peculiar manner, as it was losing the privileged position of 'the workshop of the world', which it had enjoyed up to the end of the 1860s. Accordingly, in the early 1880s, there arose even in Britain, which had long been the stronghold of free trade, a movement calling for Fair Trade to counter the 'unfair practices' of the other countries. The movement aimed at restricting the scope of free trade to the interior of the

---

13   W. Ashley 1920, pp. 124–5.

British Empire, consisting of the mother country and her colonies, while adopting protective policies externally. The Conference of Colonial Premiers held in 1887, 1894 and 1897 had dealt with tariff questions from the very beginning. It was, however, in the last of these meetings that Canada agreed to introduce preferential tariffs with regard to the United Kingdom.

Germany protested against this move on the basis of the existing treaty of 1865. Yet the United Kingdom sided with Canada by abrogating the treaty with Germany, which forced the latter to treat Canada quite separately from the United Kingdom. The British action, in this instance, in effect, heralded a switch in the country's approach to foreign trade.[14] In the 1902 Conference of Colonial Premiers, Britain was asked by the colonies to grant preferential treatment on colonial goods in its own market, in exchange for the preferential tariffs that it enjoyed on the export of its goods to the colonies. The colonial premiers were following the example of Canada, which had for a long time demanded and finally obtained preferential treatment on its goods, especially on grains, in the British market. In 1903, South Africa, Australia and New Zealand adopted preferential tariffs on the same terms as Canada. However, the willingness of the colonies to conclude such a special trade relation with Britain was predicated upon the latter's adopting a discriminatory tariff policy vis-à-vis other countries, which, however, was not easy for the mother country, inasmuch as that would have meant a radical departure from the traditional policy of free trade. The British reluctance to abandon the principle of free trade was reflected in the low-key performance of the movement led by Joseph Chamberlain (1836–1914). It became even more conspicuous after 1903, following his resignation as the colonial minister in the conservative government of 1895, since the movement had explicitly campaigned for imperialist protection policies, based, in particular, on a preferential trading system with the colonies. It was also apparent in the failure to obtain the official recantation of the free trade doctrine, which the 1907 Conference of Colonial Premiers requested. Nevertheless, in response to Germany's increasingly aggressive stance, which had been geared towards imperialism, ever since the dawn of the twentieth century, Britain was gradually pushed towards a radical switch in its own commercial policy. The renaming of 'the Conference of Colonial Premiers' to 'the Imperial Conference' symbolised a decisive shift at the helm.

To the extent that the German tariff policy was profitably made use of by cartel organisations, German industries, especially those that nurtured domestic monopolies, could not avoid the dumping of their products in foreign markets,

---

14   P. Ashley 1920, pp. 75–6.

and in a thoroughly systematic fashion. The reason that Great Britain did not choose to confront this offensive immediately (so it appeared at least), despite the repeated requests arising from the colonies, lay in the fact that her imperialism stood on a base quite different from that on which German imperialism was erected. What constituted that uniquely British base of imperialism was the expansion of colonies and overseas investment. Only in the late nineteenth century did Britain begin to pursue these two in earnest.

2   The Acquisition of Colonies and the Export of Capital

A. Supan, a geographer, whose table is quoted by Lenin in his book on imperialism, presents the following picture: Whereas, by 1876, only 10.8 percent of the African Continent had been acquired as colonies by European powers, the latter had, by 1900, carved up for themselves as much as 90.4 percent of the same territory. The table also shows that, in Polynesia, the percentage of the territory that was acquired by the imperial powers increased from 56.8 to 98.9 percent during the same period. It is, therefore, indisputable that, after the decade of the 1880s, there intervened an age of territorial acquisition and expansion by leading capitalist nations.[15] J.A. Hobson, who undertook research on extensive colonial acquisitions by Britain from 1870 to 1900, writes as follows: 'The vast increase of territory, and the method of wholesale partition which assigned to us great tracts of African land, may be dated from about 1884. Within fifteen years some three and three-quarter millions of square miles were added to the British Empire'. Great Britain, however, was not alone in expanding its territory in this period, as he goes on to say: 'The definite advance of Germany upon its Imperialist career began in 1884, with the policy of African protectorates and annexations of Oceanic islands. During the next fifteen years she brought under her colonial sway about 1,000,000 square miles, with an estimated population of 14,000,000'. Similarly, 'France was soon actively engaged in the scramble for Africa in 1884, while at the same time she was fastening her rule on Tonking and Laos in Asia. Her acquisitions between 1880 and 1900 (exclusive of the extension of New Caledonia and its dependencies) amounted to an area of over three and a half million square miles, with a native population of some 37,000,000'. Italy, Portugal and Belgium also took part in the same scramble for new territory. Although Spain and the Netherlands kept away from the race for territorial expansion at this time, Russia and the United States joined it in a somewhat dif-

15   Lenin 1971, p. 60 (p. 223).

ferent way, due to the special circumstances that then defined their interests.[16] What transpires from the above is literally 'the partition of the world' by the imperialist powers. In 1914, on the eve of the Great War, only Persia, China, Turkey and a few other old states remained free, although many of them were reduced to what may be termed as 'semi-colonies'.*

* On the partition of the world, Lenin quotes the following figures for 1914:

TABLE N-4   *Colonial possessions of the great powers*[17]

	Area (in million km²)	Population (in million inhabitants)
The Six Great Powers[a]	81.5	960.6
(Not inc. the mother countries)	(65.0)	(523.4)
Colonies of Other Powers[b]	9.9	45.3
Semi-Colonies[c]	14.5	361.2
Other Countries	28.0	289.9
Total for the World	133.9	1,657.0

[a] Great Britain, Russia, France, Germany, United States, Japan
[b] Belgium, Holland, etc.
[c] Persia, Turkey, China, etc.

I have already stated that the decade of the 1880s, which followed the depression years of the latter half of the 1870s, was the age during which European countries witnessed, on the one hand, the high tariff policies led by Germany and, on the other, a massive increase in the export of capital, spearheaded by Great Britain. These two concomitant trends were surely not unrelated. Yet, just as the German tariff policy did not directly work as the agent of the cartel-forming monopolies, neither was the British acquisition of new territories directly motivated by the simple desire to ensure the export of capital. The expansion was propelled rather as a policy in anticipation of the needs that finance-capital would encounter in the future, as it grew out of its formative stage. It cannot be denied that, to some extent, Britain aimed at securing outlets for its commodities or that it sought resources that could be used as raw mater-

16   J.A. Hobson 1971, pp. 19–22.
17   Lenin 1971, p. 226.

ials. It may have hoped as well to enlarge opportunities for direct investment of capital. However, the primary motive of Britain's expansion, in this period, was to enclose a territory for prospective use, territory which would guarantee free action for British monopoly capitals untrammelled by other capitalist nations. Indeed, the acquisition of a new territory did not *ipso facto* lead to an expansion of the scope of foreign investment or of the market for exports. As for resources for use as raw materials, these had only just been found, and their full usefulness was yet to be explored. In many cases, they had to wait for a new invention or the discovery of a new method which could be applied for their effective use. They, nevertheless, had to be laid claim to, since, as Lenin said, 'present-day technical development is extremely rapid, and land which is useless today may be improved tomorrow if new methods are devised, and if large amounts of capital are invested'.[18] In other words, an ever-larger territory had to be claimed as exclusive territory and cordoned off from possible encroachment by other competing capitalist nations.

It was, of course, not accidental that the export of capital from Britain was strongly re-activated in this period of the so-called 'partition of the world', as typified by the division of Africa. Yet, even in this period, the way in which British capital was exported could only be described as unsystematic or disorganised, even bordering on anarchic. Up to the early 1870s, the destination of British foreign investment was largely limited to the European Continent; but this practice changed during the period in question, as more and more of the less-developed nations began to join the club. Even then, the recipient areas and projects attracting British investment were various, and changing constantly. In the early 1880s, Australia and South Africa were the first (outside Europe) to absorb British funds, and then came the railway projects in Canada, the United States and India. In 1884–5, gold and diamond mines were discovered in South Africa, which certainly accelerated British investment there. However, in the early 1890s, the collapse of business prosperity in Argentina dealt a severe blow to British investments with repercussions on those in South Africa and Australia. Britain continued to invest overseas throughout the 1890s, until the discovery of a new method of refining gold-ore brought a boom to gold mines in South America and Australia, which led to an additional investment of several million pounds there. Overall, however, the increase of foreign investment in the 1890s was less than in the 1880s, as American railway bonds began gradually to be sold at home (in the United States) rather than to British investors. Still, after an interruption by the Boer War of 1899–

---

18   Lenin 1971, p. 229.

1902, British overseas investment resumed its strength in 1904 and realised an epochal new upswing, which was initiated, in particular, by investments in railways in Canada and Argentina. The leading actors in this period were Canada, the United States and Argentina, followed by such Latin American countries, as Mexico, Brazil and Chile. South Africa, Egypt, the East and the West Coast of Africa also joined the crowd, though on a smaller scale. In the period 1904–7, British foreign investment rose very rapidly and reached the phenomenal sum of £140 million, which far exceeded the previous peak of 1872. In 1908–9, there was a temporary setback in this trend; but a new expansion began in 1910. This new expansion in the early twentieth century not only increased the amount of investment quantitatively, but also diversified the countries and the projects into which British money was directed. Though the building of railways still constituted the main absorber of the British funds, other lucrative fields opened up, such as the construction of dockyards, waterworks, the supply facilities for gas and electricity, telegraph services, tramcars, etc. These were added to the older fields, such as mines, plantations, finance, commerce, etc., for which the need for capital was as strong as ever. In the meantime, funds were exported to Canada, India, Russia and the United States, for the purpose of industrial finance, in such branches as cotton and other textiles, iron-and-steel, paper, and so on.

In the above paragraph, I have followed C.K. Hobson's book to outline the ups and downs of Britain's overseas investments after the 1880s.[19] The export of capital by Britain was mainly channelled into the purchase of securities, whether it was in the form of national debts, municipal bonds, shares or debentures of a private enterprise or whatever, issued abroad in the colonies or foreign countries. The destination of British foreign investment was not limited to territories belonging to the United Kingdom.* The investment in Canada, South Africa and Australia was in no way different from that in South America or the United States. What counted for British investors of funds in overseas securities was the safety and profitability of the project and the particular location of that project. It should, therefore, not be expected that the export of capital was tied directly to the export of commodities, though the pound sterling, made available by way of investment, was often used for the purchase of British commodities, so that the export of British goods to both foreign countries and colonies was indirectly stimulated by foreign investment.

---

19   C.K. Hobson 1914, pp. 145–60.

* The Royal Institute of International Affairs, *The Problem of International Investment*,[20] shows the following table for the distribution of British overseas investment as of the end of 1913.

TABLE N-5   *The state of British overseas investment (end of 1913)*

(1) Area	Value in £ million	Percentage
British Empire	1,780.0	47.3
United States	754.6	20.0
Latin America	756.6	20.1
Europe	218.6	5.8
Other Countries	253.3	6.8
Total	3,763.3	100.0

The same total when rearranged according to the kinds of publicly subscribed securities was as follows:

(2) Invested in	Value in £ million	Percentage
National and Municipal Bonds	1,125.0	29.9
Railways	1,531.0	40.6
Public Utilities	185.1	5.0
Commerce & Industry	2085	5.5
Mines & Resources	388.5	10.8
Banking & Finance	317.1	8.4
Other	8.1	0.3
Total	3,763.3	100.0

Overseas investment within the 'British Empire' of £1,780.0 million in the panel (1) above of Table N-5 by geographical distribution was as follows:

---

20   The Royal Institute of International Affairs 1937, *The Problem of International Investment*, pp. 121–2.

(3) Areas	Value in £ million	Percentage
Canada & Newfoundland	514.9	13.7
Australia & New Zealand	416.4	11.1
South Africa	370.3	9.8
West Africa	37.3	1.0
India & Ceylon	378.8	10.0
Island Colonies	27.3	0.7
British North Borneo	5.8	0.2
Hong Kong	3.1	0.1
Other Colonies	26.2	0.7

The first two items (investment in 'national and municipal bonds' and 'railways') in panel (2) above had the following area breakdowns:

(4) Areas	Value in £ million	Percentage
	National and Municipal Bonds	
Dominion and Colonial Government	675.5	17.9
Foreign Government	297.0	7.9
Municipalities	152.5	4.1
	Railway Securities	
Dominion and Colonies	306.4	8.1
India	140.8	3.7
United States	616.6	16.4
Other	467.2	12.4

This report concentrates mainly on international investment after the First World War. In its chapter 9, however, it also gives a concise account of 'prewar foreign investment' by Britain, France, Germany and the United States, wherefrom the above tables are quoted.

TABLE N-6   *British trade with foreign countries and with British possessions*[21]

Annual averages	Imports into Great Britain from		Exports from Great Britain to	
	Foreign countries	British possess.	Foreign countries	British possess.
1855–9	76.5	23.5	68.5	31.5
1870–4	78.0	22.0	74.4	25.6
1885–9	77.1	22.9	65.0	35.0
1900–3	77.3	20.7	63.0	37.0
1913	75.1	24.9	67.1	32.9
1924–9	69.4	30.6	59.1	40.9

Referring to the figures in this table, the author states: 'Imperialism had no appreciable influence whatever on the determination of our external trade until the protective and preferential measures were taken during and after the Great War. Setting aside the abnormal increase of exports to our colonies in 1900–1903 due to the Boer War, we perceive that the proportions of our external trade had changed very little during the half century; colonial imports slightly fell, colonial exports slightly rose, during the last decade, as compared with the beginning of the period. Although since 1870 such vast additions have been made to British possessions, involving a corresponding reduction of the area of "Foreign Countries", this imperial expansion was attended by no increase in the proportions of intra-imperial trade as represented in the imports and exports of Great Britain during the nineteenth century'.[22]

Needless to say, the investments in railways, harbours, mines, banks, and so on, of many foreign countries especially in South and Central America, as well as in Asia, may be said to have contributed, not only directly but also indirectly (through the purchase of national and municipal bonds), towards the formation of the sphere of influence exclusive to British capital. Moreover, the export of capital to the former colonies, such as Canada, Australia, India, South Africa and others, must have nurtured a particularly intimate relationship between them and the mother country. Yet, for all that, it is not possible to say that a given amount of capital export entailed a corresponding strengthening of Bri-

21   This table is based on data taken from J.A. Hobson 1971, pp. 33, 370.

22   J.A. Hobson 1971, pp. 32–3.

tain's sphere of influence. Though much the same was also true with regard to the foreign investment carried out by France and Germany (especially during the nineteenth century), this feature was especially striking with regard to Britain. The fact that finance-capital in Britain did not involve itself much in the process of assembling the funds destined for overseas investment meant that it lacked, from the beginning, the power (or inclination) to co-ordinate and unify the nation's investment policy. Indeed, it was this feature that characterised the nature of British imperialism. As mentioned earlier, there arose in the early 1880s an imperialist call in Britain for unification of the colonies; yet it never succeeded in rallying sufficient political support. In the meantime, its imperialism adopted a more realistic (i.e. less systematic) approach, which could be encapsulated by the contemporary slogan: 'We shall not fall behind others, in gaining the lion's share of the partitioning of Africa'. Underlying this 'realistic' approach to imperialism was the thoroughly unsystematic fashion, in which this country's massive foreign investment was being carried out.

If foreign investment made in the United States, or in nations similarly well developed, were sailing smoothly, it was otherwise with investment made in countries at a less advanced stage of development, whether directly in the operation of a commercial project or indirectly through the granting of loans to the local government. For they frequently came into conflict with indigenous social relations. Since the latter had to be violently dissolved, a political force of one kind or another had to intervene, and, at that point, British politics could not remain disengaged. Thus, as J.A. Hobson states: 'Aggressive Imperialism, which costs the taxpayer so dear, which is of so little value to the manufacturer and trader, which is fraught with such grave incalculable peril to the citizen, is a source of great gain to the investor who cannot find at home the profitable use he seeks for his capital, and insists that his government should help him to profitable and secure investments abroad'.[23] Indeed, the annual returns on investment abroad and the enormous gain that accrued to the financiers, who mediated such investment, amounted to a colossal sum, which could be earned only because Britain possessed its overseas colonies and spheres of influence. The cost of maintenance of this huge apparatus was, of course, borne by ordinary British citizens. The politics of the country was behind this power structure, even though it did not openly recant the official support of its liberal tradition.*

---

23   J.A. Hobson 1971, p. 55.

* In a commentary on the political influence of the financiers who were the main agents of foreign investment, Hobson has the following to say: 'In view of the part which the non-economic factors of patriotism, adventure, military enterprise, political ambition, and philanthropy play in imperial expansion, it may appear that to impute to financiers so much power is to take a too narrowly economic view of history. And it is true that the motor-power of Imperialism is not chiefly financial: finance is rather the governor of the imperial engine, directing the energy and determining its work: it does not constitute the fuel of the engine, nor does it directly generate the power. Finance manipulates the patriotic forces which politicians, soldiers, philanthropists, and traders generate; the enthusiasm for expansion which issues from these sources, though strong and genuine, is irregular and blind; the financial interest has those qualities of concentration and clear-sighted calculation which are needed to set Imperialism to work. An ambitious statesman, a frontier soldier, an overzealous missionary, a pushing trader, may suggest or even initiate a step of imperial expansion, may assist in educating patriotic public opinion to the urgent need of some fresh advance, but the final determination rests with the financial power'.[24] Here, Hobson lays his finger on the powerful influence that the financiers exerted on the country's high-level politics, at a time when journalism was agitating public opinion. It is, however, noteworthy that Hobson's 'financiers', even those who could be qualified as 'grand financiers', did not seem to have manifested an overwhelmingly centripetal force in the concentration of capital, the kind that Hilferding attributed to finance-capital. That may, to some extent, explain the difference between the style of patriotism of the British and that of the Germans.

As stated above, British overseas investment was in practice operated by such agents as private financiers and investment trust companies, the business of which it was to mediate the investment by buying and selling securities. Among these agents were those who organised themselves in what Liefmann called *Finanzierungs-gesellschaft*. It was the kind that could be observed in British investment in the gold mines of South Africa during the 1880s and the 1890s. The same method was also applied to enterprises in rubber, petrol and others, and was thought to supplant, to some extent, the more traditional and simpler service of financial mediators.* Yet, even this kind of company, which held shares of other companies, did not fully exploit the power to concentrate funds in the same manner as the banks did in Germany. Thus, Britain always stood at arm's length from the German style of foreign investment.

---

24   J.A. Hobson 1971, p. 59.

* Robert Liefmann found that England's so-called 'financial company' evolved its business from simple lending pledged on securities to subscribing to and underwriting securities, and in that manner it approached his own concept of *Finanzierungs-gesellschaft*. Still he was conscious of its distinction from *Finanzerirungs-gesellschaft*, properly speaking, the main business of which was to finance the establishment of some new business companies, by completely underwriting their shares.[25] Of course, this sort of company did not always continue to hold all the shares of the companies it helped to inaugurate, but sold part of them in the market, as they expanded their own business activities. Apparently, the large firms, which dominated the management of the mines in South Africa in the 1880s and the 1890s, were the ones that Liefmann had in mind.[26] Thus, Liefmann's *Finanzierungs-gesellschaften*, which controlled the management of many other large firms, were a far more advanced form of finance-capital than mere investment agents, such as may be illustrated by England's financial company or investment trust.

In a striking contrast to the British case, the large banks played a crucial role, from the beginning, when German capital wished to move abroad. Since Jeidels offers a lucid account of this story,[27] let me summarise his main points below. A number of important banks actively took part in the export of German capital, in the 1880s, for the building of railways in foreign countries. At this point, however, these banks were mainly interested in finding profitable securities (issued by foreign governments or railway companies) in the market, and were only marginally interested in connecting themselves with German industrial firms, i.e. only to the extent that they shipped building materials to one or another foreign project. Then, the nationalisation of railways in several European countries (such as Rumania, Russia and Switzerland) added further to the cooling off of the banks' interest in foreign railway projects. However, the circumstances radically changed in the 1890s with the steady advance of organised monopoly in Germany. The interest of the banks now shifted from portfolio investment in foreign securities to direct investment, because German industries were becoming increasingly involved with foreign projects. For, by that time, large banks and heavy industries had already been integrated in an organic fusion inside Germany. An industry which was, by then, ready to spread its activity abroad needed, for its part, the assistance of the banks which, through their network of branches in foreign countries, and, through experi-

---

25   Liefmann 1924, pp. 406–17.
26   Liefmann 1924, pp. 486–502.
27   Jeidels 1913, pp. 185–9.

ence in international financial transactions, could powerfully assist it in making inroads into foreign markets. Since the export of capital involved external relations, both economic and political, in which domestic firms did not necessarily know the ropes, the services of the banks proved essential to them. The banks, for their part, had developed contact with many foreign governments and business circles, for which they had earlier arranged or contracted external loans and offered other services. The banks could thus share their skills with domestic industry.

Proceeding further, Jeidels classified into four categories the overseas investment activities of large German banks, illustrating each category with concrete examples. *The first category* consisted of the cases in which the existing domestic industrial enterprise sets up a foreign subsidiary. Banks could then assist the industry in more than one way. They could merely extend a helping hand, from behind the scene, as it were; they could more actively work together with the mother enterprise; or they could even set up a special company for the purpose of establishing a foreign subsidiary. The last method played a very large part in the development of electricity projects abroad by means of German capital. Many subsidiaries of the German electric companies were established in Italy, Switzerland, Latin America and elsewhere beginning in the late nineteenth century. *The second category* consisted of the cases in which industrial projects were started in a foreign country directly, without any particularly close ties with corresponding operations in Germany. To this category belonged the building of railways, of which the most famous example was the railway service constructed by the Germans in the Balkans and Asia Minor. Part of this construction was financed by a loan to the government of Turkey, but another part was led by the Deutsche Bank, which established both the Anatolian Railway Company and the Bagdad Railway Company. The Deutsche Bank and the Diskontogesellschaft Bank also helped establish companies in railways, mines and other operations in the Shantung Province of China. In the German colonies of Southwestern and Eastern Africa as well, large German banks set up companies for the construction of railways, the exploration of mines, and the like. *The third category* took the form of participating in an existing foreign company. Large German banks were fairly deeply involved in the mining operations in British South Africa, having acquired shares of these foreign companies. *The fourth category* consisted of the cases which went far beyond mere participation in existing foreign operations. In these cases, large German banks themselves drafted a plan to set up a new industry in foreign countries, and this constituted the most typical way in which the Germans carried out their foreign investment. The development of the Rumanian oil fields was an outstanding example of the type of involvement that large German banks had developed in industrial activities abroad, and that was incomparably more thorough and systematic than in the case of electricity. It was with this project, moreover, that Germany intended to penetrate the petroleum operation in the area, which had been, up to then, a sanctuary of American and Russian capital. Spearheading this move were the three groups which were led by the Deutsche Bank, the Diskontogesellshaft Bank and the Dresdner-Schaaffhausen Bank, respectively. The group led by the Deutsche Bank, in particular, set up the German Petroleum Company, in 1904. This company made inroads into the export and international sales of petroleum products, first by tying up with the British Shell Pipe-Line Company, then by participating in the ongoing Russian operation. Subsequently, it competed with the American Standard Oil Company for domination in the European market.[28] In 1907, it made a temporary agreement with Standard Oil which was scrapped in 1912, as the German company disintegrated[29] under Standard's pressure. The scheme for the international monopoly sale of petroleum products, which Lenin mentioned,[30] referred to movements in this period. Although, in the end, the big German banks that moved into the Rumanian oil field could not oppose the American monopoly in the supply of petroleum products, yet this case nevertheless illustrated the style that German finance-capital most typically employed in the field of overseas investment. It stood, as Jeidels describes, 'on the necessity of finding an advantageous and profitable space abroad for *free German capital*, the necessity that becomes increasingly more urgent at a given stage of development of any modern capitalism'.[31] Here, the expression 'free German capital' may be interpreted to mean 'freely available capital which could no longer be profitably employed within Germany' so long as it was held under the grip of an organised monopoly. Such (excess of) capital was exported by the banks, which had hugely contributed towards the formation of organised monopoly in the domestic market. The difference with the case of Britain was thus obvious. It may, of course, be going too far to claim a direct relation between this type of capital export and German imperialism's territorial ambition to carve out an ever-larger segment of the world's surface for its exclusive hunting ground. Yet it may be said that what made German imperialism distinctly more aggressive than its British counterpart was the fact that Germany, in the course of consolidating its organised monopoly within its national borders in the 1870s and 1880s, discovered itself painfully handicapped, relative to Britain and France,

---

28   Jeidels 1913, pp. 189–96.
29   Liefmann 1924, pp. 444–5.
30   Lenin 1971, p. 55.
31   Jeidels 1913, p. 197.

in the acquisition of exclusive spheres of action abroad, by virtue of its belated participation in the race for the 'partition of the world'.

As I mentioned earlier, the 'division of the world' by such powers as Great Britain, France and Germany reflected the general trend of capitalist development after the 1870s, when no more profitable investment outlet remained at home. Yet the configuration of the hitherto acquired spheres of influence by these powers did not quite fit the subsequent development of capitalism in the world. This does not merely signify that the world so divided proved inadequate to secure advantageous investment opportunities for the value augmentation of superabundant capital. The way in which such capital was concentrated differed in Germany and in Great Britain. The fact that Germany, which was the most methodical investor, could avail itself of only incomparably lesser access than others, such as Britain and France, to the exclusive sphere of action for its capital, led to the inevitable result, in which an aggressive Germany confronted a defensive Britain. Even if the export of capital at that time was not directly proportional to the extensiveness of colonies and spheres of influence then possessed, it was never in doubt that the space must be secured for the future export of capital, which would mortgage the glory of the imperialist nation. Thus, the struggle relentlessly intensified between the newcomer, covetous of gaining more territory, and the old faces jealously guarding their inherited possessions, until a calamitous solution imposed itself in the form of the outbreak of an imperialist war. At this point, war no longer served as the catalyst of transformation of the old social order into the new, as it often had in the seventeenth and the eighteenth century. Nor did it serve as a catalyst of transformation of dispersed backward feudal states into unified modern nation-states, as it did in the nineteenth century. War now imposed itself as the necessary outcome of the conflict, fomented among capitalistically fully developed nations, as they each and all sought the most lucrative investment opportunities abroad, i.e. the most advantageous way to utilise the productive powers already in their possession. This was precisely where the policies of finance-capital, i.e. the policies of imperialism which finance-capital originally introduced with cartel tariffs and colonial expansion, would come to in the end.

Conclusion

While pure economic theory [*genriron*] aims at clarifying the general laws of capitalism, the study of economic policy belongs to what I call the stages-theory [*dankairon*] of development of capitalism. The horizon of the stages-theory, however, must not be viewed as being restricted to a study of economic policy as has been outlined in this book. That sort of study must be complemented by more detailed investigations focusing on agriculture, industry, commerce, finance, transportation, colonial affairs and other applied features of the economy, at each of the stages of capitalist development. Particularly important, in this regard, is the study of public finance, inasmuch as the latter directly affects, and is affected by, the implementation of economic policy by the state. It is not too much to say that the economic policy, whether of mercantilism in the seventeenth and the eighteenth century, of liberalism in the nineteenth century or, for that matter, of imperialism in the twentieth century, can be studied only one-sidedly, so long as its backing by public finance is left unexplored. Moreover, it is this compelling dialogue between the study of economic policy and that of public finance that will allow us to develop a model of interdisciplinary collaboration between economics, on the one hand, and law and politics, on the other, at the abstraction-level proper to the stages-theory, thus leading to a fully satisfactory, i.e. scientific, theory of the state.

Needless to say, the study of economic policy, as distinct from that of pure economic theory, constitutes the first step into the field of the stages-theory of capitalist development. This fact has indeed been understood by many economists and economic historians, albeit vaguely, that is to say, without a lucid awareness of its methodological implication. Indeed, my own study of economic policy in this book could not have been undertaken, without prior works of many distinguished economists. Mine differs from theirs merely in that I consciously endeavoured to distinguish the abstraction-level proper to the study of pure economic theory from that proper to the study of economic policy. Thus, what I wish to affirm, at this point, is that the stages-theoretic study of economics will remain incomplete until it is duly buttressed by more detailed research into the stage-specific features of the capitalist economy in its multiple sectors, in such a way as to relate their operation with the policy-oriented allocation of public funds.*

---

*Whereas economic policy directly reflects the aim of (the dominant form of) capital, public finance cannot be explained so simply as representing such a unidirectional relation. If economic policy translates the aim of capital into political action, public finance rather achieves an economic accommodation of diverse political wills each representing its own sectional interests. Therefore, unlike economic policy, public finance cannot be understood quite as simply in terms of the stage-theoretic determinations (that is to say, in terms of the developmental need of capital). It is for this reason that the essential features of the stage must first be formulated by the types of economic policy. Only in that light can any interaction between economic policy and public finance be studied. The 1955 book by Takeda Takao, Endô Shôkichi and Ôuchi Tsutomu, entitled *Theory of Modern Public Finance [Kindai Zaisei no Riron]*, contains an interesting discussion on this subject.

My stages-theory is not, as seems to be so often misunderstood, just a simple 'periodisation' (from without) of the history of capitalist development. My aim in defining the three typical, world-historic stages of capitalist development is to employ them to mediate between the abstract-general economic theory, which is unique, and the concrete-specific (and hence multiple and diverse) economic histories of capitalism, whether in a particular country or in the world as a whole. They are, therefore, not mere 'ideal types', but the real capitalist economies of Britain, Germany and/or the United States, as the case may be, when, and to the extent that, they marked the three necessary stages of capitalist development as world-historic epochs, or as *types*, that is to say, insofar as they have been divested (or cleansed) of all their empirical contingencies. As a country adopts the capitalist mode of production, it undergoes a path of development (through the phases of birth, self-sustained growth and decline), which is different from others, because of its specific historical heritage and the specific time at which it is drawn into the capitalist orbit of the contemporary world. This fact makes it impossible to interpret its very peculiar path of development directly in the light of the abstract and unique theory that defines capitalist society in general. It is for that reason that a mechanical application of theory to history in economics has frequently resulted in many unwarranted conclusions. I deeply regret the fact that Marxists have, in particular, been liable to commit this debilitating error in their analyses of current economic conditions, despite the fact that it was Marx himself who, for the first time, formulated economic theory as the theory of a purely capitalist society. As mentioned earlier, the Marxist movement towards the end of the nineteenth century generated an intense controversy between the revisionists and the orthodoxy; and it was with such circumstances in the background that the economic meaning of imperialism was first debated, until, in the end, such important works as Hilferding's *Das Finanzkapital* and Lenin's *Imperialism, the Highest Stage of Capitalism* appeared. Yet neither one of these authors was aware that he then faced stages-theoretic issues at a distinct level of abstraction from that of purely theoretical ones. What I hoped to clarify in this book is precisely the importance of the distinction between the two levels of abstraction, as well as the relationship between them, in the study of economics. It is, indeed, that preoccupation that impelled me to write a treatise on economic policy that is so vastly different from a conventional treatment of the subject. However, as I detailed in my Introduction, all of that stems from the inevitable fact that economics is the discipline that studies the real economy as it operates under the laws of the commodity-economy.

That thesis of mine, needless to say, does not imply that pure economic theory [*genriron*] must first be perfected, and the stages-theory of capitalist development [*dankaïron*] unambiguously clarified once and for all, before one may undertake to study the history, current or past, of a national or world economy [*genjô-bunseki*], which constitutes the ultimate aim of economic studies. As a matter of fact, progress in economics has always entailed studies at all of its three levels of abstraction. In some ways, however, the recent trend in modern (bourgeois) economics is to overemphasise formal theory at the expense of history, while *sozialpolitik*, which carries on the tradition of the German historical school, tends to underestimate the need for theoretical rigour in its fixation with history. These schools, thus, render the study of economic policy either unduly mechanical or blindly historicist. Contrary to these approaches, it was my wish to present here a study of economic policy at the level of *dankaïron*, which stands between the theory and the history of capitalism as a middle term mediating between them. It is at this middle range of abstraction that, I hope, all branches of applied economics can be studied adequately, thus enriching the scientific perspective within which to situate the study of economic history, either current or past, of a real capitalist economy. Such a frame of reference, at least, militates against the conventional (and facile) idea that economic policy and/or public finance may be so 'prescribed' as to always rescue the capitalist economy from all its dysfunctions. Social science, unlike natural science, does not yield knowledge that can be technically used to suit our convenience.

Memorandum on Capitalist Development after the First World War (1970)

In the concluding part of the previous edition of this book, after the sentence: 'My stages-theory is not just a simple periodisation (from without) of the history of capitalist development', I inserted a footnote, which I am suppressing from the present edition. That footnote stated as follows:

> As the reader can see, the scope of this book is limited to the exposition of the stages of capitalist development prior to the First World War. It is surely both interesting and important to reflect upon whether or not the subsequent development of capitalism has provided us with sufficient information to warrant the definition of yet another, more recent, stage of development of the capitalist mode of production. I wish, however, to leave that question open at this point, even though my study of the world economy after the Russian Revolution of 1917 has *prima facie* led to my surmise that it is likely to be more adequately studied as the economic history of the present, pure and simple, rather than as manifestation of another (the fourth) typical stage of capitalist development.

At the time of the previous edition, I was still uncertain as to whether or not I was justified to conclude the book on 'the types of economic policy under capitalism' with the First World War. Nor had I convinced myself yet as to whether or not the Second World War could be characterised as an imperialist war, in the same way as the First World War. I was not sure either what to make of the de-colonisation of Asia and Africa, and of the drift towards socialism in China, North Korea and the Eastern European countries. Even with regard to the ongoing construction of the socialist economy in the Soviet Union, I was so poorly informed of what was actually occurring behind the scenes that I did not feel myself in a position to make any definite pronouncement of its prospects. What was clear to me, however, was that the development of the capitalist nations then, remarkable as it was, did not demonstrate sufficient vigour in blocking the expansion of the socialist sphere. This fact led me to believe that capitalism (in the sense of the capitalist mode of production) had lost the dynamism necessary to give rise to another world-historic stage of capitalist 'development', following the end of the First World War. I, therefore, felt that imperialism, which, as the economic policy of finance-capital, marked the last (or final) stage of development of capitalism proper, ended with the Peace of Versailles.

In 1957, a German Marxist named Kurt Zieschang published an article on the theme of so-called 'state-monopoly capitalism', in which he argues, based on the experience of West Germany, that the production-relations of imperialism entered a new stage, as the increasing importance of the role of the state intensified the contradiction between them (the imperialist production-relations) and the productive powers. The translation of this article was widely read in this country and debated at length by its supporters and opponents. Yet no works inspired by this debate managed to outline a convincing thesis that the concept of 'state-monopoly capitalism' could be used to define a new typical stage of capitalist development. Mr. Tsutomu Ôuchi's interesting contribution, 'A Note on State-Monopoly Capitalism',[1] started with Lenin's thesis on this topic and dealt with Zieschang's work in some detail. After pointing out several ambiguities in the theory advanced therein, Ôuchi concluded that behind the stepped-up role of the imperialist state, which Zieschang had made much of, lay the inflationary policy the state, made possible under (and by means of) the managed currency system. Ôuchi, however, failed to clarify whether or not that policy constituted a policy of finance-capital. Zieschang himself, while dealing with the problem of 'state-monopoly capitalism', never referred to finance-capital (or to anything that might have supplanted it). As for the managed currency system, it might indeed have had counter-cyclical policy effects on labour (or employment), as Ôuchi claimed; but, according to him, 'by the time the state implements such a policy, socialism has become a world-historic fact, which compels the capitalist nations, in their external relations, to take it into full account'.[2] It was rather this observation that seemed to me to be more relevant to the question at issue.

The inflationary policy that can be enforced under the managed currency system exerts a far more powerful impact on the real economy than, for instance, the customs policy of the former imperialist state. It is surely unwarranted to believe that currency, if not production, is susceptible of the state's control, even within the regime of the capitalist mode of production. Yet it is also true that the inflationary policy of the state, as it is nowadays practised, does have some influence on production through its control of the nation's currency. The question, therefore, is what to make of the *managed currency system*, which enables the state to enforce an inflationary policy. As it happens, the managed currency system is an offshoot of the profound disequilibrium that has arisen within the community of capitalist nations.

---

1   Ôuchi 1970.

2   Ôuchi 1970, pp. 270–1.

This system of managed currency was not designed as a bulwark against socialism, nor was it sought by finance-capital expressly with a view to reinforcing its grip on the imperialist stage of capitalist development. It arose rather *ad hoc*, through the disruptions in the aftermath of the First World War and in the process of haphazard reconstruction thereafter (all of which led eventually to the Great Depression of the 1930s), as something which the public finance of the time required, and which finance-capital may have wished to make some astute use of. Whatever the circumstances of its birth, however, *the managed currency system was a monetary system which was alien to the commodity-economy, and which, therefore, contradicted the self-regulation of capitalism as a historical society.* It denied commodity-money in part or in whole, in form or in substance. Yet this abnegation on the part of the capitalist mode of production was a necessity (and not a temporary expedient), if it was to continue to survive alongside the socialist camp.

Indeed, under the inflationary policy of the state, industrial workers increasingly lost their former identity, as they merged with service workers and peasants in the broader class of 'employed labour' (versus 'management'), while radical trade unions joined conservative craft unions to form larger, and less focused, labour organisations. Left-wing political parties, too, were obliged to tone down their militancy, and adopted a more conciliatory, citizen-based and nationwide electoral stance. Thus, the decline of Marxism could, in part at least, be attributed to the structural change in the economy that was occurring under the inflationary policy of the state. That surely must have had due repercussions on the so-called socialist camp as well.

It is against this background that we must now review the significance of the economics of Marx's *Capital*, which laid the groundwork for a so-called 'scientific' socialism. To my mind, however, this task involves far more than simply returning to the text of Marx's writings. For, in them, it is not immediately apparent how the general theory of capitalism (the capitalist mode of production) that he outlined may be correctly related to a study of the current trends in the world economy. Without an explicit distinction between *genriron* (pure economic theory of capitalism) and *dankaïron* (stages-theory of capitalist development), Marx himself could not guide us with sufficient clarity. Despite his unsurpassed insight into the economics of capitalism, he could not assist us in the task of comprehending the economic history of the present, that is to say, in the task of comprehending the nature and significance of the society in which we live today. I deeply regret the fact that the intellectual legacy of Marx is being neglected, not only by the activists of socialist movements in the so-called 'capitalist' nations, but also by the leaders of those self-professed 'socialist' nations that are supposedly in the process of giving birth to socialist societies.

I do not necessarily object to the use of such terms as 'US imperialism' or 'Japanese imperialism', so widespread in the press today. Yet these ready-made journalistic expressions cannot hold any scientific content, nor do they throw any real light on the nature of the society in which we now live, unless they are defined appropriately in the light of the *genriron* and *dankairon* of capitalism. It is precisely such discretion that is lacking in Zieschang's article, which, for example, irrevocably dilutes the stages-theoretic concept of finance-capital in the catch-all appellation of 'monopoly capital'. In the second section of his article, in which he deals specifically with 'some aspects of the monetary and credit system', especially as it pertains to the supply of investment-funds to industry, he makes much of the direct financing of the firm [*jiko-kinnyû*]; but I believe that his thesis puts far too much emphasis on a particular aspect of development of the system of the joint-stock company. It is true enough that at a certain stage of its development, such a tendency (a tendency for the joint-stock company to self-finance its production) manifests itself. Yet, if pushed too far in that direction, that tendency will end in a national socialism (i.e. Nazism), in the sense of the state control of business firms through a managerial revolution, which amounts to a 'capitalism that negates itself'. That would be a pure fantasy stemming from the failure to fully comprehend the meaning of the commodity-economy. For capitalism could not itself survive if it actually dissolved its fundamental contradiction, whether by means of the system of the joint-stock company or by that of any new form of the state. Of course, Zieschang does admit the fact that the imperialist state is not up to fully organising the economy by planning.[3] He also states that state-monopoly capitalism merely modifies the effects of the laws of capitalism, without being able to repudiate their enforcement with the attendant contradictory consequences.[4] However, neither he nor most other Marxists today seem to have adequately comprehended the meaning of the working of the laws of capitalism.

In the meantime, so far as such expressions in the press as 'American imperialism' or 'Japanese imperialism' are concerned, they are clearly not thematising imperialism as the final stage of capitalist development, as I have done in this book. Nor can my theory fully explain all of what these expressions intend to convey, to the extent that they imply, if vaguely, certain aspects of the present international relations involving Japan or the United States, with socialist nations in the background.

---

3   Zieschang 1957, p. 28.
4   Zieschang 1957, pp. 33–4.

Thus, with reflections such as the above, I have come to believe that the world economy after the end of the First World War must be studied not as capitalism in its highest, imperialist stage of development, but rather directly as a phase in the economic history of capitalism, which is free from such stages-theoretic determinations (that is to say, as capitalism moribund) in the sense of already presupposing the emergence of socialism, as its own negation. The study of the economic history of the present [*genjô-bunseki*] must, no doubt, be buttressed by concrete-specific details that transpire in some leading states, which are themselves influenced by the trend of the world economy. The latter, in any case, cannot be free from the increasing scope of the socialist sphere, which already exists in the present world. It is with this sort of understanding that I am suppressing the footnote in question in the earlier edition of this book.

Translator's Afterword

This translation of Uno's *Keizai-Seisakuron* into *The Types of Economic Policies under Capitalism*, I started it early in the 1980s, not so long after the publication (in 1980 from the Harvester Press) of my first translation of Uno's books, that of his *1964 Keizai-Genron* into *Principles of Political Economy*. It then took a relatively short time (for me) to finish a rough draft of the first one-quarter of the book, including the 'Introduction' and 'Part I: Mercantilism'. At that time, my hope was that the translation of the rest of the work would follow in due course, that is to say, would proceed at more or less the same pace. I was totally wrong, however; for I never anticipated that it would take as long as it actually did before reaching the present state. There were two main reasons for this unanticipated and disproportionate delay. The first was simply that, for many of these years, I was engaged in university teaching, most often in subjects unrelated, or not so closely related, to the content of this book, in consequence of which frequent and lengthy interruptions could not be avoided. Thus, it was only after my retirement from teaching in 2005 that I could finally resume, and concentrate on, this translation without being unduly diverted by other preoccupations.

The second and more fundamental reason for the delay was that I had greatly underestimated my own ignorance of the subject matter of the book I had undertaken to translate. Even my own understanding of Uno's *dankaïron* [stages-theory] at that time was still uncertain and haphazard (for only recently have I managed to come to its comprehension in the way that I am presenting in my first essay, appended to this volume), so that not infrequently I encountered certain passages in the text which immobilised me, as I failed to grasp Uno's real intent with sufficient clarity. Furthermore, this book contains detailed documentations from the economic history of capitalism, which were beyond the easy grasp of a non-historian such as myself. That is why I had to trouble a large number of persons better acquainted with the subjects than myself to enlighten me in one way or another, whenever I lost my way in the dark. These persons were so numerous that it is not possible to mention all of them. However, among those to whom I was particularly indebted and grateful were Messrs Shôken Mawatari, Katsumi Sugiura (deceased), Masahiro Fujikawa, and Seiichirô Yamane, for 'Part II: Liberalism', and Messrs. Kiyoshi Nagatani, Tetsuzô Yamamoto, Moto-o Haruta and Masanori Kuzuu, for 'Part III: Imperialism'.

More recently, after resuming this work in my retirement, I am also deeply indebted to Professor Makoto Maruyama of the University of Tokyo and Mr. Sachio Katagiri, an independent economist, for helping me to undertake some indispensable library work. The latter person lent me invaluable support in completing the list of references and compiling the index of names as well as that of subjects, in addition to overviewing the adequacy of my translation in relation to the original text in Japanese (especially in 'Part II: Liberalism'). Professor Hideo Okamoto and Librarian Yasuo Nagatani of Tokyo Keizai University also helped me mightily with regard to fine points in the list of references. Finally, Professor Toshiharu Fujisawa of Hôsei University was so kind as to check all German language references appearing in the book to ascertain that Uno either quoted from them or summarised their relevant passages correctly and with precision.

Thus, so many well-meaning and selfless persons enabled me to bring this work to the present state, each proffering his most generous assistance. To all of them I owe my most sincere word of thanks, though, needless to say, I am solely responsible for all the remaining errors and inadequacies. Last but not least, I have been the lucky beneficiary of the outstanding editorial skill of my longtime friend and associate, Professor John R. Bell, whose meticulous attention has rendered this book far more readable than I could ever hope to make it myself.

Thomas T. Sekine
Tokyo, December 2012

APPENDICES

Two Essays by Thomas T. Sekine

∴

An Essay on Uno's Stages-Theory of Capitalist Development: What Might We Learn from This Book?

I

Uno's *Keizai-Seisakuron*, here translated as *The Types of Economic Policies under Capitalism*, is undoubtedly one of the most important of his works. It has been widely read as a primary source of information with regard to his original idea of *dankaïron*, or the 'stages-theory of capitalist development', which it certainly is. Yet it has not always been easy to penetrate his abstruse style so as to focus directly on that theme. Indeed, many have ended by reading this book merely as a convenient introduction to the history of modern capitalism with focus on international trade relations. Even for that limited purpose, the book has been useful enough, but undoubtedly more so in the past than at present. For, as the author himself admits in his Foreword, its documentation is entirely based on pre-WWII sources, and fails to duly take into account many more recent discoveries that have, since then, vastly enriched the discipline of modern economic history. Indeed, it may strike the present-day reader as a somewhat antiquated introduction to the subject.

On the other hand, it will strike the reader that the book dwells on 'conceptual issues' far more elaborately and persistently than would be thought necessary or useful to simply outline the history of capitalism (in the sense of the capitalist mode of production)[1] in its three stages of development: mercantilism, liberalism and imperialism. For example, the author talks repeatedly of the stage-theoretic (as distinct from purely logical or theoretical) 'determinations' of capitalism. Surely, that sort of 'periodisation', based largely on the three distinct types of economic policies of the modern, bourgeois state in different periods, as capitalism in the West evolved from the seventeenth to the twentieth century, must have seemed apt, and was thus easily acceptable, to many in

---

1 Uno uses the term 'capitalism', in most cases (in this book and elsewhere), in the narrower sense of what Marx called 'the capitalist mode of production', and not in the wider sense of 'capitalist action in general'. See Sekine 1997a, pp. 17–19, where I called the latter *capitalism-I* *and* the former *capitalism-II*. See also the beginning of Bell and Sekine 2001, pp. 37–55; Sekine 1999, pp. 17–25.

the 1930s or 1940s, without so much conceptual and methodological ado regarding the nature of the subject matter. It must be emphasised that Uno was not interested in merely characterising the three distinct stages of capitalist development *externally*, so as to give to the novice a bird's eye view of what would inevitably prove to be a dense forest of extreme variations and complexities. What mattered to him was that, even under capitalism, *real*-economic life of society must involve some *concrete-specific* use-values, whereas, in the purely logical theory of capitalism, only nominal (i.e. substantively unspecified) use-values need (and must) be presupposed.[2]

These are the considerations that are crucially important to the economist, though perhaps not so vital to the historian. The history of capitalism abounds in use-values of all sorts, most of which are produced and circulated as commodities. Real-economic life under capitalism may, therefore, be considered as numerous (and as various) as there are different combinations of such use-values involved therein. If I may call by the term 'use-value space'[3] any com-

---

2   Economic theory must, strictly speaking, be stated *from the point of view of capital*, whereas history can only be recounted *from our own (i.e. human) point of view*. In other words, theory belongs to capital whereas history belongs to us. Thus, use-values in economic theory are merely material objects, one distinct from another, which are believed to be useful to humans in some undefined ways; that is to say, capital remains indifferent to the concrete-specific ways in which they are each useful to human life. In contrast, use-values in history are useful things for *our* own economic life, so that the concrete-specific ways in which they serve our needs and wants, one differently from another, are of vital importance to us.

3   A 'use-value space' is a set of goods or use-values, expressible as a vector $(x_1, x_2, ..., x_n)$, on the basis of which a society's real-economic life is constructed. Some elements of the set (or vector) may be commodities, others not. The use-value spaces which support a real-economic life under capitalism, however, consist of commodities in principle, that is to say, of use-values which are more or less easily 'commodifiable'. From the point of view of economic theory, or the dialectic of capital (i.e. capitalist-logically), all elements of the use-value space are somehow commodified already, and capital does not question how easy, or not so easy, the process of their commodification actually was. For such a problem belongs to the historical context. This does not mean that capital (or economic theory) does not recognise use-values at all. It does, but only as 'some distinct objects for use or consumption'. It does not approach them with human concern and passion, likes and dislikes, remaining quite indifferent to their concrete-specificity. That should make sense, since it is not capital but we, humans, who actually use and consume them to live. To put it more precisely, capital *in theory* is constrained by *some* use-values, but not by this or that specific one. Thus, for example, industrial capital represents the form of capital which is the least constrained by (or most indifferent to) use-values, because, if it is constrained by them, it is so only by the use-value of the commodity which it has itself freely chosen to produce within its technical competence. The form of

bination or set of use-values, upon which a 'real-economic life of society' can be organised, the number of such spaces must be considered countless (almost infinite), even though only some of them are fit to be 'operated capitalistically', i.e. susceptible of being subsumed broadly under the commodity-economic logic of capital. Yet even this 'capitalist subset' of use-value spaces must also, for all intents and purposes, be considered 'infinitely many', and the economic historian of capitalism must be prepared to face any of them, as the case may be, as his/her object of study. The selected 'use-value space' must, in other words, be studied in all its concrete specificity and particularity, his/her professional task being to study the historical *uniqueness* of that space in all its details. Given its geography and climate, cultural traditions and social habits, legal institution and political organisation, its *capitalist* practice may have no parallel or equivalent elsewhere. It is for that reason that the historian cannot, and does not, resort to facile generalisations. The variety of the use-values involved in each particular instance of capitalism is that which he/she is called upon to concentrate on.

For the economist, the focus of interest is understandably quite different. What he/she is interested in is the extent to which the particular instance of real-economic life under study is, in fact, 'capitalist' rather than 'non-capitalist'. To answer that question, he/she must be informed of a precise definition of capitalism (in the narrow sense of the capitalist mode of production). The latter, as I will argue in much greater detail later, must be theoretical (logical), i.e. in pure and general terms, applicable universally in one way or another to any real-economic life that can be qualified as 'capitalist'. Such a definition (rigorous conceptualisation or determination) can, however, be obtained only when use-values are 'neutralised or nominalised', i.e. when they are made devoid of substance, their *concrete specificity* being deliberately laid aside. For the theoretical definition of capitalism must be in the nature of the 'software' (*logiciel*), capable of programming *any* capitalistically operable 'use-value space', if this latter may be viewed as the 'hardware' (*matériel*). In other words, a use-value appearing in economic theory is named only 'as illustration'; that is to say, if 'x_i' is called cotton, it could just as well have been called wheat, coal, toy or anything like that, without making a substantive difference to the argument. This means that the real-economic life that one presupposes in theory is 'ghost-like', in the sense that it is not yet posited in any concrete-specific terms. It still remains a 'nominal' reality, constituting a lifeless shadow of capitalism in real

---

merchant capital which does not possess this freedom (and hence is more subject to some contingencies) is, in contrast, a theoretically less developed form.

time (as its logical theory should be). In order to inspire life therein, and make capitalism appear in real time and space, the use-value space in question $(x_1, x_2, ..., x_n)$ must be more concretely specified, as, for example, with a series of the cotton-like goods produced in abundance in mid-nineteenth century Britain, or with another series of steel-like goods produced energetically towards the end of that century in Germany or in the United States. Then and only then does economic life under capitalism become truly 'real', so that it can be placed in the historical context.

It is, therefore, necessary to first decide, even broadly, which type of concrete-specific use-values are to be presupposed by $(x_1, x_2, ... x_n)$, before one knows which type of *real* capitalist economy is under consideration. For Uno, the capitalist economy typical in the *mercantilist stage* of development would be the one in which the key commodities are like the woollen and worsted manufactures produced domestically in the farming districts of seventeenth and eighteenth century Britain, and circulated internationally; and the capitalist economy typical in the *liberal stage* of development would be the one in which the key commodities are like cotton-manufactures produced in light-industrial factories in the mid-nineteenth century Britain, and circulated internationally. If, on the other hand, the key commodities are like the iron-and-steel goods produced in heavy-industrial plants in Germany, the United States, Great Britain and other advanced Western powers towards the end of the nineteenth or the beginning of the twentieth century, and circulated internationally, then one may visualise the operation of the capitalist economy typical in the *imperialist stage* of development. Unlike the bourgeois economist to whom the *real* and *market* economy are always presumed to be the two inseparable sides of the same thing (which, in effect, ignores the historical transience of the commodity-form), Uno makes a sharp distinction (following Marx) between *commodity-economic (or mercantile) logic* (which is value based) and the *real-economic life* (which is use-value based) that it subsumes.[4] This is what compels

---

4   In this section I have endeavoured to highlight the difference between the conventional and the Unoist approach to economics. In the conventional approach, the relationship between economic theory and 'the real world' on which it is supposed to shed light is left quite ambiguous. Not only does the reliability of empirical testing in conventional economics leave much to be desired, but the presumed 'real world' itself is also highly stylised and suspect, often amounting to little more than the land of a fairytale, anecdotally recounted with a view to illustrating a (subjectively concocted) theory. There is little or no understanding that use-values in the logical space and those in real-economic history cannot be so easily related. The Unoist approach, in contrast, first determines the logical concept of capitalism (in its narrow sense), before it tries to locate its incarnation (real capitalism) in human history. The use-

him to posit the *stages-theory* of capitalist development, in which the use-value spaces are delimited (or kept under control) *as types*, standing as they do between the *pure theory* of capitalism, in which the use-value space is abstract and symbolic, and the *concrete-empirical history* of capitalism, in which use-value spaces are as diverse and concrete as it occurs in real time.

II

Marx's *Capital* is subtitled *Critique of Political Economy*. Political economy here means the economic theory of the classical school. The latter, 'beginning with William Petty in Britain and Boisguillebert in France, and ending with Ricardo in Britain and Sismondi in France',[5] made the first step towards discovering economic theory, or the logic of capitalism (always in the sense of Marx's 'capitalist mode of production'), which constituted the *substructure* of modern society. This first step was assisted by the faith in modern society, which the classical economists took to be the ideal (most accomplished and final) form of human society. This end-of-the-world faith (of bourgeois ideology), however, was not merely subjective, inasmuch as capitalism in real historical time was then in the process of perfecting itself. Indeed, by the middle of the nineteenth century, it was increasingly divesting itself of pre-modern residues (traditional customs and institutions), so as to bring much of *real-economic* life under *commodity-economic* (or mercantile) management. What capitalism itself was then accomplishing in *reality* was what the classical economists sought in their *theory* (i.e. in their idealisation of capitalism), a rare instance in which the object of study and the subject who studied it progressed hand in hand. Past the middle of the nineteenth century, however, this happy confluence was to be frustrated. As the real trend of capitalism diverged from the path of its self-*purification* (or *self-perfection*), political economy too lost its erstwhile vitality and soon degenerated into an apologetic of the existing capitalist regime. The surviving bourgeois ideology of the perfectibility of capitalism no longer enlightened vulgar economists with regard to objective reality, but blinded them to the gap between what was real and what they devoutly wished.

---

values of (capitalistically produced) commodities which stay in the logical space *and* those which actually exist in the historical context can be related only through the intermediary of the 'typical commodity' which did appear characteristically in each of the stages of capitalist development.

5   Marx 1970, p. 52.

What was needed at this point was an ideology which regarded even capitalism (the economic base of modern society) in relative, not in absolute, terms. The 'materialist conception of history', which Marx held as his 'guiding thread' in approaching economics in the middle of the nineteenth century was, according to Uno, precisely the ideology that was needed. For it did not regard capitalism itself as the 'end of the world', but rather as the last step before arriving at it. In other words, humankind was to be fully liberated not with the triumph of capitalism but with its demise. Regardless of what the *après*-capitalism was likely to be, it was the idea that capitalism too had its own end that enabled Marx to see it as a totality, whereas bourgeois economists (even the 'classical' ones), with their modernist eschatology, could see only its partial (i.e. positive and cheerful) aspects. Unlike most Marxists, however, Uno did not consider the materialist conception of history itself to constitute a critique of political economy. It was merely an 'ideological hypothesis', which Marx adopted (at the entry point of his study) as an 'antidote', so as not to be infected by bourgeois biases while learning what was true in classical economic theory. To Uno, what made Marx's works truly immortal was not his prescription of the antidote that would protect him (and those who followed him) against being infected by the bourgeois faith in capitalism, but the critique of political economy which enabled him to go beyond the classical economists towards a more *synthetic* comprehension (and so definition) of capitalism.

Uno sharply distinguished between *ideology* and *social science*, but not in general terms. What he insisted upon was that Marxism as the materialist conception of history was not equal to Marxian economics as the critique of political economy. That was the reason that he reacted strongly against the so-called 'critique of Marx' by leading German intellectuals of the time including Max Weber, which only attacked Marx's materialist conception of history (also called 'historical materialism'), completely ignoring his economics (or critique of political economy). These 'philosophers' scarcely understood economics or political economy in the Anglo-French tradition; they were not concerned with seriously criticising it. Quite unlike Marx, they thought themselves to be in a position to interpret matters related to 'the material conditions of life' and 'civil society'[6] by merely 'philosophising' about them as if from heaven (*pensée du survol*). This kind of intellectual lapse unfortunately continued until quite

---

6   'My inquiry led me to the conclusion that neither legal relations nor political forms could be comprehended whether by themselves or on the basis of a so-called general development of the human mind, but that on the contrary they originate in the material conditions of life, the totality of which Hegel ... embraces within the term "civil society"; that the anatomy of this civil society, however, has to be sought in political economy' (Marx 1970, p. 20).

recently, particularly in that part of Europe where the study of economics was held relatively secondary. Since Kant's critical philosophy, which distinguished the 'phenomenal' from the 'noumenal' world, and confined 'metaphysics' to the latter, made no reference to 'society' as a legitimate object of scientific study, social science was always left in limbo, unable to define its own field of competence, undisturbed by quasi-metaphysical discourses. Uno regretted these circumstances and sought to find a better example in Marx's method of the 'critique of political economy'. He, however, remained distinctly unsuccessful in persuading professional philosophers around him to take an interest in this vitally important problem.

Prior to the modern times, there existed no such concepts as 'society', 'economy' and 'the state'. The social sciences, including economics, which dealt with these concepts, were, therefore, products of the modern age. They were developed, in the first instance, to praise and justify the evolution of modern society, claiming its superiority to the earlier forms of human association. They were, thus, from the beginning, (even unconsciously) saturated with modernist-bourgeois-liberal biases; and economics was in no sense an exception. This being the case, it became all the more imperative for the social sciences, especially economics, to break away from such ideological constraints in order to be able to claim the (scientific) objectivity of their knowledge. For otherwise, the social sciences would forever be trapped in what Karl Polanyi aptly called the 'market mentality'.[7] Marx's critique of political economy was the first and the only adequate framework in which to achieve that end. For it was to lead to a synthetic, not a partial and one-sided, definition of capitalism, i.e. the 'laying bare' of the substructure of modern society. This important point, which was completely overlooked by ordinary Marxists and their critics (the two who differed only in looking at the one or the other side of capitalism, but who never differed fundamentally in that they both remained persistently one-sided, partial observers), constituted the point of departure for Uno.

Marx aimed at grasping the laws of capitalism as the 'economic base' of modern society, which was a historical society.[8] Now, what distinguished modern society from all other historical societies was that in it alone did the substructure tend to disengage itself from the ideological superstructure, or, to bor-

---

7 Polanyi 1968, pp. 59–77. See also Polanyi 2001; Polanyi 1977.

8 A *historical society*, for Uno, is a self-sufficient one which really exists in history and is, therefore, supported by its economic base or *substructure*; it is not something that is merely imagined to exist as a model (e.g. a society of petty producers) with its substructure (economic base or social reproduction-process) undefined.

row once again Polanyi's terms, 'the economy tended to dis-embed itself from society'. This tendency, as stated above, was real and was actually observed, when capitalism was in the process of self-purification or self-perfection, which reached its peak late in its liberal stage (concretely in the middle of the nineteenth century in Britain); but this tendency never consummated itself, as the radical, and thus more deluded, liberals would have liked to believe. The reason for this outcome was that real-economic life involving concrete use-values could never become so weightless as to 'levitate' into a purely logical, commodity-economic space. The commodity, as object for sale (value-object), which always endeavours to prove itself to be capable of becoming part of society's abstract-general, mercantile wealth, does remain a down-to-earth use-value, a portion of real-economic wealth that is far from ethereal. Nevertheless, it was the reality of this tendency for the economic substructure of modern society to disengage itself from its ideological superstructure (for 'the economy to dis-embed itself from society'), and nothing else, which founded the truth of economic theory.

III

Human life is materially supported by use-values of all sorts, some of which are more easily commodifiable than others. Often light-industry products are thought to be more readily convertible into commodities than heavy-industry products, and so also are manufactured than agricultural goods.[9] The set of use-values that characterise a particular instance of the real-economic life of society, I have called 'use-value space'. The nature of the latter depends on the society's natural environment, its technological and cultural history, its intercourse with other societies, and various other pertinent conditions. With many of those 'use-value spaces', a commodity-economy (economic life based on commodified use-values) can exist in part or peripherally; but there are comparatively few of them to which the commodity-economy is integral and in which it is self-regulating. The ones in which even labour-power (the human capacity to produce use-values while not being itself a 'produced' use-

---

9 It may be remarked in passing that when life is urbanised, the proportion of 'public goods' combined with services, which are more difficult to commodify, seems to increase as a proportion of the consumer's spending. The real-economic life of today's advanced societies tends to consume more and more complex use-value combinations that must be supplied as systems, and must also be 'serviced' as they are being consumed. Their pricing must then become quite arbitrary, as they exceed commodification in the traditional sense of the term.

value) is convertible into a commodity are the ones that are regarded as being *capitalistically operable*, i.e. subsumable under the logic of capital.

An important characteristic of the commodity-economy lies in the fact that in it, a use-value, which is originally concrete-specific wealth, and demanded as such by the buyer, tends also to be treated as a value-object (or a commodity), that is to say, as part of society's abstract-general, mercantile wealth, by the seller. Sometimes, this uncertain connection is described as the 'contradiction between value and use-value'. Capitalism (in the sense of the 'capitalist mode of production') can exist only when, and to the extent that, this contradiction (meaning tension, conflict, cleavage, gap, and so on) between the buyer's standpoint and that of the seller can be reconciled. The contradiction does not disappear, but can be controlled and reconciled to some extent, depending on the nature of the use-value space. In the capitalistically operable ones, it is (including 'is about to be' and 'is still somehow managing to be') adequately controlled or subdued, owing to the conversion into a commodity (or commodification) of labour-power; but even then, the contradiction has not completely disappeared. This disclaimer, which may offend radical liberals, echoes the earlier statement that the self-purification of capitalism will not be consummated, i.e. that the 'economy' will never be completely *dis-embedded* from society, or that real-economic life does not become so ethereal and weightless as to 'levitate' into the purely logical market-space. Yet it is also in the nature of capitalism as a global commodity-economy to aspire, and indeed to actually point, to its own perfection, *use-value permitting*. Both the ontology and the epistemology of *capitalism* crucially depend on this fact.

Marx's economic works were mostly carried out in the latter half of the 1850s and the earlier half of the 1860s. It was undeniably the time when capitalism itself tended most closely towards its perfection, which also meant that both the classical school and Marx could then safely imagine the theoretical use-value space $(x_1, x_2, \ldots, x_n)$ of capitalism to consist of such elements as were quite readily commodifiable, indeed more so than they actually were. That is to say, they could safely suppose the operation of capitalism, a global (i.e. all-embracing) commodity-economy, to be constrained by use-values only *in a general way*, but not in any specific way in each case.[10] They were labelled

---

10   In theory, not only can an individual use-value be distinguished one from another, but so also can a group of use-values be distinguished from others. For instance, means of production (capital-goods) can be distinguished from articles of consumption (wage-goods and luxury-goods), agricultural commodities from manufactured ones, ordinary commodities from the monetary one, durable from non-durable goods, and so on. However, these are formal or functional categorisations. That is to say, in order to illustrate the function of

with different numbers simply because they were qualitatively distinct and so measurable only in their proper physical units. Yet this presupposition, without which no economic theory (nor any purely logical definition of capitalism) could have been stated, was not an arbitrary assumption of the subjective 'model-maker', but was, in fact, the 'materialist copy' of that which their object of study actually pointed to. Thus, Marx worked in an ideal period to both appreciate and criticise the classical school. The latter was not just imagining a liberal utopia; they were, up to a point, 'copying reality'. Their economic theory, therefore, contained truth, even though it was partial and *one-sided* to the extent that it was misguided by its bourgeois-modernist ideology, which caused classical economists to believe that their theory could be directly applied to explain the economic base of *all* human societies. They were unaware of the fact that what they discovered was, in fact, bits and pieces of the theory of a purely capitalist society. The latter was not supposed to apply directly to all forms of real-economic life, although it was, as the synthetic definition of capitalism, meant to serve as *the referent* in studying them (in much the same way as Marx imagined that 'the anatomy of human body sheds light on that of the ape').

The above is roughly how Uno has interpreted what Marx actually accomplished by his 'critique of political economy', even though Marx himself was most probably not aware of the full significance of what his own unfinished works portended. Uno himself explains the reason why he could appreciate, even more than Marx himself, the significance of the latter's economic work in the following terms. Marx, who died in 1883, had not had the chance to see the full evolution of 'imperialism as the last stage of capitalist development', whereas Uno, who studied Marx's economics only after World War I, had the advantage of witnessing how capitalism fared in its final stage. Whereas, in the earlier stage of liberalism, it manifested the tendency to approach its own perfectible image, this tendency was frustrated and was even *reversed* in the subsequent era of imperialism, which actually contained the foreboding of its own end. Only with the realisation of its 'mortality', according to Uno, could capitalism be studied synthetically as a self-revealing whole, its internal logic being fully laid bare, such that it was possible to conclude the project of Marxian economics as the critique of political economy. In other words, only several decades after Marx's death could the synthetic definition, or the pure

---

capital-goods (or the means of production), as distinct from wage-goods or luxury-goods (or the articles of consumption), power-looms can be cited just as well (i.e. appropriately) as blast furnaces, even though their historical importance to our real-economic life has been vastly different.

theory, of capitalism (which Uno calls *genriron*) be completed as a logically closed (i.e. dialectical) system.[11] The latter, however, must be 'pure' in the sense of *not* admitting any *specific* materiality or sensuousness of use-values in it;[12] for otherwise it could not apply to all 'capitalistically operable' use-value spaces. Yet, all episodes of capitalist economic history, in real-historical time, past and present, are bound to be brimming with use-values of all sorts in their full diversity. Their empirical-situational study (which Uno calls *genjô-bunnseki*) cannot, therefore, be directly related to, or interpreted in the light of, the purely logical theory. Theory (the logic of capital) and history (our life-world) must be mediated by the stages-theory of capitalist development (which Uno calls *dankaïron*), in which use-values are introduced as *types*.

Two comments are in order here. First, many Marxists have long been subject to the delusion, perhaps under the influence of the Englesian logical-historical method, that they are somehow endowed with a miraculous 'dialectic' which enables them to 'unify theory (logic) and history (practice)' with a single wave of the magic wand. Uno, of course, refuses to be diverted by that sort of facile make-believe. He, instead, squarely faces the issue, which constitutes the crux of his methodology of Marxian economics. Even though, because of its blind faith in the permanence (immortality) of capitalism, bourgeois economics can afford to ignore the question of the 'contradiction between value and use-value', this latter question constitutes instead a crucial matter for Marxian economics, since it regards capitalism to be a historically transient society, which is not destined to survive forever. From this point of view, it must show, from the outset, how it proposes to reconcile the purely logical (abstract) theory of capitalism with the substantive concreteness of its empirical history. For Uno, the solution is to distinguish *three levels of abstraction* in the study of economics: the level of *genriron* at which use-values are merely things that are qualitatively distinct; the level of *dankaïron* at which they are distinguished into three types, according to the developmental stages of capit-

---

11   The dialectic can be logically closed, without depending on axioms or postulates. In contrast, a formal logical system can be closed only tautologically, once axioms and postulates are accepted (for example, the well-known Euclidean theorem that the three inner angles of a triangle add up to a straight line is *tautologically* equivalent to the axiom of parallel lines). When so closed, it is called an axiomatic, as opposed to a dialectical, system. Note that it is always possible to introduce into an axiomatic system as much ideological bias or one-sidedness by way of axioms and postulates.

12   In this sentence, the word 'specific' is emphasised because, from the point of view of capital, only 'materiality and sensuousness' in general terms matter, and not the specific ways in which they affect the humans individually. See the caveat above in footnote iii.

alism; and the level of *genjô-bunseki*, where they are as concrete as they appear in real-historical time. In Marx's *Capital*, these three levels are not yet clearly distinguished, so that use-values which appear there may be at any of the three levels of abstraction, as the case may be.

Secondly, Uno's stages are *material types* (although he does not himself employ such a term) as opposed to the *ideal types* for which Max Weber is justly famous. In this book and elsewhere, Uno warns repeatedly against confusion between these two 'types' of a very different nature. Each of Weber's ideal types is a social-scientific concept which the author (the social scientist) may construct *subjectively*, by associating to it only such features as *he/she* considers 'typical'. In Weber's own words: *'An ideal type is formed by the one-sided accentuation of one or more points of view and by the synthesis of a great many diffuse, discrete, more or less present and occasionally absent concrete individual phenomena, which are arranged according to those one-sidedly emphasised viewpoints into a unified analytical construct* [Gedankenbild]. *In its conceptual purity, this mental construct cannot be found empirically anywhere in reality. It is a* utopia'.[13] For Weber, a social-scientific theory is made up of these subjectively constructed ideal types ('in its conceptual purity' no doubt), and not of abstract-theoretical (purely logical) concepts such as are found in economic theory. In Weber's case, in other words, 'utopian' ideal types *replace* the abstract-theoretical economic concepts, which they, in effect, abolish.

In the construction of Uno's *material types*, too, a mental process of simplifying reality to features that are essential may be involved. Yet this simplification is not one-sided, arbitrary or subjective, as in Weber's case. For, basically, it amounts only to the selection of a particular use-value (a *material* object), like the woollen fabric, produced by the domestic industry of the seventeenth and eighteenth century England, as 'typical', in characterising real-economic life of the incipient (or rather preparatory) stage of capitalism, called 'mercantilism'. The latter may indeed be a 'mental construct' or a 'utopia', which may as such 'not be found empirically anywhere in reality', since many things other than (though akin to) the woollen goods were then also produced and consumed. Yet in order to define the material base of that stage, it does make sense to *privilege* the (actually existing) woollen products as more 'typical' than any other contemporary product, by simply dropping the latter as atypical details; this is different from arbitrarily transforming real history into our mental picture (ideal types) of what history ought to have been. In other words, unlike Weber, Uno did not abolish the history of capitalism for its ideal types. Neither did he

---

13   Weber 1949, p. 90.

abolish the theoretical definition of capitalism. On the contrary, his formulation of *genriron* (or 'materialist copy' of capitalism) is even more abstract and rigorous than Marx's own in his *Capital*. The purpose of constructing a material type is to see how capitalism, as defined by *genriron*, would operate, if all commodities were like, for example, the woollen products actually produced in the above specified time and place. In this way, the capitalist economy as a stage-theoretic type may serve as a midpoint (mediation term) at which the pure theory of capitalism (which, as the solipsism of capital, should contain no human concern) can be related with a fully concrete-empirical instance of capitalist history (which is *our own*).

Weber, who started from the study of concrete-empirical history, may have wished to eventually arrive at a fully general theory of human society by means of *ideal types*, as the latter in their 'conceptual purity' may one day become adequate for the purpose. Uno, to whom such a universal theory of human society is neither attainable nor meaningful, has, for his part, decidedly remained an 'economist', in that in seeking to relate abstract economic theory with empirical economic history, he has never stepped out of the context of capitalism. This is a point of extreme importance in understanding Uno's method of Marxian economics, since the correspondence between theory and fact in economics is not quite so simple as may be thought in the natural sciences, and thus cannot (and must not) be understood analogously.

IV

What was it then that led Uno to such a conclusion? It was that, while in Germany in 1922–4, he carefully studied Marx's *Capital* and Lenin's *Imperialism*, the two classics of Marxian economics, almost side by side, and was struck by their marked difference not only in the scope but also the style of their presentation. Marx's *Capital*, as already stated, focused on the critique of political economy, which, in effect, meant that it sought a general (or pure) theory of capitalism at its most abstract level, i.e. a *synthetic definition of capitalism by capital itself*, while surmounting the liberal limitation (one-sidedness) of the classical school. Lenin's *Imperialism*, on the other hand, aimed at outlining the prominent features of the 'highest stage of capitalism', specifically the evolution of the capitalist mode of production, after the Great Depression of the 1870s, when it swiftly shifted its base from light to heavy industries. The former was essentially a book on economic theory, whereas the latter was concerned with the characterisation of the imperialist stage of capitalist development. Neither Marx nor Lenin were aware of the distinction between the purely theoretical (logical) and the stage-theoretic (typological) determinations in economics, and the fact that these involved distinct levels of abstraction as regards use-values, such that, at the purely theoretical level, use-values were merely 'illustrative' (in the sense that one could speak of 'cotton' interchangeably with 'iron'), whereas, at the stage-theoretic level, they represented one of the three 'types', and further that, at neither of these levels, were use-values yet fully 'concrete-empirical' as they should be in the historical context.

Lenin tried to show the extent to which capitalism, by the time of the First World War, had transformed itself from what it used to be in the liberal era. The age of free competition standing on light industries (such as textiles) had given way to that of monopoly and protection based on heavy industries (such as iron and steel). Even though, during Marx's time, the pure theory of capitalism could be relatively easily illustrated in references to actually existing capitalism, it was no longer the case in the imperialist era. That, in effect, meant that if the use-value space that underlay the capitalism of the liberal stage was not so distant from the abstract use-value space that the theory must presuppose, the one that supported the capitalism of the imperialist stage was vastly removed from it. Since many Marxists of the Second International were confused and misled by that fact, Lenin must have felt it urgent to show that the recent dramatic transformation of capitalism did not materially alter or invalidate the economic teachings of Marx. Lenin had no inkling then of the Unoist methodology of economics; yet he combined his brilliant insight with what he learned from Hilferding, Hobson and others to demonstrate that imperialism represented the 'highest' (and hence final and declining) stage of capitalist development. He understood that the dominant form of capital which led the capitalist production of commodities, at this point, was *finance-capital* instead of industrial capital. The mode of accumulation peculiar to that form of capital, according to Lenin, manifested itself most typically in various monopoly organisations, which the producers of coal, iron and steel created with the help of large banks, especially in Germany. The imperialist bourgeois state, then, secured the domestic market for them, by resorting to protective commercial policies involving high 'cartel tariffs'. While this picture characterised the *aggressive side* of finance-capital, Lenin did not overlook its *defensive side* which was represented by the massive overseas investment, undertaken especially by Great Britain to its colonies and spheres of influence, which was also assisted by the state, in this case more by the navy than by the board of trade.

Lenin was not aware that the level of abstraction fit for the stages-theory of capitalist development was not the same as that which was proper to the logical theory of capitalism. Therefore, his common-sensical effort to *directly* derive the concept of monopoly from free competition could hardly be defended. Yet he quite correctly refrained from being influenced by witchcraft (or gobbledygook) *à la* Hilferding such as: 'bank-capital negates usurer capital, and is itself negated by finance-capital'! Uno appreciated that discretion on the part of Lenin, from whom he learned that imperialism had to be studied not at the same abstraction-level of the purely logical theory of capitalism, but rather at the stages-theoretic abstraction-level. At that level, the specific type of use-value that was dominant, in this case 'iron and steel', which represented the products of heavy industries of the era, had to be taken into explicit consideration. There is hardly any doubt that Lenin's little book on *Imperialism*, the German translation of which was still new when Uno found it in Berlin, gave him the first insight into what was to become his stages-theory of capitalist development.

If, however, the stage of imperialism was to be characterised with explicit reference to such use-values as 'iron and steel', so likewise was the stage of liberalism to be characterised in reference to 'cotton goods', and the stage of mercantilism to be characterised in reference to 'woollen goods'. This realisation was crucial for Uno who, upon his return to Japan from studies in Germany, was appointed to the post of assistant professor of economic policy at Tôhoku Imperial University. For, by that time, the earlier influence on Japanese economics of the late German historical school (the school, in particular, of the *sozialpolitik* led by Gustav Schmoller) was quickly fading, and many Japanese (academic) economists were beginning to take an active interest in Marx's economics. Uno could, therefore, arrange his lectures in such a way that, under capitalism, the economic policies of the bourgeois state had to undergo the three distinct types: mercantilist, liberal and imperialist, in reflection of the three stages of capitalism's world-historic development. As he admits in the Foreword to this book, the content of his lectures evolved over the ten-year period during which he annually repeated them, until their content approached that of the present book. (It is interesting to remark in passing that Uno, who belonged to the first generation of Japanese Marxian scholars, had the advantage of operating on virgin soil, so to speak, in the sense that he had no influential predecessor to follow or established authorities to bow down to, nor was there any entrenched conventional wisdom, political or academic, to divert his attention from the path of his own strictly intellectual curiosity. That was what led him to the stunning discovery of the full significance of what Marx's critique of political economy entailed and implied, which no one else later could easily duplicate. He was lucky in not being deterred by the many road-blocks which the established academic profession would cheerfully lay in the way of later-generation scholars).

I wish to suggest another striking aspect of Uno's method, even though Uno himself never openly admitted it. His view that economics should study capitalism (in the sense of the capitalist mode of production) at three distinct levels of abstraction as regards the treatment of use-values (purely logical theory, developmental theory of stages and concrete-empirical history in real time) closely parallels Hegel's tripartite classification of human knowledge into the *logic of pure thought*, the *philosophies of nature and finite spirit*, and *the empirical sciences*. Indeed, according to Hegel, 'logic coincides with metaphysics',[14] and its 'content is the exposition of God as he is in his eternal essence before the creation of nature and a finite mind'.[15] What he means is that 'logic' deals with 'the realm of pure thought' wherefrom all materiality and sensuousness must be excluded.[16] In contrast, the 'philosophies of nature and finite spirit' deal with what is 'material and real', but only to the extent that it incarnates the 'pure reason' of the Absolute. The 'empirical sciences' fall outside the realm of philosophy, since they study what is 'real and material' with all its untamed (i.e. earthly and empirical) contingencies. Thus, Hegel's often quoted dictum that 'whatever is reasonable is actual, and whatever is actual is reasonable' makes sense inside the realm of philosophy, which deliberately excludes the contingencies of the 'real and material' that exist outside that hallowed realm. In economic terms, the same dictum may be translated into: 'whatever is commodity-economic is real-economic, and whatever is real-economic is commodity-economic', the significance of which is that the subsumption of real-economic life under the mercantile logic of capital is meant to be complete in the pure theory of capitalism, and is held to be adequate in the stages-theory of its development, but not to be taken for granted (and so must be judged

---

14   Wallace 1975, p. 36.
15   Miller 1969, p. 50.
16   In Hegel's case, 'materiality and sensuousness' are literally excluded from the 'logic of pure thought'; for 'pure thought' does not include, for instance, the idea of dogs which has a sensuous connotation (see Sekine 1986, Vol. 1, p. 27). In pure economic theory, however, capital feels constrained by use-values which affect human beings, though it is not itself interested in this or that particular use-value. In the Hegelian system, the realm of pure thought, which is 'heavenly', and the empirical world, which is 'contingent', are mediated by the philosophies of nature and finite spirit, in which the necessity of reason prevails over contingencies. In Uno's system, the pure theory of capitalism, which is a *logical* definition of capitalism *by capital itself*, and real capitalism operating in *historical* time, which is full of human contingencies, are mediated by the stages-theory of capitalist development, in which use-values 'as types' enable a controlled mental experiment.

instance by instance) in empirical history. This, I believe, is not very far from Uno's view. Elsewhere, I have shown that his *genriron*, which constitutes a synthetic definition of capitalism by capital itself, bears a striking resemblance to Hegel's logic.[17] Thus, when Uno calls his *genriron* 'pure', he means it to be Hegel-pure, not axiomatically pure, as when Walras and his followers call mathematical economic theory 'pure'.

V

In the very brief Conclusion to this book on economic policy, Uno writes as follows: '*The horizon of the stages-theory, however, must not be viewed as being restricted to a study of economic policy as has been outlined in this book. That sort of study must be complemented by more detailed investigations focussing on agriculture, industry, commerce, finance, transportation, colonial administration and other applied features of the economy, at each of the stages of capitalist development*'. Then he continues in the following manner: '*Particularly important, in this regard, is the study of public finance, inasmuch as the latter directly affects, and is affected by, the implementation of economic policy by the state*'. What he then endeavours to explain in the following several highly condensed paragraphs is unfortunately less than crystal-clear. His intent may, however, be paraphrased roughly as follows.

This book does not deal with all forms of economic policies, but only with the ones that directly bear on foreign trade. For the latter must be treated first, before all other economic policies, given that the bourgeois state itself arises as a modern *nation-state*. Since capitalism is the self-regulating commodity-economy, the state does not figure in its logical definition or economic theory. It is introduced, for the first time, at the abstraction level of stages-theory, where the use-value space takes on a concrete developmental type. The bourgeois state's original function is to intervene between the internal and the external market, *like the keeper of the toll-gate as it were*, restricting or forbidding the flow of commodities at the border. This turns out to be the basic form of economic policy that the bourgeois state undertakes. By collecting taxes and granting subsidies, it intends to regulate the circulation of commodities. It grants subsidies to encourage the export of commodities produced domestically, and taxes foreign commodities to discourage their circulation inside its borders. The same pattern of imposing 'tax-subsidy combinations' is observed in the implementa-

---

17   Sekine 1986.

tion of other economic policies under capitalism, which are aimed at regulating the internal circulation of commodities.

This view implies that the economic policy of the bourgeois state limits itself essentially to 'internalising externalities', so as not to directly interfere with the working of the basic laws of capitalism, specifically the laws of value and of relative surplus population. I will, however, return to that point later, and will follow Uno, for now, in reaffirming that the economic policies of the bourgeois state are always put into practice via *public finance*, the latter reflecting an intense political process that must take place as a complex 'tug of war' played amongst interest-groups of all sorts, according to the prevailing rules. Uno emphasises the fact that only at the level of stages-theory can economics co-operate with law and politics, since they all meet in the first instance in public finance. He believes that a 'truly scientific study of the bourgeois state' can be undertaken only at the abstraction-level of stages-theory. Thus, although economic policy, be it national or international, is not (and should not be) the only ingredient of the stages-theory of capitalist development, it nevertheless plays the key role in relating economics to other branches of social science.

In his 1857 manuscript which constitutes the Introduction to the *Grundrisse*, Marx refers to the planned 'disposition of material' (which Rosdolsky calls the *1857 plan*) in five sections. In that scheme, the sections (*3*) *the state as the epitome of bourgeois society*, and (*4*) *the international relation of production,* etc. are the two important parts that seem to have been left out of the scope of the three volumes of Marx's *Capital*, as it is known today.[18] Uno writes, in 1962, that the presumed contents of these two sections cannot be derived from the logical definition of capitalism (his *genriron*), nor should they be studied only at the level of concrete-empirical history (his *genjô-bunseki*), thus suggesting that they fall precisely within the scope of the stages-theory.[19] It is, in fact, quite likely that he had these two sections in mind when he wrote this book. To quote:

> If, however, such themes as 'the international relations' and 'the state as the epitome of bourgeois society' must not be studied in the purely theoretical context, since they cannot be conceptualised at the strictly logical level of abstraction, it does not follow that they must be studied only in concrete-empirical ways as they exist in disparate episodes of history. In fact, with such an approach one would fail to grasp their real meaning. It is important to understand that, when capitalism actually arises and

18   Marx 1970, p. 214. Rosdolsky 1977, pp. 10 ff.
19   Uno 1962, pp. 44–5.

grows in any particular country, that process never occurs in isolation but always in close relation with other nations, of which the degrees of development of the commodity-economy differ rather widely. The 'bourgeois state' evolves always in the process of industrialisation of a particular developing country, under the influence of a nation (or nations) which is (are) capitalistically more advanced, even though each individual case occurs in a specific way and at a particular time. No country enters the process of capitalist development all by itself, in complete isolation from others. Capitalist development is, thus, destined to be 'world-historic', so that, in all epochs, there is an advanced country (or countries) guiding the less developed others.

Indeed, *merchant capital* first led the development of capitalism, as it encroached upon the production-process in sixteenth and seventeenth century Europe, specifically in England, thus marking the early phase of the mercantilist stage. Then *industrial capital* came to the fore after the Industrial Revolution, which began in the late eighteenth century in the same country, as it gradually developed the capacity to operate the capitalist production of commodities in a self-sustained fashion, while establishing its hegemony during the liberal stage. Finally, towards the end of the nineteenth century, the new stage of imperialism evolved, as *finance-capital* became firmly entrenched in both Germany and Great Britain. In all these cases, there was an advanced country (or were advanced ones), which typically represented the world-historic stage of development of capitalism, leading and influencing the less developed nations. Moreover, the dominant form of capital that, in each of these periods, represented the stage as a 'type' did not appear uniformly in all branches of industry. It appeared only in specific ones in each case, i.e. merchant capital in the *woollen and worsted industry*, industrial capital in the *cotton* industry and finance-capital in the *iron-and-steel industry*. Once again capitalism, in each of the developmental stages, focused on the typical industry in which the typical mode of accumulation of the dominant form of capital occurred.

Clearly, Uno's emphasis here is on the fact that in order to comprehend the process of capitalism's world-historic development, one cannot neglect the triple combination made up of (1) 'the representative commodity' and 'the industry that produces it' (together with the technological and organisational method involved therein), (2) the peculiar mode of accumulation of 'the dominant form of capital' adapted to the latter, and characterising the material base of the capitalist economy *typical* of the stage, and (3) the advanced country (or countries) which constitutes (constitute) the industrial centre(s) of the world-historic capitalist development of that stage. These considerations are (and should be) absent in his *genriron*, the purely logical definition of capitalism. Returning to his brief conclusion of this book, I wish once again to quote Uno's following passage: '*My stages-theory is not just a simple "periodisation" (from without) of the history of capitalist development. My aim in defining the three typical, world-historic stages is to let them mediate between the abstract-general economic theory, which is unique, and the concrete-specific (and hence necessarily multiple and diverse) economic histories of capitalism ... They are, therefore, not mere "ideal types", but the real capitalist economies of Britain, Germany and/or the United States, as the case may be, to the extent that they marked the three necessary stages of capitalist development as world-historic epochs, or as types, that is to say, insofar as they have been divested (or cleansed) of all their empirical contingencies*'.

VI

Let us now review, in this section, how the 'stage-theoretic determinations' of *merchant capital* and *industrial capital* differ from their 'purely logical determinations', before considering, in the next section, how *finance-capital*, which is only 'stage-theoretically determined', relates to the purely logical concept of *interest-bearing capital*. It will be helpful to first understand the subtleties of these distinctions and connections in order to adequately grasp the need to separate the stages-theory of capitalist development from the pure theory (or logical definition) of capitalism.

   Merchant capital appears, in pure theory, as the first and simplest application of the general formula for capital, $M–C–M'$. Money (M) first arises from the selling of commodities (C) as the means of purchase (active money), but that part of the means of purchase which is not immediately applied for that purpose becomes *funds* (idle money) convertible into capital. If, however, idle money is hoarded forever, the motion of value stops there, which will, in the end, contradict the capitalist principle of *chrematistic*. It must, therefore, be 'activated' so as to 'buy commodities in order to sell', and thus to be converted into capital. The capitalist, in the first instance, buys a commodity cheap and sells it dear, in the operation of either *arbitrage* or *speculation*. In this context, the 'commodities' are not specified substantively, in the sense that any of them (provided that they are not immediately perishable) can serve equally well as the instrument of arbitrage or speculation. Thus, for the purely theoretical determination of merchant capital, the use-value of the commodity remains (indeed must remain) completely neutral (anonymous), in the sense of requiring no substantive specification of one sort or another, so that any use-value can (and must) be used equally well to 'illustrate' the operation of merchant capital.[20]

In contrast, merchant capital as *the dominant form* of accumulation in the incipient (mercantilist) stage of capitalist development is explicitly tied to the products of the woollen and worsted industry in the seventeenth and eighteenth century in England. One knows from history what type of use-values these commodities were, how they were produced (the technological and organisational aspects of the industry), and how they were circulated (both domestically and internationally). They were produced in 'cottages' spread out in the farming districts, circumventing the guild regulations in cities, and were circulated through the *putting-out* system operated by merchants connected with national and international markets. In the background there stood the absolute monarchy, intent upon building a modern nation-state in close co-operation with the newly up-coming class of the bourgeoisie. It was then not unexpected that the economic policy of the mercantilist state, a joint work of the absolute monarch and merchant princes, had to be attuned to the 'primitive accumulation' of wealth by 'expropriation' (which also entailed the conversion of labour-power into a commodity), and to the formation and protection of 'the domestic (or home) market', in which arbitrage operations gradually established the principle of 'one price for one good'. The highly expropriatory nature of merchant capital, which remained so blatant throughout the age, reflected the incomplete nature not only of the conversion of labour-power into a commodity, but also of the self-regulation of the capitalist market which would subsequently blossom in the liberal era. While obviously incomplete as capitalism, with the persistent relics of traditional societies still lingering pervasively, this stage of capitalist development remained meaningful in that merchant capital, as stage-theoretically determined, successfully operated the woollen and worsted industry of the time in such a way as to prepare for the Industrial Revolution by the end of the eighteenth century.

In the case of *industrial capital* as well, it has to be determined (or conceptualised) differently at the level of abstract theory and at that of stages-theory. The form of industrial capital, M–C ... P ... C′–M′, already presupposes the full conversion of labour-power into a commodity, so that it can transform the elements of production (means of production and labour-power), C, into a commodity, C′, as desired by capital. Here, however, capital does not

---

20   Sekine 1997a, pp. 85–96.

want c′ as use-value, but only as value (not as a concrete-useful wealth to be consumed, but only as abstract-general, mercantile wealth to be sold). In other words, industrial capital should be indifferent, at least in theoretical terms, to the use-value that it chooses to produce in the form of a commodity. Not only is the capitalist indifferent to the use-value of the commodity which he/she produces, but so also is the labour-power that he/she hires to have it produced. Indeed, the whole production-process should become indifferent to the specific use-value of the commodity that it produces. The capitalist mode of production, or capitalism proper, begins to operate only when this principle of indifference to use-values is fully established.[21] In economic theory, however, this indifference to use-values is already presupposed and taken for granted, as the fully prevailing feature of the commodity market. For, otherwise, economic theory itself would be a non-starter. The definition of capitalism in the abstract does not ask what sort of 'material' condition on the part of use-values is, in fact, required to make that presupposition a reality.[22]

Yet, everyone knows that capitalism began to operate increasingly as it should only after the Industrial Revolution, which primarily involved the invention of textile machines (in spinning and weaving) as well as steam engines, during the period beginning in the late eighteenth century and continuing well into the nineteenth century. The evolution of the British cotton industry with its increasing mechanisation also entailed the establishment in the 1830s of the labour market, where numerous property-less workers sold their labour-power as a commodity. The liberal stage of capitalist development thus arrived with the establishment of the mechanised, light-industrial factories in Britain, which hired a large number of unskilled workers. These were primarily the cotton-mills. For, at this stage of capitalist development, the cotton industry was unquestionably the most important and 'typical' one. Many other industries tended to follow the same pattern, though by no means all. There were industries in which traditional, artisanal works survived, and those in which heavy and large items, such as ships and rolling stocks, were produced in limited numbers. There were also industries closely tied to agricultural production and these were, therefore, strongly affected by seasonal and other natural factors. Nevertheless, from the point of view of the stages-theory, these non-

---

21   Merchant capital, M–C–M′, is a less developed form of capital because of its failure to achieve this indifference. For, unable to choose C at will, it must always remain a middleman between the producer and the consumer. See above note 3.

22   Sekine 1997a, pp. 104–16.

typical cases must be deemed as *not essential* in defining the liberal stage of capitalist development, inasmuch as all sectors of the economy, including agriculture, then tended to develop more or less uniformly. The stages-theory, for that reason, considers them as 'contingent' rather than 'necessary' factors in defining the stage.

Here it is apparent that stages-theory operates at a level of abstraction different from that of purely logical theory, but that it, being still a 'theory', does not come all the way down to the fully concrete-empirical level of historical contingency. Thus, even in the liberal stage, during which real capitalism tended to approach its ideal (purely theoretical) image, so that the gap between facts and theory was as small as possible, industrial capital, as determined stage-theoretically, must be distinguished from industrial capital as it is determined purely logically. Thus, in pure theory, industrialisation and wage-labour are explained at the fully abstract level, in the sense that the specificity of use-values is considered irrelevant, for they are just things with different names. Industrial capital, in this context, pursues the production of absolute and relative surplus value through the dialectic of 'co-operation', 'the manufacture division of labour' and 'the mechanisation of the factory', which lays down the three key elements of the so-called 'capitalist method of production'. Theory shows that the latter also constitutes the process through which the conversion of labour-power into a commodity perfects itself.[23] It is obvious then that the theoretical factory that is supposed to embody the 'capitalist method of production' is, in fact, an abstract image of the cotton-mills in mid-nineteenth-century Britain.

Yet, the abstract theory of capitalism cannot admit this, as it has to remain 'purely logical', in the sense of excluding use-values in concrete-specific terms; it cannot privilege cotton goods and the British cotton industry of the nineteenth century. Since the abstract theory of capitalism is the 'solipsism' of capital above all human concerns, any use-value should be as good as any other in either obstructing or obeying the law of value. The liberal stage offers the material framework in which that ethereal theory (recounted by capital) can for the first time operate at the level, so to speak, of human abstraction. The latter then decides the distinction between that which is necessary (dictated by the logic of capital) and that which is no more than contingent (which escapes it). Thus, in the liberal stage of capitalist development, all factories are supposed to be like the British cotton-mills in the mid-nineteenth century. In that context, one indeed sees that both the micro law of value and the macro law of relative sur-

---

23   Sekine 1997a, pp. 146–53.

plus population were quite adequately at work, so that the self-regulation of the capitalist market was more or less realised.

Since industrial capital, based on the British cotton industry of the mid-nineteenth century, achieved the system of a more or less self-regulating commodity production, it no longer needed to rely on state power and the practice of 'expropriation' (or predatory dispossession) for its chrematistic and accumulation. Industrial capital, therefore, promptly opted to campaign for the free-trade movement, repudiating the state's mercantilist protection and the special privileges which the state once granted to merchant capital. *Laissez-faire* and *laissez-passer* became the key words. The cotton industry imported its raw material from abroad and exported much of its product overseas, and thus operated as a typical 'processing industry', and thus was not deterred by domestic agriculture. This strategy won for Great Britain the 'monopoly of industry', or the central position in the system of international division of labour, as the 'workshop of the world'. The Anglo-French Free Trade Pact of 1860 signalled the culmination of the liberal era. The small 'night-watchman state' advocated since Adam Smith meant lesser intervention of the state with business affairs, but it did not mean a complete retreat of the state. Not only was the state busy in dismantling the old mercantilist practices, it also increasingly managed civil society with the established rules of the legal state rather than with *ad hoc* discretionary policies. It was particularly active in concluding commercial treaties containing the *most-favoured-nation clause* with trade partners, so as to render the divide between domestic and international commodity market as seamless as possible. Thus, even at the liberal stage, the state functioned as 'the epitome of bourgeois society' especially by co-ordinating 'international relations'. Yet these relations had to remain in the background and to become invisible in the abstract-theoretical space; for only in such a space could classical economists perfect their doctrines, and prepare the ground for Marx's *Capital*.

VII

In the first two stages (i.e. the mercantilist and liberal stages) of capitalist development, the dominant forms of capital (respectively, *merchant capital* and *industrial capital*) were determined, on the one hand, abstract-theoretically, and, on the other, stage-theoretically. In the last (i.e. imperialist) stage of capitalist development, however, the dominant form of capital, *finance-capital*, is only stage-theoretically determined. Yet it is closely related to the purely logical concept of 'interest-bearing capital', or what Uno preferred to call 'capital, as the automatically interest-bearing force'. I, therefore, wish to begin by discussing the meaning of that concept.

The pure theory of capitalism first shows how surplus value is produced in the context of the capital-to-labour relation, both in micro and macro terms (the *doctrine of production*); but once this is done, it further explains how *surplus value already produced* is divided up, in the context of the capital-to-capital relation, into various income-forms other than wages (the *doctrine of distribution*). Surplus value is first understood as *profit* earned by industrial capital, and is distributed as 'average profits' to different branches of its activity, in equal proportion to the money-value of capital advanced in each of them. In a branch of production such as agriculture, however, in which capital must pay *rent*, that portion of surplus value must be ceded to landed property before its distribution as *profit* to different units of industrial capital. That, however, is not all. In order to make the production of surplus value as efficient as possible, part of industrial capital must be differentiated into *loan-capital* and *commercial capital*, and to the extent that they too contribute, if indirectly, to the production of surplus value, they are entitled to share part of surplus value as *interest* and *commercial profit*. The latter will also be distributed to each unit of commercial capital in equal proportion to the money-value of the capital advanced, and the rate of profit in commerce and industry must also be equalised in equilibrium. Thus, surplus value minus *rent* and *interest* will consist of industrial *and* commercial profits. When these are distributed to each capitalist, it is called 'normal profit' (or 'average profit in the second sense').[24]

Now, the commercial capitalist tends to divide his/her normal profit into two parts: the 'interest' which must accrue to loan-capital for the currently borrowed money *and* the 'entrepreneurial profit' to which he/she is entitled for the advance of own capital. This is a mere 'quantitative division' of his/her normal profit, even though it already shows the extent to which any trace of surplus value production is beginning to fade away from the consciousness of the commercial capitalist, operating away from the greasy dust and deafening noise of the factory. Yet this quantitative division soon develops further into a 'qualitative' one, in which entrepreneurial profit is understood as being a due reward (or wages) to which the commercial capitalist is entitled for his/her effort (or 'labour') in successfully 'buying cheap and selling dear' *and* interest which automatically accrues to the lender's asset.[25]

---

24   Sekine 1997b, pp. 174–7.
25   Sekine 1997b, pp. 193–5.

This division of profit into 'earned income' and 'property income' is the first step towards the commodification of capital itself. For, in this light, capital becomes an asset, the 'capitalised value' of which is equal to the expected flow of incomes accruing to its owner, discounted by the market rate of interest. This type of capitalist-rational pricing of an asset is a *sine qua non* to logically close the definition of capitalism. For even when theory has satisfactorily explained the reason why landed property is entitled to a share in surplus value in the form of *rent*, that does not justify landed property itself on a commodity-economic basis, unless land is shown to be a purchasable commodity. (For, otherwise, the ancestors of the present landowner may have 'wrested' or 'stolen' the land from someone, which may be factually true but commodity-economically repugnant). It is, therefore, necessary to claim, if only fictionally, that land can be priced 'capitalist-rationally' as an asset promising a stream of rental revenues. It does not mean that land is actually traded as a commodity in a purely capitalist society; it need not and it is not. Yet theory must provide for its conversion, if need be, into a tradable asset, or an *interest-bearing capital*. Once this concept is accepted, the aggregate value of capital in society which, in fact, exists in the three forms of *money capital*, *commodity capital* and *productive capital*, is fictionally reinterpreted as a uniform mass of *interesting-bearing capital*, yielding the whole of surplus value as 'interest' accruing to a property that is owned in the same way as land to which rent accrues (rather than as the 'profit' that capital has earned). The commodification of capital is, however, not quite as simple as that of land; for it involves the form of a *joint-stock company*, such that its equity is represented, on the one hand, by the net worth of the ongoing capitalist firm, and, on the other, by the value of its marketable shares outstanding. Due to this 'doubling', the firm can continue its value-augmenting motion *undivided*, even while its ownership is, in part or in whole, transferred from one agent to another.[26]

This form of (joint) 'stock companies', which Marx described rather elliptically as 'the abolition of capital as private property within the framework of capitalist production itself',[27] had been adopted in railways, public utilities and overseas commerce by his time, but not in manufacturing. It was only with the advent of heavy industries such as iron and steel, which required the advance of a 'bulk of fixed capital', that the joint-stock company became the normal form of business enterprise, especially in late-starting capitalist countries, such as Germany and the United States. Obviously, there arose a

26   Sekine 1997b, pp. 195–204.
27   Marx 1987, *Capital*, Vol. III, p. 436.

need to quickly assemble idle funds convertible into capital, and the system of joint-stock proved helpful. In some places (such as in the United States), open markets for stocks developed quickly; in others (such as in Germany), banks subscribed to the new issue of stocks before they were gradually assimilated by individual investors. In any case, the joint-stock company, which only *notionally* existed as an application of interest-bearing capital in pure theory, became the favourite instrument of *finance-capital* in the stage of imperialism, as the productive base of society shifted from light to heavy industries, and that because the latter, unlike the former, required massive advances of fixed capital. This form of business administration, as the German example showed most strikingly, facilitated the development of monopoly organisations, such as cartels and syndicates together with the collusion of large banks and large industrial firms.

It was clearly not possible to derive *finance-capital*, as the dominant form during the stage of imperialism, directly from pure theory. Hilferding, who first studied this type of capital, tried in vain to deduce the concept from Marx's theory of 'money and credit', and merely strayed into a labyrinth.[28] Lenin, too, who rather wished to derive it from the 'concentration of capital in general', also remained in the dark as to its relationship with interest-bearing capital. Thus, even after their remarkable contributions, the two authors did not quite settle the pervasive crisis of Marxism after the Second International. It was Uno who finally filled in the gap between Marx's economic teachings and the fact of imperialism, by distinguishing the level of abstraction proper to the stages-theory of capitalist development from that appropriate to the definition of pure capitalism.

VIII

What primarily characterised *imperialism* as the last stage of capitalist development lay in the fact that in order to operate a much more advanced real-economic life, i.e. at a much higher level of productivity than previously available, capitalism as global commodity-economy was, for its part, forced to make necessary concessions. Recall that in the liberal stage, the productivity level (with mechanised light industries) was just right for near-perfect competition among small individual firms, so that the laws of capitalism tended to work their way through the economy without much distortion. It was for that

28   Hilferding 1981, part I.

reason that theory and facts could be relatively easily bridged without anyone becoming conscious of the hidden intricacy of the problem. With the advent of heavy industries, requiring massive investment of fixed capital, especially in late-developing capitalist nations, the situation radically changed, in such a way that the so-far vigorous trend of capitalism to approach its theoretically more perfect image was frustrated, and even reversed. In other words, in order to accommodate a more advanced real economy at a higher level of productivity, capitalism was forced to diverge from its path of self-purification, and to swallow such non-liberal values as 'monopoly and protection', 'uneven development', and the like. The advance of the real-economy, concomitant with the regression of the commodity-economy (and hence of capitalism as such), therefore, had to be the characteristic feature of imperialism.

For the ahistorical view of capitalism, widely held by the liberals, this may be thought to be an unbearable contradiction. For, to them, there cannot be any divergence between progress in the real economy and that in capitalism (which materially supports modern society): economic life must become richer as capitalism perfects itself; technical progress which capitalism itself promotes cannot make it more difficult for capitalism to contain. Marxian economics, however, holds capitalism (as a global and self-dependent commodity-economy) to be a historically transient economic institution, so that it comes into being at a particular point in history and exits at another: capitalism arises at a given level of productivity of human society and fades away at another. It means both (a) that only some use-value spaces are capitalistically operable, and (b) that some use-value spaces are more easily operable as capitalism than others. Thus, if the use-value spaces were relatively well-attuned to capitalist operation at the liberal stage, the ones at the imperialist stage, which are technically more advanced, may well be *less* so. For, otherwise, capitalism would last forever. Unbelievably, a great many Marxists share the bourgeois faith in the perpetuity of capitalism, and refuse to see any foreboding of its end in imperialism (and even later).[29] Uno certainly is not one of them.

For Uno, 'infant industry protection' was a policy of industrial capital in the late-developing capitalist nations such as the United States and Germany. Many of these countries adopted this policy in the course of 'industrialisation', but only in its early phase. Once the industries which they wished to implant in their country were well-established, such a policy was swiftly dismantled, so

---

29   Maybe it is still believed that capitalism cannot cease to exist until it is violently smashed
      by a revolution that hoists the red flag, but history has shown this to be neither a necessary
      nor a sufficient condition.

that they could be exposed to fair international competition. In the meantime, the emerging capitalist nations had the advantage of importing fully mechanised large industry, practically ready-made, from Great Britain, so as to expedite their industrialisation without having to reproduce the grim process of primitive accumulation, as England had had to undergo during its bloody mercantilist era, involving the thorough dissolution by relentless expropriation of things belonging to the traditional society. By this time, enough labour-power could relatively easily be shifted from well-populated farmlands to industrial factories that were already endowed with a high value-composition of capital. Only a mild resistance, by means of infant-industry protection, against free-trade aggressively promoted by the country's agricultural interests sufficed to secure room for the emergent industrial capital, provided that the latter could promptly mobilise idle funds for investment in its business units, incorporated as joint-stock companies. In the late-developing capitalist nations, this form of business organisation had already become widespread even in light industries and had proven to be highly efficient in the period immediately prior to the age of heavy industry.

The rapid expansion of the commodity-economy in the world entailed a sustained demand for iron-and-steel goods, which led to a series of technical innovations in that sector. When, in 1878, the Thomas-Gilchrist method was made available, Germany acquired a distinct advantage over other countries in exploiting the iron-and-steel industry due to its proximity to Lorraine and Luxemburg, where iron-ores and coal were both abundantly available. In this type of industry, however, a massive mobilisation of funds convertible into capital was needed for investment in heavy plants and equipment (such as blast furnaces), which Uno described as 'bulking large of fixed capital'. This fact provided a new impetus to 'investment banking'. Unlike their previous practice during the liberal era, banks no longer acted merely as 'loan-capital', which mainly provided individual firms with circulation credits. Not only did they assemble idle funds spread out in society into their accounts, but they also used the financial resources thus acquired primarily to assist large industrial firms in heavy industries in the issuing of new shares, which enabled them to earn huge profits by sharing in the firms' *founder's gain*, which consisted of the difference between the firm's interest-bearing capital (its current revenue 'capitalised' at the market rate of interest) and its paid-in capital, that is to say, of the excess of the market value over the face value of its shares. It was, in effect, a speculative and expropriatory gain which could become proportionately larger as the firm's profit-rate exceeded the market rate of interest. Since the firm, once founded, was expected to dominate the market with its monopoly-power, its profit-rate was bound to far exceed the market rate of interest. It was through this type of 'operation in the capital market' (the market in which shares and stocks, bonds and debentures were traded) that *finance-capital* fuelled its own accumulation.

The above approach was typified in the case of Germany, where large banks and monopolised industrial firms colluded to fully control the market for heavy industrial products through cartels and syndicates. In the United States, finance-capital operated in a less organised, but equally relentless, manner to dictate the production of surplus value in heavy industries, through direct stock-market operations, often verging on outright fraud and swindles. In both cases, finance-capital controlled domestic production in heavy industries, via operations (or machinations) in the capital market, so as to realise *monopoly profits*. Under the circumstances, the imperialist bourgeois state, too, had to secure the home market for finance-capital from external competition, by means of radically protective commercial policies. The 'cartel tariffs' which the imperialist state then imposed on foreign goods so as to protect national finance-capital were much higher, and better entrenched, than 'infant-industry tariffs'. For, after thus making doubly sure of its control over the domestic market for heavy industrial products, finance-capital then resorted to predatory dumping in foreign markets, which, in turn, made it necessary that it should be prepared against similar offensives from other imperialist nations. Nor did heavy industrial goods remain the only dutiable items; tariff schedules included any goods that were traded, whether they were light industrial manufactures or agricultural produce, raw materials, or semi-finished and finished commodities. For they all became the instruments of tariff negotiations, which were constantly renewed amongst the imperialist nations. In this way, the international market for commodities was gradually divided up into *colonies and spheres of influence*, which became the only space in which finance-capital could hope to grow.

It was, however, not even necessary for finance-capital to have followed all these steps in sequence in order to finally arrive at the 'division of the world market' into colonies and spheres of influence. Due to years of surplus value production, the oldest capitalist nation, Great Britain, had by then accumulated a huge volume of idle funds convertible into capital. Not only did industrial and commercial firms in that country possess enough internal funds for their business expansion, but also landed property, large and small, and intermediate classes of all sorts, had already saved up sizable pecuniary resources that regularly flowed into the City of London for 'merchant banking'. That is to say, these resources were invested primarily abroad in the construction of railways, the exploration of mines and the building of local infrastructures, either directly or through the governments of the countries concerned. With the spectacular increase in the volume of foreign investment, enormous interest revenues accrued to Britain, by which its commercial deficit was more than covered, turning the country into a typical *rentier* state. Thus, finance-capital in Britain took the form of financing investments abroad, which assisted foreign economic development and the opening up of new markets for capitalistically produced commodities (which were, of course, mostly European), rather than developing its own heavy industries systematically.

Actually, in the 1860s, Britain was the top exporter not only of cotton manufactures, but also of iron-goods as well. Yet, as new techniques were developed for steel making, Britain had invested far too heavily in fixed capital based on the Bessemer method, relying on the import of high-quality Spanish ore. When, in the late 1870s, the Thomas-Gilchrist method enabled the use of lower grade iron-ore to make steel, the British industry, stuck with old equipment, could no longer rival its newly emerging German counterpart. At this point, however, Britain was already wealthy enough with the interest revenues from abroad to spare, and need not have persevered to win back its erstwhile manufacturing hegemony. It made better sense to maintain its political supremacy, as the greatest of all colonial powers, with formidable military resources to back it up. After all, the age of finance-capital in any country was characterised by 'uneven development among different economic sectors'. There was nothing unusual in the fact that Britain should excel in international finance, while conceding its industrial prowess to newcomers. That not only explains the frustration of Joseph Chamberlain on the one hand, but also the eventual victory of Great Britain and its allies in WWI, on the other.

IX

The outbreak of the 'imperialist war' was a *necessary* consequence of this stage of capitalism's world-historic development. For, in one way or the other, finance-capital could not continue its accumulation in the narrow confines of the domestic market in which the excess (or superabundance) of capital soon prevailed, such that domestically saved idle funds, which could no longer be lucratively invested (converted into real capital) at home, were forced to seek outlets abroad in the form of *overseas investment*. If the same situation prevailed in all imperialist powers, their international conflict would become inevitable and increasingly more acute.

All that, however, is a *stage-theoretic necessity*, which must, according to Uno, be distinguished from the *purely theoretical (or logical) necessity*, for instance, of 'decennial crises' within the abstract definition of capitalism. In the latter, industrial crises must occur since the course of capital accumulation is bound to be cyclical, undergoing in turn the phase of *widening*, in which the value-composition of capital is held constant, and that of *deepening*, in which it is raised. The aggregate-social capital introduces technical innovations in a cluster (as Schumpeter would say) during the depression phase, raising the value-composition of capital; but once the prosperity phase begins with a given composition of capital, these innovations are gradually absorbed into various sectors of the economy, first in the sub-phase of *recovery*, then in that of *average activity*. By that time the demand for, and the supply of, labour-power tend to equal each other, and, on that basis, resources tend also to be optimally allocated to different sectors of the economy, bringing it roughly to a state of general equilibrium, where average profits are earned in all industries at their margin. In the following sub-phase of *overheating*, however, the further accumulation of capital entails an excess demand for labour-power; thus real wages must consequently rise. Capital, however, cannot curb this trend, since it cannot by itself increase the supply of labour-power. As labour costs rise, a profit squeeze becomes unavoidable, which, in the face of previously contracted fixed costs and increasing interest rates, forces capital to stop further accumulation. The ensuing disarray of the social reproduction-process renders a capitalist crisis inevitable. This story, needless to say, is recounted at the fully abstract level, at which no particular use-value need be concretely specified, except that it generally presupposes the existence of some use-values (in this case, capital-goods) that are durable.[30]

However, the decennial crises, which punctuated the typical Juglar cycles at their peaks, were actually observed only about five times during the liberal era. The reason was that in the liberal stage characterised by light industries, free competition among firms prevailed and a typical textile machine lasted for about ten years. In the absence of significant monopoly power, the capitalist method of production tended to be renovated 'in a cluster' in a depression period, so that business cycles could more or less follow the theoretically expected pattern. Thus, the laws of relative surplus population and of value worked largely undistorted. In the imperialist stage, with the advent of heavy industries accompanied by the 'bulking large of fixed capital', there emerged a strong monopoly power, which distorted the working of the real capitalist economy. For a large industrial firm in a heavy industry could safely launch, at any desired time, a new company equipped with a more advanced method, while still continuing to operate the old, less productive method elsewhere,

---

30   Sekine 1997b, pp. 156–67.

since it could dictate the market price for its products regardless of how they were produced. Of course, there still remained many competitive sectors in which monopoly power did not prevail, so that industrial cycles and crises were not altogether abolished. Yet the existence and ascendancy of monopoly power in heavy industries significantly affected the regularity and the self-regulation of the capitalist economy, so that decennial crises no longer settled all the problems of the *excess of capital*. The latter then tended to become a chronic feature in the domestic market, requiring finance-capital to seek better opportunities abroad. This meant that what used to be settled more or less by the logic of capital inside the state, as epitome of bourgeois society, could no longer be. In consequence, economic and political tensions had to mount in the international scene, foretelling the necessity of an imperialist war.

The above account illustrates the crucial fact that in pure economic theory, which is a *synthetic definition of capitalism by capital itself*, there is (and can be) no germ to be found of capitalism's self-destruction (or automatic break-down), contrary to the expectation of many conventional Marxists. The end of capitalism makes itself felt only at the level of stages-theory, specifically, in *the stage-theoretic necessity of an imperialist war* to which the accumulation of finance-capital must lead. Since 'war' exceeds the logic of capital, it is quite justified to regard imperialism as the *declining* stage of capitalist development, even though, prior to WWI, the industrial prowess of both a newly emerging Germany and the United States may have appeared to promise a brighter future for capitalism. Here again, one must recall the fact that although the real-economic side of imperialism, based on heavy industries, is far more advanced (and productive) than in the previous era, its commodity-economic side has been adulterated, becoming less certain and more haphazard than pre-viously, as 'monopoly and protection' replace 'competition and free trade', and as 'uneven development' replaces the previously more uniform and balanced pattern. Thus, imperialism, on one side, shows the ability of finance-capital to overcome technical difficulties in order to handle a more advanced eco-nomy inside the nation-state; yet, on the other, it also shows that its accumula-tion sooner or later exceeds the confines of the commodity-economy, shifting the unsettled 'contradiction between value and use-value' to the international theatre. It is for this reason that imperialism constitutes the *last* (final) stage of capitalist development, after which no new (fourth) stage of capitalist devel-opment is conceivable.

The present interpretation seems to me to be consistent with Uno's con-ception of capitalism (in the sense, as always, of the capitalist mode of pro-duction), which, however, radically differs from conventional ones. In his case, as in Marx's, capitalism is defined quite narrowly and *rigorously* by economic theory, that is to say, *from the inside* by the logic of capital itself (as *genriron*), not *from the outside* by a subjective and arbitrary 'model' which *we* construct in our imagination. To Uno, therefore, only the real-economic life that *can* be subsumed under capital's logic can constitute a capitalist society, as a historical society. This is quite different from the more widely held 'protean' view of capitalism, according to which any society in which some capitalist activities are found is *ipso facto* capitalist, regardless of the nature of the use-value space upon which its reproduction-process is erected. It is obvious that such a view simply reproduces the bourgeois-liberal, modernist ideology according to which all use-value spaces are equally commodifiable, and capitalistically operable, so that all societies are, by definition, capitalist. Marxists should certainly beware of being trapped by this kind of bourgeois eschatology, if they are to truly seek to transcend capitalism.

If one follows Uno's strict definition of capitalism, then the scope of 'economic policies under capitalism' which he treats in this book becomes much clearer. The policies which the bourgeois state adopts *vis-à-vis* the (self-regulating) capitalist economy aim fundamentally at 'internalising the externalities', that is to say, at adjusting the prices of such commodities if and when the market fails to evaluate them correctly. For 'externalities' mean that which falls outside the well-performing capitalist market or that which the latter fails to duly take into account. Often *social* costs and benefits fail to be properly assessed by the market, since the private firms' myopic profit-and-loss calculus fails to adequately take them into account. The role of the bourgeois state then resides in redressing such biases so as to enhance the efficiency of capitalist society as a whole. It plays that role, in particular, by designing suitable tax-subsidy combinations in its public finance, where the economic meets the political and the legal.[31] This observation applies especially well during the liberal era, when the state did not actively involve itself in industrial promotion and protection, since the accumulation of industrial capital was more or less self-sustained.

It applies perhaps less cogently during the mercantilist and the imperialist era, when capital needed the assistance of the state more directly and urgently because it was less self-dependent than in the liberal era. In its incipient stage,

---

31   Interestingly, this view of economic policies under capitalism echoes the teachings of welfare economics, often regarded as providing a theory of micro-economic policies, as distinct from macro-economic policies, even though Uno himself is most unlikely to have had any idea as to what welfare economics was and is up to.

capitalism was still in its making, so that even if it constituted a growing sec-tor of the economy, it certainly was not the only one. It, therefore, needed to develop the manufacturing of woollen products in the countryside, circum-venting the more traditional city guilds, with the assistance of the absolute monarchy. The latter, for its part, sought both wealth and power by assisting the primitive accumulation of merchant capital with, for example, the Navig-ation Acts and the Poor Laws. In the declining stage of capitalism, the speedy accumulation of finance-capital in the monopolised heavy-industry sector did entail the 'uneven development of the capitalist economy'. The accumulation of industrial capital in the sector of more competitive light industries, though still extensive, lagged behind, often creating problems which were visited upon the inefficiency of small and medium enterprises, while traditional agricul-ture was left far behind by the rapid development of heavy industries. A pool of surplus labour arose which could not be absorbed swiftly enough by the industrial sector. Faced with these circumstances, the state had to deal with anti-monopoly legislations, on the one hand, and with *sozialpolitik*, on the other.

In all cases, however, it may be said that the economic policies of the bour-geois state tended to assist the accumulation of the dominant form of capital in each stage of capitalist development. Even in modern society, the bour-geoisie does not exercise 'monopoly power' with regard to policymaking, there being a variety of interest groups, large and small, old and new, all of which seek to achieve their own sectional ends through the instrumentality of the state. They all take part in a complex 'tug of war', pulling the rope in their own directions with varying strength, the result of which depends on not just the predictable parallelograms of forces, but also a great many unpredictable con-tingencies. Hence, not all the policies adopted and implemented by the state are necessarily in the best interest of capital. Yet if policies actually put into practice during the capitalist era proved not to serve effectively the accumu-lation of the dominant form of capital, they were bound to be screened or filtered out, and, if need be, replaced by the ones more adapted to, and effect-ive for, the purpose of capitalist development. It was the role of the bourgeois state to see to it that proper selection and elimination of policies were made through the judicious management of its public finance. In no case, however, would the bourgeois state have acted against the fundamental laws of capit-alism, such as the laws of value and of relative surplus population (which on the surface of the capitalist market reappeared as the laws of average profits and of the falling rate of profit), for that would have been suicidal. It always endeavoured to prepare, maintain and/or preserve the ground upon which the capitalist rules of the game could best be played out. To the extent that

this principle was successfully observed, economic policies may be characterised as ones *under capitalism* and implemented by *the bourgeois state*, in Uno's
sense.[32]

X

Thus, in this book, Uno distinguishes the three world-historic developmental
stages of capitalism: the mercantilist, which represents its incipient (nascent
and preparatory) stage; the liberal, its stage of maturity and autonomy; and
finally, the imperialist, its aging and declining stage. If capitalism is conceived,
as it should be, to be a transient form of human society, which arises at one
point in history, comes of age at another, and is destined to end its historical
mission in due course, the interposition of these distinct developmental stages
formulated by *dankairon* (at the abstraction-level of which use-values are 'typical') becomes inevitable as the 'mediating term' between the fully abstract-
logical theory of capitalism as stipulated by *genriron* (at the abstraction-level
of which use-values must necessarily be neutral, i.e. nominal, ethereal and
'weightless'), and the concrete-empirical, and situational, reality, analysed by
genjô-bunseki (at the abstraction-level of which use-values must be both naked
and multifarious, just as they appear in any actual historical context). It is
only when capitalism (the capitalist mode of production) is misconceived to
be something like a permanent and immutable natural order, be it a para-
disiac one, which will realise the promise of the pre-established harmony
(the bourgeois-liberal ideology), or an infernal one of internecine class wars
between the rich and powerful minority and the exploited and dispossessed
majority (the radical-revolutionary ideology), can one skip the necessary interposition of stages-theory and pretend to adopt the natural-scientific method,[33]
which presumes to directly relate a subjective 'pure theory' with the objective
'real world'. Yet, in that case, the latter (the 'real world') is bound to become
a fraud (amounting to no more than an ideological 'make-believe'). Uno's

---

32   The bourgeois state also provided capitalist society with many important public services,
      be it in education and healthcare, in the maintenance of law and order, in that of safety
      and hygiene, and so on. Without doubt, they had a strong impact on the functioning of
      the commodity-economy indirectly (that is to say, they did not directly interfere with it),
      as services are not themselves commodities.

33   On the natural-scientific method versus the social-scientific method, see Sekine 2003. See
      also Sekine 1997a, pp. 1–22.

method of distinguishing the three levels of abstraction, which is implicit in the works of Marx and Lenin, thus involves a fundamental critique of both bourgeois and conventional-Marxist economics.

There is, however, one theme that this book leaves largely unsettled. It has to do with the world economy *after* the war of 1914–18, which cannot be viewed as belonging to the stage of 'imperialism'. For that stage represents the *declining* one (the old age) of capitalism, and not its phase of *disintegration* (deathbed). From Uno's point of view, an economic policy *under capitalism* cannot possibly 'aim at suspending the working of the law of value or at circumventing periodic crises'; for such a policy would flatly contradict the preservation of capitalism (the capitalist mode of production) itself. It is, of course, true that under such extraordinary circumstances as when bourgeois society is visited by a war, a famine or any other natural or human calamity, it may become necessary for the state to temporarily suspend the normal functioning of the commodity-economy (for example, the operation of the international gold standard might have to be suspended for the duration of a war), but such interventions are destined to be removed as soon as the crisis is over, so as to restore the integrity of the self-regulating, capitalist market.

In the 1970 essay appended to this book, entitled 'Capitalist Development after the First World War', Uno quite clearly states that 'the capitalist development after the Russian Revolution of 1917 is more adequately studied as economic history of the present, rather than as manifestations of another [a fourth] typical stage of capitalist development'.[34] The reason why he decided on such a view was that, as he observed the performance of the world economy in the first two decades following WWII, it was clear to him that 'the development of the capitalist nations then, remarkable as it was, did not demonstrate sufficient vigour in blocking the expansion of the socialist sphere'. It was this fact that convinced him that 'capitalism had lost the dynamism necessary to give rise to another world-historic stage of capitalist development, following the end of the First World War'. If capitalism has ceased to 'develop' further, then the process of its dismantling, or disintegration, must also have started. In other words, the world economy after the Peace of Versailles must be studied as a process of 'transition away from capitalism to another historical society', which may, for convenience, be called 'socialism', even though what this latter will eventually be like is not yet clear even in its broad outlines. The purpose of studying this transitional process, which I have called the process of

---

34 Although, in the 1954 edition of this book, he was still vacillating on that issue, he settled more definitively on the above-quoted conclusion in the final 1971 edition of this book. See pp. 237–241 of this book.

'ex-capitalist transition', is to be increasingly informed of the signs and adumbrations of this new society as we actually approach it.[35]

Uno's 1970 essay refers to the Japanese debate on 'state-monopoly capitalism', which followed the publication of a 1957 acticle on that theme by Kurt Zwieschang, a German Marxist, in which the author argued that 'the production-relations of imperialism entered a new stage, as the increasing importance of the role of the state intensified the contradiction between them and the productive powers'. Uno was not impressed by this sort of argument, which freely mixes economic analysis with formulae of the materialistic conception of history. He was especially unhappy that no participant in the debate, who wished to deal with the theme of 'state-monopoly capitalism', as an 'advanced phase of imperialism', bothered to explain how this 'increasing importance of the role of the state' related to the need of *finance-capital*, which should remain the dominant form of capital at the stage of imperialism. On the other hand, he took note of a survey article on the debate that Tsutomu Ôuchi, then his junior colleague at the University of Tokyo, published, in which the latter observed: 'Behind the stepped-up role of the imperialist state, which Zwieschang had made much of, lay the inflationary policy of the state, that was made possible under the managed currency system'. Ôuchi also stated in the same article: 'By the time the state implements such a policy, socialism has become a world-historic fact, which compels the capitalist nations, in their external relations, to take it into full account'. With regard to this second statement of Ôuchi's, Uno writes: 'It was rather this observation that seemed to me to be more relevant to the question at issue'. This tallies with Uno's view quoted in the previous paragraph to the effect that the capitalist nations had lost sufficient dynamism to eventually swallow up the socialist bloc which then appeared to have come to stay. In view of the more recent fall of the Soviet Union, Uno has been duly criticised for having attached too much credence to the premature establishment of socialism in the world.

With regard to the first observation of Ôuchi's, Uno writes as follows:

> The inflationary policy that can be enforced under the managed currency system exerts a far more powerful impact on the real economy than, for instance, the customs policy of the former imperialist state. It is surely unwarranted to believe that currency, if not production, is susceptible of

35   This period of *ex-capitalist transition* beginning with WWI may, at first sight, strike one to be rather long; but, in comparison with the lengthy process of the disintegration of medieval society, prior to the dawn of the modern age, it should not cause undue surprise.

state control, even within the regime of the capitalist mode of production. Yet it is also true that the inflationary policy of the state, as it is nowadays practised, does have some influence on production through its control of the nation's currency. The question, therefore, is what to make of the managed currency system, which enables the state to enforce an inflationary policy.

It is thus quite obvious that, for Uno, what constitutes the key to capitalism's process of disintegration was the managed currency system which made the macro-policies of the state possible. It is both interesting and important to note that, according to Uno, such a critical (even revolutionary) change in the world economy did not occur as the result of a deliberate or considered (policy) action on the part of anyone in particular. For he says: 'the managed currency system is an offshoot of the profound disequilibrium that has arisen within the community of the capitalist nations'. Uno continues:

> This system was not designed as a bulwark against socialism, nor was it sought by finance-capital expressly with a view to reinforcing its grip on the imperialist stage of capitalist development. It arose rather *ad hoc*, through the disruptions in the aftermath of the First World War and in the process of haphazard reconstruction thereafter (all of which led eventually to the great Depression of the 1930s), as something which the public finance of the time required, and which finance-capital may have wished to make some astute use of. Whatever the circumstances of its birth, however, the managed currency system was a monetary system which was alien to the commodity-economy, and which therefore, contradicted the self-regulation of capitalism as a historical society. It denied commodity-money in part or in whole, in form and in substance. Yet this abnegation on the part of the capitalist mode of production was a necessity (and not a temporary expedient), if that mode of production was to continue to survive alongside socialism.

Thus, Uno makes it quite clear that the managed currency system, which the capitalist countries adopted willy-nilly to replace the international gold standard system, in the aftermath of WWI and during the process of reconstruction, constituted *the first decisive move away from capitalism*, though the gravity of its consequence was then hardly noticed by anyone.

There are some more interesting observations to be found in Uno's essay, but they are more cursory and impressionistic in nature, apart from the reassertion of his own methodology of Marxian economics. In his view, in order to sensibly account for the evolution of the world economy after the Peace of Versailles, it is not sufficient to simply go back to Marx's own texts for hints. For in order to fully comprehend what capitalism (the capitalist mode of production) is all about, it is necessary to investigate it at the three distinct levels of abstraction (of use-values). Only when Marx's intellectual legacy is reviewed in that light can one grasp the true meaning of capitalism, as a world-historic economic system, and, in that light, sensibly approach the ongoing 'economic history of the present'. Only then can one hope to understand 'the nature and significance of the society in which we live today'. It is thus far that Uno's major contribution to Marxian economics has taken us.

(Written in 2010 and revised in 2012)

An Essay on Transition away from Capitalism: How Might Unoists Account for the Evolution of the post-1914 World Economy?

I

In the previous essay, I tried to review, by essentially paraphrasing Uno's writings, what we might learn regarding the significance of his *stages-theory* of capitalist development (*dankaïron*). In its last section, I mentioned that, after a period of hesitation, he finally convinced himself that capitalism properly so-called (in the sense of Marx's 'capitalist mode of production') ceased to further 'develop' into a new world-historic stage after the war of 1914–18, and hence that the world economy thereafter must be studied as being in a 'transitional process from capitalism to a new historical society'. We may, therefore, regard this perspective of Uno's as providing a hint as to his 'theory of transition away from capitalism (*katokiron*)' which was *yet to be elaborated*. However, the Memorandum on this subject, appended to the 1970 definitive edition of the present book,[1] was written in the twilight years of his intellectual career, and can hardly be said to embody his mature, fully worked-out thought; rather, it represented his tentative foray into a new territory. For that reason, that piece of work, when it suddenly appeared in print, as much inspired as puzzled his students. Indeed, his arguments in it were often more mystifying than convincing. That being the case, most Japanese Unoists at the time apparently found the interpretation by Tsutomu Ôuchi (1918–2009) of capitalism after WWI more congenial than Uno's suggestive but not yet fully elaborated, and so opaque comments on it. Ôuchi was a junior colleague of Uno's at the University of Tokyo, and his 1970 book entitled *State Monopoly Capitalism*,[2] which, while indicating respect for Uno, also retained to a considerable measure the conventional views on the subject, was widely read and also turned out to be quite influential thereafter. Uno's 'Memorandum' does refer to Ôuchi's earlier 'Notes on State Monopoly Capitalism' from 1963,[3] but not to the later book, in which the author elabor-

---

1 See pp. 237–41 above.
2 Ôuchi 2007.
3 See Ôuchi 1970.

ates on his own thought in the Note. Uno never commented on Ôuchi's book in public, nor was he aware of its subsequent influence. In any case, there were certain obvious differences between the views of the two authors. I, for one, could not and cannot accept Ôuchi's idea that 'state-monopoly capitalism' constituted a mere variation and continuation of the 'imperialist stage of capitalist development', even though the latter had lost its prewar vigour and had become more defensive under the post-WWI climate of the so-called 'general crisis' of capitalism. For Uno was quite unambiguous in his view that WWI was an imperialist war that irrevocably terminated the further 'development' of capitalism. Yet, I could not myself figure out how Uno might have developed his own *katokiron*, had he had the opportunity to live and work for, say, ten more healthy years.

After a long search in the dark, however, I have recently felt enlightened on this matter by the works of Mitsuhiko Takumi (1935–2004) and Hyman Minsky (1919–96). Takumi, after his extensive study on the World Depression of the 1930s,[4] came to the conclusion that the crisis of 1929 in the United States could not be viewed as another instance of 'capitalist economic crisis'. This view is diametrically opposed to that of Ôuchi, who believed that it was just another capitalist crisis, and thus, as was to be expected, that capitalism had not lost its self-healing (or recovery) power, even though, because of the uncommon severity in the prevailing climate of the so-called 'general crisis of capitalism', rather expeditious political interventions could not be avoided, which had inadvertently but decisively changed the future course of the world economy. Takumi's view, in contrast, is that the crisis of 1929 initiated a *deflationary spiral*, involving a quantitative fall in output and employment (physical downscaling of production) in leading industries. Normally, a capitalist crisis is followed by a sharp fall of product prices in the leading branches of industry, so that, in the stage of imperialism, for instance, a crisis meant a catastrophic fall in the prices of such products as coal, iron and steel. Thus, while the low prices of these products persisted for some time during the stagnant period following the crisis, innovations were introduced in the method of producing them, which eventually enabled them to be produced at lower production-prices than before. This was sufficient to re-launch the whole reproduction-process of capitalism under a new system of values. Yet there is no sign that this mechanism operated after the crisis of 1929. This is not to say that the prices of many important commodities (especially those of food and primary commodities) did not fall. They did, and indeed catastrophically. What happened, however, is that, even before

---

4   Takumi 1994; Takumi 1998.

these prices fell, the physical scale of operation (output and employment) in the leading branches of industry shrank, because these were 'Fordist' producers, meaning that their products had to be sold at rigid supply-prices equal to the unit-cost of these products with a suitable mark up.

After the First World War, the centre of commodity production shifted from Europe to the United States, where Fordist industry was becoming increasingly prominent. I use this term, Fordism, in the special sense of representing the 'oligopolistic' industry that (often) produces durable goods by means (always) of durable capital assets. In other words, Fordist production embodies the Minskyian characteristic of crucially involving and depending on 'durable capital-assets'.[5] However, the production of durable commodities by means of durable commodities cannot be so easily operated in a capitalist-rational fashion, inasmuch as the 'contradiction between value and use-value' can no longer be so easily surmounted. Both the 'micro law of value' and the 'macro law of (relative surplus) population', the two basic laws that constitute the crux of capitalism, were, therefore, paralysed, and so too was the self-recovery power of capitalism from its periodic industrial crises. The intervention of the national (or federal) government in economic affairs consequently became an unavoidable feature of the era, as did what is now commonly termed the 'mixed economy', with Minsky's so-called 'Big Bank and Big Government' thus prevailing. This truth was yet to be recognised in the interwar period. Uno, who was never well informed of the writings of Keynes, Kalecki or Minsky, could not lay his finger, even by the end of the 1960s, on the real cause of the evolution of the world economy in the post-WWI era, although he was viscerally aware of it more than anyone else, and that is why he was convinced that WWI *terminated* 'capitalism properly so-called', a stunning conclusion that left even those who were close to him practically speechless.

Indeed, it was in 1913–14 when Henry Ford first introduced the assembly-line system into his factory to prove that such 'complex' use-values as automobiles, which must be constructed by assembling many component parts, and which therefore had previously been only 'custom-made' by skilled master-artisans in small numbers of units, could now be mass-produced by ordinary factory workers, and sold as extensively as many other commodities in open markets. Indeed, this revolutionary discovery unexpectedly added to the longevity of capitalist commodity production. The fact that the United States alone was blessed with a decade of prosperity in the 1920s may also have assisted with the advent of this new style of production, and clinched the shift of the centre

---

5 Minsky 2008a; Minsky 2008b; Minsky 1984.

for commodity production from Europe to the United States. Perhaps, it was to the credit of the French school of *régulationnistes*, led by M. Aglietta, to have first realised the key importance of Fordism, and to have subsequently popularised this term as representing industry under so-called 'state-monopoly capitalism'. But, unlike Takumi, they have not related this fact with the downward rigidity of prices, already made much of by Keynes and Kalecki, of the commodities produced in Fordist factories (be they goods for consumers or for producers). Unlike such simple use-values as coal or iron-and-steel products previously, 'complex' use-values such as automobiles, airplanes, helicopters, tractors, power-shovels, and the like, which combine many engineering parts, cannot be sold in large quantities at lower prices when the demand for them flags. (No one has ever heard of a post-Christmas sale of brand new cars, even if the factory is about to close down!). The physical scale of production must be contracted with layoffs of the personnel, which, if massive, would further reduce earned incomes and destroy employment opportunities, leading to an even severer decline in aggregate demand. Thus, in the early years of the 1930s following Black Thursday in 1929, a 'deflationary spiral' began to operate and could not be stopped. Even with some public works inspired by the New Deal, which the Roosevelt administration eagerly promoted after 1933, the depression became protracted and could not be fully surmounted until the production of arms and munitions were activated with the approach of the Second World War.

II

The period between the two World Wars (the so-called interwar period) may be regarded as constituting *the first phase* in the process of the disintegration of capitalism, or the process of 'ex-capitalist transition' for short. This phase, as is often said, can be rather distinctly divided into the two rather contrasting decades. In the 1920s, the prevailing mood was for a swift return to the prewar 'normalcy', predicated on due restoration of the old international gold-standard system (which Peter Temin calls 'symmetric'),[6] while, in the 1930s, as that hope was rudely dashed by the protracted depression decade, there arose a sudden trend towards blatant collectivisms both of the right (fascism) and of the left (bolshevism) that besieged the faltering Western democracies, 'faltering' because, though emerging as winners from the war, they were unable

6   Temin 1989, p. 32.

and unwilling yet to reconcile the new principle of the 'self-determination of peoples' with the old legacy of extensive imperialist possession of territories, to which was inevitably associated the sense of supremacy of a perceived white race in the world.

The First World War was a large-scale total war, fought with modern weapons mainly on the European soil, with untold sacrifices of both human lives and much of the heritage of past generations. Neither the winners nor the losers could have foreseen the extent of the devastations that they would eventually have to sustain. Thus, on the morrow of the ceasefire, all European nations woke up to find their coffers practically empty of money for postwar reconstruction, but rather filled with a pile of deeds stipulating obligations to pay back their debts of one kind or another. Germany had to worry about paying reparations of a then incalculably enormous sum, which would only be determined in more detail later, while others were concerned about debts they had contracted mostly with the United States, directly or indirectly, for the prosecution of the war, which they were obligated to repay with substantial interest. Whereas the United States wanted to withdraw as soon as possible from European squabbles, pertaining especially to the complicated problem of the 'reparations', it turned out that only the inflow of US money invested into Germany could support its postwar economic reconstruction as well as its partial payment of reparations. Some of that money further circulated in Europe (and perhaps also in European colonies) before returning to the United States. In the meantime, however, the repayment of the European war debt to the United States, which was sometimes estimated to amount roughly to 1.9 billion in the British pounds of the time, progressed if gradually. Thus, gold as specie money flowed massively from Europe to the United States. It was by foreseeing this trend, that the United States alone was able to restore its gold standard as early as 1919. Although all other major nations, which had suspended their gold payments during the war, wanted to follow the American example, especially after the Genoa conference of 1922 which urged them to do so, the process was delayed inordinately. Even Great Britain, which prided itself for having been, in prewar years, at the centre of the international gold standard system, could not lift the ban on gold export until 1925, and then only at a crippling cost of deflation. The period between 1925 and 1929 is sometimes described as the years of 'relative stability in Europe', but this stability was secured only to the extent that American investment in Europe remained lucrative and so renewable. As the US boom in the 1920s gained momentum, however, the American money available for investment in Europe tended to diminish, if it was not actually withdrawn, rendering the gold standard regime recently restored there that much more precarious. Overall, as gold flooded into America, Europe was bled white and suffered from anemia as gold fled. That was the general situation of the world economy prior to the collapse of the American boom in 1929. I need not add here that, a while after that point, Washington too chose to suspend the conversion of the US dollar into gold, 'sterilising' its enormous stock of gold in Fort Knox. Other major countries followed suit and abandoned the recently rehabilitated gold standard one after another, until France did so somewhat belatedly in 1937.

The above picture explains why the restoration of the prewar international gold standard, the pious hope of all Europeans then, could not really be accomplished in the 1920s, before the decade-long depression of the 1930s made it even more decisively impossible. Gold is 'commodity money' in that it is originally one of the many ordinary commodities exchanged in the self-regulating market, though chosen automatically and necessarily in the end to act also as the 'general equivalent' because it is the commodity which has use-value qualities that best suit it to serve as means of purchase (and so of exchange), in addition to continuing to satisfy its original non-monetary use. I suggest that the reader refer to the 'theory of the commodity' in the dialectic of capital for more detail on the logical necessity of the emergence of such a special commodity.[7] But the important point of the theory is that a 'commodity money' emerges automatically from the operation of the market for commodity exchanges, when the latter is not unduly disturbed by, or interfered with, by factors that are not 'mercantile', that is to say, by factors that are completely alien to commodity-economic considerations, such as inter-governmental transfers of funds of enormous magnitude due to reparations or to the repayment of past debts. Unlike in prewar years, the international markets for trade and investments after WWI were too readily exposed to, and perturbed by, the massive flows of funds due to non-mercantile operations, which resulted in the radically uneven distribution of gold in the world as just mentioned, and which thereby rendered the working of the time-honoured 'price-specie flow mechanism' a near joke. This indeed is what rendered a restoration of the good-old international gold standard system an anachronism after the war of 1914–18.

The problem is that people were not aware of the 'economics' of the changes that had taken place during and after this war. Changes often take place swiftly, one after another, whether people comprehend their nature and significance correctly or not, and become venerable historical facts, the causes of which are left (or kept) unknown. When all attempts at rehabilitating the prewar monetary system that had become literally 'anachronistic' failed, the inter-

---

7   Sekine 1997a, pp. 34–49.

national economy quickly disintegrated, as all major nations, in order to survive under the stressful climate of protracted depression, now shifted their
attention and priority to the internal rather than the external economy and
to the policies that might stabilise their new objective. In other words, they
no longer hesitated to resort to 'beggar-thy-neighbour policies', such as was
illustrated, for instance, by the notorious Smoot-Hawley tariff act of 1930, adopted by the United States. Moreover, the international economic disintegration
quickly translated itself into an international *political* one as well. Clearly, the
peace of Versailles did not adequately sort out and settle on the rules of the
game in terms of which all countries could reasonably survive. Rather the
grudges and grievances that could not be contained inside the country found
expression in desperate fantasies of replaying imperialist games, by inflaming
racial prejudices and xenophobia, which prepared the ominous grounds for the
Second World War. Indeed, it appeared that the only way to overcome the Great
Depression of the 1930s was to fight another world war, even more destructive
and cataclysmic than the previous one. This sad conclusion to the era, however,
should not obscure the fact that at the root of all these sad happenings lies the
crucial fact that the gold standard ceased to function, so that thenceforward
the supply of money had to be managed by a discretionary policy in each nation.
This important point that paralysed capitalism was not fully grasped, in part
due to the fact that whatever happened during the war could be regarded as
part of the emergency (and so temporary) measures, and that, after WWII, the
Breton-Woods IMF system of the 'gold exchange standard' based on the US dollar prevailed, so that a more 'genuine' experience of the 'managed currency
system' emerged only after the full de-monetisation of gold in 1974. Prior to
overviewing these details, we must first study and understand the 'economics'
of the difference between commodity and non-commodity money.

III

There are basically two kinds of money: commodity money and fiat money.
Gold, as already stated, is an example of *commodity money*. From among many
commodities, it has been selected over time to act as money (means of purchase), or as the *general equivalent*, in which to express the value of commodities, and thus to mediate their mutual exchanges, even while continuing to
retain its former, non-monetary use-value. On the other hand, there is *fiat
money* issued by the sovereign state with an express view to letting it mediate
commodity exchanges. Not being itself a commodity, however, it has no use-
value of its own, apart from its use as money to circulate commodities within

its national territory. There is controversy as to which is historically the primary form of money, but here I shall not delve into that question. What matters to us now is their difference. The supply of commodity money, as of any other commodity, is regulated by the law of value, while the issue of fiat money reflects the discretionary *seigniorage right* of the sovereign state. The word 'seigniorage' suggests that it is a prerogative of the sovereignty of the state.

In the dialectic of capital there are several places where the production of gold for monetary and non-monetary use is explained.[8] But in all cases it always refers to the same application of the law of value, such that the production of gold (whether for monetary or for non-monetary use) is bound to be stimulated, if and when the prices of commodities other than gold fall sufficiently, so as to make it advantageous to allocate more resources for its production, and *vice versa*. This is a perfectly familiar theory. In reality, of course, there are many countries in which gold is not produced; but they can always acquire it by generating a surplus in their balance of payments, provided that the international market remains free and self-regulating, that is to say, it is largely undisturbed by factors that are not commodity-economic or mercantile. In that case, the individuals and firms, when they acquire gold-money by selling commodities, will most likely deposit it with a local commercial bank in exchange for its banknotes or for its account wherefrom they can withdraw it as need arises. Originally each commercial bank used to issue its own banknotes, and safeguarded the deposited gold. But gradually over time the note-issuing function as well as the safekeeping function of customers' gold were both transferred to, and concentrated in, the hands of the central bank in each country. Now freed from the troublesome functions of safekeeping customers' gold and of issuing and managing its own banknotes, the commercial banks then became *member-banks* under the umbrella of the central bank. At that point, they merely opened their own demand-deposit account with the central bank, from which they could withdraw cash whenever they saw fit. However, this account opened at the central bank constituted the only 'non-earning asset' which was called 'cash or reserve money' in the balance sheet of the commercial bank. As for its 'earning assets', they consisted first and mainly of the 'discounts and loans' which it offered to its own customers, and secondly of the 'investments in securities available in the market' on which they earned some modest interest. Obviously, it was to the advantage of the commercial bank to minimise 'cash' which earned it no interest at all, and to maximise the 'earning assets' in such a way as to make the operation of the bank most

---

8   Sekine 1997a, pp. 181–2, 183–4, 202–4; Sekine 1997b, pp. 158–60, 164–6.

profitable. Against these items on the asset side, there were the liability-side items, which consisted of the customer's 'demand and time deposits'. For an ordinary commercial bank, the asset side exceeded the liability side in value by the amount of its 'net worth', or things that it directly owned. Corresponding to this T-account of the commercial bank, there was the balance sheet of the central bank, of which the asset side roughly consisted of the stock of monetary gold in safekeeping entrusted to it by the member banks, loans to the member banks and loans to the (central or federal) government, much of the latter being in the form of national bonds outstanding. On its liability side figured the central banknotes in circulation or held by banks, and the demand deposits of the member banks and that of the (central or federal) government.

Now in this system, it is the amount of gold in the vault of the central bank which figures on the asset side of its T-account, and which for all practical purposes assembles the whole stock of monetary gold within the country that sets the limit to the maximum quantity of money supply in it. This latter quantity equals the central banknotes in circulation and the money deposited at member banks, i.e. the cash that the public can withdraw at a moment's notice from its accounts at the member banks. This amount in theory is roughly equal to the $M = b^* G > 0$, where $G > 0$ is the national stock of monetary gold in the vault of the central bank, serving as reserve for the credit creation by the banking system, and $b^* > 1$ is the coefficient of the bank-multiplier, which indicates the extent to which the banks can safely create their credit either in the form of their discounts or of their loans (we call it 'credit money'). During the so-called 'sub-phase of average activity' that intervenes in the prosperity period of business cycles, and within which *the value of labour-power is supposed to just equal its reproduction-cost*, while the law of average profit prevails in all industries (that is to say, when the allocation of resources to all industries is just right), the capitalist economy is supposed to be in general equilibrium and at its best activity level corresponding to (or made possible by) the available technology. The optimum money supply will then be more or less equal to $M = b^* G$ as defined above. This quantity will be automatically achieved under a genuine capitalism when its gold standard system is operating properly.[9] Moreover, the price level then observable will also be just right, so that there is no need or room for a discretionary monetary policy of the government to intervene. Prior to the sub-phase of average activity, however, when the economy is recovering

---

9 That quantity should also be equal to $M = k Y_f$, where on the right-hand side of the equality is shown the estimate of potential GDP of the nation, Y_f, multiplied by the so-called Marshallian-k.

but not yet firmly on its feet, the supply of bank credit may still remain insufficient, with the actual reserve ratio to back up the bank's credit falling short of
the correct one (meaning the level corresponding to the 'fully loaned-up position' of the banks) at: $b < b^*$, so that the money supply falls below its optimum
level. Past the sub-phase of average activity, when the economy tends to over-
heat, there will be a tendency to over-supply bank credit, which will cause the
actual bank multiplier to exceed the correct one: $b > b^*$, thus portending a financial panic.[10]

Under a fiat currency system in which gold is already 'de-monetised', a near
optimum money supply cannot be achieved automatically as it will be under
a genuine capitalism. There is need for a discretionary monetary policy of the
(national or federal) government in order to achieve price stability, that is to
say, in order to create a near 'optimum money supply' in such a way as to
enable the real economy to achieve its best activity level, corresponding to full
employment or potential output. Indeed, when monetary gold disappears, it
also disappears from the balance sheet of the central bank. There will be no
more gold on the asset side of its balance sheet. Will there remain then only
loans to the member banks and to 'the (central or federal) government' as
'earning assets' of the central bank? Where is the cash or 'non-earning asset'
of the central bank? To answer that question, we must learn how the central
bank under the fiat currency system can operate to supply the full amount of
money to meet the need of the economy at its full-employment or potential-
output level. Normally, it is thought to be sufficient for the central bank to
grant enough 'base money' (H) to its member banks, by simply purchasing
from them outstanding government bonds in their portfolio. For that will
increase *their* cash account at the central bank, while reducing their (member
banks') holding of government bonds correspondingly by the same amount.
(That is what is called 'base money'). On the T-account of the central bank,
the corresponding changes will be reflected by (1) the increase of its liability
vis-à-vis the member banks by the amount of the base money, and (2) the
corresponding increase on the asset side in terms of its (the central bank's)

---

10   The gold standard system presupposes an economy operating under capitalism still in
      its process of 'development', and not in that of 'disintegration'. There, the size of public
      finance is expected to be quite modest in any case, and the economic activity of the
      'government sector' as distinct from that of the 'private sector' is, in effect, practically
      non-existent. Therefore, even though the central bank always acts as the banker of the
      government (central or federal) by managing its deposit account, the money paid in by
      collection of taxes will soon be paid out as a budget item, so that we need not specifically
      deal with that part of the central banking operation explicitly.

holding of government bonds. In other words, it is a simple rearrangement of the balance sheets both of the central bank and of the member banks at the same time that makes it possible to increase the 'base money', which can be used by the member banks to extend their credit creation (supply of 'credit' money). It is as though we can thus be assured of achieving $M = b^*H$ in much the same way as $M = b^*G$ under the gold standard. *But that is not the case.* For there is no reason that the central bank's policy to increase H will always result in a proportional increase in M with a fixed bank multiplier b^*, unless there is a corresponding increase in the *demand* for bank credits in the form of 'loans and discounts'. Recent experience with the so-called policy of quantitative easing (QE) has demonstrated that, when the economy is depressed, an increase in base money (H) will at best lead only to an increase in commercial banks' holdings of marketable securities (including national bonds) without leading to more 'loans and discounts', and hence this *fails to increase the supply of credit money due to lack of demand for it.* In this case, the money supply will remain at a low level $M = bH$, with $b < b^*$, and will fail to raise the level of the economy's activity to its full potential (with banks being 'fully loaned up'), giving a false impression that the discretionary policy of the state cannot do any more to boost the post-capitalist economy deprived of an automatic power of self-recovery.

However, the central bank under the fiat money system can always increase the supply of money in the national economy more directly, that is to say without going through (or depending on) its 'banking channel'. For, as the bank of the (national or federal) government, it already has the deposit account subject to checking of the sovereign state (be it federal or national), which it (the central bank) can credit with a new issue of fiat money, provided that it has the authorisation to do so by the state, the sovereignty of which is represented by a duly elected government. That is what may be called the 'government channel' of monetary creation now available to the central bank. If the government now needs $100 billion more for whatever reason, *the central bank need only to buy from the state a 'certificate of authorisation to newly issue $100 billion on its behalf'* and to hold that certificate on the asset-side of its T-account, while on its liability-side the money that the government can withdraw by checking increases by the same amount. Under the fiat money system, it should of course be possible for the state to directly issue inconvertible paper money of its own, apart from the notes issued by the central bank. But, in that case, it will be like letting circulate $100 bills of different colours simultaneously in the market, one for the bills issued by the government (printed, say, in red) and the other for those issued by the central bank (in blue) when it purchases good-quality bonds in the capital market. That will not only be confusing for those who use them, but they must also be scrupulously managed so as not to let the exchange rate between them depart from 1 in the slightest. It is much better and easier to so arrange that only the central bank will issue banknotes for circulation (as legal tender) by either purchasing outstanding bonds in the capital market, or by purchasing directly from the state 'its sovereign right to issue money on its behalf' piecemeal in appropriate amounts as occasion demands. There should be no mystery about it, for *this is precisely what a 'fiat money system' means.* It should also be apparent by now that the central bank's 'cash or non-earning asset' turns out to be the 'certificates of authorisation to issue fiat money of this or that sum on behalf of the sovereign state'. This now replaces the 'metallic cash or monetary gold in the vault of the central bank' in the old, familiar system of the gold standard. Thus, the money supply under the fiat money system should correctly be written as $M = bH + B$. Only this amount, $M = bH + B = kY_f$, where all symbols here being positive (> 0), and Y_f is an estimate of 'potential or full-employment GDP' and k is an estimate of the constant often called the Marshallian-k, can be regarded to equal the 'optimum money supply'. I will come back to this point later to show that 'mixed economy' on a permanent basis implies, and is implied by, this fact. Yet, so many persons seem still to be averse to and unaware (or uncertain) of this fact, and do not want to believe it. The reason is that it is unfamiliar to them, just as in the 1920s so many persons were unaware of the fact that the restoration of the old gold standard system would be impossible, because *they did not want to* believe what was then all too 'unfamiliar' to them. People generally do not like to see things that are radically different from the commonsense pattern of a genuine capitalism.[11]

If indeed capitalism is in the process of its development, rather than in the process of its disintegration, the 'actual accumulation-process of capital' (which best represents the chrematistic of capital) can be expected to alternate between *widening* (in which the value composition of capital is unchanged as technology is given) and *deepening* (in which it is elevated as new technology is adopted). The same process is reflected, if I may repeat, in the capitalist market in the alternation of *prosperity* and *depression* in business cycles. The period of prosperity is divided into the sub-phases of recovery, average activity and

---

11   To my knowledge, the only respected economist known to me, who is fully cognisant of this method whereby the central bank can increase the money supply through its 'government channel', and who has been vigorously advocating its importance and usefulness both in public speeches and in writing, is Professor Haruki Niwa of Japan. I will, therefore, speak of the 'Niwa-effect' in relation to the method of regulating the money supply in the contemporary national economy, in what follows.

overheating, before ending in a periodic crisis. Only in the sub-phase of average activity does the capitalist economy approach a state reminiscent of 'general equilibrium', because the *macro law of relative surplus population* and the *micro law of value* are both more or less satisfied. This theoretical pattern is, of course, not reproduced exactly in real capitalism, but its two basic laws *tend to* work behind all the deviations and contingencies, so that between the sub-phases of recovery and of overheating in the prosperity-period of business cycles, there is always the one of 'average activity' relative to the existing level of technology. As mentioned already, this automatic pattern is lost with the coming of Fordism, since capitalism no longer retains the power of self-recovery, once it is caught in a spiral of deflation.

IV

The world economy enters the *second phase of ex-capitalist transition* with the end of the Second World War; and this phase will continue until the last year of the 1970s. If the first phase of the transition, the interwar period, may be described as the 'Age of Great Transformation', borrowing Karl Polanyi's celebrated expression,[12] this second phase may be characterised as the 'Age of Pax Americana, wherein there were some experimental forays in the direction of creating to a full-fledged welfare state'. When hostilities ended, the economic supremacy of the United States was unequivocal and unchallenged. Even prior to that moment, the Allies had met at Bretton-Woods and deliberated on the possibilities of launching an ITO (International Trade Organization) and an ICU (International Clearing Union), both proposed by Keynes, but they were blocked by the United States which preferred rather to see the IMF-and-GATT regime define the postwar world economic order. These Anglo-American initiatives, however, were not viewed favourably by the Soviet Union, as East-West tension mounted in the meantime. In 1949, the United States, determined not to repeat the sad experience of economic disorder in the 1920s, offered to help Europe's reconstruction by means of the Marshall Plan, which was accepted by 16 nations of the West, but not by the Soviet Union and the East-European countries under its influence. For all practical purposes, this set off the Cold War, which was to last till the end of the 1980s. Thus, all the more, the American economic leadership in the reconstruction of the world economy in the West became evident. The IMF regime was, in effect, a 'gold

---

12   Polanyi 2001.

exchange standard' based on the US dollar. It worked fine as long as the 'external convertibility of the dollar into gold' was deemed secure. But the Cold War imposed on the United States the heavy responsibility of Western defence, the onerous burden of which led to the two 'dollar crises' of the 1960s, whereby the gold that once flooded to America returned to Europe with a vengeance. That is why, in the 1970s, the Bretton-Woods IMF regime based on fixed exchange rates could no longer be defended. Under the following 'freely fluctuating exchange-rate system', trust in the US dollar was rapidly undermined, until gold had to be altogether 'de-monetised' in 1974. Up to this point, one could talk of 'managed currency system' in the broad sense of any departure from pure gold standard, so that even the Bretton-Woods IMF system, which was in fact indirectly and circuitously dependent upon gold, was generally understood to be a managed currency system. But after 1974, with the unambiguous 'de-monetisation of gold', the true face of that system as the 'fiat money standard' became quite obvious.

What is remarkable about this second phase of ex-capitalist transition is that it began with the Employment Act of 1946 in the United States, wherein it was expressly stipulated that to achieve both full employment and price stability was a duty incumbent upon the federal (or central) government of the nation-state. At that time, there still was a fear that a severe economic depression might return, when the wartime controls were lifted and the private economy in peacetime was left again to its own devices. The experience of the New Deal and some influence of Keynesian economics may have backed this view. At any rate, there was a clear sign of admission (or recognition) that a national economy could no longer be run by the unregulated, profit-seeking private sector alone, and that a government sector of significant size must intervene and co-operate with the private sector so as to form a 'mixed economy', in order to stabilise the base of a nation-state. This, in effect, was an admission of 'social democracy', which must then have strongly encouraged the New Dealers, but would also have been met by an irate repulsion on the part of the conservatives, who still stuck to the principle that the economy should be left to private businesses. But the spirit of the time was such as to favour the former, especially as the signs of the Cold War became more apparent. The United States at the centre of the Western Camp could not afford to renew and intensify the prewar 'class struggles' which, as it was thought, would necessarily return under an untrammelled capitalism. It was rather to its advantage to replace class struggles with 'industrial peace', that is to replace the labour market with collective bargaining in determining wages. Thus, the trend was to encourage the mutual accommodation between 'organised labour' and 'business managers' (reinvigorated by their embrace of the 'managerial revolution'), both of which were then regarded as being well abreast of the times. As the Labour Government in Britain also made a decisive move towards a welfare state at this time, the two major nations in the West seemed to have set the trend for social democracy in order, ironically, to defend so-called 'modified (or renovated) capitalism' against the outright communism of the Eastern camp.

But this ideological reset was not the only trend that marked Western economies in the second phase of ex-capitalist transition. More important, perhaps, was what I would call 'petrolification', that is to say, the extensive use of oil not only directly as energy replacing coal in both industry and transportation, but also indirectly, through the application of petro-chemistry, to produce 'synthetic' materials, capable of replacing the ones based on scarce natural resources such as fibre, resin and soap. Surely, the war must have encouraged the advance of such petro-technology, but the conversion of the war economy into a peacetime one did not in any sense slow it down. On the contrary, post-war civilian life, which became more urbanised, affluent and educated, proved itself even more attuned to the same trend. As the age of petroleum thus came to stay, the so-called Affluent Society became the symbol of superiority of the Western democracies vis-à-vis the Soviet regime in the East.

Only in 1957 was that complacency shaken a bit as the latter launched *sputnik* into space first. Though it caused a minor crisis, it also offered a chance to overhaul the system of higher education to make it fit for a mass society in the making, first in America then throughout the West, so as to be able to compete with the demonstrated Soviet prowess. The area of study was not restricted to science and engineering, but all branches of knowledge, including economics, which were also subject to this new educational overhaul. For under petrolification, urbanised societies were becoming more intellectual, affluent, and overwhelmingly middle-class. Such societies cannot be maintained with a handful of intellectuals. They need a number of qualified university graduates or equally competent intellectual workers. By this time, Samuelson's 'neoclassical synthesis' had become part of the accepted curriculum in economics. Keynes had thought that his *General Theory* would in due course have wholly repudiated the neoclassical doctrine, but such a radical position could hardly be accepted in the country where he was at times suspected even of being a covert communist. For classical economics had embodied a sacred tenet of bourgeois-liberal ideology that the Invisible Hand of Providence would lead us all to a pre-established harmony, even if we are each left free to pursue our own differing and conflicting interests. It was, therefore, necessary for Samuelson to make a concession to the effect that only macro (income) theory was Keynesian, while micro (price) theory remained integrally neoclassical. This was by no means a logically convincing synthesis, but rather a makeshift concession for coexistence of the bourgeois-liberal faith and a veiled Keynesian social democracy, whereby the latter would at least put one foot in the door. It was this concession, however, that gutted the true worth of Keynes's teaching, according to the later claims of Minsky and his followers. For, as it happens, Keynes was soon to be evicted from mainstream economics with the resurgence of conservatism.

With such reservations notwithstanding, the influence of Keynes in economics was still quite secure in America, so long as fiscal policies inspired by him appeared to work as well as expected; and that was the case, if not better, until about the middle of the 1960s, since the 'unit labour cost' kept declining up to that time, no doubt in part under the influence of productivity gains due to petrolification. However, that trend was reversed later, and that was no doubt critical. There were other factors, of course, that were as damaging to the US and Western economies. For instance, the international prices of food and primary resources suddenly turned upward in the 1970s, in part due to such contingent reasons as the large-scale Soviet purchase of wheat in international markets (which was due to some crop failures in the Soviet Union). But it also reflected the awakening of certain developing countries to what may be called 'resource nationalism', inspired by the formation in 1963 of UNCTAD (United Nations Conference on Trade and Development), which adopted the resolution called NIEO (New International Economic Order) in 1974.[13] The first Oil Crisis that OPEC (Organization of Petroleum Exporting Countries) staged in 1973, which tripled the price of crude oil overnight, was no doubt the first outburst of this new trend. The economies of the United States and of other major Western nation, by now irrevocably 'petrolified', yet so smugly dependent upon the low import price of Arabian oil, were truly stunned and devastated. For the first time since WWII, the US and Western economies were exposed to the peril of 'cost-push inflation' as opposed to 'demand-pull inflation'. The circumstances relating to the fall from grace of the US dollar, already described above, was an additional impediment that reversed the trend that the second phase of ex-capitalist transition had established and had sought vainly to maintain. Misfortunes never come singly.

---

13   There is much to learn in this and related matters from the works of Michael Hudson; see
       Hudson 2003; Hudson 2005.

V

The second phase of ex-capitalist transition which sought to reconstruct a stable world economy under Pax Americana was rather short-lived. It was over, as explained above, by the end of the 1970s. There were both necessary and contingent reasons for that unhappy outcome. Yet it was not a complete failure. On the contrary, it left many lasting marks that are valuable in that they suggest, or point to, some essential features of the future historical society to which we may be heading. By far the most important fact was that capitalism (in the sense of the capitalist mode of commodity production), if it still survived as a rump, could no longer wholly or integrally subsume a national economy and be stable. The bourgeois nation-state, which constituted the 'carapace' within which proper capitalism could survive integrally and 'develop', was no longer present after WWI. Yet, in the 1920s, no one could (nor wanted to) understand that fact, and so in the 1930s diametrical, anti-capitalist oppositions arose both of the right and of the left in the form of collectivist states railing against the erratic attempts at reviving bourgeois democracies, which eventually led to yet another scourge of world war. After the Second World War, it was agreed that another global conflict had to be averted, and indeed such a tragedy was averted, albeit under the dicey atmosphere of the Cold War. In order to achieve this result, it was necessary for each nation-state to stabilise its economy without harming its neighbours, and the leading western democracies chose to do so *by abandoning the bourgeois nation-state*. For the latter minimises the intervention of the state in the self-regulation of the capitalist market, which is deemed to have an unlimited capacity for self-regulation. Of course, in reality, the bourgeois state could not always afford to be content with being simply a 'night-watchman state'. Both the mercantilist and the imperialist bourgeois states surely had to do much more. But, in all cases, their primary function was always to set the stage, on which the 'dominant type of capital' could most readily accumulate, that is, could best pursue its own chrematistics. For that reason, the administrative works of the state (in peacetime) was kept to a bare minimum. The scale of public finance in peacetime was quite modest, and money was ordinarily directly linked to gold prevailing as the world-money. The belief was that the smaller the government, the better for the national economy. Only the decade-long depression of the 1930s taught otherwise. Minsky's 'Big Government and Big Bank' would both be necessary to stabilise the national economy. The Employment Act of 1946 in the United States admitted this fact.

The fundamental cause of this sea change in outlook on the economy is the fact that the Fordist economy is prone to long depressions that do not cure themselves automatically. Once caught in a depression, neither the macro law of population, nor the micro law of value will automatically work to put the private sector of the economy on a new path of accumulation; for its *ex ante* investment tends to fall short of its savings. Even if the firms earn enough profit, they hesitate to invest enough, while idly accumulating their 'internal reserves'. The conversion of the firm's accumulation funds (idle money) into real capital formation stagnates, as the firm tends to lack 'animal spirit' according to Keynes. And this is *not* just a cyclical matter so that, in the long run, aggregate (*ex ante* or intended) investment is not expected to tend to equal aggregate savings. It goes without saying, of course, that they will always be equal *ex post* as the matter of accounting, but that is not the issue here. The prevailing trend was for the private sector of the national economy to tend to spend less than it earns ($I - S < 0$), so that unless either the foreign or the government sector compensated for that deficit in spending, that is to say, unless the foreign sector exported more than it imported ($X - M > 0$), or the government sector spent more than its revenues ($G - T > 0$), the aggregate spending of the economy (GDE) would fall short of its aggregate production (GDP), which would end by depressing the latter. But why is that a rule rather than an exception under the Fordist economy? The reason is that Fordist production depends heavily on 'investment in plants and equipment' in the form of 'durable capital-assets', the financing of which, as Minsky explains, involves oligopolistically competitive firms with highly risky commitments. Once an expensive piece of capital-asset is acquired, the firm has committed itself to repay its value by instalments over an extended period of time, during which any unexpected thing can happen in the market so as to upset its original plan. It cannot always pay what is due out of its fluctuating expected incomes; it may have to borrow in the capital market sometimes in the worst possible conditions. It will, therefore, have to be alert to changing conditions of the capital market and to make sure not to become inadvertently saddled with heavy debts, which will be difficult to get rid of later. These considerations will tend to promote precaution, rather than a reckless gambling for ordinary non-financial firms, unless the boom has already lasted so long that it is already turning into a bubble. Thus, *uncertainty* increases in a mature Fordist economy, tending to discourage investment in plants and equipment, by rendering non-financial firms more cautious and hesitant in investing in real assets than previously. They would rather accumulate their internal reserves, while 'parking' them in more readily marketable securities.

If this is the case, the presence of a significantly large government sector will become mandatory for the national economy to avoid its secular decline, unless it is prone to export more than import, that is to say, unless it can use its $X - M > 0$ to compensate for its $I - S < 0$. But no country can permanently count on this method without provoking international frictions. Thus, as a rule, it must solve its internal problem internally, that is to say without resorting to a 'beggar-thy-neighbour' policy. Consequently, a nation of which the economy is primarily Fordist will sooner or later be obliged to solve the same problem by means of $G - T > 0$, that is, by the method of *deficit finance of the state*. This is why, as Minsky claims, a Big Government becomes a necessary method of stabilising any contemporary national economy. Indeed, as can be roughly estimated, G in the postwar Western countries which adopted the method of the 'mixed economy' was around 20 percent of GDE, whereas it was smaller than 2 percent apart from military spending during the 1930s.[14] However, if deficit finance ($G - T > 0$) continues *permanently* as a trend, and not just cyclically in such a way as to make $G - T = 0$ in the long run and on average (in which case the 'mixed economy' itself will be unnecessary in the long run), this national economy must somehow 'finance' the deficit of the state (of the government sector) *permanently*. It is thought normally then that the annual deficit of the government sector should be financed by borrowing money from the private sector, that is to say, by issuing new national bonds. That is the view of Samuelson's neo-classical synthesis as well as that of the currently mainstream Chicago school, which has by now completely abjured Keynes. However, *that is evidently an impossible proposition*. For, if we must on average have $G - T > 0$ every year, however modest the size of that excess spending may be, we will be destined to eventually accumulate a massive stock of national debt, which the state will never be able to repay. Our posterity will agonise in vain under the ever-accumulating burden of un-repayable debt. Surely, we need another way to finance this absolutely unavoidable deficit, which the permanent 'mixed economy' logically presupposes. That way is to enable the state to finance its permanent deficit *not by borrowing but by directly issuing new fiat money* in the way already explained. For *it is precisely for that reason that we left the gold standard behind, and adopted the fiat currency system*. As I have explained above, the money supply under the fiat money system need not be increased only through the 'banking channel'; it can as well be increased directly through the '(national or federal) government channel', by letting the central bank *purchase* the deed from the state that stipulates the extent to which it is willing to confer upon the central bank part of its 'seigniorage right to issue fiat currency' in the amount B, when legitimate need for it arises.[15]

---

14   According to Minsky, 'Federal government purchase of goods and services was 1.2 percent of GNP in 1929 and 11.3 percent of GNP in 1962'; Minsky 1984, p. 12.

15   In other words, the *Niwa effect* can always be counted upon to finance $G - T > 0$ without

In the meantime, what was most remarkable about this second phase of ex-capitalist transition is that, for the first time, it introduced the idea of a 'non-market reproduction of labour-power'. For the reproduction of labour-power as a commodity was the crux of capitalism (in the sense of the capitalist mode of production). It is said that the Roman Empire perished almost instantly when the supply of slaves to work in its *latifundia* farms (large estates where slaves worked in agrarian labour) could not be renewed, whether the Vandals attacked or not. As I mentioned in my first essay (Appendix 1), the reproduction of labour-power is the existential condition of any society. Capitalist society reproduced itself by reproducing its labour-power, in this case specifically 'as a commodity', which meant that the wage-worker who leaves the factory this evening will return to its door tomorrow morning 'in the same condition as regards his health and strength'.[16] At the time when Marx wrote this, the core of labour was a 'productive' one (i.e. capable of producing a use-value), which was predominantly physical (if in part intellectual). It was overwhelmingly represented by 'factory labour' in newly growing industrial cities. Thus, if in their 'slums' the core of factory workers could be easily recruited for wages that permitted their ordinary family lives to continue, that was about sufficient for the reproduction of their labour-power, and hence of capitalism itself. That indeed is about all that was needed, judging from what Engels wrote on the state of the working class in England in 1844–45.[17] All that, however, could be left to the automatic working of the capitalist market, so that the bourgeois state had little to do directly for the maintenance of labour-power in order for capitalism to perpetuate itself. The First World War, however, changed that situation radically, especially under the climate of the 'general crisis'. Trade unions grew distinctly more powerful, and tended to be politicised, inflaming the sense of 'class struggles' among factory workers. This was the reason why the New Dealers realised the importance of 'industrial peace' based on the

---

imposing any cost (interest) or even the burden of eventual repayment on the government. The popular objection to this claim to the effect that 'it is bound to end in an uncontrollable inflation' is not founded on any sound economic theory, and hence (despite its corrosively demagogic effect) need not be taken seriously by responsible economists, since all we need to provide against possible inflation due to an excessive $B > 0$ is to stipulate that it shall be subject to the limiting condition: $'M = b^*H + B$ must not exceed kY_f, which number can be easily calculated'. There is no reason to believe that this condition is more easily infringed upon by excessive B than by excessive b^*, that is to believe that the bankers are more law-abiding than the government officials.

16   Marx 1987, p. 169.
17   Engels 1952.

system of 'collective bargaining' between employer and trade unions. Industrial peace could not, however, be achieved automatically through the working of the capitalist labour market, in which wages and other labour conditions were determined. In other words, the reproduction of labour-power could no longer be left to the automatic working of the capitalist market, and hence to the 'bourgeois nation-state' which refused to interfere in the matter. Thus, in the second phase of ex-capitalist transition, *a new challenge arose, which demanded a switch from the bourgeois state to the 'welfare state' as a new form of the nation-state.*

The idea of achieving 'industrial peace' by co-operation or co-ordination between organised labour and the managers of the enterprise is not in itself incorrect by any means, though the extent to which government may be involved to mediate disputes between them may still be open to discussion. But it may have the risk that collusion between the two parties (labour and management) could lead to a bureaucratisation and eventually to a sclerosis of the economy. This tendency was first noticed and widely discussed in the United States and Britain, the two leading nations in the West, when they were put on the defensive in the international trade scene by West Germany and Japan, as these two countries vigorously recovered from their postwar prostration, and emerged as formidable competitors of the two leading countries. In the United States and Britain it was thought that if workers were generously protected from (or even in) unemployment, they would tend to lose their incentive to work, and the firms, which foresaw little or no chance of bankruptcy, would fail to compete for excellence. But the problem did not remain at such a peaceful level. As inflation became excessive, it exacerbated the problem and obstructed the attempt to rescue the inflating economy from stagnation in the second half of the 1970s. The simultaneous presence of (cost-push) inflation and economic doldrums was a new experience in the postwar western economies. As the climate of 'stagflation' deepened, the pursuit of industrial peace proved increasingly dysfunctional. Both in Great Britain and the United States, labour disputes, which became frequent and radicalised, were often getting out of hand as strikes were repeated in waves. That provided an opportunity for conservative forces, for so long disgruntled at postwar developments along social-democratic lines both in politics and in economics, to strike back against the idea of 'industrial peace' under the new banner of 'neo-conservatism', based largely on middle-class antipathy towards over-protected labour and the now bureaucratised and incompetent managers of large businesses.

VI

The *third and the last phase of ex-capitalist transition* began with the 'neo-conservative counter-revolution' in the last years of the 1970s, spearheaded by Thatcherism and Reaganomics, and it still lingers on at present. They both hark back to the nostalgic image of the 'good old days of vigorous (dynamic) capitalism' before World War I, which were so sentimentally portrayed by Austrian scholars such as von Mises and von Hayek, who conjured up an idealised image of pre-1914 Great Britain from a distance. The main thrust of their argument was that 'the smaller the government sector and the larger the private sector in the national economy, the more invigorated, reactivated and prosperous will the latter be'. They wanted less taxation of free enterprises and individuals as well as more 'de-regulation' of the economy. While not completely denying the presence of the government sector, they would certainly reject the idea of Big Government à la Minsky. Even though they engaged in hyperbole, there was a kernel of truth in what they said with regard to the situation that the two leading nations of the West were involved in at the time. Yet, their claim has no general validity as an economic doctrine. Actually, 'neo-conservatism' as such is no more than a moral philosophy or ideology and contains no dependable lesson on the subject of economic theory. What was then called 'supply-side economics' included, apart from some flippant arguments, little more than anti-Keynesian rallying cries, so that, despite its strong political appeal and impact, represented by the simultaneous accession to power of Margaret Thatcher and Ronald Reagan, there was not much to learn in terms of economics as such directly from either Thatcherism or Reaganomics. Yet the development that has taken place under their influence in the real world economy thereafter (including their callous disempowerment of trade unions) must be carefully studied in order to understand where we stand at present.

First, there was the fact that the inflation was arrested by the Federal Reserve policy under the influence of 'monetarism'. Even before President Reagan's accession to office, Mr. Paul Volcker, who was appointed as a new chairman of the American Federal Reserve Bank in 1979, took a 'monetarist' stance in severely curbing the supply of 'base money'. Since, under the prevailing inflation, there existed a strong demand for further bank credit at the time, this policy of strictly limiting an increase of base money successfully put an end to it, though at a mortal cost to non-oil producing developing countries. To what extent Mr. Volcker was under the influence of Milton Friedman was not clear. But the latter's view that inflation was 'strictly a monetary phenomenon' appeared to be shared by many at the time and also to be thoroughly vindicated on this occasion. Unlike most neoclassical economists who tended to choose to concentrate on price theory, while Samuelson's 'neoclassical synthesis' held sway, Milton Friedman was an outstanding exception in that he focused on macroeconomic theory along neoclassical lines, essentially by extending the 'quantity theory of money' to overcome the idea of the 'dichotomy' between monetary and real economic theory. His 'monetarist' thesis claimed that inflation was a strictly 'monetary phenomenon' in that, unless an 'optimum supply of money' is achieved policy-wise, the economy will suffer from either inflation or deflation. I believe that he was correct in that claim. I believe, however, that he erred in believing the money supply, $M = b^*H$, itself to be a policy variable. The base money, H, may indeed be considered to be a policy variable, but the money supply, M, cannot be, because $1 < b \leqq b^*$ is not expected to be a constant. Friedman especially emphasised that in monetary policy 'one does *not* push a string', meaning that $b = b^*$, presumably even by postulating that $b = b^* = 1$, being faithful to the Chicago tradition of promoting 100 percent reserve banking. For only in that case can $M = H$ be regarded as a policy variable. The history of capitalism, however, shows that there is no meaningful commercial banking without a fractional reserve system. Capitalism can produce more surplus value than otherwise because 'loan-capital' expedites the circulation of commodities by means of fractional-reserve banking.[18] Thus, if Friedman was correct in how to stop inflation, he was not in how to start it (i.e. how to 'reflate' a deflationary economy). In other words, by restricting base money, it was possible to control inflation (as Paul Volcker successfully did), but by simply supplying more 'base money', it would be impossible to rescue an economy from out of a deflation (as one would hope that Bernanke and Kuroda should by now have learned).

Moreover, even though Volcker's 'monetarist' policy managed to stop inflation, it was not without some unforeseen side effects with grave consequences for the future of the world economy. There was a spectacular rise in interest rates never before witnessed in the civilised world, which first hit the heavily indebted, non-oil producing developing countries, as I have already suggested, rendering NIEO instantly a dead letter. An even more stinging effect, however, was that, as interest rates rose above the legal limit payable on time-deposits by commercial banks, the latter began swiftly losing them to other financial firms capable of paying more, which threatened the very existence of the commercial banks and similar deposit institutions. It was thus urgently necessary to amend the Banking Act that had been in force since the New Deal, and this led first to an amendment with regard to the maximum interest rate payable on time-deposits. However, by this time the financial interests nestled in

---

18   See Sekine 1997b, pp. 134–67.

Wall Street, and hitherto severely regulated by several New Deal laws, such that they could act freely and profitably only in offshore banking, had been gaining strength even at home, especially by having acted skilfully in 'recycling oil money', following the Petroleum Crises of the 1970s. Thus, at this point, the liberalisation of the interest rate led to demands for a more general 'liberalisation of finance' including the de-compartmentalisation of financial business into banking, securities and insurance. During the same decade, similar moves took place in Britain under the banner of a financial Big Bang. Thus in the two leading nations of the West, the economic outlook radically changed in the mid-1980s, in such a way as to *let financial interests prevail over industrial interests*. The free business enterprise which had so far been thought to be at the disposal of its 'managers' was now suddenly returned to its majority shareholders who, with the help of 'financial engineers', could buy it, sell it, or do whatever they liked with it, as can readily be observed in the many A&M operations that have proliferated ever since. This change was widely recognised and often described as the 'financialisation of the economy'. But its real import was poorly understood.

To me, the above signals the birth of 'casino capital' and the concomitant abandonment of Keynes's 'euthanasia of the rentiers'. This is what really characterises *the third and last phase of ex-capitalist transition*. I have, of course, borrowed this attractive term from Susan Strange's *Casino Capitalism*,[19] but here I must begin by relating it with Uno's theory. Many persons believe erroneously that casino capital is in some sense a variation of 'finance-capital', but it is not. Finance-capital was the dominant form of capital in the imperialist stage of capitalist development. It first assembled monetary savings from all the nooks and corners of the then capitalist society into the hands of a monopoly firm to be invested in one whole (i.e. as if it wholly belonged to it) in fixed capital, then beginning to 'bulk large' in the age of heavy industries. Later, when the 'idle funds' thus assembled no longer found lucrative outlets for real investment at home, finance-capital exported them abroad in order to be used for economic developmental projects there. Its theoretical underpinning is to be found in the concept of 'interest-bearing capital' in the dialectic of capital (or Uno's *genriron*), which exposes capital's own aspiration and need to self-commodify.[20] Casino capital has nothing to do with that form of capital. For it is not even a full-fledged form of capital. The dialectic of capital points to two *primitive* forms of capital: merchant capital and money-lending capital, both

19   Strange 1986.
20   Sekine 1997b, pp. 195–204.

of which are not even self-subsistent in a purely capitalist society. They are both absorbed (or 'sublimated') in the form of industrial capital, which, after having been established, differentiates itself later into 'loan-capital' and 'commercial capital' respectively in order to rehabilitate part of the functions that merchant and money-lending capital used to concentrate on. Merchant capital profits from price-differentials, but in a purely capitalist society, in which arbitrage is supposed to have already worked itself out, price-differentials for the same commodity would in principle already have been eliminated, so that merchant capital would no longer be able to earn its profit or to continue to subsist by itself. Neither could money-lending capital exist in a world in which merchant capital does not survive, since it could no longer earn interest by intercepting merchant's profit. Thus, once industrial capital is well established, only some functions of what money-lending capital used to perform can be rehabilitated in the form of loan capital. This being the case, *the appearance of full-fledged 'money-lending capital' is possible only before or after the age of capitalism's full (industrial) development.* Unlike finance-capital, casino capital is a direct descendant of money-lending capital. That is why the reappearance of the latter as 'casino capital' and as the dominant form of capital at this point in the world economy forebodes to me an impending demise of capitalism (in the sense of the capitalist mode of production) itself. For it means that, to borrow the Keynesian locution, the 'rentier', far from meekly acquiescing to solicited euthanasia, has come back triumphantly with a broad Cheshire-cat grin. But why is that so inconvenient to capitalism? Long before Keynes, Wicksell had already taught the lesson: If the 'natural rate of interest' (rate of return on real economic activity) were to be less than the money rate of interest (rate of return on money), would (or could) any 'industrial capitalist' be made to work? The capitalist economy would then be caught in a downward 'cumulative process' to naught.[21]

VII

Neo-conservatism, as I described it, was merely a counter-ideology that inspired an antithesis to the 'industrial peace' that was to be achieved social-democratically. It believed that labour should be more exposed to the 'discip-

---

21   Wicksell 1962. In this book Wicksell meant the rate of interest for the rate of return on money. Today the latter means the rate of return on "money games" which often exceeds the rate of return on real business.

line of the market' and wake up from its idle dream of being over-protected by the welfare state. Thus, for instance, Reagan's stringent anti-union policies, enforced in the early 1980s as inflation was about to subside, had the immediate effect of stopping a rise in money wages, so that the upward trend of unit labour costs was reversed, which even led to an unexpected success through his military-Keynesian policy of heavy spending on arms. In Britain, Thatcher too was working hard to suppress militant trade unions in order to make them accept the privatisation of large nationalised firms. Thus, in those two key countries of the West, it appeared as though a return to the age of old-fashioned class struggles was imminent. But the key figure that emerged in both countries during this decade and that was destined to dominate the future course of the world economy was not the old-fashioned, union-allergic and irascibly exploitive industrial capitalist, as the believers of neo-conservatism might have imagined. It was 'casino capital' that suddenly loomed in the background, took over 'neo-conservatism' and transformed it into 'neo-liberalism'. The difference between the two is that 'neo-conservatism' is basically an ideology of the industrial interests and, as such, it is 'nationalist' rather than cosmopolitan, whereas to 'neo-liberalism' national borders are irrelevant from the outset. As the ideology of casino capital, it is attuned to 'borderless' and 'global' orientation.

The fact that the transition from 'neo-conservatism' to 'neo-liberalism' was so seamless as to be hardly noticed was both interesting and important. For I believe that if an industrial state had officially adopted neo-conservatism as its leading ideology, it would not have lasted for much more than a decade or so. The extreme longevity now bordering on forty years of neo-conservatism can be explained only by its inconspicuous merging and blending with 'neo-liberalism', which no longer insists on bourgeois nationalism. In the background, there was the end of the Cold War which was accomplished towards the end of the 1980s, though the trend in that direction was already apparent in the middle of the decade. After the fall of the Berlin Wall, the United States, which remained the only economic super-power, eagerly sought to adopt 'globalism' as the *leitmotif* of the new world order. In the age of Reagan and Bush (the father), the United States still wanted to retrieve its industrial hegemony of bygone days. But the persistence of its 'twin deficits' made it increasingly clear that the American strength in the world economy depended rather on the US dollar remaining as the key international currency. Even in the first term of the Clinton administration, the strong advocacy of so-called 'strategic trade policies' indicated the still lingering nostalgia for the traditional industrial supremacy of America. But in the second term of the same administration, as the influence within the cabinet of M. Robert Rubin increased, there appeared a clean break from wistfulness for industrialism and a definitive shift towards

ICT (information and communications technology) as the goal towards which America should aim, since it would dominate both industry and finance. By thus grasping the leadership in this technology, the United States secured its unshakable position of world economic (and military) leadership.

By this time, however, the importance of the nation-state has faded away from the consciousness of people at large, by being rather excessively de-emphasised in public speeches. Since neo-conservatism wanted to reactivate the private sector at the expense of the government sector, it also wanted the role of the nation-state in the economy to diminish proportionally. That also suited the neo-liberalism of globally oriented casino capital. Indeed, the state has been drastically impoverished by a series of tax cuts, and perhaps even more crucially by tax evasion. Thus, in most countries, the main source of tax revenues had shifted from income tax (both corporate and individual) to general consumption taxes such as GST, VAT and SZ (or their Japanese version *shôh-izei*). These new indirect taxes actually have proven themselves to be strongly regressive, weighing heavily on the vast majority of the population which earn modest incomes and are always resident within the national borders, in order to compensate for the loss of fiscal revenues due to the all too easy evasion of income taxes by the rich and powerful, rendering the 'redistributive function' of the state by taxation almost completely ineffective. As a result, the middle-class population, which was on the increase during the second phase of ex-capitalist transition, has been precipitously decreasing in its third phase, the disparity of earnings between the rich and the poor widening, as the inequality in the standard of living between them has increased. Thus the welfare state, if it ever existed, now appears to many as having been no more than an illusion never to be realised in this world.

That, however, presents a very deceptive picture, the importance of the nation-state being unreasonably downplayed. It appears as though the vague idea of 'governance' in the world economy derived from some unidentified authority is good enough for the international community of civilised nations to survive and prosper together, even in the absence of a clear-cut world government. In reality, that sort of image unjustifiably imparts a dangerous illusion, since the nation-state has not yet 'withered away' in the least. It gives the false impression that the main economic activity nowadays occurs on a world-wide scale beyond and above nations, without being in any way constrained by national rules and organisations. But the privilege of operating and participating in the economy at such an ethereal level, so high above the nations, is reserved only to some very large international firms, the CEOs of which may be invited to Davos from time to time to talk about inanities. But by far the greater majority of ordinary citizens who work in these and many smaller firms, as well as in public offices of all sorts, namely, the modest 'employees' or 'workers' at the bottom layer of society, who live by regularly earning wages or salaries and consuming their own labour-power, lead their daily lives within a nation-state, pay their taxes to it, renew and reproduce their labour-power largely within their national borders. It is these people who constitute the mainstay of the world economy even today.

Since the 'invisible hand' of Providence is no longer to be trusted to take care of the reproduction of their labour-power 'as a commodity' in the market, it devolves on the nation-state to see to it that it should now be reproduced 'as a non-commodity', and that must be done within the framework of the nation-state, which cannot remain the bourgeois one, but must now evolve in one way or another into a welfare state. As a matter of fact, despite the years of neglect and rejection by neo-conservatism and neo-liberalism, the welfare state never died, nor even receded or contracted. Not only does it continue to exist today, but it has also developed into one that is equipped with an enormous machinery of public administration, the reason being that *it is the only competent framework within which the 'reproduction of labour-power as a non-commodity' can realistically be accomplished.* It has to make sure that the currently employed or employable workers, at all levels of productive or unproductive (manual or intellectual) labour, in agriculture, manufacture, services, or information, whether they are male or female, full-time or part-time, in the private or governmental sector, must all be able to reproduce themselves in their respective family lives. It means that *the state must see to it that they are happy and satisfied with their work and remunerations, so that, tomorrow morning, they will all come back to their respective workplaces with renewed energy, health and full of incentive to work.* For that to be possible, the state must manage the child-raising and educational systems, ensure public hygiene, health and medical care services, provide all who want to work with fair employment opportunities, oversee their working conditions and mediate conflicts and disputes among them, encourage their cultural and leisure activities, ensure their old-age pensions, securities and post-retirement activities, among many other things. Even under the long sway of neo-conservatism, the welfare state has not ceased its operation. On the contrary, it has grown both in its sheer size and in the variety of its involvements. *It is only that attention has been deliberately and persistently diverted away from this fact.*

The reason for this outcome, it seems to me, is that the welfare state is expensive, and the powers that be in the present society do not wish to bear its burden. It is obvious, however, that whether they want it or not, *this cost must be borne by our society*, if we wish to survive and improve our lives in it, together with our cherished civilisation as we have inherited it. I also believe that we are not in any way lacking in physical resources and productivity to enable us to do so. Yet, somehow we are made to believe that there is some inevitable economic logic integral to the present world economy that dictates its being caught in the slough of a long period of stagnation, out of which we cannot be easily rescued. In particular, it is said and believed widely that no nation's public finance can bear the burden of the welfare state. This is where the ideologies of neo-conservatism and of neo-liberalism become dangerous. Let us examine in the following if there is any veracity in that claim.[22]

VIII

Now that we have roughly outlined the main features of the process of ex-capitalist transition in its three phases, I wish to focus at this point on the very nature of the world-economic problem that confronts us today. I began this essay by stating that with the advent of Fordism, as the novel style of com-modity production, capitalism began its disintegration by losing its power of self-recovery in the face of a periodic crisis. If the speed of production under capitalism accelerates even when aggregate demand fails to catch up with it, the national economy will hit the wall and an industrial crisis will break out. But if the prices of the main products fall and stay at a low level for some time, a search for a new technology will automatically be set off during this period of stagnation, and that will soon enable a few firms to supply the same products at significantly lower production-prices than before. This kind of innovation can be described as 'quantitative', since it is like introducing a more productive spinning machine, equipped with a greater number of spindles than before, or introducing a more productive blast furnace with greater capacity than before. It is different from 'qualitative' innovations such as can be illustrated by replacement of a natural wood board for a plastic one in construction, of

---

22 So far as the constant reminder of ubiquitous 'fiscal crises' today is concerned, we already know that it is a radically malevolent, false alarm. Given the facts that our monetary system is *not* based on gold or any other commodity money, and that, in that case, as long as we abide by the above-stated restriction that '$M = b^*H + B$ must not exceed kY_f', that is to say, so long as we have not yet achieved full employment or full potential GDP, we can print any amount of fiscally spendable money, $B > 0$, without inviting the slightest shade of inflation. Surely, 'fiscal crisis' is a made-up bogeyman propagated by the moneylenders (now under the modern guise of casino capital) who benefit from deflation. It is a ghost or spectre that invites 'quack' economists to the chorus of a psalm in the service of casino capital, leading honest but uninformed people to ruin. *Eveillez-vous!*

coal for oil as fuel, or of horsepower for engine power in industry and transportation. During the developing era of capitalism, 'quantitative' innovations
occurred regularly more or less at ten-year intervals, so that typical business
cycles also roughly displayed the 'decennial' pattern such as was represented by
the so-called Juglar cycles. Uno believes that the durability of a typical spinning
machine in the nineteenth century was about ten years. The 'qualitative innovations' occurred more irregularly in different ways. For instance, when trade
in cotton goods expanded quickly over extensive territories, whether domestically or internationally, the need for railways and steamships increased for
their transportation, which in turn entailed strong demand for iron and steel
products. In this case, technical innovations of the 'qualitative' nature occurred
that eventually changed the core of capitalism from light to heavy industries, to
such an extent that they even marked a different stage of its development. This
kind of innovation cannot be fully accounted for in terms of economic theory
alone, or, for instance, as a mere 'rise in the organic composition of capital'. One
sometimes talks of such innovation as a 'transformational' change, which must
be treated as a 'contingent' or 'exogenous' factor that affects our economic life
irregularly and from the outside.

Marx talked about the 'periodic or decennial capitalist crises' based on his
experience of the liberal stage of capitalist development. Uno also mentions
in this book and elsewhere that the typical ten-year rhythm in the occurrence
of capitalist crises could be observed distinctly only during the liberal stage,
whereas in other stages that regularity tended to be distorted, presumably as
a result of various contingent reasons. Nevertheless, a typical industrial cycle
under capitalism was regarded as normally lasting for about ten years or so,
unless there were some exceptional circumstances that were recognised as
having disrupted the regular behaviour. Thus, during the second phase of ex-
capitalist transition, economists were puzzled to find out that business cycles
then appeared regularly in a much shorter span of time, repeating the 'boom-
and-recession' pattern, without even being punctuated by any 'crisis' to speak
of. That is probably due to the fact that during the booming phase of the cycle,
the government intervened before it got excessively overheated and burst out
in an industrial crisis, and guided private firms operating in the Fordist environment to replace their 'plants and equipment' in such a way as to enable them
to introduce due quantitative and/or qualitative innovation, without having to
incur too heavy a private cost because of the sudden destruction of their capital.
But that would mean that Big Government acted in order to ensure that a recession did not degenerate into Minsky's 'It', meaning a great depression reminiscent of the one in the 1930s. For, by then, the private sector of the economy
was regarded as being incapable of resetting itself on its own and rebounding

back onto an appropriate path leading to the next 'boom'. I would not say that a recovery of business by itself would never happen. For there is always a windfall bonanza such as, for instance, the discovery of a new technology enabling one to pump out 'shale gas' at a dramatically reduced cost, which will then stimulate significantly greater private investment. On the other hand, the advent of neo-conservatism definitely put an end to the age of 'boom-recession cycles'. For with its misguided and specious idea of 'reactivating' private economic activity at the expense of the government sector, it systematically impoverished the latter, by depriving it of its due fiscal resources. That means, however, that the private sector once caught in a recession had to stay there, in principle permanently, due to the erosion of a Big Government, since the latter's compensatory spending had been the only way to rehabilitate the anemic private sector. Yet the trouble does not end there. For, by this time, neo-conservatism had been absorbed by neo-liberalism, meaning that, after the liberalisation of finance was completed, casino capital rules over industrial capital. Indeed, since about the mid-1980s, 'boom-and-recession cycles' have been replaced by a 'bubble-and-bust sequence'. The latter can no longer be called 'cycles', since although a bubble always ends in a bust, the latter is not necessarily followed by another bubble.

Although from about the mid-1980s one began to talk about a 'bubble-like boom' (notably in Japan), indicating the fact that casino capital was beginning to increasingly meddle in and dominate economic activity, it was only in the 1990s that the idea of the 'bubble-and-bust sequence' replaced that of the 'boom-and-recession cycle'. In the last years of the 1980s, the Japanese bubble was already overblown to its limits, with the prices of shares and of land reaching an unprecedented height, while the Bank of Japan continued to persist in its low interest-rate policy. It then burst in 1990 with devastating damage throughout the economy, *after which there has been no visible sign of economic recovery to this day, for nearly a quarter of the century.* In the United States, in contrast, the Clinton administration performed much better in the management of its economy. It successfully induced casino capital to co-operate with the government in renovating the core of the American economy from the old, decrepit heavy industries to the new ICT, or internet-based, one. This policy was sometimes applauded for officiating at the advent of a 'new economy', which may to some extent be justified, inasmuch as *informatisation*, just as *petrolification* earlier, will certainly have a very profound and far-reaching 'transformational' effect on our lives and industries. Moreover, when it ended in a bust, a new, subprime-mortgage bubble started only a few months later in 2001, presumably due to the policy adopted by Mr. Alan Greenspan, then in his third mandate as chairman of the FED, of keeping interest rates unreasonably low. This bubble, which involved more toxic and venal elements than the previous one, ended in 2007 with the collapse of Lehman Brothers, the well-known Wall Street investment banker. Since then, the world has seen neither a new bubble nor economic prosperity. When President Obama was elected, many hoped that he might be able to inspire the launching of a new bubble with, say, the environment or public health as a new theme. It is, however, obvious that such a theme is far too 'clean' to conceivably entice casino capital into a joint venture. The private sector thus remains adamantly powerless to recover by itself.

IX

Now, after the eviction of Keynes, mainstream bourgeois economics is stuck with the false idea that since fiscal policy has proven to be ineffective, only monetary policy remains to be of any use in uplifting the stagnant private economy, by somehow increasing the supply of money. Thus, both in America and Japan, the central bank has vigorously pursued the so-called policy of quantitative easing (QE) to combat deflation, though only with miserable and pathetic results. This policy consists of the central bank's operation to purchase outstanding good-quality (national or private) bonds in the capital (securities) market in exchange for newly issued central banknotes or equivalent central-bank deposit money with a view to increasing the supply of money. This is called the 'infusion of liquidity into the economy', most of which will result in adding to the base money, H. It is then expected to produce the credit money up to $M = bH$, where the size of the banking multiplier, $b > 1$, in a deflationary environment, is certain to remain less than b^* ($> b$), which will enable the banks to achieve a state of being 'fully loaned up'. This means that firms cannot spend as much as they would otherwise do (that is, invest). In other words, the level of economic activity still remains less than its potential, the supply of money being less than optimal ($b < b^*$). Many central banks have been frustrated when they learn that their indiscriminate 'infusion of liquidity' by the method of 'QE' always ends in failure, forcing them once again into a cul-de-sac. Obviously, they do not see where the problem lies. The reason is that they do not distinguish between 'active money' which buys commodities (real goods and services) and 'idle money' which does not. No textbook in bourgeois economics teaches this crucial distinction between the two sorts of money, and repeats the same useless lesson that 'inflation means too much money chasing too few commodities'. Thus, presumably, deflation would mean that 'too many commodities are left unsold in the market because there is not enough money to buy them'. Whence derives the call for more 'QE' so as to 'pump indiscriminately more liquidity into the system'.

In 1947–8, however, Uno wrote two essays on the importance of the distinction between 'currency' (*tsûka*) and 'funds' (*shikin*) in connection with debates over the postwar Japanese inflation, claiming that the problem then lay in 'the abundance of the former concomitant with the scarcity of the latter'. The distinction between *tsûka* and *shikin* corresponds exactly with that between 'active' and 'idle' money to which I just referred. Some imprint of this distinction remains even in an expository note on a very early page of this book.[23] In applying his insight to the present context, I claim that the problem with the present worldwide spread of 'deflation' lies in *an excessive shortage of active money simultaneous with the super abundance of idle money*. The trouble with the policy of 'QE' lies in its failure to generate more 'active money' (means of circulation of commodities), while uselessly contributing to the supply of 'idle money' which is already superabundant, and is, therefore, not simply useless but positively harmful. Trying to increase the money supply through the 'banking channel' by increasing base money will always hit the wall, since b remains always far less than b^*, given that no bank would want to be stuck with bad ('non-performing') loans when the business climate remains sluggish. If unnecessary reserve money is forcibly pumped into the banking system by more 'QE', it either remains in its original form as a non-earning asset, or it will be 'parked' in safe securities to earn low interest. It will never increase 'loans and discounts' that constitute the main business of banking. That is to say, instead of creating any more 'active money', it will only add to the pool of 'idle money'. In its proper sense, 'idle money' means 'money at rest for the time being', awaiting a chance for investment in the sense of real capital formation. It is something 'convertible into real capital' in due course. Its abundance, in other words, is a sign that no one wants to invest it in real capital, namely, to use it for the creation of real goods and services. Thus, the abundance of 'idle funds' is by definition equivalent to the presence of deflation. If so, it follows that 'QE' creates more deflation instead of combating it. Do I have to ask who the beneficiaries are of the excessive supply of idle funds? The obvious answer is that it is the moneylenders (or casino capitalists in the present context) who love deflation. Casino capital wants to make use of 'idle money' directly as the means of its chrematistics, instead of converting it into real capital first, and then engaging in genuine capitalist chrematistics. That, moreover, is possible only when Wicksell's 'natural rate of interest' is lower than the 'money rate of

---

23   See pp. 3–4.

interest'. I have the impression that so-called 'financial engineering' has been
able to invent a situation, in which what Wicksell's 'natural rate of interest',
or the rate of return on investment in real economic activities, must compete
with is no longer the 'money rate of interest' in the original sense, but the
rate of return on speculative *money games*, which has become a routine and
massively lucrative instrument of chrematistics in the hands of casino capital.

If it is thus apparent that monetary policy such as 'QE' recommended and
endorsed by mainstream economics remains powerless to solve the present
problem of deflation, we must then seek a genuine solution by attacking the
problem from a radically different angle, i.e. from an entirely unorthodox point
of view. For otherwise, unable to extricate ourselves from the same (or similar) conundrums that the world once faced in the 1930s, we will be destined to
tread on that fatefully devastating path leading to another tragic apocalypse.
Thus, in what follows I will suggest an Unoist solution to the problem of deflationary spiral in which we are increasingly caught up at present, even though I
am quite aware that it will initially face repulsion as a knee-jerk reaction, since
it flies in the face of the 'commonsensical' view of capitalism still so dear to
many. The problem itself is in fact quite simple. We need to supply more 'active money' instead of increasing 'idle money'. The distinction between these
two kinds of money is absent in mainstream neoclassical economics. Keynes,
in contrast, did distinguish between 'money held to satisfy the transactions or
precautionary motive' from the same 'to satisfy the speculative motive'. These
can be regarded as distinguishing the demand for 'active money' from that for
'idle money'. But he did not specify how these two kinds of money are each
separately supplied. That is the question we must now face. We have, however,
confirmed already that, under deflation, the central bank cannot supply a sufficient amount of 'active money' through its 'banking channel'. That is to say,
if the central bank merely creates new 'base money', H, it will not induce the
banking system to step up its credit creation such as to provide the commodity
market with sufficient 'active money', $M = b^*H$. It will only increase the banking
system's holding of more outstanding marketable securities at best, meaning
that it will only pump more liquidity into the securities market, where only 'idle
money' (held to satisfy the 'speculative motive') increases.[24] It is then clear to
me that the only way in which the central bank can infuse liquidity into the

---

24   The reason that 'QE' does not increase 'active money' is that the central bank operates
      exclusively in the capital market through its 'banking channel'. Money is created only
      by buying securities from the market. For that to be possible, however, there must be
      the sellers of securities to the central bank. But the reason why they already had some

national economy as 'active money' is to go through its 'other channel', namely to create B directly by purchasing an appropriate portion of the state's 'seigniorage right to issue currency' *as money to spend fiscally*. Any part of B that is spent by the central (or federal) government through its publicly approved budget item, whether for investment or for consumption, will necessarily be used as 'active money' and so will be certain to have the effect of activating the real economy. Certain ways of fiscal spending may be more effective than others, depending on the extent to which leakages will occur in the chain of transactions that the fiscal money, once spent, will eventually entail. But that is only a matter of detail, and not of the substance of the issue. By the way, Friedman's metaphor of 'helicopter money' to activate the economy can be interpreted to the same effect. Moreover, given the present monetary institution at our disposal, that is the only way available to us whereby to arrest the sinister deflationary spiral and the debt deflation that will follow, which, if left unattended, will certainly worsen and will eventually lead us to fatal disaster.[25]

---

securities on hand to sell is that they purchased them before. And the reason that they did so in the first place is that they did not need to buy commodities either for production or for consumption. They, therefore, 'parked' their 'idle money' in those securities. That would mean either that they would not sell their securities to the central bank, or that they would once again use that newly created money to buy other securities, not commodities. Why should we suddenly expect that they will spend the new money to buy commodities either for production or for consumption, which they did not? If they buy securities again, the only result will be to raise the prices of securities, and so depress the (already low) rate of interest even closer to zero. The availability of money at an excessively low interest rate will only stir up more speculation, while commodities will continue to be left unsold since 'active money' remains short.

25   Yet there is a kind of subconscious aversion to this kind of approach, since this mechanism cannot be explained by the IS-LM curves analysis, supposedly so inspirational to mainstream economists. This famous device proposed by Hicks and adopted by Hansen is, however, a negative legacy of the neoclassical synthesis, which teaches that the IS-curve that may be shifted by the fiscal policy of the treasury, and the LM-curve that may be shifted by the central bank, must each be obtained separately and independently from each other. But that convenient hypothesis breaks down when the central bank purchases from the treasury a certificate of 'authorisation to print more money'. No 'licensed' macroeconomics textbook would dare suggest that possibility, which follows from the fundamental difference of the fiat money system from the commodity money system. Is there a conspiracy of silence or just an innocent slumber of ignorance?

APPENDIX 2

X

My experience so far has been that when such a solution to the problem is suggested, it always meets an expression of consternation and incredulity, if not suspicion and hostility, especially among those who are better trained and educated in 'economics'. Did we, however, not observe the same kind of reaction in the 1920s in the face of any suggestion that the restoration of the good old, international gold standard system would never be possible then? So fond and deep is the nostalgia for the contrived beauty of a commonsensical view of capitalism in the psyche of economists. Actually, there is good reason for that. Economics as a systematic body of knowledge is a product of modern society, the material base or 'substructure' of which is capitalism (in the sense of Marx's 'capitalist mode of production'). But the latter was not built by us, according to any previously drafted, human-devised plan or design. It rather emerged, grew and declined spontaneously. The reason why it first emerged in seventeenth- and eighteenth-century Europe is that by far the most important use-values that determined the mode of life in society at the time (such as woollen goods) could be produced more readily as commodities than otherwise. This fact led to the formation of the 'home market' within nation-states, which were then beginning to be established here and there. Soon labour-power itself adopted the commodity-form, which made it inevitable that a whole society must be organised as 'capitalism' according to the mercantile principles of capital. The absolute monarchy in alliance with the then budding bourgeoisie accelerated this process of formation of capitalism, though neither party was yet aware of who would eventually prevail over the other. By the middle of the nineteenth century, it turned out that the bourgeoisie triumphed; but, by this time, it had transformed itself from its early form as merchant capital into its mature form as industrial capital. By the end of that century, the bourgeoisie as industrial capital had further transformed itself into finance-capital to finally bring its glorious saga to an end with the imperialist war of 1914. It was during this capitalist era that economics developed as a systematic body of knowledge. There had, of course, been many fragmentary pieces of knowledge on some facets of economic life before. But only with the evolution of capitalism, which supported the whole modern society at its base, did economics become a systematic body of knowledge. The reason was that capitalism always exists in two ways: first as the empirical history of the capitalist era which (as hardware) can be described only from the outside, and secondly as a logical whole or system, i.e. as that which makes capitalism what it logically is (as software). True economics has to do with the latter.

In practice, however, the study of economics began in the formative period of capitalism to show that it was a much better and more reasonable (both rational and civilised) way of organising human society than any other previous one. As such, it was inseparably tied to the *ideology* of upholding modern values, such as individual freedom, equality of all human beings regardless of birth, universal human rights, and the like. The mercantile logic of capital did not appear to contradict any of these moral values, though being perfectly consistent at the same time with the promotion of sectional bourgeois interests in particular. Thus, economics, in explaining the objective logic of capital, could also serve to promote the interests of the bourgeoisie in society. Now all societies have a *power structure* of their own and *the hierarchy and vested interests* to support and perpetuate it. While the operation of the material (economic) substructure will automatically support them, the latter must also be reinforced and justified at the spiritual (human) level by the ideological 'superstructure' of society to ensure its stability. The ideological superstructure includes religion, law, culture, education, and all that pertains to the conservation of the spiritual values of society. These are often highly institutionalised, often to a monumental dimension, and inculcated vigorously as justifiable at all levels of the population. In the past, only a few intellectuals were needed to guide a large number of common people. But as society progresses and becomes largely middle-class and enlightened, a more sophisticated organisation of its ideological superstructure becomes both necessary and costly. I have mentioned above how the 'sputnik crisis' in 1957 led to an abrupt overhaul of higher education in Western mass societies. What I have been driving at is that economics as 'social science' is made to pursue two different objectives. One is that it must study and expose the logical structure of capitalism quite objectively, that is to say without involving any ideological biases. The other is to support and defend the bourgeois-liberal ideology which says that the values of modern society so far unsurpassed must be cherished and carefully preserved forever. By about the middle of the nineteenth century, these two objectives were perhaps not so far apart and thus were not often in conflict with one another, in that the objective (material) trend in the evolution of capitalism was also beneficial to all, i.e. to society as a whole. But past that point, a gap between the two sides became increasingly apparent, first in the declining stage of capitalism and then even more so in the process of its disintegration. Objective reality of capitalism and the fiction that its idealistic image should continue forever begin to fall apart. Reality and ideology must then part company, however traumatic that may be.

Adam Smith is believed to have used the expression 'Invisible Hand' twice, once in *The Wealth of Nations* and once again in *The Theory of Moral Sentiments*. He did not use the term 'Providence', nor did he expressly refer to Leibniz's philosophy of a 'pre-established harmony'. Yet he certainly knew that the capitalist market, if left un-interfered with, could under given circumstances automatically tend towards a state of general equilibrium, as the so-called 'Harmonists' thought after the disintegration of the Ricardian school, which broke up unable to explain the compatibility of the labour theory of value with the law of average profit. The neoclassical school adopted the Harmonists' view and reconstructed the classical economics of Smith and Ricardo on a mathematical basis without the labour theory of value. The school's representatives then concentrated on refinements of the classical theories of competitive equilibrium over forty years between the Franco-Prussian war and WWI, even though real capitalism by then had entered the developmental stage of imperialism, in which monopoly and protection prevailed over free competition. It was nevertheless important for the neoclassical economists to rigorously prove the classical tenet that free competition under capitalism (Pareto-optimally) 'harmonises' the conflicting interests of all the participants in the capitalist market. Their efforts should be credited in that the economic theories of the classical economists (and those of Marx), which previously could only be 'numerically illustrated', could now be mathematically stated with more generality and rigour as demonstrable theorems. In so doing, they enabled economists to speak the same scientific language as physicists, at the same time as they brought economics closer to religious faith than to scientific investigation. For instead of accounting for how real capitalism aged in its declining years, they rather contrived the Parnassian beauty of what capitalism ought to be. Even when capitalism ends its process of development and enters that of disintegration, neoclassical economics cannot stop thinking of 'rational expectation', and what not, so as to vindicate the automatic achievement of 'full equilibrium' in their imagined capitalism.

But, in effect, this amounts to reducing 'capitalism' to something that is ultimately 'unknowable', like nature (or the physical world), just as Galileo's 'mathematisation of nature' rendered the latter unknowable.[26] We are ourselves part of nature; but in order to 'know' the latter, we must stand outside it and face it as being out there and over against us. Then, all we can know about it will be its 'phenomenal' aspects, exclusive of any 'thing-in-itself', as Immanuel Kant taught us many years ago. I recall having read a mimeographed essay written by a very eminent mathematical economist, in which he admits that the concept of 'capitalism' belongs to 'economic sociology' since it cannot be defined in 'economics' as science. This admission cannot be more 'true' so far as the 'bour-

---

26   Husserl 1970, part II, chapter 9.

geois economics of the neoclassical school' is concerned, inasmuch as the latter belongs to the ideological superstructure of modern society to serve as a 'spiritual tranquilliser' in support of the latter. As long as it belongs to the ideological superstructure of modern society, economics must defend capitalism which constitutes its base. It is for this reason that bourgeois economists keep harkening back to the glorified myth of capitalism, always constructing with artistry a mathematical model of the economy that circumvents all of the problems it might face in reality. Nor is it satisfactory to criticise this practice from the point of view of a diametrically opposed ideology, such as Marxism, by constructing equally subjective (or arbitrary) counter-models of capitalism. The reason is that capitalism can always be axiomatically defined to be good or bad, heaven or hell, anything that we like or hate; and any number of formally consistent (i.e. tautological) models based on the chosen axiom can be produced at will. But that cannot be the correct way to learn what capitalism really is. For capitalism is not like nature that has already existed prior to our coming into being, and so can keep concealing the 'thing-in-itself' from us. It is a human drama, the scenario of which *we* have collectively played out, whether consciously or unconsciously. Therefore, we cannot pretend to our incapacity to know this 'thing-in-itself'. *In interiore homine habitat veritas.* The only correct economic theory then must be based on the discovery of the logical *definition* of capitalism, *not dictated by us* according to our chosen ideology as an axiom, but as it is exposed by capital itself trans-ideologically as the 'dialectic of capital' (or as Uno's *genriron*). In this essay, I have tried to show how one might extend Uno's first foray into his *katokiron*. Regardless of whether or not I was successful in that enterprise, I have never departed (or deviated) from the true teaching of Uno's economics, which lies in his grasp of capitalism as something that exceeds the confines of formal (i.e. tautological) logic.[27]

(First written in 2010, entirely revised in 2015)

---

27   Elsewhere, I have written in more detail about this aspect of Uno's theory; see Sekine 2013, Part I: Methodological Essays.

References

Ashley, Percy 1920, *Modern Tariff History, Germany – United States – France*, 3rd edition, London: John Murray.

Ashley, Sir William James 1920, *The Tariff Problem*, 4th edition, Westminster: P.S. King & Son.

Baines, Edward 1835, *History of the Cotton Manufacture in Great Britain*, London: H. Fischer, R. Fisher and P. Jackson.

Bell, John R. and Thomas T. Sekine 2001, 'The Disintegration of Capitalism: A Phase of Ex-Capitalist Transition', in *Phases of Capitalist Development*, edited by R. Albritton et al., London: Palgrave.

Bland, A.E., P.A. Brown and R.H. Tawney (eds.) 1921, *English Economic History: Select Documents*, London: G. Bell and Sons.

Bowley, Arthur L. 1905, *A Short Account of England's Foreign Trade in the Nineteenth Century, Its Economic and Social Results*, revised edition, London: Swan Sonnenschein & Co.

Brentano, Lujo 1927–9, *Eine Geschichte der Wirtschaftlichen Entwicklung Englands*, 5 vols., Jena: Fischer.

Cole, G.D.H. 1932, *British Trade and Industry, Past and Future*, London: Macmillan.

——— (ed.) 1935, *Studies in Capital Investment*, London: Victor Gollancz Ltd.

Cunningham, W. 1912, *The Growth of English Industry and Commerce in Modern Times*, Cambridge: Cambridge University Press.

Davies, Ernest 1935, 'Foreign Investment', in *Studies in Capital Investment*, edited by G.D.H. Cole, London: Victor Gollancz Ltd., pp. 213–64.

Edwards, G.W. 1938, *The Evolution of Finance Capitalism*, New York: Longmans, Green & Co.

Ellison, Thomas 1886, *The Cotton Trade of Great Britain*, London: Wilson.

Engels, Frederick 1952, *The Condition of the Working Class in England in 1844*, translated by F.K. Wischenewetzky, London: G. Allen & Unwin.

Ernle, Right Honourable Lord 1922, *English Farming, Past and Present*, 3rd edition, London: Longmans, Green & Co.

Gladstone, W.E. 1863, *The Financial Statements of 1853, 1860–63, to which are added, a Speech on Tax-Bills, 1861, and on Charities*, London: John Murray.

Gregory, T.E.G. 1921, *Tariffs: A Study in Method*, London: C. Griffin.

Hasbach, Wilhelm 1908, *A History of the English Agricultural Labourer*, translated by Ruth Kenyon, Westminster: P.S. King.

Heymann, Hans Gideon 1904, *Die gemischten Werke im deutschen Grosseisengewerbe*, Stuttgart: Cotta'scher.

Hilferding, Rudolf 1981, *Finance Capital: A Study of the Latest Phase of Capitalist Develop-

ment, translated by Morris Watnick and Sam Gordon, edited with an Introduction by Tom Bottomore, London: Routledge. [1955, *Das Finanzkapital, Eine Studie über die jungste Entwicklung des Kapitalismus*, Berlin: Dietz], translated into Japanese by Jirô Okazaki: 岡崎次郎訳『金融資本論』(岩波文庫) 1970.

Hobson, John A. 1971, *Imperialism: A Study*, with a New Introduction by Philip Siegelman, Ann Arbor, MI: University of Michigan Press. Translated into Japanese by Tadao Yanaihara: 矢内原忠雄訳『帝国主義論』岩波文庫、上 1951 下 1952.

Hobson, Charles K. 1914, *The Export of Capital*, London: Constable. Translated into Japanese by Katsumi Yanai: 楊井克己訳『資本輸出論』日本評論社 1968.

Hudson, Michael 2003, *Super Imperialism: The Origin and Fundamentals of US World Dominance*, London: Pluto Press.

——— 2005, *Global Fracture: New International Economic Order*, London: Pluto Press.

Huskisson, William 1831, *The Speeches of the Right Honourable William Huskisson*, 3 vols., with a Biographical Memoir, Vol. II, London: John Murray.

Husserl, Edmund 1970, *The Crisis of European Sciences and Transcendental Phenomenology*, translated by D. Carr, Evanston, IL: Northwestern University Press.

Ikukawa, Eiji 1952, 'Industrial Finance under the Formation of Monopoly', *Bulletin of Economics* (Society for Economic Research, Osaka City University), 27(4–5).

——— 1953, 'On the Appearance of Industrial Finance', *Management Research* (Faculty of Commerce, Osaka City University), 8: 31–56. 「工業金融の発生について」『経営研究』（大阪市立大学商学部）第 8 号

——— 1954, 'Deposit Banks and Industrial Finance', *Bulletin of Economics* (Society for Economic Research, Osaka City University), 30(1–2).

——— 1956, *Formation of Financial Capital in Britain* [*Igirisu Kin'yû-shihon no Seiritsu*], Tokyo: Yuhikaku. 生川栄治『イギリス金融資本の成立』有斐閣

Itoh, Makoto 1973, *Credit and Crisis* [*Shinyô to Kyôkô*], Tokyo: Tokyo University Press. 伊藤誠『信用と恐慌』東京大学出版会

Jeidels, Otto 1913, *Der Verhältniss der deutschen Grossbanken zur Industrie*, 2nd edition, Munich: Dunker & Humlot.

Jones, Eliot 1922, *The Trust Problem in the United States*, New York: Macmillan.

Koga, Hidemasa 1952, *Concentration of the Control of the Firm* [*Shihai-shûchû Ron*], Tokyo: Yuhikaku. 古賀英正『支配集中論』有斐閣

Kojima, Seiichi 1928, *The Development of the Iron and Steel Industry* [*Tekkôgyô Hattatsu Shiron*], Tokyo: Nihonhyôronsha. 小島精一『鉄鋼業発達史論』日本評論社

Kuczyinski, Jürgen 1952, *Studien zur Geschichte des deutschen Imperialismus*, Berlin: Dietz.

Kumagai, Hisao 1964, 'Issues of Economic Policies', in *Development of the Theories of Economic Policies* [*Keizaiseisaku Riron no Tenkai*], Tokyo: Yûhikaku. 熊谷尚夫・横山正彦「経済政策論の問題点」『経済政策理論の展開』（山中篤太郎・豊崎稔監修『経済政策講座』第一巻）有斐閣

Lenin, Vladimir I. 1971, *Imperialism, the Highest Stage of Capitalism* (*A Popular Outline*), in *Selected Works*, Moscow: Progress Publishers. Translated into Japanese by Motosuke Udaka: 宇高基輔訳『帝国主義』岩波文庫 1956.

Levi, Leone 1880, *The History of British Commerce and the Economic Progress of the British Nation 1763–1878*, 2nd edition, London: John Murray.

Liefmann, Robert 1923, *Beteiligungs- und Finanzierungs-Gesellschaften*, 4th edition, Jena: Fischer.

———— 1927, *Kartelle, Konzerne und Trusts*, 7th edition, Stuttgart: E.H. Moritz. [*International Cartels, Combines and Trusts*, with an Introduction by Charles T. Hallimann ('A record of discussion on cartels at the International Economic Conference and a summary of legislation on cartels'), London: Europa Publishing].

Lipson, E. 1921, *The History of the Woollen and Worsted Industries*, London: A. & C. Black Ltd.

———— 1931, *The Economic History of England*, 3 vols., London: A & C. Black.

List, Friedrich 1841, *Das nationale System der politischen Ökonomie*, Stuttgart und Tübingen: Cotta'scher Verlag.

Marshall, Alfred 1923, *Industry and Trade*, London: Macmillan.

Masuchi, Yôjirô. *Treatise on Corporate Finance* [*Kabushiki-gaisha Zaimuron*] 増地庸治郎『株式会社財務論』 (Masuchi was a prolific author in the field, but in the list of his works currently available the title that Uno quotes is not found. The latter may be referring to either one of the following publications in Japanese: 1954,『経営財務論』(東洋出版社), Tokyo; or 1937,『株式会社：株式会社の本質に関する経営経済的研究』巌松堂書店, Tokyo.)

Marx, Karl 1970, *A Contribution to the Critique of Political Economy*, Moscow: Progress Publishers.

———— 1976, 'Speech on the Question of Free Trade' [*Discours sur la question du libre échange*, prononcé à l' Association démocratique de Bruxelles, 9 janvier 1848], in *Collected Works of Marx and Engels*, 1845–1848, Moscow: Progress Publishers.

———— 1987, *Capital: A Critique of Political Economy*, 3 vols., Unabridged, edited by Frederick Engels, New York: International Publishers.

Matsuoka, Kinpei 1913, 'German Coal Syndicate', in *Kokka Gakkai Zasshi*, 27(3). 松岡均平「独逸石炭シンジケート」『国家学会雑誌』第 27 巻第 3 号・

McCulloch, J.R. 1847, *A Dictionary, Practical, Theoretical and Historical, of Commerce and Commercial Navigation*, London: Longman, Green & Co.

Miller, A.V. 1969, *Hegel's Science of Logic*, London: George Allen & Unwin.

Minsky, Hyman P. 1984, *Can 'It' Happen Again?* Armonk, NY: M.E. Sharp.

———— 2008a, *Stabilizing an Unstable Economy*, New York: McGraw-Hill.

———— 2008b, *John Maynard Keynes*, New York: McGraw-Hill.

Ôno, Eiji 1951/1953, 'The Structural Characteristics of German Finance-Capital', *Keizai-Ronsô* (University of Kyoto), 67(6), and 71(1). 大野英二「ドイツ金融資本の構造的特質」『経済論叢』(京都大学) 第 67 巻第6号と 71 巻第 1 号

Ôuchi, Tsutomu 1970, 'A Note on State-Monopoly Capitalism', in *Basic Issues of Social Science* [*Shakai kagaku no Kihon-Mondai*], the Institute of Social Science, University of Tokyo. 大内力「国家独占資本主義論ノート」『社会科学の基本問題』東京大学社会科学研究所 [大内力『国家独占資本主義』東京大学出版会 1970 所収]

———— 2007, *A Study of State-Monopoly Capitalism* [*Kokka-Dokusen Shihonnshugi*], Tokyo: Kobushi-shobô.

Page, William 1919, *Commerce and Industry, A Historical Review of the Economic Conditions of The British Empire, 1815–1914, based on Parliamentary Debates*, 2 vols., London: Constable.

Palgrave's Dictionary of Political Economy 1963, edited by Henry Higgs, Vol. I, entries on 'Company' and 'Joint-Stock Company', London: Palgrave.

Polanyi, Karl 1968, 'Our Obsolete Market Mentality', in *Primitive, Archaic and Modern Economies: Essays of Karl Polanyi*, edited by G. Dalton, Boston, MA: Beacon Press.

———— 1977, *The Livelihood of Man*, edited by H.W. Pearson, New York: Academic Press.

————2001 [1944], *The Great Transformation: The Political and Economic Origins of our Times*, Boston, MA: Beacon Press.

Rickert, Heinrich 1926, *Kulturwissenschaft und Naturwissenschaft* (Sechste und Siebente durchgesehene und ergänzte Auflage), Tübingen: J.C.B. Mohr. [1962, *Science and History: A Critique of Positivist Epistemology*, translated by George Reisman, edited by Arthur Goddard, London: D. Van Nostrand Co.].

Riesser, Jakob 1912, *Die Deutschen Grossbanken*, 4th edition, Jena: Fischer.

Rosdolsky, Roman 1977, *The Making of Marx's 'Capital'*, translated by Pete Burgess, London: Pluto Press.

Royal Institute of International Affairs 1937, *The Problem of International Investment*, Oxford: Oxford University Press. Translated into Japanese by Shin'ichi Matsumoto: 松本真一訳『国際投資の諸問題』

Schmoller, Gustav von 1884, 'Studien über die Wirtschaftliche Politik Friedrichs Grossen', in *Schmollers Jahrbuch*, VIII.

———— 1900–4, *Grundriss der allgemeinen Volkswirtschaftslehre*, 2 vols., Leipzig: Duncker & Humblot.

———— 1911, 'Volkswirtschaft, Volkswirtschaftslehre und Methode', *Handwörterbuch der Staatwissenscaften*, VIII.

Sekine, Thomas T. 1986, *The Dialectic of Capital*, 2 vols., Tokyo: Toshindo.

———— 1997a, *Outline of the Dialectic of Capital*, I, London: Palgrave.

———— 1997b, *Outline of the Dialectic of Capital*, II, London: Palgrave.

———— 1999, 'Une réflexion sur les tendances actuelles de l' économie mondiale', *Chiiki-Bunseki* (Aichi Gakuin University), 37(1): 17–25.

———— 2003, 'The Dialectic, or Logic that Coincides with Economics', in *New Dialectics and Political Economy*, edited by R. Albritton and J. Simoulidis, London: Palgrave.

————— 2013, *Towards a Critique of Bourgeois Economics: Essays of Thomas T. Sekine*, edited by John R. Bell, Berlin: Owl of Minerva Press.

Souda, Kiichirô 1922, *Issues of Economic Philosophy [Keizai-Tetsugaku no Shomonndai]*. 左右田喜一郎『経済哲学の諸問題』第3版(改訂版) 東京(岩波書店)

Strange, Susan 1986, *Casino Capitalism*, Oxford: Basil Blackwell.

Suzuki, Kôichirô (ed.) 1971, *Studies on Imperialism*, Tokyo: Nihon-Hyôron Sha. 鈴木鴻一郎編『帝国主義研究』日本評論社

Takeda, Tadao, Shôichi Endo and Tsutomu Ouchi 1955, *Theory of Modern Finance [Kindai Zaisei no Riron]*, Tokyo: Jichôsha. 武田隆夫・遠藤湘吉・大内力『近代財政の理論』時潮社

Takumi, Mitsuhiko 1994, *World's Great Depression: The Causes and Manifestations of the 1929 Crisis [Sekai-Daikyôkô, 1929-nen Kyôkô no Katei to Gen-in]*, Tokyo: Ochanomizu Shobô. 侘美光彦 『世界大恐慌 –1929 年恐慌の過程と原因』 御茶の水書房

————— 1998, *Great Crash [Daikyôkô-gata Fukyô]*, Tokyo: Kôdansha. 侘美光彦『大恐慌型不況』講談社

Taussig, E.W. 1923, *The Tariff History of the United States*, 7th edition, New York: Putnam. Translated into Japanese by Taizo Hasebe and Shoichi Aki: 長谷部泰三・安芸昇一共訳『米国関税史』弘文堂 1938.

Tawara, Kuni-ichi 1918, *Iron and Steel [Tetsu to Kô]*, Tokyo: Maruzen・ 俵国一 『鉄と鋼』丸善.

Temin, Peter 1989, *Lessons from the Great Depression*, Cambridge, MA: MIT Press.

Tohara, Shirô 1960, *The Advent of Finance-Capital in Germany [Doitsu Kin'yû-shihon No Seiritsu Katei]*, Tokyo・戸原四郎『ドイツ金融資本の成立過程』東京大学出版会

Tooke, Thomas and William Newmarch 1928 [1857], *A History of Prices and the State of the Circulation during the Nine Years, 1792–1856*, London: P.S. King and Son.

Uno, Kôzô 1946, *Value Theory [Kachi Ron]*, in *Collected Works III*. 『価値論』（宇野弘蔵著作集 第三巻）岩波書店

————— 1947, 'The Tariff Argument of the German Socialist Party', in *Introduction to Agricultural Problems*, in *Collected Works VIII*. 「社会党の関税論」『農業問題序論』付録（宇野弘蔵著作集第八巻）岩波書店

————— 1950/1952, *Principles of Political Economy [Keizai Genron]*, 2 vols., in *Collected Works I*. 『経済原論』上下（宇野弘蔵著作集 第一巻）岩波書店

————— 1953, *Theory of Economic Crises under Capitalism [Kyôkô Ron]*, in *Collected Works V*. 『恐慌論』(宇野弘蔵著作集 第五巻) 岩波書店

————— 1962, *Keizaigaku Hôhôron [Methodology of Economics]*, in *Collected Works IX*. 『経済学論』(宇野弘蔵著作集第九巻) 岩波書店

————— 1969, 'Theory of Crises', in *Issues related to Marx's Capital [Shihonron no Shomonndai]*, in *Collected Works IV*. 「恐慌論の課題」『資本論の諸問題』所収 （宇野弘蔵著作集 第四巻) 岩波書店

————1980, *Principles of Political Economy: Theory of a Purely Capitalist Society*, Sussex: Harvester Press. Translated by Thomas T. Sekine, [*Keizai Genron*], 1 vol., 1964. 『岩波全書版　経済原論』(宇野弘蔵著作集　第二巻)岩波書店

United States Department of Commerce 1934/1949, *Statistical Abstract of the United States.*

Voigt, A. 1928, 'Volkswirtschaft und Volkswirtschaftslehre', in *Handwörterbuch der Staatswissenschaften* (4. Aufl.), VIII Band.

Wallace, William 1975, *Hegel's Logic*, Oxford: Oxford University Press.

Weber, Max 1949, 'Objectivity in Social Science and Social Policy', in *The Methodology of the Social Sciences*, translated by E.D. Sils and H.A. Finch, New York: The Free Press. ['Die Objektivität sozialwissenschaftlicher und sozialpolitischer Erkenntnis', in *Archiv für Sozialwissenschaft und Sozialpolitik*, Band 19 (1904), Tubingen: Mohr]. Translated into Japanese by Y. Tominaga and Y. Tateno: 富永祐治・立野保男共訳「社会科学と社会政策にかかわる認識の客観性」社会科学方法論』岩波文庫 1936.

Wicksell, Knut 1962 [1898], *Interest and Prices*, translated by R.F. Kahn, New York: Augustus M. Kelley.

Wieser, C.W. von 1919, *Der finanzielle Aufbau der englischen Industrie*, Jena: Fischer.

Wilbrandt, Robert 1924, 'Das Problem der Vokswirtschaftspolitik', in *Einführung in die Vokswirtschaftslehre*, Band IV, Stuttgart: E.H. Moritz [an original version in typescript, translated by Nakayama Ichirô into Japanese and published in Shôgaku-kennkyû (Hitotsubashi University): 『商学研究』（一橋大学）第 4 巻　第 1 号 1924.

Zieschang, Kurt 1957, 'Zu einigen theoretischen Problemen des staatsmonopolistischen Kapitalismus in Westdeutschland', in *Jahrbuch des Instituts für Wirtschaftswissen-schaften*, Deutche Akademie der Wissenschaften zu Berlin, Band 1. Translated into Japanese by Tamaki Yoshinori as 'Kokka Dokusen Shihonshugi no Jakkan no Riron Mondai', in *State-Monopoly Capitalism* [*Kokka Dokusen Shihonshugi*], edited by Takuichi Ikumi, Tokyo: Ôtsuki Shoten, 1958. 井汲卓一　『国家独占資本主義』大月書店

Index

usurer's 174
value-composition of 278
variable 72
capitalism 1–7, 9–13, 17–28, 63–65, 72–76,
140–45, 169–74, 233–37, 239–42, 247–68,
273–74, 279–83, 285–91, 295–99, 319–26
abstract theory of 269
birth of 48, 99
declining stage of 31, 281, 323
economic histories of 235, 266
evolution of 11, 26, 32, 75, 138, 322–23
formative period of 19, 37, 39, 49, 64, 128,
154, 323
general crisis of 288
industrial 58, 163
logical definition of 256, 262, 264, 266,
325
modern 232, 247
pure economic theory of 28, 32
real 10, 21, 113, 171, 250, 262, 269, 299, 324
self-propelled growth of 58, 67, 69, 71, 73,
75
self-regulation of 239, 285
capitalist society 5–6, 8–13, 16, 18, 21, 23, 29–
32, 64–65, 67–68, 97, 113, 170–71, 235,
280, 310–11
Carnegie 204–5
cartel price 131, 178, 183
domestic 218
fixed 184
cartels 131, 146, 164–65, 175–81, 183–84, 186,
195, 200, 208, 216–17, 273, 276, 328
comprehensive 182
domestic 209, 216
early 175
formed interlocking 194
regional 181
short-lived 175
casino capital 310–12, 315, 317, 319–20, 330
central bank 3, 160, 191, 294–98, 318, 320–21
chrematistics 123, 266, 270, 298, 303, 319–20
circulation 5, 37, 67, 96, 263, 295, 298, 330
internal 264
City of London 192, 276
classes 16–17, 22–23, 57, 64, 83, 150, 163, 170,
178, 215, 239
feudal ruling 37
landed 107, 112, 133
working 21, 23–24, 71, 172, 306

classical political economy 9–10, 12, 21–22,
64, 133–34, 148
class struggles 300, 306
Clinton administration 312, 317
coal 83, 87, 100, 118, 120, 138, 144, 165, 177,
180–87, 194, 211, 218, 288, 290
colonies 48, 54, 58, 100, 115–16, 120, 209, 220–
22, 224, 226–28, 233, 260, 276
commodities 5–8, 18–19, 35–39, 63–65, 67–
69, 73–76, 127–29, 149, 151–52, 178–79,
248, 254–55, 266–68, 292–94, 321–
22
agricultural 255
capitalist production of 260, 265
circulation of 3, 37, 157, 263, 309, 319
exchange of 35, 68, 149
overproduction of 147
competition 73–74, 79, 125, 127, 132–33, 140,
159–62, 179, 204
concentration 53, 108, 144, 162, 164, 166, 180,
187, 194, 200, 203, 229, 327
Corn Laws 56, 99–100, 107–10, 112–15
new 107
protectionist 101
cotton 54, 77–78, 80, 82, 87, 89, 92, 116, 118,
125–27, 141, 174, 211, 215–16, 224
credit 4, 15, 93, 95–96, 157, 160, 290, 295, 297,
327
bank's 296
long 93
short-term 191
crisis 18, 71, 73, 83–84, 93–97, 175, 180–81,
204, 207, 211, 279, 283, 288, 327, 330
decennial 277–79
dollar 300
fiscal 315
general 288, 306
periodic 11, 64, 141, 283, 299, 315
theory of 330

debentures 151, 157, 162, 198, 202, 205, 224,
276
corporate 194
private 191
debts 73, 153, 191, 198–99, 291–92
heavy 304
national 48, 192, 224, 305
un-repayable 305
deflation 4, 291, 299, 309, 315, 318–20